⫰ **W9-CBQ-677**

"Winsome and beautifully written...superb."
—David J. Garrow, *Washington Post Book World*

"This engrossing narrative...is forthright and honest. A memorable book." —Annelle R. Huggins, *Library Journal*

"Reads like a fast-paced novel...gripping."
—Joanne Wasserman, *Daily News*

"Admirable....A rich account of the life of a remarkable inner-city school." —Lis Harris, *The New Yorker*

"An honest portrayal of the life of a high school teacher [and] a celebration of the many teachers who give of themselves for the sake of their students. Freedman's work is required reading."
—John Hyland, *San Francisco Chronicle*

"*Small Victories* [is] a big win."
—Benjamin DeMott, *Entertainment Weekly*

"A colorful, fast-moving stream of lives and hopes, raised or dashed, dramatizing the contradictions and deficiencies of the American educational system...vividly drawn."
—*Kirkus Reviews*

"Memorable....Seward Park High becomes at once a brilliantly rendered setting and a way of comprehending larger universes." —David L. Kirp, *Mother Jones*

"Beautifully written." —*Seventeen*

"[*Small Victories* is] an engrossing beautifully described account...a pleasure to read."
—Ellen Guiney, *Boston Sunday Globe*

Small Victories

THE REAL WORLD OF A TEACHER, HER STUDENTS, AND THEIR HIGH SCHOOL

Samuel G. Freedman

HarperPerennial

A Division of HarperCollins*Publishers*

Grateful acknowledgment is made to the following for permission to quote from copyrighted material:

Lyrics from "Pink Houses," by John Mellencamp. Copyright 1983 by Riva Music Inc./Windswept Pacific Entertainment Co. d/b/a Full Keel Music Co. All rights reserved. Reprinted by permission of Full Keel Music Co.

Excerpt from *The Great Gatsby*, by F. Scott Fitzgerald. Reprinted with permission of Charles Scribner's Sons, an imprint of Macmillan Publishing Company, from *The Great Gatsby*, by F. Scott Fitzgerald. Copyright 1925 by Charles Scribner's Sons; renewal copyright 1953 by Frances Scott Fitzgerald Lanahan.

Lyrics from "Un Cibaeno en Nueva York," by Luis Kalaff. Copyright 1965 by Deer International Corp. Copyright renewed. International copyright secured. All rights reserved. Used by permission.

"Honor Role of Heroic New Yorkers." Reprinted by permission of the author and the *Village Voice*.

Excerpt from *Murder in the Cathedral*, by T. S. Eliot, copyright 1935 by Harcourt Brace Jovanovich, Inc., and renewed 1963 by T. S. Eliot, reprinted by permission of the publisher.

Lyrics from "English Teacher" by Lee Adams and Charles Strouse. Copyright 1960 (renewed 1988) by Lee Adams and Charles Strouse/Strata Music. All rights of Strata Music administered by the Songwriters Guild of America. International copyright secured. All rights reserved.

Excerpt from "Police Kill Woman Being Evicted: Officers Say She Wielded a Knife," by Leonard Buder. Copyright 1984. Reprinted by permission of the *New York Times*.

Excerpt from "Police and Victim's Daughter Clash on Shooting," by Selwyn Raab. Copyright 1984. Reprinted by permission of the *New York Times*.

A hardcover edition of this book was published in 1990 by Harper & Row, Publishers.

SMALL VICTORIES. Copyright © 1990 Samuel G. Freedman. All rights reserved. Printed in the United States of America. No part of this book may be used or reproduced in any manner whatsoever without written permission except in the case of brief quotations embodied in critical articles and reviews. For information address HarperCollins Publishers, 10 East 53rd Street, New York, NY 10022.

First HarperPerennial edition published 1991.

Designed by Helene Berinsky

The Library of Congress has catalogued the hardcover edition as follows:
Freedman, Samuel G.
    Small victories: the real world of a teacher, her students, and
their high school/Samuel G. Freedman.—1st ed.
        p. cm.
    ISBN 0-06-016254-6
    1. Seward Park High School. 2. High schools—New York (N.Y.)—
Case studies. 3. Siegel, Jessica. 4. High school teachers—New
York (N.Y.)—Biography. 5. Minorities—Education (Secondary)—New
York (N.Y.)—Case studies. I. Title.
LD7501.N525F74   1990
373.11'0092—dc20   89-45654

ISBN 0-06-092087-4 (pbk.)
91 92 93 94 95   FG   10 9 8 7 6 5 4 3 2 1

In Memory of Robert W. Stevens
and
With Love to Cynthia

This is my world and I have banished darkness from it.

It is not madness, Marius. They say mad people can't tell the difference between what is real and what is not. I can. I know my little Mecca out there, and this room, for what they really are. I had to learn how to bend rusty wire into the right shape and mix sand cement to make my Wise Men and their camels, how to grind down beer bottles in a coffee mill to put glitter on my walls. My hands will never let me forget. They'll keep me sane. It's the best I could do, as near as I could get to the real Mecca. The journey is over now. This is as far as I can go.

ATHOL FUGARD, *The Road to Mecca*

Contents

no hardcover?

Acknowledgments

Although this book contains scores of characters, it would never have been written had not Jessica Siegel, a fiercely private and self-effacing person, accepted the risk of letting me camp out in her life. She was honest and critical in evaluating herself and unfailingly charitable in directing attention and acclaim to her friends, colleagues, and students. At every turn, she emphasized that no teacher succeeds in solitude and no school succeeds only because of one teacher.

Noel N. Kriftcher did the bravest thing any public school principal could do—allow an outsider with a notebook untrammeled access—and readily shared the lessons of his own decades in the New York City school system. Bruce Baskind enlightened and provoked me with his ideals, both within the classroom and without. Jules Levine patiently deciphered the mysteries of school finance for a neophyte, and Ellen Silva did a thousand and one favors that made my life in Seward Park easier.

I owe not only thanks but apologies to Helen Cohen, Rafael Figueroa, Victor Ng, Ian Ponman, Francisco Ramirez, Mike Ramos, Ira Shankman, and Norman Wong. These administrators, teachers, students, and alumni gave unstintingly of their time and insights and are not represented in this book in fair proportion to their generosity. But none of their words left me, and they informed my own perceptions.

Michael Shapiro and Michael Norman provided me ceaseless support during the process of writing this book and intelligent and ruthless commentary when I mistakenly thought it was completed. Jude McNeela was a tireless and outstanding researcher. Sam Roberts, Cliff Krauss, and Katie Quan lent their expertise in New York political history, Latin American affairs, and Chinese immigration, respectively, to the chapters involving those subjects. My trip to the People's Republic of China was made possible by Huang Zhizheng of the Chinese consulate and Libby Sung of China Express. Kwong Chi Chang in Taicheng and Katharine Sid, Helene Dunkelblau, and Juan Chien-ping at Seward Park assisted with translations of interviews and written materials. In the Dominican Republic, the families of Ernesto Galan and Maria Campos offered knowledge and hospitality. José Santana served as an emergency interpreter in New York on many occasions.

My appreciation also goes to Angel Franco, Dawn McClendon, Rosalind Lichter, Dick Shepard, Myra Forsberg, Bill Hampton, Marty Gottlieb, Robert Wagner, Jr., Richard Riley, Suzanne Trazeoff, Agent Bob Strang, Lieutenant David Linott, Lieutenant Joseph Lisi, Professor Stephan Brumberg, Doctor Irwin Redlener, Tom Bird, Richard Meislin, Maria Fortunato, Elizabeth Bogen, Frank Vardy, Bill Utter, Elizabeth Brackett, Scott Terranella, Lisa Ward, Wayne and Donna Carpenter, Beverly Cheuvront, Linda Amster, Robert Vare, Regina Myer, Manny Azenberg, Howard Stein, Ron Baskind, Simeon and Fanny Siegel, and Lorraine Mulligan.

I never would have undertaken a book without the learning experience of seven years of reporting for *The New York Times,* and I thank such exemplary editors as A. M. Rosenthal, Arthur Gelb, Jeff Schmalz, and Marv Siegel, who were in many ways my teachers.

Once I entered the realm of books, I was blessed to have an agent as warm and humane as Barney Karpfinger and an editor as committed and thorough as Rick Kot.

Through better than two years of research and writing, my family gave love, ballast, and diversion in abundance. I am most especially beholden to my sister Carol, doyenne of the hard disk.

Nobody has lived through the emotional oscillations of this book more than Cynthia Sheps, whom I met and married during its creation. She has boosted sagging spirits, challenged easy assumptions, and always demanded my very best labors. I only hope *Small Victories* justifies her faith and her love.

Small Victories

Introduction

THE PATH THAT led me to an overcrowded, underfunded, dilapidated public high school in a notorious immigrant slum on New York City's Lower East Side began in a setting seemingly remote from any such social or educational ills.

The place was Wheaton, Illinois, a county seat perched on the fringe of the prairie, a national center of charismatic Christianity, a suburb made prosperous by corporate capital. I landed there as a reporter for *Suburban Trib,* an adjunct of the *Chicago Tribune,* assigned to cover education. "The two most important things to people are their kids and their taxes," my editor told me on my first day. "Public school is the place they both meet."

I was soon to learn how troubled was that intersection of interests. To my eye, the Wheaton school system was good, perhaps outstanding. Classes were small, buildings were new, teachers were devoted. There was a measure of racial integration and tolerance rare for metropolitan Chicago, thanks to Wheaton's former role as a station on the Underground Railroad. All but a handful of high school graduates entered college, and a significant number attended the elite private colleges on each coast. The superintendent, Kenneth W. Olsen, a Mormon with a doctorate in education, brought to his office a believer's faith and a missionary's zeal. When I first met him, he was deploying teachers and administrators in a top-to-bottom evaluation of the entire school system.

The schools in Wheaton, I often thought, could have been the schools I attended in Highland Park, New Jersey. My hometown, with its main street of drug stores and delicatessens, with its high school topped by clock tower and cupola, with its Shakespeare-in-the-Park performances and McGovern for President potluck suppers, always struck me as a convergence of Middle America and Eastern Intellectual, *Our Town* reimagined by Irving Howe. People moved to Highland Park, and endured the high property taxes, for its public schools. I remember the municipal boast that Highland Park had the "second-best" school system in the state, as if claiming the very top rung would have been arrogant. I remember as a fourth- or fifth-grader helping my parents stuff mailboxes in the successful campaign to raise taxes to build a new junior high school. I remember the column in our high school newspaper listing each senior's college acceptances. It was called "Ivied Hauls."

How dumbfounded I was, then, to cover a Wheaton school board meeting one night in May 1980 and hear Olsen and his schools pilloried by the very people who seemed to have most benefited from them. One critic was the mother of a freshman at Stanford University, another the mother of a freshman at Duke. Both children had availed themselves of advanced placement courses in high school, and both had won substantial scholarships to college based on their high school records. Yet to those two mothers, and to the 939 fellow parents who signed a petition they submitted to the school board, public education in Wheaton was mediocre. Some of their proof was as clinical as a decline in scores on the Scholastic Aptitude Test (SAT) by Wheaton students; some of it was as subjective as the contention by the Stanford freshman that several college classmates had arrived knowing more Dickens.

Personally, I was less interested in the immediate debate than in what it suggested and in what it came to signify in my mind. It was one thing to hear generalized mourning for the demise of public education, another to discover myself surrounded by those shouting out the obituary. By various measures, American public schools were indeed in trouble. Average scores on the SAT fell steadily from 1963 through 1980, before beginning a negligible rise. Forty percent of minority youths, it was estimated, were functionally illiterate. Teachers were drawn disproportionately from the bottom quarter of their college classes and were paid salaries so low that the best left the profession. Yet none of those trends was new. Not even the perception of crisis was new. Every generation or so, it seemed, America had indulged itself in a spasm of conscience about the state of the public schools. The last one had commenced in 1957, when the Soviet Union threw a 185-pound satellite named Sputnik into the heavens. The Cold War became education's ally, loosening Washington's purse, in the form of the National Defense Education Act, in the interest of staving off Russian conquest. As potential defenders of democracy, my friends and I were instructed in something called "New Math" and steered into algebra and chemistry while in junior high school.

So the imbroglio in Wheaton touched my sense-memory as well as my news judgment. When I left *Suburban Trib* in 1981 for *The New York Times,* I found that the criticism of public education was only increasing, the bill of indictment only lengthening. I contributed to the corpus of horror stories, reporting on the expulsion from Bridgeport, Connecticut, high schools of two seventeen year olds for carrying and firing guns, and on a state court's subsequent ruling that the young criminals be provided home tutoring. If felonious behavior was rewarded by the individual attention that urban schools could so rarely bestow on deserving students, then something was severely wrong. At about the same time, I heard news from Highland Park that was, in its way, almost as disturbing. An elderly woman, who lived next to the high school, had died and willed her home to the Board of Education. After years of operating from rooms wedged between the high school gymnasium and cafeteria, the board would have its own building, free of charge. The single formality was that voters had to approve the transfer of title. Fewer than one hundred people cared enough to cast ballots, and a majority of those who did refused the gift, incorrectly assuming there had to be a catch. How great and how reflexive had grown the suspicion of public education, even in the sort of suburb that existed for its schools.

These random, inchoate impressions found a focus in April 1983. The National Commission on Excellence in Education, appointed by President Reagan, issued a thirty-five-page bombshell of a report, entitled, *A Nation At Risk.* "The educational foundations of our society," it contended, "are presently being eroded by a rising tide of mediocrity that threatens our very future as a Nation and a people." A critique of public high schools by the Carnegie Foundation for the Advancement of Teaching, released within months of the federal declaration, waxed only slightly less apocalyptic. "There remains," the foundation said, "a large, even alarming gap between school achievement and the task to be accomplished. A deep erosion of confidence in our schools, coupled with disturbing evidence that at least some of the skepticism is justified, has made revitalizing the American high school an urgent matter." In the years that followed, attacks on public education would become a staple of serious political discourse and expedient demagoguery. Both Allan Bloom's *The Closing of the American Mind,* a denunciation of feminism, rock and roll, and other alleged crimes against academe, and E. D. Hirsch, Jr.'s, *Cultural Literacy,* a laundry list of purportedly vital knowledge for all Americans, resided for months on bestseller lists.

Like anyone who cared about public education, I applauded the good intentions of all these efforts, however much I disagreed with their conclusions. It seemed to me that Bloom and Hirsch, the Reagan Commission and the Carnegie Foundation, functioned most importantly as evangelists, thundering from the pulpit for a life free of sin. No mortal would ever equal the challenge, but in the effort existence could be raised to a higher plane. The only problem was that the public response to the alarms was so fitful, so self-defeating, and sometimes so plainly craven. The Reagan Commission's report, for instance, amounted to a compelling argument for increased federal funding of public schools, the sort of funding that was enacted after Sputnik. Yet at the same time, the Reagan administration was cutting back aid to schools, reducing related programs ranging from Head Start to low-interest college loans, advocating tuition assistance for families of private school pupils, attacking the entire concept of bilingual education, and attempting to jettison the U.S. Department of Education itself. The solution to this seeming contradiction was a bit of image adjustment. On the advice of his pollsters, President Reagan staged visits to several public schools, posing with adorable children and inveighing against Washington's "misguided policymakers." Now he was *perceived* as a champion of public education, and perception was all that mattered.

Piecemeal reforms did pop up during the mid-1980s on a state-by-state basis—merit pay for teachers here, minimum-skills tests for high school seniors there—but without any sense of cohesion and often without the money to support them. A subsequent study by the Brookings Institution of school reform in thirty-eight states found that the initiatives either left unchanged or damaged the quality of education because in every case the schools, already overburdened, were being asked to take on still more responsibilities; and even were these measures effective, they could, by definition, address only the educational problems inside schools, while the schools themselves had to contend with the full spectrum of societal forces. When the Congressional Budget Office investigated the decline in standardized test scores, for instance, it concluded, in a 102-page analysis, that the descent derived more from social, cultural, and demographic factors than from educational policies.

Such common sense was welcome and all too rare. Since its founding, America had been torn between its belief in the perfectability of all citizens and its longing for a British-style elite: It wanted to be both Eton and Eden. Already saddled with those impossible and irreconcilable expectations, the public school system from the 1960s on was handed every problem being abdicated by family, church, and community. The public school was seen as a bathosphere, tethered to the ship of society but bobbing peacefully undersea, somehow unaffected by whatever mutinies or hurricanes wracked the vessel. As Diane Ravitch wrote in *The Schools We Deserve:*

> Horace Mann, Henry Barnard, and other founders of the common school movement could not have imagined the social situation of the schools in the 1980s; could not have imagined the condition of the family, the divorce rate, the rise of child abuse, the widespread neglect of young children by their parents; could not have imagined the spread of addictive drugs to young children barely in their teens; could not have imagined the soporific and powerful effect of television. . . . How could they have foreseen the social disintegration that would force upon the school the roles of parent, minister, policeman, social worker, psychiatrist and babysitter?

I agreed with Ravitch, and I resolved to find out how a school indeed struggled with its massive challenges, both inherent and inherited. I wanted to learn what I thought the parents in Wheaton and the politicians in Washington did not truly know—what form education took inside a public school, and what forces outside school affected the process of learning. I considered returning to Wheaton, but ultimately decided against it, because I knew the furnace was hottest not in affluent suburbs but in city slums.

In July 1986, I wrote an article for *The New York Times* about a Bronx child who had fallen to her death because a landlord had not installed the required safety barrier in her apartment window. I received a congratulatory letter a week or two later from someone named Jessica Siegel, who identified herself as an English and journalism teacher at Seward Park High School on the Lower East Side of Manhattan. I wrote back to thank her and to offer, in return, to speak before her journalism class. She invited me the following fall, and when I rode the subway down to Delancey Street that October for the first time, I expected to encounter a dangerous school filled with disaffected students. Without revealing too much about Seward Park, let me say that I was proved wrong, which intrigued me. It intrigued me, too, that when I chatted with Jessica Siegel after class, it became apparent that she knew a great deal about her students' lives beyond the classroom, and that those lives were filled with drama and tragedy. The overwhelming majority of her students, and Seward Park's, were immigrants or the children of immigrants, and so both she and the school were engaged in the most fundamental act of American education, creating intelligent citizens.

My idea was simple: I would spend the entire 1987–88 school year in Seward Park—not masquerading as a student, not attempting to teach, but taking notes and conducting interviews as a sort of reporter in residence. I would follow Jessica Siegel, but with the intention of widening my aperture to include many teachers, students, and administrators, for I wanted to explore a community, not create a personality cult. I would observe classes, parent conferences, disciplinary hearings, faculty meetings, basketball games, and the entire pageant of school life. I would pursue Seward Park's people to their homes, their second jobs, their old neighborhoods, and perhaps to their birthplaces abroad. Having secured from Jessica Siegel a promise of cooperation without payment or preconditions, I approached Dr. Noel N. Kriftcher, the principal of Seward Park. He approved my plan, provided I also gained the support of Robert F. Wagner, Jr., the president of the New York City Board of Education. In June 1987, Wagner granted me permission.

By the time classes began, three months later, I had resigned from *The Times* to research and write this book. During the last free days of summer, I flew to Chicago, in part to see Ken Olsen, with whom this whole enterprise had begun. I telephoned his office in Wheaton and was given without enlightenment another number to dial. When Ken answered, he gave me directions to his new office in a different suburb, and once I arrived he explained. Those mothers in Wheaton, those petitioners I had seen seven years earlier, those perfectionists for whom having their children admitted to Duke and Stanford was not sufficient proof of fine education, had driven him out of town. The school board had refused to renew his contract, and he was now completing a one-year stint in another district. The Wheaton experience had blackened his reputation so completely that this marvelous, gifted educator was facing unemployment. For the first time in the years I had known Ken, he appeared afraid. Returning to New York City and to my immersion into the real world of public education, I took his worried face as an omen.

Bobby Pins
and Tissues

you write in present tense

I T IS JUNE 24, 1987, Graduation Day for Seward Park High School, and Jessica Siegel has a pocketbook full of bobby pins and tissues. The bobby pins are for her students. The tissues are for herself.

The high school sits empty and silent in the late afternoon, a breeze nudging litter down the streets outside, for the commencement is being held eighty blocks farther north in Manhattan, at Hunter College. Here the streets unfold with boutiques and diplomatic mansions and elegant apartment buildings, with awnings and doormen and gilt doors that glint in the summer sun. The college itself looms like a fortress castle, all turrets and archways, medieval grandeur reincarnated amid the metropolis.

With footsteps both urgent and tentative, the students and their families arrive. Six rise from the Lexington Avenue subway, palms shading their eyes. Five pile out of a Dodge Dart piloted by an uncle. Four emerge from the gypsy cab on which they have splurged, with its smoked windows and air freshener. All of them pause to gape, and the cabbie, too, waits an extra moment before driving on, leaning out the window to admire the promised land. Their world is the Lower East Side, its streets crammed with tenements and bodegas and second-story sweatshops, its belly bursting with immigrants, its class and tongues and customs so foreign here at Hunter, only twenty minutes from home.

And so they wait and fidget a bit—seniors in their graduation gowns, sisters with cameras, mothers with the afternoon off from the factory. Some don the blue formality of Sunday church, others the heels and sequins of a merengue club. A little brother wiggles in a tuxedo, and an older boyfriend prances in a sweatshirt marked "Slick." A girl cradles a Polaroid snapshot in both her hands as if it were an heirloom locket. A workman maneuvers through the mob and into the auditorium with a floral arrangement balanced on his head. A hot dog vendor works the crowd, scented steam rising from his aluminum cart. It is all confusing, and not a little daunting, and so the air fills with Chinese and Spanish, the languages in which most of the families find solace and take refuge.

These seniors have traveled to a border, to a frontier. Some will never cross it. They will take their diplomas and shrink back southward, back to the comforting, familiar things, back to the many menaces. But others will wield their diplomas as passports and will step into the new, the strange, the almost inconceivable. A few of them will even attend college here at Hunter, descendants of a sort to the immigrant daughters of Crown Heights and Morrisania and East Harlem and indeed the Lower East Side and Seward Park High School, who a half-century ago entered this edifice just as exhilarated and just as intimidated.

From down the block Jessica Siegel watches, identifying students outlined by the western sun. She has had perhaps 325 of the 450 graduates in her English and journalism classes. She has been teacher, adviser, mentor, and mother. Now, as she has every June for the past nine years, she must say goodbye and farewell. There is no mistaking her, even from a distance. You can see that mop of dirty-blond curls bouncing in cadence with her step. You can see that multicolored smock from Mexico, the one with two birds flanking a fruit bowl. And as she moves into the mob of seniors, you can hear her shout, "Anybody need bobby pins?"

The first taker is a lithe young woman named Sharon Queen, only the acne on her cheeks betraying her as a teenager. Somewhere in the crowd, wearing a tiny white suit, is the son she bore two years ago, at age fifteen. Child or no child, Sharon refused to quit school, never in Jessica's memory missed a single day, and now she is bound for college. Jessica slides a pin up under her mortarboard, then kisses her.

She spots a boy, his head almost clean shaven in this month's fashion.

"How you gonna keep this on?" she asks, tapping his mortarboard.

"No problem," he answers. "I got some glue."

She reaches the plaza outside the college auditorium, where the ceremony will be held. She greets Bruce Baskind, a history teacher who is her closest friend on the faculty, and Nancy Wackstein, the guidance counselor with whom she has schemed many a student into college. Baskind and Wackstein are both wearing black gowns because the seniors have elected them marshals. Neither of them can figure out how to wear the ceremonial hoods, though, and so it falls to Jessica, who was not voted a marshal, to drape the black and purple cloths properly. A third marshal arrives—social studies teacher Terry LaSalle—and Jessica performs the same rites for her. As the marshals saunter off to line up the seniors for their entrance, Wackstein and LaSalle sling their purses over Jessica's shoulders.

Behind Jessica waits a cluster of her favorite students. There is Salome Junco, the Colombian-born girl who won a national journalism contest while writing for the Seward Park newspaper, which Jessica advises. She will enter the honors program at City College. There is Alex Iturralde, the son of a truck driver from Ecuador, headed for Skidmore College. Jessica worries about that—a shy, working-class Hispanic surrounded by well-heeled whites for whom Skidmore might have been a "safety school." There is Celia Torres, who will attend Baruch College in New York. Jessica wanted her to try the State University of New York at New Paltz, but her father vetoed the idea. He was afraid that if Celia went away to school, far from paternal discipline, she would end up pregnant like her sister.

Celia wants a white bobby pin to match her mortarboard, and Jessica digs one out of her bag. After Jessica affixes it, a Chinese boy comes forward to kiss Celia. And as he does, he knocks off his own mortarboard.

"Bobby pin!" Jessica declares, starting in on his short hair.

"Oh no, Miss Siegel," he says, wincing.

"Quit being such a macho man," she says, and the deed is done.

"Next," she shouts, like a delicatessen counterman slicing lox for the Sunday-morning mob.

A thin, brown-haired boy with a wisp of a mustache runs up to Jessica. He is clutching the graduation ceremony program.

"Did you have anything to do with the English award?" asks the boy, Rafael Gerena, who has taken three of Jessica's classes in the past year.

"What do you think?" she answers, hands on her hips, as if daring him to throw a punch. Sure, she put him up for the award, but with a few misgivings. A studious sort for most of his time at Seward Park, Rafael became something of a miscreant by the end of the year, cutting class, missing assignments, chattering during lessons. In striking such a severe pose now, Jessica wants him to leave high school with the image of her monitoring him and prodding him branded in his brain. He is going far away, to the University of West Virginia, and he will need her help and more to survive.

"What a teacher," Rafael says to Jessica, sighing like the smitten. "I gotta get a picture of you." He leads her by the hand to meet his parents.

Back from the photo session, Jessica methodically moves down a line of seniors. By now, she is carrying four handbags. "I feel like *Death of a Salesman* here," she mutters, lumbering along Sixty-ninth Street.

"Stop complaining," she tells one girl whose hair is pulled too tight by the pin. "The hard part's over."

To another: "I know, I know, it wrecks your hair."

And yet another: "You're graduating? I can't believe it."

Nancy Wackstein tries to prepare the procession, shouting, "Gentlemen of Line Three, could we have three steps back, please?" She must bellow a second time before there is even a desultory retreat, and as soon as the line straightens, it snarls anew into knots for group portraits. Moving down the column, Nancy counts off bodies, weeds out the imposters, and begs the rest, "Please throw away your chewing gum." Finally, from the back of the line, she waves to Bruce Baskind, and from the portal of the auditorium he hollers, "Hey, folks, here it is."

And with Bruce in the lead, gliding athletically in the waning daylight, the Class of 1987 strides into the Commencement Exercises of Seward Park High School and into the rest of their lives. As they march past Jessica, she fastens a final mortarboard, squeezes a few arms, and accepts yet another handbag. Soon the seniors are all inside, filling the first twenty rows of the auditorium. Jessica remains on the sidewalk, where it is suddenly quiet, empty, and just a little lonely. Eight pocketbooks hang from her shoulders. She carries two award certificates under her right arm. Three last bobby pins rest between her lips.

Only now, with everyone else seated and the strains of "Pomp and Circumstance" fading, does she enter the auditorium, waddling under the weight. She finds a seat, lays down her load, and reaches for her tissues. It has been a good year, a very good year, and on Graduation Day it deserves a cry to match.

*   *   *

On the morning after graduation, the next-to-last morning of the academic year, Jessica gets to work at seven-fifteen. As usual, she is the first of the English teachers to arrive. On the streets outside Seward Park, a shopkeeper sweeps his sidewalk and a junkie weaves up the gutter, shouting to no one particular, "Go see my rabbi." Inside the school, a rare stillness hangs in the air like some wondrous vapor. Jessica sits at the sturdy wooden desk she shares with several colleagues in the English Department. Spread before her are an attendance book and a dozen homemade note cards. Next to her rest eight boxes filled with compilations of the oral histories and family recipes that she requires of students in the class she and Bruce teach about the Lower East Side. Today is the last time she will see her seniors, or at least the last time she will see them as her students. Sluggish from their Graduation Night revelry, they trudge to the third-floor office later in the morning to wish her farewell.

The first to appear is Sammy Ryan, his tired eyes obscured by round mirror sunglasses. Sammy was one of Jessica's special projects this year. He is an imposing, even threatening presence, big bones wrapped by muscles that cling like kudzu, head shaven clean except for a thicket on top. Sammy's favorite spot in class was in the rear right corner, as far from the blackboard as possible, and he generally spread himself across two or three chairs. He carried a 69 average, forecast a future in professional basketball, and claimed few champions besides Jessica. She can remember visiting him in the hospital during Christmas vacation, bedridden with an infection of his lymph system, a frightened child bunking with two withered old men. Jessica pressed Sammy's mother to see him, but the woman insisted she could not afford to travel the thirty blocks from her apartment. So on Christmas Day, Jessica brought Sammy a tin of cookies and a biography of Bobby Knight. Sammy telephoned her several days later to say he had checked out, against his doctor's orders, to study for final exams.

As they grew closer, Sammy confided to Jessica that he lived at home only part time and did little more than sleep there when he did. He had spent several years with a grandfather, until the grandfather died, and several more with a foster mother, of whom he spoke with affection. As for his real mother's inconsistencies, he would say merely, "Well, that's just the way she is." To Jessica, it seemed clear that Sammy had essentially raised himself, and knowing that, she comforted and chided and motivated and mothered, and ultimately managed to win him admission to the State University of New York at New Paltz. This weekend, he will leave for the campus to attend a special summer program for economically disadvantaged students.

Sammy lifts copies of the oral histories and family recipes out of a box on Jessica's desk. Then he reaches into his backpack for a sheet of dry-cleaner's cellophane, probably the same cellophane that had covered his graduation gown, and wraps the two booklets in it for protection. He places the package in the backpack, turns to Jessica, and says, "Off into the sunset."

But he lingers in the English office, his head bobbing with nervous energy and unexpressed emotion. This moment is, for Sammy, perhaps more wrenching than leaving home, for both he and Jessica know his mother did not bother to attend his graduation. After all Jessica's pleas, she simply said, "I'm too busy."

Finally, Jessica breaks the silence. "I put my address in the card," she says. "So write."

"I'll be back by July Fourth," Sammy responds. Behind the joke lies the fear that he will fail at the college's special summer program, and that before the regular students reach New Paltz, he'll be back with his troubled mother on the Lower East Side. He steps out of the office and slinks down the hallway toward the stairwell.

Jessica sits still for a moment, comprehending. Then she leaps up, dashes into the hall, and shouts at the silhouette of Sammy: "Bullshit!" And his laughter echoes back to her.

Already, another student, Ai Que Jiang, awaits Jessica. She failed him in English for plagiarizing a book report, and he was just as inadequate a thief as he was a scholar: For a course in American literature, he submitted a friend's paper on *The Hunchback of Notre Dame,* a *French* novel. Now Ai Que wants Jessica to raise his grade to a D. That way, he can spend July visiting his relatives in Los Angeles instead of taking English in summer school.

"I can't change your mark," Jessica says.

"Why?" Ai Que asks, pulling the word out into a long, slow whine.

"Because you failed my course."

Ai Que says nothing. He fidgets in his fashionable clothes.

Jessica opens her grade book. "Forty on one test. Fifty-five on the next test. You never revised that essay. Your book report was forged. Someone else wrote it for you. I mean, how can I pass you? How can I?"

Ai Que does not answer.

"Go talk to Miss Wackstein," Jessica offers as a compromise. "If she wants us three to talk, we'll talk. But I can't change a fifty-five to a sixty-five."

Ai Que scurries away, in search of the guidance counselor.

By now, a few other English teachers are at work, filling out their grade books at a long wooden table. Ben Dachs, the department chairman, takes orders for coffee and leaves for the restaurant across the street. Bruce Baskind sidles in wearing a blue jersey emblazoned with "Boys of Summer," the garb of his stickball league. Then, soundlessly, Alex Iturralde slips into the room. He is wearing a sleeveless T-shirt, baggy pants, and sneakers, and he shifts his weight from side to side. His twin brother stands beside him, silent and adoring. After a few minutes, Jessica notices Alex, pressed against the wall.

"Alex," she says softly. "You see?" She points to her gold necklace. Iturralde's parents gave it to her as a present at graduation. "And this is for you." She hands him a wrapped box that contains a leather-bound datebook. As he delicately accepts the gift, she opens one of her homemade cards and begins to write. Then she passes it to Alex and he reads the inscription:

It's hard for me to get down all that I have to say to you, but then I think that we've known each other for two years and you've experienced/undergone many of my classes. I'm sure I've tried to communicate what I want to say on this.

I don't worry about you at all at Skidmore. They're lucky to have selected you. You're the kind of person who thinks and wonders about the world, questions and gets excited about literature and ideas. I hope you realize how rare and precious those qualities are!

No matter how many people you meet who act like they know it all or seem sophisticated or expect everything to be coming to them, don't be impressed. Never lose faith in yourself. I know you won't.

When Alex finishes reading, he simply turns to Jessica and hugs her. Then he loosens his arms and starts to blush, hiding his head behind a bank of file cabinets. After recovering, he regards her again. He has no words, only a face as open as clear sky.

"I know you'll be fine," she assures him.

"Yeah, well," he says, fumbling for something appropriate. "See ya around." And he withdraws into the hall, exiting as unassumingly as he had entered, his twin following on his heels, shadowlike.

It is nearly ten-thirty, and all the seniors are gone. Now it is Jessica's time, that rarest of things, Jessica's time. It was odd how little she cried during graduation; she herself isn't sure why. But now she reaches into her bag for a tissue, and the tears begin to flow.

"It's sort of like sadness," she says, becoming as tongue-tied as her students. "Just to say goodbye." She dabs at her cheeks. "I guess I put so much into haranguing and harassing the kids." She looks away, trying to gather herself. "There is something very postpartum when they go. I put so much energy and so much emotion into those kids. Sometimes I think my job is being a professional mother."

But the tears attest to more than that. She gazes at the few leftover notecards on the desk. "I used to be an artistic person," she says. "In a past life." She pauses. "That's what I yearn for." She stops again. "That and a few other things."

At the age of thirty-eight, Jessica is unmarried and childless. She has not had a steady relationship in two years. Everything that represents a fantasy to her exists as a reality for most of her friends and colleagues—a spouse or lover, enough spare time to read, a job that can be left at the end of the day. A couple of Jessica's best friends from college have kids. Her younger brother Steve, whom she practically raised, wed nine months earlier. Even Bruce Baskind, as hard as he works, has his wedding ring and his stickball jersey, evidence of a life beyond Seward Park.

"Am I too based in reality?" Jessica wonders aloud. "Maybe I am. If I sound like I have low-level fantasies, maybe it's because I've been denying myself so much. What I want are the normal things, the things that most people already have. I want an easier life. I want a life where I don't just give out without getting anything back."

She knows she is going to have a splendid summer. In two days, she will leave for Santa Barbara, California, where she has won a fellowship to study *Moby Dick*. She will visit old friends in Berkeley. She will get a tan. She will resume running three miles a day, the way she did several summers ago when she studied Shakespeare in England. *Great, fine*. But the summer is the summer. Labor Day already looms, and Labor Day means back to school.

Many times, Jessica has thought about quitting, imagining that in the absence of teaching her life might regain some ballast and some balance. Each time she has reached the threshold, however, she has decided not to cross. She has stuck with the fourteen-hour days and the seven-day weeks. Teaching still touched that idealistic part of her, that 1960s part of her. All these newspapers and politicians yammered about "the underclass" while she helped cultivate the new middle class, blossoming from the rocky soil of the Lower East Side. She watched her students march off to Syracuse and Sarah Lawrence and the University of Chicago, her own alma mater; she watched them become union organizers and architects, teachers and biochemists. She knew she had made a difference.

The realization brings her peace. But it is only momentary peace, illusory peace. The question is not whether teaching gives her a sense of worth, of value, of importance. Of course it does. The question is the price she pays. You grind yourself to dust for $29,442, and all you hear about in return are lousy kids and lousy schools and lousy teachers. You read an article in *The New York Times* about single women in which somebody says it's tough to get dates if you're a teacher, because men are looking for professionals. *Professionals.*

"I understand I'm doing really good work," she says, wiping her tears and then balling up the tissue. "But I'm sacrificing my life." And so when Jessica Siegel walks out the doors of Seward Park High School on a blindingly blue June morning, she has to wonder if the next school year will be her last.

1

Tough Cookie

JESSICA SIEGEL SLEEPS in the bed of her childhood. It is a tidy single bed with a gleaming brass frame. A trunk rests at its foot and a vanity table sits beside the window. Outside the window, horse chestnut leaves rustle in the breeze from the river. An antique china cabinet stands against the wall opposite the window. Behind curved glass, its hardwood shelves brim with the fans and dolls that Jessica and her mother have bought at flea markets and church bazaars on their special days together.

Jessica wakes with a start. She has forgotten something; she has forgotten to write a term paper. But for what course? At what school? She is unsure exactly what she owes, and to whom. Only the fear is certain. It cripples her and binds her to the bed; she cannot rise. *How can I be so stupid?* she asks herself again and again. *How could I let this happen?* It is the last day of the school year, and now she will fail.

*   *   *

When Jessica Siegel stirs at four-thirty on the morning of Monday, September 14, 1987, she is in her own bed, in her own apartment in New York City. It is not the last day of the school year; it is the first. Everything else was a dream, her recurring dream. Tossing, listing, tugging at the pillows, she extracts another twenty minutes of repose. Then, still ten minutes shy of the alarm clock's call, she surrenders and rises. *So much,* she thinks, *for not being nervous after seven years.*

In the blink between night and day, the hot water in her apartment has vanished, the way it so often does in a sixty-year-old building with a curmudgeonly boiler and an indifferent owner. Looking out the kitchen window onto the dark, concrete courtyard, Jessica opens the cold tap, fills two pots, and lights the burner to heat her water, like some modern Manhattan version of the frontier schoolmarm. One pot will clean last night's dirty dishes and the other will make this morning's bath.

At five feet three, Jessica is big boned and well proportioned, and a summer of California jogging has tuned her legs and browned her pale arms into a nebula of freckles. But when she looks in the mirror, she can only see her hair and think, *Oh, my God!* She let a new stylist talk her into a body wave, even though nature gave her a headful of curls, and $105 later she was left with less a coiffure than an aura of excited amber strands. Now she is stuck with the fiasco for six months. *The kids'll laugh at me,* she thinks, as she rakes through her hair with an Afro-Pik. *And what if Prince Charming comes?*

She stacks the dishes and irons her dress as the sky outside lightens from black to purple. Still in her morning robe, she types out the year's first assignment for her journalism class. Only afterward does she don her school clothes, hoping to have spared herself a few wrinkles. She collects her brand-new school supplies—a stiff-spined green grade book, cream-colored binder paper, blue ballpoint pens not yet gnawed—and places them in her nylon tote bag. This she stows in the wire basket of her bicycle. She bought the bike on the street from a man who said he built it from spare parts. Of course, he might have stolen it five minutes earlier, but Jessica wants to believe people. She wheels the black five-speed bike out of her bedroom, guiding it between the bookshelves, the chair, and the loom, then out the door and down the hall and finally onto the sidewalk, where she stands alone in the cool, serene daybreak.

From her own block, with its elm trees and brownstones, she pedals east through the jazz clubs and pottery stores of Greenwich Village, then south past the galleries and bistros of SoHo. Turning east again and crossing Broadway, she leaves the world she inhabits and enters that of her students, the Lower East Side. Boutiques give way to garment factories, track-lit lofts to walk-up tenements, gourmet groceries to family bodegas, condominiums to housing projects. Signs now appear in Spanish and Hebrew and Chinese, Hindi and Arabic and Cambodian, for the streets in this single corner of Manhattan form perhaps the most famous immigrant neighborhood in the world, home to waves of foreigners for 150 years. Here lived Jacob Riis's "other half" a century ago, and here live the other half of New York City today, manual laborers and welfare mothers, struggling newcomers and junkies beyond hope.

Jessica rides past Prince Street sweatshops and Bowery flophouses and finally onto Delancey Street, her last leg of the journey toward school. The air reeks of wet trash. Curbside garbage cans are lashed together with chains so the drunks and junkies cannot borrow them for use as braziers on cold nights. She passes Sara Roosevelt Park, a narrow, unkempt strip of playground flanked by sooty tenements. Yet there, amid graffiti and rubble and weeds, three graying Chinese ladies slowly bend and scissor through their daily t'ai chi, unfurling their limbs with an elastic grace, like honey poured on a cool morning. Jessica smiles at the sight. It is such brilliant, fleeting miniatures that sustain her.

At the corner of Delancey and Orchard, two blocks from the school, Jessica hoists her bike onto the curb. She walks past shops selling quilts and work gloves, zippers and threads, the sky ahead of her arching pink and orange above the Williamsburg Bridge. As she enters a donut shop for coffee, Bruce Baskind is just leaving.

For most of Jessica's time at Seward Park, Bruce has been her closest friend and best foil, and for the past three years, they have jointly taught a class they designed on the history and literature of the Lower East Side. Bruce wears jeans, running shoes, and a short-sleeve oxford shirt. His eyes droop in their deep sockets, but his step is jaunty.

"Couldn't sleep," Jessica tells him.

"Same," Bruce answers. "I've been up since five-thirty."

"A regular Calvinist."

"The only difference between Jonathan Edwards and me," Bruce says, "is that he's older."

Coffee in hand, Jessica skirts a supine body on the sidewalk between an Off Track Betting parlor and a methadone clinic, averts a pile of broken auto glass from a car burglarized the previous night, and finally brings her eyes to the gray stone school. One block square and six stories tall, unadorned except by wire mesh window guards, squeezed tightly among stores, a parking lot, and a housing project, Seward Park seems like a larger building that has dropped into a defensive crouch. At age fifty-eight, it is a clean and sturdy structure, but one badly served by its landlord, the Board of Education. As the new year begins, there is a huge hole in the roof, a crumbling ceiling in the faculty smoking lounge, and a shortage of 200 window panes and glass panels, all on order for months. At the nearby annex that serves 900 freshmen and sophomores, a metal fence dented ten years ago has yet to be repaired. And when the board did replace the annex's wiring, it bungled the job so badly that turning on two percolators short-circuited the entire second floor. Jessica remembers that last spring a boy ran for student government on the slogan, "Are you ashamed to go to Seward?"

Ashamed or not, dozens of the 2,600 juniors and seniors who attend the main building are already gathering, an hour before the bell. The dutiful cluster on the school steps. The diffident linger in the parking lot. The daring breakfast alfresco on the hoods of the staff cars, parked in reserved spaces on Ludlow Street. "Hey, Red Shoes," one boy calls to a passing girl. She continues walking, trailed by laughter and snickering in Spanish. Periodically, a young drug dealer, some-one's buddy or cousin or someone Seward Park has lost to the streets, will circle the school in a BMW or Mercedes. The dealer will drive slowly, less to conduct trade than to impress and recruit. Temptation travels with smoked windows and fur seats; temptation wears a beeper and a gold chain braided as thick as marine rope.

Jessica enters the lobby, passes the security guard station, then turns her gaze toward the retinue outside the guidance office. Even from a distance, she knows these are new immigrants, entire families of them, here to register their children for school. The scene recalls a border crossing, a wartime frontier—mewling infants, mothers in shawls, frayed clothing, suspicious and longing eyes. Hands clutch green cards, passports, telephone bills, utility receipts, report cards, di-plomas, or any other proof of former education and current where-abouts. As if to reassure them, and their teachers as well, artifacts of Seward Park's immigrant tradition hang all around the first floor, from the bronze plaque etched with German and Irish names and installed when the school opened in 1929 to the Hall of Fame display case with its largely Jewish occupants from the 1930s and 1940s to the photographic portraits of outstanding students of the 1980s: Sean Singh and Pura Cruz, Chun-On Cheng and Anton Vidokle.

But this morning of all mornings, Jessica will permit herself no dallying. She turns her back on the guidance office line and strides into Room 130, formally known as the Teachers Work Room, where she rejoins Bruce on a different sort of queue. This one leads to the time clock, which every teacher in every public school in New York City must punch on arrival and departure every day. *A steel mill,* Jessica thinks as her time card is stamped 7:11 A.M., forty-four minutes before she is due to report. *Might as well be working in a steel mill.*

She replaces her time card in a metal slot on the east wall of the room, then turns to the north wall. Each teacher at Seward Park has one mailbox here and one in his or her department's office. Jessica is famous for her mailboxes. They bulge; they groan; they threaten spontaneous combustion and spontaneous generation. Her box in the English office is twice the size of any other teacher's, and even so, the papers shove above and spill below. Jessica makes more of an effort to prune her downstairs mailbox, but after a summer without tending, it, too, is wildly overgrown. Besides innumerable catalogues for textbooks and educational films, she finds a complimentary note for her work on the Lower East Side class from the principal, dated June 30; a form letter from the superintendent of Manhattan high schools, congratulating her on perfect attendance; a copy of a State Legislature resolution commending Seward Park High School for donating 500 pints of blood in some drive or another; and an Army recruiting advertisement worth $300 to *Seward World,* the high school newspaper, which she advises.

"Pisses me off," she mutters to herself. She glares at the photograph of a teenager in a helmet and uniform, machine gun at the ready. Above the soldier's head, like skywriting, floats the slogan, "Be All That You Can Be." The advertisement comes from an agency in suburban Chicago that represents all sorts of clients anxious to reach high school students. It seems no coincidence to Jessica that *Seward World,* serving a student body that is overwhelmingly poor and nonwhite, never gets ads for records or movies or study aids, only for the military. As desperately as the newspaper needs income, she refuses to run the ads. She imagines her male students, so eager for manhood or a steady paycheck, enlisting and being shipped off to die far from home; she remembers the Vietnam War veteran she interviewed during her days as a reporter, the one who was crippled by machine-gun fire at age nineteen. The advertising agency can expect an incoming round, in the form of a letter, from Ms. Jessica Siegel.

Jessica and Bruce part at the third floor, he bound for the social studies office in Room 308, she for the English office in Room 329. The English department occupies an L-shaped room of about 160 square feet. The fiction is that this room can accommodate two dozen teachers, plus the department chairwoman, Emma Jon. The fact is, that with Seward Park operating far above capacity, no teacher in English or any other department gets a desk, and the newcomers do not even qualify for a file drawer. Most teachers work out of canvas or nylon tote bags, migrating from room to room. One of Jessica's friends, Denise Simone, must lug an oak lectern and thirty-five textbooks from one room to another to teach the identical speech class in consecutive periods.

By some combination of stubbornness and seniority, Jessica generally controls the wooden chair just inside the door of the English office, and as she sits drinking her coffee, the room around her begins to fill. Denise Simone runs the duplicating machine. Shawn Gerety, who teaches advanced placement English, works on a computer terminal. Louise Grollman writes out the requirements for her drama class as her Walkman plays *Eine Kleine Nachtmusik*. Mark Fischweicher, a teacher new to Seward Park, arrives with a volume of literary criticism about *Moby Dick* for Jessica. He is followed by Steve Anderson, like Denise, one of Jessica's close friends in the department. Anderson is a displaced Kansan with the fair skin and straw hair of farm country but the corrosive wit of a native New Yorker.

"Boy, do you look relaxed," he tells Jessica. "You look like a college kid . . ." She starts to thank him. ". . . all ready to burn down a building."

She laughs and then volleys.

"You get your hair cut?"

"I just washed it," Anderson says.

"That's an idea."

Watching the bustle and listening to the banter from the far wall is Harriet Stein, a willowy twenty-six-year-old with a somber beauty. This is her first year as a teacher, and she looks duly terrified, both hands anchored on her left hip, right leg stiff as a mast, lips taut. Even when she hazards a smile, she looks capable of tears. She eavesdrops as Jessica and Denise talk.

"I couldn't sleep last night," Jessica says.

"It doesn't change," Denise says, grinning.

"I'm always looking forward to meeting my kids."

"Me, too."

Harriet slowly draws toward them. "Maybe that's experience," she says wistfully.

"Are you apprehensive?" Jessica asks.

"Yes," Harriet says very softly. She bites her lip and fidgets a bit, bending sideways at the waist like a shy teenager at the big dance. Her eyes drop. "I don't look nervous, do I?"

Jessica, remembering how it was seven years ago, smiles at Harriet and says, "No."

At a few minutes before eight, the hall is almost serene, the only sounds the whirl of the duplicating machine, the click of new heels on waxed floors, and the laughter of reacquaintance. One teacher unlocks the sepulchral storage room next to the English office, and out seeps the rich, musty, familiar smell of books, the aroma of *The Pearl, Hamlet,* and *Huckleberry Finn.* Despite the broken typewriters in Room 334, despite the shortage of chairs in Room 431, despite the fact that no two clocks tell the same time, all in Seward Park is, more or less, well. Nothing will seem so still and orderly again until July.

Then the moment comes and the doors swing open and the students burst into Seward Park, sending alarums of arrival up stairs and around corners. Before the first face appears on the third floor, Jessica can hear a wall of sound, a compression of sound, massive if indistinct. It reminds her of a huge bowling alley, with the steady wooden thunder of pins falling. A newcomer might mistake the racket for anarchy, but Jessica, a veteran, welcomes it as the audible expression of possibility, of hope.

She stands outside the English office, near the stairwell, in the T-shaped intersection of hallways known as Times Square. Like its namesake in midtown Manhattan, Times Square is both a venue for such relatively innocent indiscretions as cutting class and trading insults and a flashpoint for realer dangers involving fists and knives. Against all efforts to dislodge it, a gang called Here To Chill has claimed Times Square as its turf.

It has been an eventful morning for Here To Chill. Neither Jessica nor most of her colleagues know it yet, but ten minutes before school opened today, one of the gang's members was beaten with a baseball bat only a block from Seward Park. By now, he is in the hospital receiving twenty stitches to a head wound. The details and motives are vague, but the attack seems to have stemmed from a shooting on the Lower East Side over the weekend. And the shooting, in turn, came in response to a knife fight at an August dance between two suitors for the same girl.

Because the antagonists belonged to two gangs from different neighborhoods and with different racial roots—Here To Chill composed of Puerto Ricans from Avenue D, a half-mile north of Seward Park; the opposing Smiths composed of blacks from the eponymous housing project a half-mile southeast—the cycle of retaliation could well sweep inside the school. A combination of administrators and police officers is seeking to ensure it does not, in large part by quashing the rumors about who hurt whom and how badly. A school that is the de facto crossroads for so many racial, ethnic, class, and neighborhood groups affords kindling galore for any spark of sectarian violence.

Inside Seward Park, Jessica sees only the wonders of diversity. The hallway before her blurs into a melange of soul shakes and high-fives, bursts of Spanish, spiky bits of Chinese, bobbing shoulders, flagging shirttails. While the unofficial Seward Park uniform consists of acid-dyed jeans, unlaced high-top Reeboks, and a baggy, brightly colored cotton shirt adorned with a declaration like "Always Ready" or "Surf Club," there are deviations by the score. A black boy wears a red plastic alarm clock like a pendant. An Indian girl, emerging from a bathroom, tugs on the designer jeans she favors beneath the *kamiz* her parents dictate. Rick Rowley, an English teacher who has just transferred from New Dorp, a white middle-class high school on Staten Island, joins Jessica in the hallway. He marvels at how much less cursing there is at Seward Park than at New Dorp. "I love this place," he announces to no one in particular.

Another piece of fashion, less popular but more disquieting than most, is "big gold." This newly minted noun covers gold cables, gold tooth caps, multifinger gold rings, and similar accessories fetching from $75 to $600. Like a lot of inner-city haute couture, big gold started with drug dealers, particularly the teenage entrepreneurs in the new, lucrative crack business. One New York high school, Thomas Jefferson in Brooklyn, has already banned big gold, identifying it as the cause of numerous fights, thefts, and armed robberies. If big gold has not proven similarly incendiary at Seward Park, it remains a reminder of the world outside and its many inducements.

Sometimes it gets hard for the teachers to remember that these faces and bodies are just fifteen or seventeen years old, just kids. They have so much style, so much attitude. Jessica spots a boy wearing a T-shirt emblazoned, "Frankie Says Use Condoms." Her eyes alight on a girl in a clinging cotton minidress, sheer black stockings, and stiletto heels. Jessica wags her head in disbelief—or is it perverse admiration for the chutzpah?—and then fights back a laugh. Last year, she and Steve Anderson struck upon an explanation for such junior divas: The Smurf Theory. It holds that any girl who dresses like a forty-year-old divorcée also secretly carries a notebook featuring the toadstool-shaped cartoon characters. Behind the joke resides a truth that the best teachers at Seward Park understand: No matter how sophisticated or how imposing the students seem to be, within most of them yawns the huge chasm of adolescent insecurity. Because Jessica has already touched that secret place in so many of her students, they start their year by seeking her in the hall.

"How you doin', Miss Siegel?"

"Hey, Miss Siegel."

"'s up, Miss Siegel?" This salutation is accompanied by spastic flailing of the right arm and hand, with thumb, index finger, and pinkie extended like crooked, hand-rolled cigars. It is the Seward Park equivalent of a secret lodge handshake.

"I got you for humanities, Miss Siegel."

"I heard you give a lot of homework, Miss Siegel," one boy says.

"You heard right," she replies.

"But I heard at the end you're a snap." A *snap*, in Seward Park parlance, is something or someone good, funny, enjoyable. Jessica is honored to be part of snapdom.

"Where's three-thirty-two?"

Jessica points straight ahead.

"Where's three-twenty-five?"

Jessica points around a corner.

Behind her, in the English office, Harriet asks Denise, "How do I put in my Delaney cards? They always fall out." Denise shows her the trick. Harriet, hastening past Jessica toward her first class, sighs, "I want to go home."

Then a girl strides up to Jessica. She says nothing, simply stands and waits to be recognized. Jessica cannot quite place her. She squints, focuses, remembers. Then she opens her arms to the girl and, her voice rising up the register, says, "Oh, my God."

*   *   *

Like her 300 colleagues, Jessica learns more precisely the odds she faces at the first staff meeting of the year. It begins as a deceptively social occasion, a summer's end reunion in the school auditorium. Jessica compares tans with one friend as they amble down the aisle, waves to several others as she settles into an eighth-row seat, and once there skims through a neighbor's photo album from a Hawaiian cruise. Whispers persist even as the gathering is brought to order.

On the auditorium's side wall, above Jessica and the rest, stretches a mural of the deity Education passing books of wisdom to an acolyte on bended knee. The man before them, Dr. Noel N. Kriftcher, the seventh principal of Seward Park High School, clutches in his own hands not the knowledge of the ages but a computer printout analyzing the demographic and academic backgrounds of Seward Park's 667 incoming freshmen and sophomores. And nothing could make that mural seem more ironic.

Dr. Kriftcher paces as he speaks, pivoting on his heels to make eye contact with the teachers and counselors on each side of the center aisle. He has ruddy skin and arms bowstring tight from a summer's golfing. Even at the age of forty-eight, with glasses and an ebbing hairline, he can project arrogance and force effortlessly, and it is said by friends that in his professional life Noel Kriftcher does not care about being liked, as long as he is respected. Now he gestures with his right hand for emphasis, thrusting it into his pocket, swirling it in great circles, stitching the air like a seamstress. His voice grows faster, more insistent.

One-fourth of all new freshmen, Dr. Kriftcher says, are already seventeen years old, suggesting they have been held back several times or have only recently reached America. Nearly 20 percent were absent for more than eight weeks of the preceding school year, and half of them are officially considered high risks of dropping out. Some 155 require bilingual education or courses in English as a Second Language. And all these numbers, Dr. Kriftcher reminds the teachers, are bound to increase. If recent history repeats itself, 600 more students, most of them new immigrants, will register at Seward Park during the academic year, pushing the school toward 150 percent of capacity.

To Jessica and the teachers and counselors around her, these statistics are as distressing as they are familiar. Among Seward Park's continuing students, nearly nine in ten live with parents who do not speak English. Half come from single-parent families and 65 percent from families who are eligible for public assistance. About 30 students inhabit welfare hotels or homeless shelters and as many as 150 have been deserted or evicted by their parents and left to raise themselves. Virtually all attended elementary and junior high schools that are among the poorest in the city. When the current seniors entered

Seward Park, only 13.8 percent were reading at grade level, and for the current juniors, the figure was 7.5 percent.

It comes as no surprise, then, that from two-thirds to three-quarters of Seward Park's upperclassmen read below grade level and that more than one-tenth drop out. Last year's seniors scored a mean of 288 points, on a scale of 200 to 800, on the verbal section of the Scholastic Aptitude Test, placing Seward Park in the lowest 20 percent nationally. (Significantly, those same seniors had a mean of 457, in the highest third nationally, on the mathematics portion of the same test, in which a facility with English matters far less.) A New York State task force, noting Seward Park's drop-out rate and its scores on a standardized reading test, ranked the school in late 1985 among the worst 10 percent in the state.

The report made no mention of the nature of Seward Park's student body, a subject with which Dr. Kriftcher is all too conversant. He has seen a bright girl fail because her immigrant parents insisted on returning her overseas for an arranged marriage. He has seen the victim of a knifing stumble into his office seeking refuge. Fettered by a variety of board regulations and union contracts, he cannot select his own faculty or even give orders to the janitors. Since becoming principal at Seward Park in 1980, he has reflected often on one piece of advice from a friend in public education: "You can't look at the big picture. It's too frightening. You have to look at one small picture. And then another. And then another."

Dr. Kriftcher holds the microphone in his right hand and crosses his legs just above the ankle. "During the course of the struggle," he says, "we can't always see the forest through the trees. We can't always see the success we're having. The truth is, we have been successful." Retreating several steps, he plucks a letter from atop a folding table, then reads aloud. The superintendent of Manhattan high schools is congratulating Seward Park on its attendance rate, its improved scores on statewide examinations, and its comparatively few violent crimes. Faint praise is better than none. Dr. Kriftcher reminds the teachers and counselors that more than 90 percent of Seward Park's graduates last June went on to college, trade school, or the military, carrying with them more than $100,000 in scholarship money. He likes the shape of that number, round and six figures long.

Once again, he refers to the statistical profile of the incoming students, but this time he raises the sheet aloft. "They need the nurturing we've given in the past," the principal says. "So what do you do? Do you say, 'I could win the NBA if I coached the L.A. Lakers, but I coach the Indiana Whatevers.'" He pauses, grinds one heel, and smiles slyly at Jessica Siegel and 300 others. "The question is: What can you accomplish with the Indiana Whatevers?"

*   *   *

The bell at Seward Park does not ring. Instead, it emits a tubular, metallic sound, something out of a World War II submarine movie. And for Jessica, immersion is an appropriate image. This term, she will teach five classes in four periods—about 140 students in all, or nearly twice the load of a teacher in a suburban high school. The first and second periods of the day, she teaches two rounds of English 7, a required course in American literature. The fifth period, she teaches the Lower East Side class, officially known as humanities, with Bruce. The seventh period, she teaches both beginning and advanced journalism. She cannot have a separate class for her six advanced students, even though they have already taken and mastered the beginning course, because Seward Park literally cannot afford to maintain a class with fewer than fifteen pupils. Given the choice to double up or not teach the advanced class, she chose more work.

This schedule requires Jessica to prepare three different lesson plans each day, a task that can easily consume three hours, and to decide how to deploy the advanced journalism students. In addition to teaching and to advising *Seward World,* she serves as assistant chairwoman of the English Department, an appointment she received two years ago from Ben Dachs, who was then the English chairman. Officially, the job required Jessica to perform clerical chores in exchange for teaching four periods a day instead of the normal five. In reality, Ben allowed—encouraged—her to spend the free period working on *Seward World.* He understood that her $800 stipend as newspaper adviser hardly compensated her for the hours she devoted; he appreciated how she used the newspaper to teach writing and thinking. Ben Dachs was Jessica's friend and mentor. But he is gone now, beginning a try-out as principal of Beach Channel High School in Queens, and Jessica will answer to his replacement, Emma Jon. And that will probably mean paperwork, by the book.

Committed to duties in three different classrooms, plus the English office, Jessica conducts business out of a nylon tote bag that Steve Anderson calls "Big Black." It weighs well over twenty pounds and contains grade books, attendance books, homework assignments, a looseleaf binder of handwritten lesson plans, spare chalk, a stapler, an official school calendar, and a separate manila folder of papers to be graded for each class. This morning is one of the few times all year that the folders will be empty.

Since Jessica's two English classes meet in the same room, 336, she sets up a sort of home there. She removes a grammar teacher's cartoons of anthropoid commas and semicolons from the bulletin board and posts in their place a Red Grooms illustration, a color photograph of a knish bakery, a former student's drawings of Lower East Side markets, the seal of the Dominican Republic, and a flyer for a history exhibit about Chinese laundries. By Siegel standards, this is minimalism. The thumb tacks have barely settled into the cork when the first kids walk in the door for English 7. Naturally, they slump in the last row.

"Come on," Jessica says. "Move to the front. We've got a nice small class." Then she remembers what always happens to nice, small classes—late registration; new immigrants; and, before you know it, the class has its maximum of thirty-four. "We'll see how long it lasts."

She wants to draw in the students, to thrill them a little. The bulletin board is part of the strategy, and so is her penchant for bright, funky attire. Today she wears four earrings and five rings, two silver on her left hand and three gold on her right, and a dress from Pakistan, bonewhite cotton printed with blue designs that are as cryptic and angular as cuneiform. Jessica's style always made Ben Dachs think of *The Wizard of Oz*. A student once asked, "Miss Siegel, do you water that dress?"

Even as Jessica tries to captivate her students, she wants to control them—not to dictate or deaden, but not to abdicate authority, either. She constantly judges herself against an internal spectrum whose extremes are marked "Fascist" and "Bleeding Heart." It took her years to develop a classroom presence that felt organic, for she was naturally a listener, a backbencher, a person who began countless sentences, "I don't know a lot about this, but. . . ."

Gradually, she created from pieces of herself a persona that might best be called The Tough Cookie. She stands this morning with right hand on hip, head cocked slightly, eyebrows arched in mock disbelief; every so often, she shoots a phrase Jersey City style out of a gulley at the corner of her mouth. "Gimme a break," she says to a lying latecomer.

Her students will hear her say the same thing a hundred times before the term is over, hear her bite down hard on "Gimme" and stretch "break" into an aria of annoyance.

There is a truism among New York City teachers that holds, "Don't smile till Christmas," the idea being that kids treat kind teachers the way sharks treat wounded swimmers. Jessica cannot subscribe to that viewpoint; if the Law of the Jungle governed Seward Park, she would never have survived. On the other hand, kids want grown-ups to be grown-ups, to set standards and to mete out discipline. The Tough Cookie gives unconditional love, conditionally.

Room 336 is spartan, which is to say it is better than many at Seward Park. Thirty-five wooden desks, arrayed in five rows of seven, appear to be the school's originals. One expects to find such desks in a Vermont antique store, sanded and laquered and ready for second childhood as planters, rather than bolted to a classroom floor like an army frozen at attention. In gouges from penknife and ballpoint, in cartoons and hearts and the doggerel verse of scatology, the desks reveal their ancestry. Here sat "Wild" and "Cesar" and "P. F." Here Rosa proclaimed her love for Tony. "Mucho, mucho," it says beneath the heart.

The wooden floor is clean but bare, its varnish long ago abraded by a million squirming sneakers. The two closets at the rear of the room bear the rubrics "Day School" and "Night School," a reminder of Seward Park's original mission to educate immigrant children in one shift and their parents in another. The southern side of the classroom consists of two radiators topped by six tall windows, which can be opened only from the top. The task goes to whichever student proves capable of wielding a ten-foot pole as dexterously as an Arthurian jouster.

From their seats, the students can look across Grand Street at an abandoned apartment building, a couple of clotheslines, and a warehouse with brown boxes stacked behind greasy windows. On clear days, they can spy the two steel towers of the World Trade Center, gleaming in the southeastern sky. Room 336 is rarely quiet. A din of engines, alarms, sirens, brakes, radios, arguments, and firecrackers intrudes through the windows and then resonates off the bare walls. Trying to teach amid the tumult is like trying to exchange romantic pleasantries at a drum-corps competition.

The first order of business is the most elemental, and, typically, it is clerical. Jessica passes out rectangular pieces of paper measuring 3¼ by 1⅝ inches, about the size of a baseball-ticket stub. These are Delaney cards, so named for their inventor, and they serve as the DNA of school life in New York, carrying the essential genetic coding. Each student writes his name, nickname, homeroom, address, telephone, and one parent's name on the card, and then returns it to Jessica, who arranges the cards in the slots of a specially made cardboard sheet to conform to the class's seating pattern. She will use the cards to learn names, to take attendance, and to record latenesses. For now, these bits of paper provide what little Jessica knows about her new students, which isn't much.

Looking down the aisles and across the rows, Jessica sees the usual Seward Park stew, all the confusion an immigrant society can offer—an American-born black alongside a Panamanian who has the same pigment but speaks Spanish at home; a Chinese in pleated trousers and aviator glasses in front of a compatriot with crudely hacked hair and a secondhand sweatshirt; a Wilberto next to a Wilfredo; three Robertos, one of whom wants to be called Domingo. She strives for any connection, however faint. "Aren't you Carlos's sister? . . . You're Mei Ling's friend, right? . . . You live on Claremont? I used to live right around there."

After collecting the Delaney cards, she proceeds desk by desk, signing the computer printout of each student's schedule, again offering some personal touch. "You're taking physics? I'm impressed" . . . "You have Miss Lasalle for history? She's great!" . . . Some of what she discovers on the program cards, as the schedules are known, she deliberately lets pass without comment. Any student who failed at least three classes last term receives the designation "YRO" for "Youth Reach Out." Students with the class entitled "Resource Room" require intensive remedial instruction. Jessica silently notes that one girl has listed a shelter as her home address.

But just now, there is no time to question or pursue. There is time only to begin.

"So you came back from your vacation and you saw 'English Seven, J. Siegel' on your program card," she says, prowling the front of the room. "What did you think?"

Silence.

"Say it. I can take it. 'Not again. Oh, my God!'"

More silence.

"Well, what'd you think? Lisa?"

"Nothing."

"You didn't ask your friends?"

Lisa nods her head no.

"Angel? What about you? What'd you think."

"I really don't like English."

"So?" Jessica says, stretching her arms and turning her palms skyward, tugging the word into two syllables. "None of you checked me out with your friends? You people haven't learned any sneaky techniques yet." The class laughs, giving her an opening. "Because, you know, you come into any relationship with expectations." She pauses. "Whether it's a blind date or a class, it's better if you know what the expectations are from the start. Right? Your friend says, 'I'm gonna fix you up with this beautiful girl.' Don't you want to know what she looks like? Gorgeous? Sexy? Great personality? Blah, blah, blah?"

"Liz Taylor," someone shouts from the back.

"What else?" Jessica says, seizing the joke. "Specifically." She spots a hand in the back of the room. "Alex?"

"Oh, man," the rotund Chinese boy protests. "I was just fixin' my hair. I wasn't raisin' my hand."

"Too late. You got a blind date. What do you hope she's like?"

"Um, nice eyes." Pause. "Nice mouth." Another pause. "A good personality."

Alex sounds like an Ann Landers column, and Jessica knows seventeen-year-old boys better than that. She waits, and the silence becomes her ally. Finally, Alex speaks.

"A nice . . . um . . . body." The class cracks up, but Jessica smiles with satisfaction. She has wrung out a little truth.

"OK," she continues. "So you *do* have expectations built up. And if someone doesn't live up to them, then . . ." A hand rises. "Julio?"

"You're let down."

"Right, you're let down." She jostles a piece of chalk in her palm, sustaining the moment for emphasis. "Now, you have expectations of me, and I have expectations of you." Again, she toys with the chalk. "And it's best we know what they are."

Turning to the blackboard, Jessica writes the graduation requirements, including the much-feared New York State examinations. Every student must pass a battery of minimum-skills tests in mathematics, reading, and writing—the Regents Competency Tests, more commonly known as "the RCTs." Beyond those loom the much more rigorous Regents examinations in English, social studies, and several other subjects. Students can graduate without passing the Regents, as only one in four at Seward Park does, but the failure will be recorded on their transcripts and indicated on their diplomas by the conspicuous absence of the Regents endorsement. Graduating without having passed the Regents, Jessica's students know, is graduating second rate. And the colleges and employers whom they will beseech for higher education and decent jobs know it, too.

Jessica assures the students she will prepare them for the Regents tests. Still, she can sense their worries. These kids are a cross section of Seward Park as a whole—Hispanics, Asians, and a few blacks, from families who are working class at best and case studies of social dysfunction at worst. The Regents is the test on which they must compete, however indirectly, against the offspring of Long Island and Westchester and Park Avenue. She asks how many in the class want to go to college. A few thrust up their hands. Most leave their arms on their desks and gingerly open their palms. Their physical language tells Jessica that, yes, they want to attend college, even desperately, but that they are not sure they can make it, or that they deserve it. Almost every year, Jessica has a moment in class when someone asks her about her background. When she explains that she has a master's degree, the questioner invariably says, "Then what are you doing at a school like Seward?" That challenge is a commentary not on Jessica's worthiness, but on the students' sense of their own.

"I know, I know," Jessica says. "College seems vague and intimidating. You have so many questions. Majors? Money? Forms? Applications? Deadlines? SATs?" She mimes tearing her hair, then eases into a smile. "But don't start staying up late and worrying about it now. We'll be working on it in class."

Jessica now passes out a list of her expectations. Most of them are commonplace—regular attendance, homework, writing assignments, participation in class. But the final item crystallizes her own approach. "If you have a problem, a question, a thought, or a joke or you need extra help or you just want to say hello," Number 11 reads, "see Ms. Siegel."

When she feels the eyes lift from the paper up to her, Jessica resumes. She wants to stress the importance of the writing assignments, some to be written in a journal during the first five minutes of class, some to be prepared in answer to homework questions. To Jessica, writing is a case of the emperor's new clothes. She never lacks students who are aware, who read and speak well. And, certainly, some students arrive as natural writers. But it is more common for her twelfth graders to write one-sentence answers on homework and one-paragraph essays on tests and then to wonder why she demands more for a passing grade. Most of the students grew up without English in their households and without books in any language at home. They learned to avoid writing, and they began to fear writing, because writing revealed their nakedness, and the first impulse of the un-clothed is to grab the nearest fig leaf. Somehow they end up in twelfth grade—exactly how often mystifies Jessica. In eighteen weeks, she cannot redress eleven years of neglect or bad habits or cultural dis-location. And so, rather than marshal her efforts toward vocabulary and grammar, she tries to disarm the fear and soften the shame that surround writing and to trust that somewhere, sometime, the me-chanical skills will follow. She practices the art of the possible.

"Let's face it," she says, spreading her arms in a gesture of con-fession, "we don't write much anymore. And I include myself here. It's too easy to turn on TV or go to the movies. Even writing letters. You want to talk to your uncle in Puerto Rico, you pick up the phone. Same with Hong Kong, probably. So the only thing most of you write is your homework. And you hate it. Well, just like an athlete has to warm up, our journals will be a way for you to warm up, get your thoughts going without worrying about spelling and grammar. It's a way to get your ideas on paper."

She leans forward, elbows locked and palms braced against the desktop. "I want you to write what you feel. You want to write how much you hate this class? Fine with me." She stands back from the desk, shrugs and tosses her curls, all insouciance. "I will never say, 'Hey, you misspelled that word—ehhhh.'" The sound is of the final buzzer on a game show. "I will never say, 'You failed, you're stupid.'" She delivers "stupid" as a playground taunt, the way a third grader calls someone a "retard," and the class laughs. "The idea is to get you to write."

She pauses.

"I had a kid last year who was *allergic* to homework. *Morally opposed* to homework. Whaddaya think, I give you homework just to keep you off the streets?"

"It works," someone shouts from the back of the room.

"I think if you want to be on the street, homework won't keep you off it," Jessica answers. "I'm giving you a chance to loosen up and get your thoughts on paper. And to get ready for the next day, to direct your attention to the important aspects of the book we're working on. I won't ask you, 'What color is the coat on page forty?' I want to make you think." She sits on the front left corner of the desk. "Now I spent all this time laying out 'You gotta do this, you gotta do that, or I'll fail you.' But, like I said, it's a two-way street."

Pause.

"So now there's something I want you to do for me."

The room buzzes with anticipation.

"I want you to write me a composition . . ."

The buzz becomes a groan. Jessica rises from the desk and moves to the board, grabbing a piece of chalk on the way. She talks as she writes.

". . . on what makes a good teacher."

She hears muffled words in the back, followed by laughter.

"What?" Jessica asks, turning to face the class.

"Someone who passes you," comes the reply.

"Gimme a break."

She returns to the board and writes in her looping hand: "What are your expectations for Ms. Siegel and English 7? What do you hope to get out of the course? In your estimation, what makes a good teacher and class?"

She hears the bleating behind her. She pivots, freezes everyone with a stare, and adopts her best Tough Cookie tone to say, "Here's your chance to lay it out to me the way I laid it out to you. Remember, you've been in school for twelve years already. You're the experts."

*   *   *

During the one free period they share, Jessica meets Bruce amid the rain buckets and fallen plaster of the faculty smoking lounge. They need to recruit more students for the Lower East Side class and they need to decide the sequence of their lessons. But first Bruce needs Jessica to punch his time card when she departs, so he can leave school early and visit 65 Court Street in Brooklyn. Once he gives the address, Jessica needs to know no more to sympathize. Bruce is bound for the Board of Education's Placement Bureau, its famously coarse hiring hall, in an ongoing quest to be formally appointed to the school where he already teaches.

Bruce began working at Seward Park as a substitute in 1980, using the income to support his doctoral studies, but soon grew so engaged by the challenge of educating slum children that he set aside his dissertation and earned a temporary license. Since joining the faculty full time in September 1983, he has developed the Lower East Side class with Jessica, designed a course using drama to teach history, and produced a student play about immigration entitled *José, Can You See?* A number of his colleagues may regard Bruce as a brash radical— he answers the telephone in his departmental office, "Socialist Studies" and asks boys in his classes, "Get laid much this summer?"—but few can criticize his innovation or vigor. Seward Park's seniors vote each June for graduation marshals, two men and two women from a staff of nearly 300, and twice in four years they chose Bruce.

The Board of Education, however, seems far less desirous of his services. It did not offer a licensing examination in high school social studies for more than five years, from January 1982 until it bent to legislative pressure and held a closed test in February 1987. After all that waiting, all Bruce had to do to prove his fitness as an educator was to answer three questions about history and pedagogy. It took thirty minutes. Four months later, he learned he had passed with a score of 85, entitling him to a full license. He asked Dr. Kriftcher for a letter requesting that the Placement Unit assign him to Seward Park. He delivered both the letter and the formal notification of his test score to the Placement Unit more than a month ago. He has come today to find out why he still is unappointed.

"Steerage," he mutters when he walks into the hiring hall. It is the second week of the academic year and the first week of classes, yet 331 teaching positions in the city remain unfilled, and nearly as many teachers remain unassigned to any school. Many of the fifty supplicants in this room have been waiting since morning, and a few are into their second or third day. "I was so motivated last year," one man is telling a friend. "I didn't miss a day. I loved my job. People kept telling me, 'Wait till the board fucks you, then you'll change your mind.' And that's what's happening here."

The hiring hall is a long, rectangular place, with a low fiberboard ceiling and a gray linoleum floor dotted with coffee stains, paper clips, and fragmented potato chips. Were it not for the wall maps, the room could be mistaken for the intake office of a Medicaid clinic. The maps show the locations of each high school and the borders of all thirty-two community school districts, and they bear the smudges of many searching hands. Through blurry windows, the teachers can see shadowy forms scurrying, and through the room divider they can hear the stutter of ringing telephones and bleeping computers. Next to the closed door of Room 603, the office for high school placement, a brightly colored sign advises, "Feel Good About Yourself."

Bruce enters to find a short, pudgy white woman seated at a metal desk. From past visits, he knows that hers is the face of authority. Sometimes the teachers languishing outside joke about sending her a letter-bomb.

"I was checking on the status of my application for appointment," Bruce says humbly.

"What are you talking about?" she snaps. "There's no such thing."

Bruce squints, as if he heard wrong. His thick eyebrows press down.

"What I mean," he says, "is that I gave you these documents over the summer."

"Well, you have to get on the list that you're available."

"But what does that mean?" Bruce asks. He leans a bit over her desk. Some minor-key irritation creeps into his tone, although any behavior except submission is risky. "I gave the documents in July. I've been teaching at the school for four years."

"That doesn't matter," she says. *"You obviously don't understand."* She glances at Bruce's face, which is blank in confusion. "You have to be on the list. We'll call you when we start appointing off the July list."

"When will that be?"

"Whenever we do it."

She pauses, as if expecting Bruce to excuse himself. A clock ticks. He does not move.

"All right," she says. "Room 601."

Room 601 bears the designation "Central Processing and Approval." Bruce finds a young black man at a desk. Starting afresh, he returns to his earnest voice.

"I want to be placed on the available list."

"Were you ever unavailable?"

"No."

The man swivels his chair to face a computer. He punches several keys and green type floods the screen. He searches for Bruce's identification number.

"You're available," he assures Bruce. "They haven't called you yet?"

"No. What do I do?"

"Go to Room 603."

"They sent me here."

Baffled again, Bruce returns to Room 603 and the straw boss.

"I'm on the list."

"Fine."

"Is there any way of knowing when I'll be called?"

"No one could tell you that."

"Even though I'm working at Seward already and the school wants me?"

She starts to explain that people must be hired in order of their grades on the licensing examination, as a safeguard against patronage. Bruce wonders why no one told him that before he took the test. Now, he realizes, his job at Seward Park could be given to anyone who scored higher, and he, in turn, could be shunted to any high school from the Bronx to Staten Island. Until Bruce is appointed somewhere, which might be next term or next fall, his salary will be frozen at $28,922 a year, $1,200 less than he is entitled to as a licensed fifth-year teacher. And his four years of full-time employment with the temporary license will not count toward pension and sabbatical benefits.

Bruce leaves the hiring hall shaking his head and calling himself a shmuck. His wife, Melicia, seven years his junior, earns more than he does as a sous-chef. His younger brother, Ron, makes $40,000 a year as the dean of boys at a private school on Long Island and pays $150 a month less for a subsidized campus home than Bruce does for a Queens Boulevard apartment. Twice already, the private school has approached Bruce, dangling a better salary and class sizes of ten or twelve in rooms where the desks aren't bolted to the floor.

He has said no. So far.

*   *   *

Now the day is done, day one. Jessica walks to the basement, passing the metal shop and the swimming pool on the way to the storage room, where she keeps her bike. She lugs it up the stairs to Room 130, where she punches out. Outside, the late summer sky curves over Ludlow Street like a blue dome.

Jessica makes a stop four blocks from Seward Park, at the University Settlement. The settlement house, founded when the surrounding streets formed a Jewish ghetto, runs a community-service program for high school students called Pathfinders. The members meet three afternoons a week to discuss problems, study leadership, and ultimately undertake a project to improve the neighborhood. Those who last the year receive a $1,000 grant for college. One of the program's staff members, Elaine Taylor, asked Jessica to recommend some juniors and seniors. Elaine did not know Jessica personally. Jessica just has that kind of reputation.

She chats with Elaine awhile and promises to start recruiting potential Pathfinders this week. As long as she's in the University Settlement, she decides to look up Sammy Ryan's beloved foster mother, Isabel Rivera, who is a social worker here. She finds Isabel in an airless fourth-floor office. She is a portly woman with olive skin, short gray hair, and a smile as comforting as a down pillow. The two women have never met, but each has heard a great deal about the other from Sammy, most of it adulatory. Jessica tells Isabel how proud she is of Sammy's hard work at college. Why, he had expected to flunk out of summer school, and the last she heard from him he was reading John Locke. Isabel beams at Jessica and says that whenever she can spare twenty dollars she sends it to Sammy. Otherwise, he has no money to eat out, and on Sunday the cafeteria serves only two meals. And you know Sammy's appetite.

By the time Jessica returns to her bike, early evening shadows fill the street. She retraces her morning journey, but now with the rest of the world awake. Bums wash windshields at the corner of Delancey and the Bowery, departing once they've earned their pint. The second shift marches into a garment factory on Spring Street. At the outdoor cafes lining Seventh Avenue South, actresses between roles serve capuccino to poets between muses.

Jessica pulls her bike onto the curb and then up three steps into the lobby of her building. It is not a bad building because it has, in Manhattan lexicon, location. It is near poets, actresses, and cappuccino. It is not, however, an especially distinctive building. Red bricks and beige mortar rise six stories from the street. The lobby sports three shades of green—sea green for the door, lime green for the trim, pale green for the walls. Nothing offends; nothing charms.

Jessica's apartment rests at the rear of the ground floor, providing her no direct sunlight, but easy access to the garbage cans. The apartment is shaped roughly like an elongated "S," with the living room leading to the kitchen and bathroom, which, in turn, lead to the bedroom. The parquet floor is gouged and scuffed. A fault line runs up one wall of the living room and across the ceiling, giving the impression that the room was at some point sawed apart and then hastily glued back together. Gaffing tape seals leaky pipes. Plaster patches blemish the walls.

Jessica pays the relative pittance of $280 a month for the apartment, a feat she managed by having consecrated a "paper marriage" with the then-tenant in 1976, entitling her to his rent control. Without dissembling, she could not have remained in Manhattan, where a comparably modest apartment commands $1,000 or more a month. Eventually, Jessica's landlord sued to evict her. Jessica had no case, but she hired an energetic lawyer with large fangs. The landlord dispatched his regular counsel, who was in his eighties. An agreement was struck: Jessica could stay in the apartment until December 1988 and then would receive a cash settlement for obediently getting lost. For the next fifteen months, though, she anticipates often boiling her bathwater.

As Jessica slides her key into the door, she can hear her cat, Marmalade, crying for food. Entering the room, she comes face to face with a poster of Harpo Marx, pensive beneath blond curls, the model for her costume on several Halloweens. A Chinese paper lantern hangs from the living room ceiling, obscuring the bare bulbs above. No surface goes unadorned by a weaving, a paper cut, a cloth doll. A statue of Don Quixote stands on the windowsill, between the air conditioner and the corn plant. Masks of gods and demons stare from the walls. An oil painting by her mother dominates one corner, still photographs by her brother fill another. These seem more than decorations; they are talismans.

Records and books line the far wall, arranged on the shelves that Jessica has jerry-rigged from cinderblocks and raw lumber; the motif might be called Early Graduate Student. Toward the right side of the record collection is the Bruce Springsteen shrine—all nine of his albums, six cassette tapes, three benefit records featuring him, two twelve-inch singles, and one bootleg. A two-foot poster of Springsteen hangs just around the corner. Springsteen buttons appear on several walls. Jessica loves music of ideas and adult passions—Los Lobos, Tracy Nelson, Robert Cray, Maria Muldaur, Al Green—but she loves Bruce Springsteen's beyond all others.

When Springsteen sings about the people who labor in car washes and auto plants, the forgotten Everymen, his words assure Jessica that hard work is a value and that values are worth having. When Springsteen sings love songs to single mothers and Jersey Shore waitresses, he promises Jessica that here stands one man who will love you for all the goodness that nobody else notices. When Springsteen married a twenty-five-year-old model, Jessica cursed her luck.

In the hallway near the kitchen, Jessica has a cork board. Every inch is covered with photographs. Here Sammy Ryan adjusts his blue mortarboard, giving a "Number One" sign with his right hand. There Bruce Baskind teaches the humanities class, clasping a window pole to his side like a shepherd's staff. Jessica's firmament holds Norman Wong and Salome Junco, Sue Lee and Alex Iturralde, Juan Gonzalez and Teri Chan, all the stars of *Seward World,* all the favorite students of years gone.

One photograph explains all the rest. It shows five women in cutoffs and T-shirts sitting at a grassy campsite. The two women on the right wear shirts with the word "PESSIMIST." The woman in the middle wears a shirt that says, "ON THE FENCE." The two women on the left wear shirts declaring "OPTIMIST." Jessica is the farthest on the left, her shirt lettered in brilliant yellow, her thumb thrust skyward.

The photograph was shot in 1984, during the annual camping trip Jessica used to take with two of her college roomates, Ilene Kantrov and Ellen Bogolub, and two of Ilene's friends from high school, Debbie Olshever and Teri Newman. The trips celebrated "sissy camping," in Ilene's phrase, with chilled chardonnay and fresh-ground coffee and the occasional lobster. Over those meals, the women talked about their lives, charting their relationships and their careers with a mixture of truth and fantasy. Sometimes, to spare hurt feelings, they would refer to each other with make-believe names, silly anachronisms like "Doris" and "Ida." The T-shirts arose from one particular conversation on the 1983 trip, a conversation built around the question, "Are good things likely to happen to me?"

Jessica passes the photograph on the way to feeding Marmalade. If the photograph were taken again, she thinks, she might position herself elsewhere. Even Ilene has kidded her about that, saying that Jessica's "OPTIMIST" shirt needs a footnote. It would say, "For other people."

With Marmalade occupied by 9 Lives, Jessica plays back the messages on her answering machine. Teri Newman is coming to the city for a wedding. Sue Lee has a new boyfriend at college. Sammy Ryan wants to read her his class essay about the Lower East Side. She decides to call them back later or tomorrow. She sits in a kitchen chair, dishes and pans and recipe books looming above like turrets. What does she want for dinner? She had salad for lunch. She usually has salad for lunch.

These twilight hours are rarely easy. Jessica can divine the efforts of the day deep in her chest, where the muscles ache from talking, talking, talking. Her head feels full of the lives of others, too full to leave room for her own. The sensation is of a vessel about to fly apart from the pressure of its contents. *Always on,* she thinks. *I'm always on.*

In the past, she took night courses in Spanish and squash and the history of fabric. A few years ago, she had a boyfriend who loved to cook, and she would bicycle to his house in midevening for homemade shrimp scampi. That was a way to live. But the price of teaching writing is reading writing—journals, homework, test essays, *Seward World* articles, with at least a paragraph of commentary in red ink for each one. If she goes to a play or to dinner with a friend, Jessica knows from experience, she may be up until 2 A.M., grading and writing lesson plans. Either that, or go to bed at midnight and wake up at 4 A.M. and then stagger through the day. When she falls behind, and the kids start asking where their papers are, the fearsome critic inside her scolds, *You're a lousy teacher. You're not living up to expectations.*

Meanwhile, there is work to do. Jessica opens the leaf table in the living room, draws up a chair, turns on a lamp, and dives into the compositions. The subject, of course, is expectations.

"My expectation is that Ms. Siegel will be a teacher give the students less homework and sometime tell the students a joke."

"What I really want from English is to learn and pass the course."

Jessica sees the name on the top line and remembers that this girl already has a baby.

"I want to get more skills in the english field, so that when and if I go to College I will be able to hold my owne."

"I expect a teacher to keep a student involved. I expect her to do this by having fun and interesting lessons that are not just lectures. There must also be a little comedy in the lessons, which will keep us awake. A teacher must be understanding of her students' problems."

Now there, Jessica tells herself, *is a boy who thinks about things.*

"I want to learn as much as my brain can handle."

"I hope you'll help me to understand myself and to understand that I have the greatest opportunity in life, and that is to learn."

Jessica had the girl in journalism class last spring. It's hard to believe she came from Ecuador just a couple of years ago.

"I did of wrong thought. To me it was just another class for me to pass even if you was hard or not. I didn't her nothing about you this the first time I heard about you, so I thought you was a old lady that can't teach."

Oh, my God, Jessica thinks. *Oh, my God. Didn't anyone ever stop to teach this kid English?*

"A good teacher is a teacher who cares. A teacher who wants to help a student in class and out of class. A teacher that you can talk to. A teacher that will take the time to talk to you. A teacher whom you can also be friends with."

Jessica touches her red pen to the paper and writes in the margin, "I agree!"

Sixty compositions later, Jessica pushes back her chair and collapses onto the couch. Marmalade has pricked the brown fabric until it bleeds white stuffing; Jessica would have it reupholstered if she had the money. She puts up her feet on a steamer trunk. At 10:30 P.M., she opens the morning paper. Beside the couch are two piles of newspapers and magazines, each nearly two feet tall. She subscribes to both the Columbia and Washington journalism reviews; she has never quite rid herself of the desire to return to her earlier career as a reporter. She gets magazines about music and fashion and crafts, the hobbies for which she wishes she had more time.

As Jessica pads into the bedroom, she passes her loom. She had begun weaving a shawl for her mother the week before, then ran out of that good yarn she'd bought last year in Cape May. She wants to finish the shawl in time for Hanukkah. Or maybe before. Her mother gives so often and gets so rarely, Jessica thinks. Now that school has started, she worries that the shawl will lie suspended in the wooden frame for weeks and months, like Penelope's winding sheet, ever unfinished.

2

Lamplight

Jᴇssɪᴄᴀ sɪᴇɢᴇʟ ᴛᴜʀɴs her back to the thirty-five desks in Room 336 and spies a chunk of chalk in the grooved tray beneath the blackboard. As she hears footfalls of the arriving class behind her and seats creaking beneath the students' weight, she writes in four-inch-high letters, "Journal Topic: Who Am I? Describe Yourself." She dips into Big Black for a folder of rexos—the Seward Park term for dittoes—as the bell rings.

By now, two weeks into the term, the students know they are expected to check the journal topic upon entering Room 336 and to scribble away for a few moments. Jessica says nothing during this time except a barbed "Elvin!" or "Steve!" when someone reads the *Daily News* sports section instead of writing in his journal. She leaves the front and rear doors open into the hall, so the room catches a dry fall breeze. This is one of Seward Park's few times of grace between a summer without air-conditioning and a winter with hyperthyroid radiators. Jessica gleams like neon in a yellow rayon dress and shocking pink stockings; a necklace of tiny Crackerjack toys—a locomotive, a wristwatch, a lemon, a clothespin—rests on her chest. Suddenly the sound of fenders colliding rises from Grand Street, followed hard by horns and cursing. Today, grace lasts shorter than usual.

The students seem perplexed. Journal topics are usually clearer in scope and intent. "Who Am I?" The question is both simple and complex, obvious and elliptical. Pens sputter and stall in their journey across notebook pages. Fingers scratch scalps, sighs fill the air. Still, Jessica says nothing, for a certain confusion, even a discomfiture, is part of the plan. Before the week is over, each of her seventy English 7 students will have handed in an autobiography—well, at least begun one. Only after these lessons will Jessica proceed into her survey of American literature, only after she begins to know who she is teaching. She has memorized names and faces, but characters remain indistinct. In the course of writing an autobiography, each one will gradually turn, like a Polaroid photograph, from a dull brown emulsion to a focused and fully colored portrait.

School explains only so much about a student, Jessica believes. The largest clues to success or failure lie beyond Seward Park's portals, in the home and on the street. Some of Jessica's colleagues think the less they find out about their kids's outer lives, the better; the beauty of the teacher-student relationship to them is its circumscribed nature. These teachers realize that tragedy, real tragedy, exists outside Seward Park, but at worst they really do not care, and at best they fear they could not demand academic excellence from the weepy position of a confidante. Jessica respects some of these teachers—she herself reels from the war between head and heart—but she cannot share their ways. She must know more. It is the journalist in the teacher; it is the humanist in the journalist.

Just the other day, Jessica was telling Harriet Stein that the kids with whom she often becomes closest are the troublemakers. She pulls them out of the room for impromptu conferences. She calls their mothers. She meets their mothers. Once in awhile, the mothers send her cake. The result is a depth that Jessica less easily achieves with pupils who sit decorously at their desks, doing the right thing. The ingrate, after all, only wants attention, which is an understandable object in a high school of 3,500, and even more so for a teenager living almost by definition in what the novelist George Lamming called "the castle of my skin."

Jessica depends on youthful vanity and self-absorption. They are her allies in encouraging her students to write. "Presumably, it's a subject they care about—their lives," Jessica once said in explaining her emphasis on autobiographies. "It's not 'What I Did on My Summer Vacation' or 'What I Think about Capital Punishment.' I'm asking them for *their* feelings, *their* thoughts. Which may be powerful enough to break down the writing blocks. I mean, how is someone who was in a car accident going to learn to walk again? Not by sitting in a chair. By trying out muscles. However painful that is at first. So the next time, it doesn't hurt as much."

The more immediate benefit is college admission. Jessica constantly stresses college to her classes, yet she does not teach advanced sections and she harbors a particular fondness for underachievers, for fine minds trailing Cs and Ds like tin cans from a mutt's tail. She has seen a moving autobiography pry open the gates of academe. She trusts in the power of words as much as she ever did when they were her words as a reporter, and perhaps more.

She surveys the class. Not a pen stirs.

"OK," Jessica says, "I want you to imagine you're an admissions counselor at Harvard. You're evaluating two hundred students for admission. Here are three. Which one would you pick."

She passes out a rexo, with the academic records of three fictitious students. Student A has a score of 1,150 on the Scholastic Aptitude test, a 97.6 average, ranks first in the class, and participates in chorus and basketball. Student B is the president of the senior class and a member of the volleyball team, with an SAT score of 1,200, a 93.2 average, and a class rank of fifteenth. Student C, who ranks eighth in the class with a 96.7 average and a 1,060 score on the SAT, appeared in the school play and was vice president of the Student Organization.

"Well?" She puts her hands on her hips. "Who would you let in? Why?"

" 'A,' " someone says. "First in the class."

"Forget about it," another adds, and Jessica recognizes this not as a dispute but, in the Seward Park glossary, as an affirmation. " 'B' only has a 93."

"Word!"

In rap-music terminology, then, a consensus has been reached. It always amazes Jessica how the students seize on "A" and mercilessly judge the two competitors. When one girl says of C, "I'd give that person a chance," she is ridiculed by the rest. Jessica quiets the class.

"The fact is," she tells them, "all these people could get into Harvard. They're all qualified. So how would you decide? They're all about equal in their grades and test scores and activities. The difference is their interview, their teacher recommendations." She shifts gears briefly. "So if anyone wants a college recommendation, just ask me." Come March, she will regret the offer. "And one of the most important things is the autobiographical essay."

She returns to the board and writes the aim of the day's lesson, "How Can We Prepare to Write an Autobiographical Essay?" There are murmurs as they begin to see the point. Then Jessica refers to the journal topic. "I asked you to write 'Who Am I?' What kind of things did you include?"

"Age."

"Interests."

"My high school average."

"Remember," Jessica says, moving in front of her desk, "the college has your transcript. This is your chance to tell them about *yourself.*" She pauses. "So?"

"I got a good personality."

"My hobbies."

"Like partying."

Everyone laughs and two boys slap high-fives.

"How my family affected me."

"That's good," Jessica says. "That sounds good."

The static of laughter, though, still crackles in the air. The students joke about college because humor disguises doubt. College is too much to ask. And Harvard. Harvard is a sweatshirt you buy if you want to dress like a preppy. Harvard is those guys on the subway carrying briefcases and the *Wall Street Journal.*

"There are two students I had who had sixty-nine averages," Jessica goes on, "who got into college at New Paltz." She waits. The laughter subsides. She can practically see that bit of information penetrating like dye into linen. She feels their fragile hope, and she thinks of those two students, Sammy Ryan and Vinnie Mickles. Sammy she pushed into New Paltz on a sort of package deal with a classmate the college dearly desired. But Vinnie won admission entirely alone, which was how he had accomplished everything in his life.

Jessica met Vinnie three years ago, when he took English 7. He attracted her notice in part because he appeared so irregularly, missing class eleven times in the first two months, and often arriving late and without homework. He told anyone who asked that his father was dead and his mother was a nurse, explanations that neatly accounted for one's absence and the other's frequent trips to hospitals. His ambitions, and those of his friends, ended with graduating high school, working as a security guard, and finding his own apartment.

Yet Vinnie had a harsh wit and an argumentative streak, and both convinced Jessica he was worth pursuing. She discovered that he had never met his biological father, that his stepfather had divorced his mother years ago, and that his mother had been in and out of psychiatric wards a half-dozen times. Vinnie lived with her in a tenement that had neither heat nor hot water, the cold cracking his hands until they bled and freezing his wet hair into an icy helmet. The reason was only too typical on the Lower East Side: The landlord was withholding services from his tenants in a war of attrition, trying to force them out so he could either rent their apartments at far higher rates or sell the entire building for several hundred thousand dollars.

It was hard to concentrate on homework, Vinnie confided to Jessica, when all you could think about was staying warm. Sometimes it felt colder in his apartment than out on the winter streets, where, at least, the sun brought a little warmth. And since none of the tenants except Vinnie and his mother spoke English fluently, they were incapable of taking the landlord to court, and in some instances afraid that if they sued, the landlord would report them as illegal aliens. So Vinnie kept shivering through his cold shower every morning and making due.

He expected Jessica to fail him in the first marking period, for he had accumulated twice the permitted absences for an entire term. But she passed him, and he recognized the grade as her wager on his potential. He stopped cutting and started reading and he often stayed after class to talk. One day he asked her if, in the 1960s, she had been "a flower girl." "A flower child," she corrected him, and the malapropism became their private joke.

Vinnie graduated and enlisted in the Marine Corps, and, for once, Jessica endorsed a military future. Anything that could whisk Vinnie away from his mother and his landlord was worth trying. She attended the farewell party the night before he left for Parris Island. When Vinnie was discharged two years later, he returned to Seward Park to look for Jessica and Bruce Baskind, his other favorite teacher. He wanted to go to college. Although she reckoned that his average was too low for him to gain admission, even under special programs for economically disadvantaged students, Jessica thought that a college had to understand what it took for Vinnie to have graduated, to have stayed sane, to have stayed alive. She had him write an autobiography, and he delivered a devastatingly dispassionate tale of his mad mother, his absent father, his icy apartment. The State University of New York at New Paltz accepted him.

Jessica's watch warns her the period is almost over. She returns one final time to the board. "HW: Write a paragraph or two describing yourself to a college." The bell rings. She thinks again of Vinnie. He is already in his second semester at New Paltz and he says he is in love. It seems he finally found a flower girl. Her name is Sunshine.

*   *   *

"Let's go back to being Harvard's admissions officer," Jessica says as she trawls up and down the aisles the following day, collecting homework. "We're going to look at a few autobiographies and see which ones make you want to read more."

"Im a Senior at Seward Park H.S. I would very much like to attend you college," she reads from the paper of one of her "YRO" students. "My major is studying Criminal Law. I also have several interests such as: Track & Field, Dancing, Aerobics, skating and singing. My future Plans are attending a 4yr College to study the field of Law. Hope you can help make this wish Come True."

As Jessica replaces the paper, she spots an addendum: "Dear Ms. Siegel, I will be taking my SAT on Nov 7. Please help and give me some preparation." She makes a mental note to tell the girl about the free SAT review courses available on weekends.

"My name is ——— let me tell you about myself," Jessica goes on. "I have a good personality if I do say so myself." She laughs until her cheeks redden. "I like to have fun make people laugh and have a good time." She falters, trying to correct the boy's grammar in the instant the words travel from eye to mouth. "My interest are girls video equipment. and I also like football and basketball. I like to hangout and I love money and music."

She skips the rest of the page. She cannot catch all the errors and she prefers not to repeat them and expose the boy to derision. But meanwhile, what is she supposed to do with a high school senior who cannot punctuate a sentence or prevail upon noun and verb to agree? She shuffles through the pile, trying to skim each paper before reading it aloud, until she comes upon one that looks safe, even dull. It starts, "I'm a senior at Seward Park H.S. I'll be graduating in June of 1988. My interests are English, Psychology and Nutrition." Then she is stopped. "Due to family problems, I no longer live with my parents. I live in a group home called. . . ." Jessica pretends to drop the paper, supplying the pretext for reading a different one, but her act convinces no one. Students shoot glances at each other, as if guessing who among their number is the unfortunate. Jessica's hands sift through the papers, passing those beginning "My name is. . . ." or "I'm five-foot seven. . . ." or "I'm a brown-skinned Puerto Rican." Finally, she sees the name "Wilfredo Ayala" on the top right corner of a sheet and withdraws the page. Wilfredo wrote that paragraph on expectations that she liked so much.

"I'm a person who is a hard worker," she reads. "When I set out to do something, I want nothing to stand in my way, I want to get it done. I want to lead a succesful life. I don't want to be just another person out there struggling to get by in life, looking for an answer to life. To me life isn't a question to be answered. It is a mystery to be lived, and I want to live it in the best possible way that I can."

There is more, but Jessica has found a port of embarkation. She rolls up Wilfredo's homework and clutches the paper tube like a scepter.

"What you did last night was *prewriting*," she says, inspiring a few quizzical looks. "Sometimes you can use part of that for your final autobiography, sometimes not. Autobiography doesn't necessarily start with age one and go through to the age you are now. You have to explain how you got from there"—she stamps both feet on the bare wood floor, then crosses the room with Groucho Marx gait—"to here."

"No one wants to hear about your family," one boy interjects.

"Why should anybody care if your parents got divorced?" puts in a girl.

"What do you think?" Jessica asks, mirroring the question back to the class. "Don't those things affect who you are?"

"It's OK to talk about your parents," a student in the back offers. "If they got a profession."

"So your parents are only worth talking about if they're lawyers or doctors?" Nobody dives for the bait. "Otherwise just stick 'em in the closet?"

The exchange, such as it is, gives Jessica some useful grist for the lesson, but it also troubles her. She can address the literary issue well enough, but shaking poor minority teenagers out of that inchoate, enveloping belief in their own insignificance demands more than pedagogy. Jessica can only hope that the very act of writing an auto-biography will help a few kids discover the validity in their lives.

"It's important to communicate not just the outer you, but the inner you," she says, knowing that she is answering only half the real question, the easier half. "The outer you—you're in chorus, what your average is—they'll see on the application. You have to get across what makes you unique, interesting."

She draws breath.

"I know that a lot of people find it difficult to start writing," she says. "So we're going to do something called 'free writing' that can help."

"No charge?" someone calls out.

"I want you to write without worrying about grammar and punctuation." She switches into the whine of a Woody Allen *kvetch.* " 'Oh my God, where does this comma go?' 'Did I spell this right?' 'I'm terrible at this.' " Now she returns to her own, assuring tone. "And so you get afraid of expressing your ideas. But there's no right or wrong answer here. It's your life."

"I can't write anything," one boy insists.

"Just put your pen on the paper," The Tough Cookie answers. "Something'll come out."

As the students begrudgingly begin, she paces the aisles, sowing ideas.

"Think about your past experiences," she says in the soothing monotone of an amateur hypnotist. "Jot down ideas, memories, key words, whatever thoughts come to mind when I'm talking. Think of a personal object that's important to you. Why? Think about someone who has had a big effect on you. What happened? What did they say? List four or five words that describe your feelings. Pick one and illustrate with a memory from your past. List five things you're proud of. Choose one and say why it's important to you. Remember the first time you did something that stands out in your mind. Describe the incident. How did you feel about it? Have you changed in the last five years? Why? How? What made you the person you are today?"

She completes the circumnavigation of Room 336, and finally the bell rings. She will devote one more lesson to the method of autobiography, quoting Albert Camus, Helen Keller, and Maxine Hong Kingston. She will assign the students to write a minimum of three pages, and when they moan, she will remind them they have the whole weekend. There won't even be professional football to offer distraction, thanks to the players' strike. "Memory plus distance," she will remind them as they leave, "equals true autobiography."

*   *   *

By ones and twos, straining at their mothers' arms, the girls hurried into Jessica Siegel's house. The new girl in second grade, the one with strawberry blond curls and freckles from cheek to cheek, Jessica had invited her classmates to her seventh birthday party. It was late September 1955, only a few weeks into the school year, so none of the girls knew Jessica well or had ever met her mother, Fanny. They anticipated a Saturday afternoon of chocolate cake and Pin the Tail on the Donkey.

Fanny Siegel and her daughter led the girls into the living room. The sofa had been moved aside, opening space for a low table covered with homemade placemats. No chairs surrounded the table, only pillows on the rug. Paper fans hung from the ceiling, and tiny parasols rested in porcelain teacups. Nearby were a dozen more fans, which would be given as favors. Between arrivals, Fanny dashed into the kitchen to finish the birthday meal of teriyaki, green tea, and rice cakes. Store-bought sweets and box games just weren't distinctive enough to suit Fanny Siegel; she had the idea of a party on a Japanese theme. It would be one of her little triumphs, hers and Jessica's.

In the weeks after the party, Fanny encountered several other mothers in the market or at PTA meetings. They thanked her, of course, but always with a sidelong gaze, as if taking her measure. Few of their daughters subsequently invited Jessica to their homes. Fanny figured they felt intimidated by her creativity. How could they compete? Their only solution was not to try.

Isolation suited the Siegels. It wasn't that they were cold—they were, in fact, quite hospitable—it was that they were brightly plumed in a gray flannel decade, free thinkers in an America of loyalty oaths and the Red Scare. In New Milford, New Jersey, a suburb of $15,000 tract houses bought on GI Bill mortgages, the Siegels lived in a 250-year-old Dutch Colonial with sixteen rooms and four fireplaces, separated from neighbors by tall trees on one side and the Hackensack River on the other. Simeon Siegel was a doctor in a town where most fathers were plumbers or letter carriers or salesmen dutifully riding the morning bus to "The City." The Siegels were Jews in a town composed of Irish or Italian Roman Catholics, and while the two dozen other Jewish families clung together for purposes of solidarity and matchmaking, the Siegels, self-proclaimed atheists, refused the essential gesture of joining the New Milford Jewish Center.

They would create their own idyll. They would be family and more than family, a community unto themselves. Simeon Siegel provided the financial fuel, and his wife supplied the spirit. Simeon was a cautious man, most content when he was most safe. It was one reason he remained a general practitioner instead of adopting a medical specialty; it was why, early in his career, he had liked living above his office with his wife as receptionist and nurse. Fanny Siegel was more like some force of nature, stout and tireless, often bursting into raucous, raspy laughter. She had enlisted in the Army as a young nurse, serving in a field hospital during World War II, and then attended the University of Chicago because some novel she had been reading had extolled it. Marriage and motherhood interrupted her studies, but she resumed them at Columbia University at age 48, earning both a bachelor's and a master's degree. And from the copper plates and weather vanes adorning its walls to the flower beds and stone fence outside to the evenings of Charlie Chaplin movies and "mystery dishes," the Siegel home was Fanny's handiwork.

As much as Jessica played kickball with the kids across the street and brought classmates after school to investigate the "spook house," a warren of tiny rooms above the kitchen, her life came to center on one person. Jessica was her mother's daughter, the instrument of her inspirations, the sorcerer's apprentice. "I had no internal life," she says now, looking back. "I hung out in the kitchen with my mother." They cooked and they painted. When Jessica joined the Girl Scouts, her mother signed on as troop leader. Together they concocted wacky, macabre costumes for Jessica—Madame Nhu, the Imelda Marcos of South Vietnam, for one Halloween; Vashti, the beheaded villainess of a Bible story, for the Jewish festival of Purim. Every weekend brought a trip to an auction house or a rummage sale, and Fanny taught Jessica to bid on pieces she wanted, jewelry and dolls and a treadle sewing machine. Then they went to their favorite diner for a hamburger, just the two of them.

Only with her brother Norman, two years her junior, did Jessica enjoy a comparable intimacy. They saved their allowances for journeys to Manhattan for Broadway shows, climbing to cheap balcony seats for hits like *Mame!* and dogs on the order of *Ben Franklin in Paris.* Back home, they performed their favorite numbers from the musicals, Norman on piano and Jessica singing. They devoured the Sherlock Holmes mysteries, purchased both English and American periodicals on Holmes, and joined the New York chapter of the Baker Street Irregulars. The Siegel household soon included a dog named Sherlock and a cat called Watson. So complete was the world Jessica and Norman constructed that it existed without any concession to popular culture or, more accurately, without a recognition that popular culture existed. In a home without a record by Elvis, the Beatles, or the

Rolling Stones, they listened to Stravinsky and Sondheim. While other teenage girls subscribed to *Seventeen,* Jessica read *Theater Arts.* Norman wrote an opera based on *Animal Farm* and was selected for instruction at Juilliard. Jessica declared her ambition to be a drama critic and adopted the middle name Stevenson, in homage to her parents's political hero, Adlai.

New Milford High School, circa 1962, did not know what to make of her. "Everyone had the same ambition," remembers Joanne Kaplan Tilove, who first met Jessica in junior high school. "To be a cheerleader and date the captain of the football team and get married. It was 'Leave It to Beaver.'"

Jessica was assigned to a homeroom for honors students, and she spent all four years of high school with the same thirty-five classmates. Although they stood apart from the more conservative, blue-collar "townies," the honors students had created a conformity all their own. Boys wore plaid, button-down madras shirts, chino slacks, white socks, and penny loafers. Girls wore black cardigan sweaters buttoned up the back, pleated skirts hemmed at mid-thigh, black knee socks, and penny loafers. Everyone listened to the Beatles, the Kingston Trio, and Peter, Paul, and Mary. The McDonald's in nearby River Edge, a locus for less refined elements, was to be avoided. Grades mattered, but reading except on assignment was frowned upon. The gestalt was of the Mouseketeer Club gone faintly beatnik.

As one of the rare rebels, Jessica was preceded by a kind of legend. Her family lived right on the town border, and people thought the geography appropriate. "She didn't live near anyone else," Joanne Tilove recalls, "and she didn't live like anyone else." Jessica sewed her own clothes from fabrics printed with purple sunflowers and pink dandelions. She made a Sherlock Holmes cape and hat. She ornamented herself with jewelry from Greenwich Village. And her iconoclasm exceeded attire. When the Board of Education suspended a high school student for having long hair, Jessica wrote a letter of condemnation. "She had a personality and she had a belief system," Tilove says. "She had the confidence to be herself at a time when being yourself is the hardest thing."

Jessica, unfortunately, did not feel nearly so self-assured. All her life, her family had imbued her with the importance of being an individual, and she had believed in their values as the only values. Now she found that a genuine individual was as suited to a suburban high school as a barmaid to a cotillion. Her confidence eroded in small ways, normal ways for a girl reaching puberty—stumbling through gym, not having dates, hearing a particular tone of dismissal when a classmate sighed, "Oh, that's Jessica."

Then, person by person, the family armor that had so sustained her began to fail. Jessica had heard Norman hailed as a musical prodigy for years, and she had stood obediently in the background when he was summoned to the piano to perform at family occasions and public events. Jealousy had not occurred to her; she had already laid claim to literature as her bailiwick, so she could still be the best in her family at something. But during her freshman year of high school, when Norman was a seventh grader, he was thrust ahead of her and into twelfth-grade English. The day Jessica found out, she trudged home from school in tears. "This is my field!" she cried to her mother. "How can they do this to me?"

During her sophomore year, her father almost died. His decline began innocuously enough, when he apparently strained a chest muscle while pulling an abandoned rowboat out of the Hackensack River. He had, in fact, torn part of his diaphragm, and after a mistaken diagnosis and a bungled operation, his body began poisoning itself, toxicity spreading into his legs, his blood, and his brain. Nearly a year transpired before the infection could be quelled, and for most of that time, Fanny Siegel was either commuting to see Simeon in the hospital or nursing him at home. At age fifteen, Jessica served as the mother of the house. She seemed, superficially, to perform with aplomb, cooking and washing and scrubbing, caring for seven-year-old Steve, and designing homemade get-well cards for Sunday visits to their father's hospital bed. Inside, however, Jessica shriveled with terror at the thought of losing her father, and she longed for the warmth she had always known at her mother's apron.

Just as the household began to return to normal, Norman took his annual optical examination. The doctor noticed unusual pressure from the rear of one of his eyes and recommended further tests. These produced a diagnosis of astrocytoma, a malignant and fatal tumor of the brain. Norman's life span was reckoned in months. Fanny and Simeon rushed him to a neurological hospital the very next day for an operation, and although the growth proved benign, they monitored their son's condition closely for months. Once again, Jessica was left to manage the household, and once again, it seemed that Norman had usurped her birthright. All her parents had ever said, in trying to spare her, was that Norman had had surgery to correct his crossed eyes. What could be such a big deal about that?

One afternoon Jessica was in her bedroom when Fanny entered to tell her how well Norman was doing.

"That's all you talk about," Jessica answered.

"Well, Jessica," Fanny said softly, "we thought he was going to die."

"You told me it was his eyes! Why didn't you tell me the truth? Why didn't you trust me enough?"

The word "trust" brought Fanny up short. In some ways, she suddenly realized, she had trusted Jessica too little, while in others, she had trusted her too much. The lesson Jessica learned from Norman's illness and from her father's before it was that her role in life was to do for others, "to be available," as she puts it now, "to serve."

"Jessica was so able, *so able*," Fanny Siegel says in retrospect. "I never thought she had reservations about having to take over as the mother, or that she saw it differently than I did. I think the experience gave her many resources. But it came at a great price. The price was that I don't think she thought that she was valued. I don't think she felt loved."

The one person who could transport Jessica was Gloryia Lenzi Okulski, her English teacher. Gloryia was a fittingly flamboyant name for the Grace Kelly look-alike who prided herself on never wearing the same outfit twice. Mrs. Okulski loved Bergman films, Puccini operas, and Bergdorf fashions with equal passion. She proudly claimed descent from an Italian anarchist grandfather. She lived in New York City and painted from her rooftop. Since the life of the mind is so exciting, she theorized, why leave it to matrons with eyeglasses and hairnets?

And Mrs. Okulski had the substance to support her style. She had been fired from a prior position in Hanover Park, New Jersey, for teaching such "wicked" works as *The Good Earth* and *Romeo and Juliet* and for writing students' hall passes in the names of the literary characters they were studying. It developed that the daughter of the superintendent of schools, one of Mrs. Okulski's pupils, was spying for her father. In a tableau from *Inherit the Wind,* students picketed for her reinstatement and her husband argued her case before the Board of Education. She ultimately lost the appeal and endured an informal blacklist for several years.

New Milford, although it chanced hiring the known firebrand, did not exactly sparkle with enlightenment. One English teacher felt compelled to cloak *Catcher in the Rye* in a brown-paper wrapper, with the class sworn to secrecy, while a science teacher required each of his pupils to construct a crystal radio, the better to communicate during a Soviet attack. Yet Mrs. Okulski was unrepentant in her innovation. She signed hall passes "Circe." She convened a murder trial for Brutus in teaching *Julius Caesar.* She introduced *Lord of the Flies* not by discussing the book's plot or theme but by asking her students what they thought would happen if some strange disease killed all the adults within a seventy-five-mile radius. Their sanguine comments served as an ironic prologue to William Golding's vision of marooned choir-boys reverting to savagery.

A lot of students loved her, christening her "Mrs. O. K." and saluting her, in the parlance of the time, as "real tough." But of all her charges in freshman English in the 1962–63 school year, Jessica Siegel stood out. She arrived early each day and grabbed a seat in the front row, and Mrs. Okulski thought of her as "my shining star." Mrs. Okulski loathed the "grade grubbers" of the honors class, and she saw in Jessica vast sensitivity and intellectual courage. She always remembered the day the class was discussing patriotism. She had the students list the advantages and then asked if patriotism had any drawbacks. Predictably, none dared whisper a dissenting word, until Jessica raised her hand and asked, "What if we saluted the flag of the world every day?" The other kids couldn't have glared at her harder if she'd broken into the "Internationale."

Mrs. Okulski thrilled Jessica in so many ways. Taking a chance and venturing an opinion felt safe in her room. There was never a sense of Right and Wrong. Class whirled along with the freewheeling spirit Jessica had felt in better days around the dinner table at home. At the same time, Mrs. Okulski seemed to Jessica so unlike anyone in her family—unrestrained, instinctual, a vision of life danced without doubt—and the more compelling for it. She was Isadora Duncan as English teacher.

Jessica did not take another class with Mrs. Okulski, but she visited her after school and once on a weekend traveled to the teacher's apartment in Riverdale. They were not confidantes; they did not need to be. New Milford was small enough for a teacher to know of the tragedies in a student's family without a word being said. Jessica counted herself blessed simply to bask in her teacher's approval. It lit a lot of dark corners. Then, midway through Jessica's junior year, the year of Norman's illness, Gloryia Okulski became pregnant and, as required by the school board, submitted her resignation. Her students threw a surprise party, presenting her with books by James Thurber and Bertrand Russell and with dozens of individual testimonials. One of them was a poem by Jessica:

A YEAR WITH MRS. OKULSKI

We have clambered through the Odyssey,
(Of course the Illiad, too).
We have researched with Dr. Arrowsmith
And murdered Julius Caesar, too.
From similes to epithets,
From slanting to themes.
And like Mr. Freud, she has made us analyze our dreams.
From Oscar Wilde to Shylock,
From Shelley to Buck.
You may pass a culture test with a little bit of luck.
Brave New World and *Animal Farm,*
Hamilton and Shaw.
The list is growing longer and I'm thinking of more than I did before.
Vance Packard and Jupiter,
Circe and the Bard.
I can think of more I've learned, it wouldn't be hard.
Lancelot and Steinbeck,
Hemingway and O'Neill.
I think I'm getting boring, and long-winded I feel.
This year was very productive,
This year was a lot of fun.
But before I get very mushy,
Let us eat all and one.

After the poem had been read, the gifts opened, and the cake cut, Mrs. Okulski spoke. "I won't be your teacher any longer," she told her young disciples, "but I'll be your friend forever." And then she was gone, never to return to New Milford High School.

When it came time a year later to select a college, Jessica chose the University of Chicago. It was her mother's first college, and Jessica had never made a decision, large or small, without her mother. The classmates and teachers who signed Jessica's yearbook, the *Emerald,* repeatedly used the words "admire," "respect," and "individual." Two girls mentioned the Japanese party, which had been held a full decade earlier. "Never stop saying and doing what you feel is right," wrote one of the most notorious grade grubbers in the honors homeroom. "I wish I had the nerve."

If all the praise was true, then why did high school hurt so badly? When friends around Seward ask Jessica about her student days, she replies, "I don't remember." She is not prevaricating; she suffers from amnesia, incomplete but extensive. The gaps cover a period of years, formative years, both in school and at home. A human mind can accomplish many remarkable things, and Jessica's mind, as if to protect her living core, has chosen to forget.

*   *   *

Jessica sits in a straight-back chair at the living room table, her arms moving in a pool of lamplight. She is clearing a spot to conform to the circle of illumination, shunting aside piles of unmarked tests and journals. These piles, in turn, push her folders of lesson plans farther into the shadows. Across the floor, flanking her stocking feet, she has strewn a pile of rexos, several *New York Times* clippings, a manila folder of *Seward World* submissions to be typed, an article about the filmmaker John Sayles that she has been meaning to read, and a promotional postcard for an upcoming crafts fair at Columbia University. She would love to go, but she has already promised to represent Seward Park at the city's High School Fair that Saturday afternoon.

Into the open space on the tabletop, Jessica pulls a stapler, several pens, a cup of lukewarm coffee, and seventy autobiographies. She arranges the autobiographies in a "T"—those from first-period English in a vertical pile, those from second-period English horizontally. She thumbs through each stack, instantly identifying the candidates for revision, those papers stretched to three pages by means of obese letters and bloated margins. She finds to her satisfaction that most of the students have exceeded the minimum and have draped their stories in a sort of grandeur. The autobiographies arrive in clear plastic folders with orange bindings; they arrive with flourishing script and computer graphics; they arrive beneath titles like "The Way I Was and the Way I Am Today" and "School, Streetwise, and Love." Jessica smiles at such precious affectations.

Then she burrows into the mounds. She is already two weeks late in returning the graded papers, an uncomfortably common state of affairs, and the guilt stings. She reads accounts of near-starvation in

China and rat infestation on Delancey Street. She reads two separate contemplations of suicide. She reads one girl's adoring analysis of her father's physique, naked from the waist up, and wonders about incest. Divorces, beatings, adultery, fatherless children—these appear as commonly as sports exploits and prattle about boyfriends. One or two autobiographies do brighten Jessica. There is Eunice Espinal, who wants to become an electrical engineer, and there is Maribel Mendez, who works through a Seward Park program as a home aide for an elderly Jewish lady, Mildred Mednick. Mrs. Mednick, Maribel writes, calls her "Bubbelah." Maribel does not know what "Bubbelah" means, only that the word conveys love. Jessica wishes she had more stories like Maribel's; she wishes her students had more joy in their lives to share. Sometimes the sheer weight of sadness overwhelms her. She gasps like one nearly drowned, and she rises and paces her apartment, waiting for her breathing to slow. She is the custodian of feeling and memory. *How do you grade these?* she asks herself. *How do you ask somebody to revise their emotions?*

"My family consists of six members, my mother, 2 brothers, 2 sisters and me. We have always been very close." Jessica is in the second paragraph of Aracelis Collado's autobiography. So far it is stylish, correct, and almost detached, which is to say quite like Aracelis herself, whom Jessica has in both English 7 and advanced journalism.

> I remember the time when we were younger and had to stay home alone. It was during our summer vacation and we had nobody to care for us. My mother was a factory worker and left to work early each day. We would wake up early each morning and find breakfast ready for us. At noon, our mother always came home to check up on us and bring us ice cream. She once told me that she would try and rush home so fast that one day she was almost run over by a truck. This she did for our safety. After she departed, we would sit in our small, snug living room, eating ice cream and watching a soap for children. For us this was great. This knitted a love so close and wonderful between us that today the bond is as strong as ever. As the years went by, the love between my mother, siblings and me increased tremendously.

Aracelis moves Jessica, with the allusion to a mother cooking breakfast in the predawn darkness, with the phrase about "knitting a love." So warm, so writerly. Yet it hardly prepares Jessica for what follows.

Another factor that influenced me towards who I am today and made me stronger was almost losing my mother. I was about 10 or 11 when she became pregnant. She ran some risks, due to the fact that she was pregnant but was aging and for 9 years had not had children. Yet she gave birth naturally and had not run into any danger. We were immediately told at home that everything was fine. This occurred at about 11:00 P.M. I fell asleep happy and content, not knowing what I would soon encounter. At 1:00 A.M. we were called and told that our mother was dying. The word rang in my ears. I thought my head would explode. My world crumbled upon me and my dreams and hopes were shattered. I couldn't believe this was happening to me. For several days, my mother remained ill and I lived a life full of agony. Thank God, she finally recuperated and came back home. To me, this seemed a new beginning.

To the bone, Jessica thinks, *right to the bone.* Aracelis had always appeared so self-assured, so controlled, perfectly kind but almost aloof, and here is this reservoir of sentiment. With all that Jessica reads and hears about the failure of the single-parent family—the pathology—she finds herself often amazed by her students' mothers. She meets some of them on Open School Night, with their tired factory eyes, their patchy English, and their unalloyed wills, the wills to pull their children through. "I'll always keep trying," Aracelis writes in the last paragraph. "So that someday I can prove to my relatives, teachers and society that I can do something for myself and others. I also want to be one of many minorities who thanks and proves to the U.S. that we want to learn and that we also have hopes and dreams which we want and can obtain." Jessica hears in those words the voice of a mother, a mother who would run home from the factory at lunch, carrying ice cream for her children.

The next autobiography, José Santiago's, promises no similar passion. Jessica sees that José wrote his name on the top line, the class and date on the second, then skipped a line, then wrote "Autobiography," and then skipped yet another line before beginning, with very large letters and no more than five words abreast. The composition opens agreeably, with Jose recalling baby-sitting his little sister and taking his first job in a pizzeria. It's all very affable, like José himself, a big kid with an on-again, off-again beard and a penchant for sweatpants and T-shirts. Jessica reads rapidly, scribbling in the margin her standard pleas for more depth and detail. This paper has all the earmarks of a first draft dashed off in homeroom.

Then, toward the bottom of the second page, José wanders back to the subject of baby-sitting, and matter-of-factly drops his bomb: "because it turns out to be that at the age of 18 I became a father." Jessica dashes ahead, impatient to learn more. The only activity outside school that José had ever mentioned to her was collecting stamps. "I have a daughter. Her name is Rebecca Luz. She is so beautiful. The experience of seeing her come out of her mother's womb was the most wonderful moment of my life. Well, about being a parent, it is very hard, but I've learned to hang on and be tough for both my wife and my daughter. We are happy."

Jessica now writes a fuller, more personal response, suggesting that José explain how fatherhood changed him. The question hovers, even after she has placed another autobiography in front of her. Every term she has at least one girl with a baby born out of wedlock—there is one, in fact, in José's class—and over the years she has had perhaps a half dozen confide their pregnancies to her. Many of the girls whispered that they wanted abortions but that their boyfriends insisted that they bear the children. Jessica has seen the same phenomenon in her journalism class, whenever she has asked the students to write an opinion article about legalized abortion. The girls tend to split on the subject, but the boys invariably invoke the Right-to-Life and the Holy Roman Church. Jessica has rarely known a Seward Park boy to truly accept his parental obligations. One week, the young father carries his newborn through the halls, a bauble in pink flannel, and the next, he parks himself back outside the bodega, hustling anyone with ovaries. But here is José, who actually stayed in the delivery room, who warms to responsibility. Jessica has no illusions about the struggle ahead, yet she cannot help rooting for José and his wife, Frances, and Rebecca Luz. Not that it will help his grade any.

It is now past eleven, and two unread papers remain. Jessica collected the assignment by rows, so one of these autobiographies belongs to Lun Cheung, occupant of the most distant corner in her second-period class. Lun contributes intelligently when he deigns; the rest of the time, he slouches in his chair, Nikes resting on the empty seat ahead, a bemused grin spread beneath his aviator glasses. He is not insolent, merely enigmatic.

Nothing in the first page and a half especially enlightens Jessica. Lun writes that he had "ups and downs." He says he could have taken "the wrong road in life." He recalls fighting and reconciling with an older brother. And then, in what Jessica is beginning to recognize as a pattern in these autobiographies, he slides casually into catastrophe.

At around the age of 14, I became sort of a rebel. I never used to listen to my parents and I played hooky a lot. I considered myself a rebel because I did everything people told me not to do. Also I joined a gang because I thought it would give me prestige and power. At this particular time if you were Chinese and living in Chinatown, being in a gang was the thing to do. Also many were taken unwillingly, but because they did not want to join, many were forced. I was a volunteer and I realize I was stupid and wrong!! At this period I was doing a lot of illegal things. I robbed, I mugged and I beat up people. At this age I can say now that I was stupid and immature. I was still mugging and beating up people and at times taking drugs because I thought this was fun.

Jessica knows the type. When she eats lunch at the Grand Street Dairy, across the street from school, she invariably encounters two or three tables of Chinese gangsters, sullen and blemished boys, splinter thin from their silk socks to their spiked hair, smoking cigarettes and tapping ashes into coffee saucers with practiced indifference. The Lower East Side is the land of designer knockoffs, and these boys are imitation James Deans. They would be laughable if their menace were not so genuine.

She resumes reading Lun's paper.

I would have stayed this way if it wasn't for my friend Steven. Steven was a true friend who was smart and tried to get me out of the gang. I did not listen. One day Steven and I were walking down some street. Enemies from a rival gang attacked us. It must have been like nine guys. Many of them had bats. They started to beat on us, we tried to fight back, but there were too many.

The next thing I knew I was in a hospital. I had survived. I asked my parents how Steven was doing. They had a cold look on their face. They told me Steven did not make it. I was devastated. My heart felt like it ripped in two. I wished I had been the one who died. For the next two years I tried to put this behind me. I could not forgive myself. When I finally had the courage to face Steven's mother, I explained the wrong person died and if I could I would take his place. Steven's mother forgave me and told me life must go on. Although to this day I cry when his birthday comes and I hear a song on the radio which he liked.

Jessica's right hand lightly cups her neck. Short of crying, this gesture communicates her deepest anguish, but unlike crying, it brings no catharsis. The sensation starts inside her throat, with the feeling of raw flesh, of abrasion. The muscles clench. She cannot

how does he know?

summon a sound. Although she has not shed a tear, her throat throbs as it does after she has sobbed for an hour. So, unconsciously, her hand rises, to soothe, to comfort, as if she had absorbed this pain from the page, from this other life, and it were in her power to heal it. She possesses no such power, she realizes. She is a teacher. She meets a student as one being among 34 in a period, among 140 in a day. She can tell herself she believes in the transforming alchemy of literature, and yet there is a world outside, day to day, impervious to art's uplift, and as many times as she has heard horror stories from the frontier around the corner, she has never lost her capacity to be shocked. She has written barely a word on the page. What is there to say? "Wow!" she finally scrawls. "What an experience!" The words stare back, mocking her with their inadequacy.

She proceeds, and Lun tells of his parents' unhappy marriage, his mother's diabetes, and, finally, his own overpowering need to prove his worth, as if in penance. "I am a very good person at heart," he writes, with the insistence of an uncertain soul convincing himself, "and I cherish the things which I love the most. I know that there is a lot of love inside of me and I am not afraid to show it. I hope in the future I can give this love to the one who molded me and to the ones I can help."

Now Jessica must offer her own summary response. She feels devoid of words, barren. What can she say? "Oh my, God." "How could you have done that?" "That's the worst thing I've heard in my life." She peers ahead, eyes unfocused, Lun's presence so palpable in this moment, he could be standing before her, eye to eye. She turns to the first page of his paper and begins to write. "This is an incredibly moving autobiography. You not only have been through a lot, but clearly it has helped you grow to be a much more mature and insightful person. You obviously picked some very important turning points in your life. I'd like you to expand this a bit more. How have these experiences helped you to form your goals for the future? What are your goals? I think this doesn't need much work to make it great."

Mary Tam's is the last of the autobiographies. Mary takes English in the first period, and her paper would have been among the first batch that Jessica read had she not submitted it two weeks late. Jessica has been engaged in a battle with Mary all term long—well, not a battle as much as an often-futile effort to connect. From the earliest days of the term, Mary had shown herself to be one of the finest writers in the class and one of the few students who read real literature on her own.

Wasn't it *Ethan Frome* she had mentioned to Jessica? She had cherubic cheeks and glistening cobalt eyes and she chose to sit in the front row, a sign of devotion that Jessica could appreciate from her own past. Then she stopped coming to class more than two or three times a week. Cutting always afflicted first-period classes, but Jessica would not have expected it from so seemingly motivated a student. Although, when Jessica thinks about it, the clues had been there from her first glance at Mary's Delaney card, which listed a group home as her residence. Mary had written of living in a group home again on the homework assignment that anticipated the full autobiography. Jessica remembers stopping herself just short of reading the paper aloud to the class. When Mary missed the deadline for the autobiography, Jessica nudged her, and when Mary let two more days pass, Jessica reminded her that the autobiography counted as much as a test in her grade for the term. That afternoon, Mary appeared in the English office after school. She told Jessica she could not write an autobiography, told her she did not want teachers to know about her life. When Jessica asked why, Mary managed a few phrases about pressure at school, pressure at home, her parents fighting, and then her composure fled. She stood unmoving, tears rolling down her cheeks, dropping off her chin, and for seconds staining her collar. She cried in an abject, passive way, like a dense cloud unburdening itself of a slow, soaking rain. Mary tried to speak once or twice, but her mouth could form only plaintive oval sounds. There was nothing for Jessica to say. She simply wrapped her arms, winglike, around Mary's body, which had begun to shake.

Now she holds the paper Mary handed in ten days later. Above the title "Autobiography" is the word Mary had obviously written first, "Diary," slashed with a single pen stroke.

> I was adopted when I was a baby in the Far East. It took nearly three years for my biological mother to make up her mind if she wanted me or not. She was a teenager when she gave birth to me. That wasn't all the reason why it took a slow time before I could come to America. Basically the legal process of adoption overseas was very time consuming. Cutting through red tape and being put on the waiting list made my foster parents lose patience as well as hope. But somehow they got a call to meet at an airport to receive me.

> My life started when I was aged 3 on the arrival here to America. My foster parents were so happy to see that I wasn't retarded or very ugly. All my foster mother noticed that I was very quiet and tired. Right away they

named me Mary Tam, yet they refused to give the name the biological mother gave to me as Gnook Yuen Wong. Soon at age 4 I learned to talk and walk. Boy, I soon became a big mouth as a little kid. I just loved to walk up to any friendly stranger and start chatting with him or her. When I was 4–5 my foster parents took me on trips to show off to their relatives that I was their kid. I got the impression that life would be like this, so nice and so endearing.

My dream was turned into a nightmare. The dark ages came when we settled down living in an apartment. I was sent to school. My foster mother went to work full time. My foster father already worked for the city. My foster mother hardly ever had time to take care of me. So often she sent me to the babysitter and their family. After work my foster mother would come & take me home around 7 P.M. My foster Dad was already home lying in bed reading a newspaper. Around 8 P.M. dinner would be ready. Then by 10 we're all asleep. This schedule was our daily ritual, which I found so boring. They refused to take me to a friend's house so I couldn't play with other children at all. Often at babysitter's house all I could do is just sit and wait for my mother to come & pick me up. I felt as though I was a ghost when I'm there at the babysitter house. They just see through me or pity me.

The home situation was no better than at the babysitter's. Constantly fights would break out over food costs, rent, or it's not clean enough, etc. My foster dad is stingy, lazy and sloppy. My foster mother is a neat freak, big mouth, aggressive, and a perfectionist. They're completely opposite. Arguments that start out verbally end up physically violent. Cause when my foster mother is angry at my foster father she will take whatever she has in her hand and throw at him. He in return bangs her head or body against the wall. All I could do was to stand in between them trying to push them apart, splashing them with my hot flowing tears. That way I sort of distract them from the argument to have some concern for me. These kinds of fights happened any minute or hour of the day. Sometimes it is so serious that neighbors must step in to control it and cops too! I made the mistake of taking sides cause the other one will end up hating me more. Often my mother would take her frustration on me by beating me or tying my hands behind my back forcing me to stand in a corner for several hours. While she's hitting me all over with the stick she cursed me off as dirt scumbag etc. She would even dare do this to me in front of my friends. The humiliation hurts more than the pain she inflicts on me. Often my father is too scared to stop her fearing she might attack him.

As I got older I rebel against this tyrany in this so call family. My mother was very strict. For example she did not allow me to grow my hair past my chin. She would cut my hair as short as a guy's. She would not allow me to read any fictious books. She was afraid imagination would make me lose control of myself. She would buy only the necessities when it comes to clothing. I never had an article of clothing that I can enjoy wearing until now. She always taunts me to leave that the door is always open! I thought realistically I couldn't. What does she expect me to do, look up in the yellow pages & find an answer right away. Damn, life doesn't work this way!

Finally my foster parents split or divorced for good. I happily joined my foster mother. But I never can conceive the idea that we can't live in harmony too! The reason I decided to live with her is that it's more convenient than living with a male. My father consistently try all means to get me to live with him. I refused after how he treated my foster mother. I will not be his slave. But when I refused he would say that my mother poisoned my mind with all her vile thoughts of him. I thought oh no, there they go again, fighting even after they divorced. The part I hate the most is that I am a mirror reflecting of the past. Every single time my foster dad sees me he sees my foster mother. Actually he doesn't see me at all. Same thing with my foster mother. Again I'm caught in between this tug of war. It is a vicious cycle. Again I felt guilty myself for stirring up the past. How I wish I can turn the clock back to the day I was born. I felt as though I'm a bomb just waiting to be activated to explode. I felt that I'm doomed for self-destruction.

This is a warning. This is a telephone call in the night, a figure crouched on a ledge. Jessica knows because she lost someone once before, someone as intelligent and despairing as Mary Tam. She writes in the margin, "I hope not! You have too much to add to the world."

The worst is to be confirm that I was adopted. I had a gut feeling that I was. I felt even more miserable knowing that I'm somebody's leftover or bastard child. It made me more wretched and lonely knowing that I have no blood related relatives. I slowly lost interest in myself. How I look and the friends around me. All of the sudden I just lost complete control of myself. I didn't care about living or dying. I started to rebel against everything my foster parents say. I didn't care about school or about learning any more. What's the point of more knowledge more truth when it can only cause more pain.

"It doesn't have to," Jessica writes. "You can learn the truth and then use it to grow more."

There was a social worker I have been seeing recently. She recommended that I should live in a group home. In a way she wants me to put some distance between my parents & myself. She thinks I can get a better grip on myself being away from them. She recommended after my birthday to go to this temporary group home for about 4–6 weeks. I was willing to try it. Later a couple weeks passed I grew to like it very much. It's just the atmosphere was so warm friendly & family like. So I thought for sure it's better to go to a permanent group home than to continue to stay and argue with my mother. It's been 2 months and a half that I have been in a group home. I still don't feel any change has happened. Physically I'm apart from my parents but mentally I don't think we are. I just feel my past is haunting me more now than before. And at the same time I feel as though I was Ethan Frome. I have had troubles pile up on top of me that I can never get out of.

Her hand quivering, Jessica draws an arrow from *Ethan Frome* to a vacant space at the bottom of the final page. "Yes," she writes, pressing the pen down hard to steady herself, "but Ethan Frome accepted things. He didn't try to change them. You did." She underlines those two words. "That's a big step, especially for someone your age. You've taken control over your life instead of being a victim—like Ethan accepting . . ." She turns the page, the snap of paper the only sound in the room. " . . . what life has offered. This shows you have the strength to deal with some of the 'raw deals' life has given you. You also have the intelligence, sensitivity, thoughtfulness, insight to make it in college. I think that will be the start of a new and easier"—she underlines the word—"life for you, which you deserve."

How do you put a grade on this? Do you circle the misspellings? Do you remark on the shifts in verb tense? Do you ask her to revise this when she is feeling more composed?

"Thank you for opening up & sharing this with me," Jessica concludes. "It must have been painful to write. You can tell by the mark what I think of your abilities."

Then, on the top of the first page, Jessica writes "100."

Her shoulders pull back and her head rolls upward, so that her eyes fix on the crease where the wall meets the ceiling. Every year she finishes the autobiographies feeling the same way. Her students are heroes. Her heroes, even some who fail the coursework. Could anyone else understand that? How they fill her with awe. How they, yes, inspire her. How their struggles and survivals distract her from the lonely alleys in her own life. And sometimes that is a blessing. When she reads their words, when she hears their voices, when she can practically grasp their urgent breath in this empty room, she knows her life has a reason, at least one reason. And then she turns the switch, and darkness reclaims the pool of lamplight.

She places the autobiographies in a folder and inserts the folder in Big Black. Tomorrow she will ask every student except Mary Tam to make additions and improvements. In the days before she collects the final drafts, Jessica will carve a bit of time for herself, and she will write a letter, the first letter since she became a teacher, to Gloryia Okulski.

3

Slumber Party

Are you allways ably her "that they Pe smell make you find of et? what coryn tris new? enoymatte?

USING THE KEY that Ben Dachs gave her several years ago in defiance of school rules, Jessica Siegel unlocks the English Department office. It is six-thirty on a September morning, the morning of the first staff meeting of *Seward World*. Six students are due to arrive in forty-five minutes, and Jessica wants time to prepare. It is not uncommon for her to start the day alone; she has often begun work earlier than this, scuttling through the darkness at five-forty-five on the day marks are due.

Solitude is a necessity, not a choice. She does not enjoy the office when it is empty; all the silence brings is an ineffable sadness. She prefers the room when feet shuffle, shoulders bump, and voices clang, when the rexo machine whirls like a cotton gin, spitting out homework assignments in fresh purple ink, each page moist and redolent of duplicating fluid. Somehow that smell pleases her, with its acrid ambrosia of things familiar, things known.

A beige canvas shade droops over the office's only window. Shadows shroud the brown linoleum floor. One long table, all dusky smudges and zigzag grooves, dominates the center of the room. Seven chairs, three wooden and four plastic, surround it. One built-in closet holds coats, another supplies; neither suffices for the faculty of thirty. Unmatched file cabinets of gray and green line the walls, except where their formation is broken by old oak shelves, sagging under their loads. Piles of books mount like stalagmites up the blue walls and toward the ceiling, all but obscuring the magazine photographs of John Steinbeck, Lillian Hellman, Ernest Hemingway, and Tennessee Williams. The room is neither welcoming nor forbidding. It is the triumph of efficiency over art; with a few adjustments, it could pass for the tool crib in a machine shop.

Ben Dachs recognized a certain lack of personality, and he decorated what vacant space there was with souvenirs of the English Department's finest moments. At the highest stratum of one wall, where grammar guides and poetry anthologies had yet to climb, he arranged posters from the last six school plays and plaques commemorating Seward Park's participation in the Academic Olympics and the Lincoln-Douglas Debates. Across the room, he hung photographs of three *Seward World* reporters. Two of them, Sue Lee and Ricardo Enriquez, are shaking hands with Ethel Kennedy, Robert Kennedy's widow, as they receive honorable-mention citations in a national journalism contest named for the late senator. The third, Salome Junco, holds a bust of Kennedy, symbolic of first prize in the competition. Jessica can be seen in one of the pictures, standing to the side.

She drops Big Black with a thud, then places quarts of orange juice and milk in the office's half-size refrigerator. She reaches into the storage closet for paper plates and on them arranges sugar donuts from the shop on Delaney Street. The donuts feel thick and stony to her touch, like chunks of petrified wood. Next time, she will bake. She raises the window shade. The sun has just scaled the housing project across Essex Street, and orange light glows in the office window like fire in a hearth.

Taking a seat at an electric typewriter, one of two available to the entire department, Jessica inserts a sheet of Seward Park stationery. This letter, to the agency that submits military recruiting advertisements to *Seward World*, calls for formality. She begins by citing *Seward World*'s press run of 5,000 four times a year. She lists the awards her students have won—the Kennedy prize three times, scholarships from the American Society of Newspaper Editors for Alex Iturralde and from the Asian American Journalists Association for Sue Lee. She mentions how many Seward Park kids hold jobs, giving them money to spend on records, clothes, and books. Then she stops being polite.

"Every single advertisement you have sent us has been for the military." She types with the frenzy of a jazz pianist whose drummer has suddenly doubled the time. "Those are the *only* ads you have ever sent us. I feel strongly that my students, living in New York City, and especially on the Lower East Side, are constantly bombarded by come-ons—on television, on the radio, in magazines, in newspapers, on billboards and in person—to join up rather than being directed toward educational and career goals that will benefit them, rather than putting them into the position to become cannon-fodder in the Persian Gulf or Latin America." She charges past the run-on sentence, oblivious in her fury. "If I sound strident on this subject, let me tell you that a good part of my time is spent talking to students about college, an enormously big decision for them, especially since for the majority of them, they will be the first in their family to go. They don't need more exposure to the inundation of military advertising that already engulfs them." Is that a mixed metaphor? Is "enormously big" redundant? She is too enraged to tell. She folds the letter and addresses the envelope.

By now it is seven-fifteen. She smooths her teal skirt, straightens the blouse on which a tiger stalks amid bamboo. It is one of her Oz outfits. She is still alone.

"See what happens when you call a meeting before school," she says, weakening for a donut. "You're the only one at it."

She expects a tough year. At least the kids could be punctual. Just once. She has no Alex this year, no Salome or Sue. Those people were found money. They arrived with a natural gift for leadership and a love of writing, and Jessica simply refined both traits. This year is another story. Of the six seniors in advanced journalism, who form the core of the *Seward World* staff, five do not speak English at home. The language gap alone would not be an unprecedented impediment for Jessica, but two of the students lag so far in their studies that they may not graduate on time, and a third probably belongs in the Resource Room, although she argued her way out of the remedial placement, wrongly deeming it a family disgrace. Wringing plausible prose out of that student—forget the other five—will be a job in itself. And if there are too many typographical errors, Jessica worries, Dr. Kriftcher will get mad at her, perhaps mad enough to resume his former practice of reading the articles before publication.

She would never utter her doubts aloud; that is a matter of pride. She hates the way some teachers at Seward Park complain about "the material," as they call it, and she senses their skepticism about the source of *Seward World*'s quality. The paper has its champions, of course, in Richard Katzke the baseball coach, who sends a nice note after almost every issue, and in Dr. Kriftcher, who is always asking for extra copies to press on visitors. And yet. And yet. One time a teacher was posing Jessica's journalism class for a portrait and complained under her breath, "I hate these group shots. People who can't write a sentence get their picture in the yearbook." After the paper won a Kennedy award, another teacher said to Jessica, "Congratulations. I know you had a lot to do with it." The words cheered Jessica at first, but the more she remembered their tone, the more the kindness curdled.

At seven-twenty, Helen Moy walks into the office. She wears jeans, a paisley shirt, and Annie Hall glasses. The perm in her short black hair, listing severely to one side, resembles the trial-and-error coiffures of China after the Cultural Revolution. Jessica knows Helen from last year as a compulsive worker, a girl who had to be talked out of attending summer school, a girl who substitutes for her mother some nights in a garment factory.

"How was your summer?" Jessica asks.

"Boring."

"What'd you do?"

"I worked. I kept a journal."

"Can I see it?"

"No."

"You want some orange juice?"

"No."

"Milk?"

"No."

Jessica offers a small plastic cup.

"Don't you like my shot glasses?"

Helen does not get the joke.

"Donuts?"

"Yes."

Shahin Ali, who goes by the nickname Moonie, enters to rescue Jessica. Moonie wears skintight pink jeans and a "Care Bears" T-shirt. She leads her younger sister, Jasmine, by the hand. Moonie's father, a laboratory technician in his native Bangladesh, waits tables in New York. He came to America for his daughters, not for himself.

"Have you seen anybody else?" Jessica demands. "Is anybody else coming?"

Moonie, mouth full of donut, shrugs. She and Helen walk into the hall and gaze down the corridors north and south. They return empty-handed.

Jessica checks her watch—seven-thirty-five. Why bother?

A few minutes later, Gregg Gross strides through the door. A lanky black boy with large, searching eyes, he wears khaki slacks and a red cardigan emblazoned with a big blue "G." Jessica taught Gregg's older sister, Penny, who is now majoring in education at Baruch College. She wants to believe Gregg could be this year's star. There is just this certain indifference of his to deadlines.

"I got up early enough," he blurts to Jessica. "It was the train."

"Famous last words." She pauses. "And don't you take the bus?"

"But Miss Siegel—"

"I have a feeling about you," she says, wagging a finger. Gregg curls his shoulders inward, steeling himself for a reprimand. He gets something worse, a prophecy. "This could be a very good year for you."

"Hope it'll be my last."

It is now seven-forty-five, and teachers have begun to filter into the office. They stare at their work table covered with food, at their chairs occupied by children. A few shake their heads with the resignation of parents chaperoning a slumber party, surrendering their living room to a tribe of teenagers with flashlights, sleeping bags, and boom boxes. "Already," one teacher moans to Jessica. Jessica, hunched over the table with her students, does not hear.

Without fully realizing, she maintains an uneasy equilibrium with her colleagues. They don't like having to stand in their own office, but they concede that Jessica and her reporters got here first. They don't like people dining on their work table, but they never complain about inheriting leftover bagels or banana bread. They respect Jessica, and so they tolerate her slumber parties as they tolerate her rain forest of a mailbox. At least they make the attempt.

"Miss Siegel," says Emma Jon, as she negotiates a path toward her desk, "can you tell me what this gathering is?"

"Advanced journalism class."

"I'd offer you another room," Emma says. She pauses as if adding a column of figures. "But there isn't one."

Jessica ponders the alternatives. Can anyone meet ninth period? Helen has a class. Tenth? Moonie has to leave for her job at McDonald's. Third? Gregg has Spanish. How about first period? Helen asks. Jessica teaches. Gregg suggests that Jessica write them all notes so they can be excused from class the same period. Jessica knows that is a fast way to make enemies; she's vowed not to write many notes this year. She slumps to the tabletop, chin sagging into her palms.

"What did you do about this last year?" Moonie asks.

"We met before school," Jessica says in a flat voice, "and it was like this. I was screaming at the kids all the time." She smiles a little. "Couldn't you hear me screaming?" Now she laughs. "And I spent all my money buying breakfasts."

Finally, at seven-fifty, the three girls who form the remainder of the staff arrive. Standing in the doorway, they purse their lips, close their eyes, and exchange busses, lightly rubbing cheeks in the process; this elegant ritual is the Dominican hello. Jessica remembers how these three girls clustered last year in the beginning journalism class, how they seemed intimidated by the more experienced writers around them, how they communicated by a language of whispers and motions. Lydia Pagan, the tallest of the three, has high cheekbones and sad eyes, circled by dark rings. Since her family moved from the Lower East Side to the Bronx, she has traveled three hours a day to and from Seward Park, where she has stayed because of the other two girls. Aracelis Collado has fair skin, blue eyes, and auburn hair smoothly swept in a "V" from forehead to shoulders. She is womanly for eighteen years, with something of Rosalind Russell about her. The shortest of the three, Rosie Sanchez, also appears to be the youngest, her wiry black hair raked into a tomboy's pigtails, her eyes shining like drops of chocolate syrup in a saucer of cream. Now Jessica can see a fourth girl edging into the portal, Aracelis's sister Damaris. Like Moonie, Aracelis is responsible for guiding her junior safely to Seward Park every day.

It is already seven-fifty. Jessica hastily doles out donuts, milk, and orange juice. A garbage truck on Essex Street pours a dumpster into its metal belly, wafting the aroma of rot into the English office. Jessica reminds the students that each must produce one article a week — good practice for working independently in college. She speaks briefly of the need to raise more than half the newspaper's $7,000 budget. She sets up a meeting for the following week.

"Now," she says, "let's get some ideas for the paper. What should we be covering?"

"Fashion tips," Rosie says.

"A lotta girls need them," Lydia seconds.

"Anything else?" Jessica asks.

"Horoscopes," Lydia says, nodding her head gravely.

"Here we go again," Jessica mutters. "What about you, Gregg? Anything you're interested in?"

"I don't know."

"Think about the things you're interested in."

"Girls, music, and basketball."

"All right," Jessica says, smiling. "The tough life of a man on the Lower East Side." She pauses. "Well, can you do a piece about the basketball team?"

"Ah," Gregg groans, waving his hand as if shooing a fly. "I don't like basketball so much anymore."

This is as stuporous as a first-period class, Jessica thinks, and she has one of those starting in ten minutes. Next time maybe she'll bring dexedrine instead of donuts.

"C'mon, folks," she says. "There's always one thing I tell my English Seven classes. You people are all experts on education. You're in school for twelve years now. . . ."

"She'd be such a wonderful mother," Larry Schwartz, an English teacher, announces to the office. "She knows how to nag. Got it to an art."

Jessica likes Larry, and so she laughs with the rest, before returning to the sales pitch. ". . . and the people who write books about education are college professors. Maybe they know what they're talking about. Or maybe they don't know. Anyone want to read one of their books and write a review?"

There are no takers. Her time dwindling, Jessica runs through some ideas collected from teachers. The Great American Smoke-Out. A student adviser to Manhattan Borough President David Dinkins. A student who won a free trip to London in an essay contest. Charlotte Hirsch, a paraprofessional who lives in the neighborhood, has been eavesdropping, and mentions the city's proposal to moor a jail barge on the East River not far from Seward Park.

"What ever happened to the good old days?" Gregg asks. "When we got ideas from other journalism classes? Are we the only one?"

Jessica nods. "Alex graduated. Salome graduated. Joy graduated. You're it now. You're the experienced journalists."

"How about interviews with students?" Gregg says. "Those'd be easy."

"No one in this school is interesting," Aracelis replies.

"Gimme a break."

Jessica thinks for a few seconds, then starts to grin a crooked grin. "How about continuing our series on good-looking male teachers?" Lydia giggles and says, "There are a few."

Jessica signs her up for a profile of Steve Barry, who teaches criminal law and wears tight jeans. It has taken forty minutes to fill the first line on her assignment pad. Thank God for crushes.

"College," Aracelis says.

"What about it?"

"How you can get in, how you can get the money for it."

"We do a lot of articles about college," Jessica says. "We have to think of a new theme."

"Surviving," Moonie says.

"Everybody's so scared," Rosie adds.

With schools closed two days next week for the Jewish New Year, Jessica says, a lot of Seward Park graduates will be home from college. Why not interview one? Rosie volunteers. Aracelis asks to write a more general article on admissions and student loans. Jessica notes both assignments.

Helen has been silent. Now she explodes, speaking in snippets and fragments and curlicues. Her Chinese accent is harsh, and she may have a speech defect, as well. A couple of the girls snicker. Jessica narrows her eyes and cocks her head, as if trying to translate a foreign tongue. Finally, her aural radar fixes on Helen's voice. "Those guys on the street," Helen nearly shouts. Her mouth races to keep pace with her mind; her lips flutter. "Dealing alcohol!"

There is a moment of palpable relief. Helen has made herself understood.

"That's a good suggestion," Jessica says. "Everybody's talking about drugs, but alcohol is cheaper and more available and you can get just as out of it as on drugs."

She adds it to her list.

"Speaking of drugs," Jessica says, wheeling back to Gregg. He slouches in his chair, eyes at half-mast. Feeling her gaze on him, he straightens. "You live on Tenth Street. What about Operation Pressure Point? Did that get rid of the drugs?"

"Oh, you know, the people were off 'The Ave' for awhile," he says, meaning Avenue D, the most infested byway in his neighborhood. "Then they were back. Dust. Crack. All that stuff."

"So you want to write about it?"

"Give me somethin' to do."

"Don't do anything *too* dangerous."

The bell rings for the first period. The students rise.

"Just five more minutes," Jessica says. "I'll write you all notes."

*   *   *

Jessica had never intended to advise the school newspaper and, in some respects, had started teaching as a reaction against her background in journalism. When Hannah Hess, Jessica's friend and colleague, left the *Seward World* advisory post in 1984 and recruited her as a replacement, Jessica resisted. She still had too much to master as a classroom teacher—lesson plans, discipline, performance—and she saw her past and present lives as incompatible, envisioning a chunk of ice too large for a glass. It was time to conform, time to get with the program. Once Jessica bent to Hannah's blandishments, though, she discovered that if the ice would not melt, at least the glass would expand to accept it.

It was while covering the Chicago Eight trial for her college newspaper that Jessica first heard about Liberation News Service, a left-wing press agency run as a collective. With no firm plans after graduation, she packed up her Marx Brothers posters and her Army overcoat and rode the train twenty-two hours to New York. Arriving at LNS, she found the entire staff sitting on the stoop because the electricity had been cut off. She was hired.

LNS supplied nearly a thousand eclectic subscribers in the alternative press—feminists, gays, Black Panthers, auto workers, Chicanos, Marxists, potheads, and sundry combinations thereof—with twice-weekly packets of news, photographs, and illustrations. The news service covered the Vietnam War, naturally, but it also waded into coal-mining safety, steel-industry pollution, student activism in South Africa, labor organizing in India, and even a strike against abusive blood banks by the drunken donors on Los Angeles's Skid Row. Certainly, LNS published rather too much of Ho Chi Minh's poetry, and it could blather breathlessly in praise of a slain Irish Republican Army commander. But for the times, it was refreshingly free of dogma—no "AmeriKKKa," no "male chauvinist pigs"—and was always able to laugh at itself. An LNS Christmas card, punning on a revolutionary bromide, counseled, "Dare to giggle, dare to grin." The notation above the staff roster read, "Table of Malcontents."

All this emerged from the self-contained confines of a cellar at 160 Claremont Avenue, in the narrow netherworld between Columbia

University and Harlem. The office had bare cement floors painted industrial gray and chairs and desks scavenged from the street. The copy camera and plate-burner were both homemade, and the staff Toyota had tallied 200,000 miles. Leftover LNS packets drifted across the floor like blizzard snow and subscribers' newspapers groaned in a canvas laundry cart. It was not uncommon to find a cockroach bathing in the coffee. Yet the walls burst with a psychedelic palette and the radio sang out Dylan, Van Morrison, and the Band. There was a poster of Che Guevara and a refrigerator painted with a National Liberation Front flag. Cuban diplomats stopped by with rum and cigars, while FBI informants occasionally arrived in the guise of college students preparing term papers.

So encompassing was life at LNS that the running joke had it that none of the staff ever ventured below Ninety-sixth Street. Everyone worked sixty-hour weeks for $25 apiece, and everyone lived together in a few $120-a-month apartments on Claremont Avenue. They shared chili and tuna curry, anything that could be cooked by the basinful, and they divided the baby-sitting for the daughter of two members. Demagogues fared poorly with LNS, generally stalking off, clutching manifestos. The collective guaranteed two-thirds of its dozen positions to women, and the men tended to be soft spoken. "We were self-effacing, underconfident people," one member, Ron Sirak, recalls. Amid the big talkers and harebrained bombers of the New Left, LNS stood out as a confederation of the meek.

Jessica started out meeker than most. When others arrived in the morning, she was already ripping open the mail; when they left at night, she was transcribing tapes; in the hours between, she often rooted through gutters and garbage heaps for LNS furniture. She wrote about the Attica prison uprising and the Wounded Knee revolt; she covered Frank Rizzo's mayoral election in Philadelphia and J. Edgar Hoover's funeral. The others nicknamed her "Siegel the Legal Eagle" for her dogged reporting on trials; she habitually filed her copy long and late, and many times a printer had to tear pages from her typewriter on deadline because she had not yet satisfied her own standards. Jessica had a finely tuned ear, both for irony and for the eloquence of the untutored, like the ghetto woman whom she quoted telling Rizzo's blueblood opponent, "You ain't much, baby, but you're all we got." Almost all Jessica's articles, in fact, opened with epigrams and quotations, and many read more like oral histories than reportage. "I felt my challenge as a journalist was to disappear," she says. "I wanted to make things that happened in very different places be accessible and understandable. Make people come across as real human beings. Let them speak for themselves."

Perhaps she succeeded too well at absenting her ego. She typically complimented her comrades with the plaint, "I could never have done that." When articles were assigned, she was likely to volunteer, "I'll do whatever no one else will." In political discussions, she often lamented, "I don't know why I'm here; I'm just a liberal," which in the New Left was as welcome as a black in the Ku Klux Klan. "People tried to convince her that she didn't see herself right," remembers Andy Marx, who worked at LNS for eight years. "After awhile, some people got really annoyed at her. But you can't yell at someone who, in effect, was already yelling at herself."

If others did not notice it, Jessica felt herself gradually growing more confident. It was a matter of knowing who to call, where to find information, what question to ask. In her idiosyncratic style, she had begun to challenge the conventional wisdom around her, asking as she typed the latest appeal to free a prisoner, "But did he *do* it?" Newer members of LNS aspired to Jessica's attention to detail and her manner of correcting reporters' errors without insulting their intelligence. Years later, when Andy Marx obtained files from the FBI's surveillance of LNS, he was halted by one agent's observation that in this self-proclaimed collective, it seemed that two people did most of the work—Andy Marx and Jessica Siegel.

LNS gave its members one month's vacation a year, and for most, it shimmered in the distance like a mirage, sustaining them through all the fifteen-hour days until they could borrow a car or stick out a thumb and vanish. So when Jessica resolved to spend her holiday in August 1973 covering a trial, her friends simply said, "That's Jessica."

Seven members of Vietnam Veterans Against the War and one sympathizer faced charges in Gainesville, Florida, that they had conspired to disrupt the 1972 Republican party convention in Miami Beach. Their purported plot transcended the bizarre: Firing ball bearings and marbles from slingshots that they had secreted in the bell bottoms of their jeans, the veterans would provoke the police into attacking demonstrators, setting off a riot. When reinforcements tried to quell the violence, the veterans would attack stores with firearms and homemade bombs, inviting a looting spree that would draw police away from the first riot, which could proceed merrily along. It was partly the fear of such an assault on the convention, at which Richard M. Nixon was to be nominated for his second term as president, that led several of his subordinates to break into the Democratic National Committee offices in Washington.

On its own terms, then, the "Gainesville Eight" trial commanded attention; its testimony would inevitably examine and quite possibly link America's two greatest traumas, the Vietnam War and the burgeoning Watergate scandal. For Jessica, though, more than history called. She had already interviewed one of the defendants in New York—that was a part of it. She had written about a health clinic begun by Vietnam Veterans Against the War in tiny Bogue Chitto, Alabama. Only a month before the Gainesville trial, she had reported on the suicide of a twenty-four-year-old Vietnam veteran and former prisoner of war. The man shot himself after he and seven other veterans had been charged with aiding the enemy by making propaganda broadcasts while in North Vietnamese captivity. Shortly after his death, all the indictments were dropped. The story, like the impending Gainesville Eight trial, suffused Jessica with a certain anguish, the anguish of the sheltered and judgmental.

She cobbled up air fare to Florida, bedded down on various floors, dined at potluck suppers. For ten sultry August days, a sleepy college town became a carnival of the heartbreaking and the infuriating. Jessica sat in court the day two FBI agents were discovered trying to bug the defense lawyers' conference room. She scribbled the testimony of a defendant whose best friend had been exposed as a government informant. She heard the defendants tell of throwing away the fifty-seven medals and citations they had won during 111 months of combat. She saw 150 of their supporters march, led by two veterans in wheelchairs and one tethered to his Seeing Eye dog. "We are the living, walking, talking Pentagon Papers," one veteran told her. "We are guilty only of having tried to tell the truth about our experience in Vietnam."

When Jessica returned to New York, one day before all eight defendants were acquitted, one figure from Gainesville haunted her. He had appeared as a witness, not in the legal sense as much as the biblical. His name was John "Gunny" Musgrave. Jessica wondered if the nickname was from Vietnam, but she never gathered the nerve to ask. Musgrave had grown up in small-town Missouri, a member of Youth for Christ and president of a Methodist student group. When he was seventeen, his mind roiling with patriotic fervor, he prevailed upon his mother to sign his enlistment papers for the U.S. Marines. Musgrave often walked point in Vietnam, and he suffered three wounds in eleven months. The last, a barrage into his chest, cost him two ribs, numerous nerves and muscles, and the use of his left arm and left lung. After seventeen months in a Navy hospital, he limped away with a decoration for valor and a 70 percent disability.

"I was nineteen years old," he told Jessica when she interviewed him for LNS, "and they told me I was going to be crippled, that I wasn't going to be the same young man I had grown up like, and that all the plans I had made were in fact going to be changed with two bursts of machine gun fire." His next words lingered in Jessica for years; when time flushed the rest from her memory, these clung like trace elements in her soul. "It really hurt me when I had to look at myself and say, 'This was such a waste because it was for nothing.'"

Jessica resigned from LNS ten months later. The New Left had been withering ever since the killings at Kent State, and internecine battles wracked the remains. LNS's subscribers dropped by half, and the collective sometimes could not pay rent, electric or telephone bills, and even its minuscule salaries. Most important for Jessica, the cellar on Claremont had become a metaphor for isolation—the isolation of leftists in a nation of centrists, the isolation of watchers in a land of doers. She wanted to test her own ideals by rubbing them against their antagonists. She wanted to share the work of society, rather than review its progress like a Saturday matinee. She had a vague sense, nothing she could quite articulate, that LNS, like the University of Chicago and the suburban home of her childhood, could not feed her hunger for "a larger taste of reality." This feeling left her with two questions: What exactly is reality? And where, in the great wide world beyond Ninety-sixth Street, may one find it?

* * *

"Where were you, Angel?"

"I'm just five minutes late," says Angel Fuster, breaking into a grin.

"But you were late."

The school year may be young, but when it comes to *Seward World,* Jessica is not in the giving vein. On this, the morning of her thirty-ninth birthday, she is again waiting for her wayward flock. Louise Grollman gave her flowers and Steve Anderson gave her a kiddie pen with a triceratops on the side, and still no students showed. They tend to appear in shifts—three at one meeting, three at another, almost as if they plan it for maximum annoyance. Jessica recalls Bruce Baskind's joke that Seward Park kids attend class on the odd-even license-plate system used for buying gasoline during the 1974 oil embargo. Except that Angel Fuster was four years old then. Clearly this is a case of parallel evolution.

"I slept over at my father's house," he persists. "In the Bronx."

"Yeah, but what about last Wednesday?"

"My hamster ate this college stuff I had." Jessica grimaces. "You want me to show you the tooth marks?" He starts to unzip his black tote bag.

"All right, Angel. I don't need to see. Why don't we start all over. But no more red-carpet treatment."

Angel walks out of the English office, pirouettes in the hall, and reenters. He is one of those boys who reached physical maturity early, a seventeen year old who is fully bearded and, at five feet three, fully grown. Like many short males, he survives on wit and guile. Lately, for instance, he has been visiting his best friend, Ivan, in Ivan's homeroom, explaining to the teacher that he is Ivan's mentor in the Adopt-a-Student program. Which, as the teacher has yet to learn, does not exist.

Bruce calls Angel "the Puerto Rican Michael J. Fox," but Sammy Glick or Duddy Kravitz would be more accurate. Angel is a hustler, an operator, a critic of the same materialism he wants to enjoy. With his parents divorced and his mother on welfare, he has held one job or another since he was twelve, guarding his tender places with a wall of one-liners. When Jessica asked Bonnie Kowadlo, a business teacher and the business-club adviser, for a financial whiz for *Seward World*, Bonnie recommended Angel. He is president of the club and, although not a member of Jessica's advanced journalism class, he is one of her pupils in English 7.

"Miss Siegel," Angel says, tucking in his shirt, "we have to talk about my title."

"King of *Seward World*."

Angel doubles over laughing.

"Anything that's *long*. That's what the colleges like."

"I don't know," Jessica says, fiddling with the pen nestled above her ear. "Advertising director? Director of advertising? Business manager? Manager of business?"

"Something big."

"How big?" She catches herself. "Wait a second. How about talking about your responsibilities?" She pulls a rate card from a pile and tosses it on the table before Angel; she could be dealing blackjack. "Your responsibility is to sell ads." She opens a manila folder containing past advertisements. "You can start by following up these."

Angel asks Jessica exactly what is involved, and she explains. *Seward World* receives $3,000 in student-activity funds—more than any single enterprise in the school, but roughly the same amount the paper received in Hannah Hess's day, when it published twice a year, not quarterly as now. The difference must be made up by selling advertisements or by running special promotions. Last year, two journalism students designed *Seward World* T-shirts, and the rest of the class sold them. All manner of candy had been preempted by the athletic teams.

"We could sell slush puppies," Angel says. "Nobody's done that yet."

"Where are we gonna get a slush machine?" She pauses. "Who's gonna stay in the cafeteria selling? What's gonna happen when someone goes to class with this junk dripping down his arm?" She shakes her head. "Think ads."

"What about McDonald's? Or Macy's? Miss Kowadlo's taking our marketing class up there."

"But the school's on the Lower East Side, Angel. What you want to think of is people who've advertised before. And think of the stores around here. You have the right drive to sell ads. You have a little . . ." She searches for a synonym for chutzpah. ". . . push." She pauses and thinks. "What would you say if you went to the Grand Street Dairy?"

"That place where the guy smokes cigars?" Angel screws up his face. He is a young man of fragile sensibilities. He listens to LITE-FM on his Walkman.

"But if you were selling," Jessica says, stretching the last word taffylike. "What would you say?"

"I'd say, 'This place is disgusting. I don't want your ad.'"

"Angel!"

"I'd tell 'em how many students eat there. The power of advertising. He could do like a two-for-one coupon. He . . ."

Angel starts scribbling multiplication tables and percentages on the back of an envelope. Jessica looks on, uncertain if this is brilliance or bullshit. The bell rings.

"Tell you what, Angel. We'll meet tomorrow and pick this up."

What she will not tell Angel or anyone else is that *Seward World* still owes its printer $500 from last year. Deficit spending is not permitted in New York schools. Without Jessica's guile, *Seward World* would not be in a position to publish this fall.

*   *   *

For all Jessica's self-doubt upon assuming its leadership, *Seward World* instantly bore her signature. Her first issue as adviser, published in January 1985, included articles on abortion, gay rights, and Chinese youth gangs, subjects that many journalism teachers pointedly avoid in the pedagogical tradition of "CYA"—"cover your ass." Still, Jessica thought she had been more lucky than good in inheriting two experienced editors, Sue Lee and Ramón Dalmasi. As their graduation approached, however, she had to begin grooming successors.

Ricardo Enriquez seemed an unlikely candidate. As he sat in her English and journalism classes in the spring term of 1985, he reminded Jessica more of the stereotypical Chinese kid than of a Hispanic. He was so quiet, so proper, right down to the carefully executed curves of his penmanship; he wore out-of-date clothes and slicked his hair straight across his head. Even if Jessica had not known Ricardo had just been transferred out of bilingual classes, she would have recognized him as a recent immigrant.

Ricardo's mother had come to New York in 1971, working weekdays in a garment factory and weekends as a housekeeper, and sending the earnings to her three children in El Salvador. The children lived with their aunt because their father, an electrician, had begun keeping company with a new woman and could not be bothered with paternal obligations. Ricardo and his older brother, Eduardo, watched *Rocky* and "Dallas" and dreamed of joining their mother in the land where everybody ate steak and drove a big car.

But Mrs. Enriquez had long overstayed her initial visa and she rarely returned to El Salvador for fear of being apprehended on reentry to the United States by the Immigration and Naturalization Service—*La Migra*. She visited once in 1977 and again in 1981 for her daughter's wedding. By then, Eduardo had been writing letters to her pleading, "Ma, please take us," for the government had begun conscripting young men for its war against leftist guerrillas. After the wedding ceremony, she told her boys, "OK. It is the time to see what will happen with us."

The three boarded a bus for Guatemala and from there, another bus for Mexico City. They hid in a hotel room, under orders not to step outside or open the door, while Mrs. Enriquez called her sister in

California. The sister would arrange for the *coyote.* A twenty-four-hour bus trip brought the Enriquezes to Tijuana, where they registered in a hotel and waited. Two men knocked on the door. They did not resemble the men Mrs. Enriquez had been told to expect, but they insisted her sister had sent them. They took all the money the three had, $160, and vanished behind an unkept promise.

Mrs. Enriquez called her sister that night. Stay put, the sister said, the real coyote is on his way. The coyote arrived the next afternoon, warning the Enriquezes they had to move immediately. They crawled beneath blankets in the coyote's van and listened to his instructions. If you get caught, say you're Mexican, not Salvadoran. If they ask where in Mexico, say Cuatemo. If they ask how far away that is, say two days. And never mention my name. Because if La Migra thinks you know a coyote, you will be held and questioned for a long time.

When the van halted, the Enriquezes found themselves on a barren hilltop, within eyesight of a ten-foot fence, which they soon scaled. Immigration officers suddenly swarmed, circling above in helicopters and advancing on horseback. A car drew near, its headlights drilling through the darkness, and the coyote fled. Ricardo, Eduardo, and their mother were captured. La Migra plopped them on a bus back to Tijuana. As they debarked, they saw their coyote waiting three blocks away.

The next night, they succeeded. Two weeks later, on October 10, 1981, the Enriquezes made it to New York. Mrs. Enriquez hurried to her factory to learn that she had been fired. She borrowed $400 from her sister, but it wasn't enough, and Christmas passed without presents or a feast. Finally, Eduardo found work on the loading dock of a kosher bakery. He made $4 an hour and even earned overtime in the busy season before Passover. As he always would, he broke his first paycheck into two parts, the larger for his mother and the household, the smaller for Ricardo.

"Brother," he said, handing over a $20 bill, "I'm working now. To help you. I'm going to give you some money every week. Please, be a good person. Don't look for trouble. Be nice. When you're in school, don't waste time. Learn what they teach you."

Ricardo was frightened of Seward Park—so big, so many floors, so many people racing from class to class. It hurt him to be called Ricardo rather than by his middle name Roberto, which Hispanics use as an endearment. By his second year at Seward, Ricardo began to change. He wanted to be somebody, to go to college, to have a career. Conquering English, he realized, was the key. He stood out immediately to Elisa Muñoz Feder, who taught bilingual history, as opinionated, active, eager to learn. "He embraced this country," she says. "That was one of the reasons he learned English so fast."

When he moved from bilingual courses into regular classes, though, the old reserve returned. Invisibility came especially easy in Jessica's journalism class, which featured a Madonna wanna-be, a jilted girlfriend threatening suicide, and a boy who wrote news stories on imaginary massacres. One day, Jessica asked the class for story ideas for the spring issue of *Seward World*. Ricardo raised his hand; he wanted to write about gentrification, a subject far more ambitious than she had been seeking. Too stunned to say no, she said yes.

In his own subdued way, Ricardo had been developing a social conscience. He worked after school at a day care center and often told Eduardo how it upset him to see Puerto Rican children fighting with other Hispanics; he joined Seward Park's Latin-American Club, which Muñoz Feder advised, to try to build that missing unity in school. As for gentrification, his family had teetered on the brink of eviction in its first months in New York, and he had seen several neighbors ousted by rent increases or harassment by landlords as the Lower East Side became one of the most lucrative real estate investments in the city.

From February to May, Ricardo reported and wrote and rewrote. He conducted interviews around the neighborhood on Sundays after church, dashing down the stairs of his building shouting, "Don't worry, Mom. I won't do anything bad." He clipped photographs and housing advertisements from newspapers to illustrate the article. Jessica took Ricardo to the Metropolitan Council on Housing, an advocacy group, and to meet *New York Times* reporter Martin Gottlieb, a Seward Park alumnus who had written about real estate speculation on the Lower East Side. Unlike almost any other journalism student, Ricardo refused further help. He said he would not show Jessica the article until it was perfect. Just as LNS colleagues had done with her, she finally tore the article from Ricardo's hands. It was an impressive piece of work, but a bit too much of a diatribe against Mayor Koch, who enjoyed close relations with large real estate interests. Jessica suggested Ricardo call up the mayor to get his side of the story. He tried not only Mayor Koch but several mayoral agencies, none of which chose to answer the questions of a high school journalist with a Spanish accent. Jessica instructed Ricardo to narrate his fruitless efforts in the article, and he did so.

The final version appeared on a full page of the June 1985 *Seward World,* beneath the headline, "Where Do You Go When There Is No Place to Go? Gentrification on the Lower East Side." Ricardo described the escalation of one family's rent from $400 to $1,000 a month; he charted the "flipping" of one building from a sale price of $5,700 in 1976 to one of $202,500 in late 1981. Like Jessica, he let people tell their own stories; many of them were his classmates at school. "When people lose their homes, they don't know where to go," he quoted one senior as saying. "If they don't know where to go, what happens then?"

Jessica recruited Ricardo for advanced journalism the following fall—truthfully, he needed little persuasion—and she found him a part-time job in a local arts agency. Leafing through a journalism magazine, she saw an advertisement soliciting entries for the Robert F. Kennedy Awards for Coverage of the Disadvantaged. She entered Ricardo's article, along with a piece by Sue Lee about Chinatown's history. But the Ricardo who returned to Jessica and Seward Park in September 1985 had changed. The boy who had always done his homework now submitted just enough assignments to pass. The country bumpkin now styled his hair and affected "Miami Vice" pastels. When he asked his mother for a tuxedo, she scraped together the money for one. "I want to be on top," he told his brother. "I want to get what I want. If I have five dollars, why can't I have ten dollars?" He had embraced America, perhaps, a bit too completely.

One afternoon that winter, Jessica noticed Ricardo idling outside the English office. She recognized such ennui as a wordless summons. Lately, Ricardo had been complaining to her that his mother was too strict, that she never let him go out. Jessica invited him to walk with her along Grand Street.

"There's something I want to tell you," he said.

"OK."

"You may be really shocked."

It seemed to Jessica he was testing her before proceeding. She remained opaque, unthreatening.

"I'm gay."

"There's nothing wrong in that," Jessica said. She made certain not to stop or swing toward Ricardo, but to continue walking at an even, untroubled pace.

"Are you surprised?"

She thought instantly of Ricardo's intimacy with one of the girls on *Seward World,* an intimacy matched by his discomfort with most boys.

"Not really."

"I thought you wouldn't be."

Ricardo insisted that he was still a virgin. Jessica had said nothing to prompt the issue; it obviously mattered to Ricardo. He said he had one gay friend in Seward Park, and it was good to talk to him. Then he and Jessica parted.

As months passed, Ricardo confided more to Jessica. He had begun going to clubs and gay discos. Older men liked him and bought him things—a watch, clothes, even a weekend in Miami. And always, always, he concluded by assuring Jessica he was still a virgin.

It was now May, only a month before Ricardo was to graduate, and he was hardly coming to class. "I can't make it," he told Jessica when she confronted him. "I was out till three or four." He was becoming, Jessica hated to admit, something of a caricature, effeminate in his short shorts and jewelry, mincing and laughing a bitchy little laugh. He talked about how his friend picked someone up at the disco and disappeared for three days; he talked about how so many men wanted to dance with him.

"What about school?" Jessica asked. "You've got to graduate. Make sure." She paused and swallowed. "I don't even care if you pass my class." She grabbed his arm, held him squarely so his eyes could not dodge her own. "Just graduate."

When Ricardo won a Kennedy award several weeks later, Jessica thought it might help. He would see the rewards for hard work; he would pass his classes and graduate. She received money from Manhattan school officials to attend the awards ceremony in Washington with Ricardo and Sue, who also had won. But on the train south, he mimed blow-jobs on a hot dog, winking at Jessica all the while. During dinner with Jessica and Sue, he theatrically flirted with a waiter. Jessica was rattled. The era of AIDS was dawning. "It's one thing to be gay," she said to Ricardo. "But what's this with picking up all these guys? You can be gay and have one relationship. You can be gay and still go to school."

Back in New York, Ricardo handed Jessica two articles for the year's final *Seward World,* both on the subject of his sexuality. Together they were the voice of Ricardo's doppelgänger, the confused child inside the tuxedo. In the first article, Ricardo related having been molested as a child, implying that being gay was not a choice but an imposition, the brand of a terrible trauma. Yet the second article evidenced not shame but pride, endorsing monogamy, professing concern about AIDS, and concluding on a commonsensical note: "Gay teenagers want to tell people, 'Hi! This is what I am. I'm not superior or inferior. I'm just like you. I'm just like anybody else.'" Jessica published only the second article, sans byline, judging it a more palatable presentation of a risque subject. But the first article was the one that kept clawing at her.

Ricardo did not graduate that June, having failed physical education, a fact that amazed Jessica. Here was the boy who danced the *cumbia* and the *joropo* in Seward Park's Latin American Festival, and he couldn't drag on clean sweatsocks often enough to pass gym. But Ricardo had confessed to Elisa Muñoz Feder that he was afraid to strip in front of other boys in the locker room. Besides, he told Jessica, he was convinced he would not be allowed to attend college because he was an undocumented alien. The United States did not grant legal status to the refugees of the Salvadoran civil war it supported. "I need college, and I want it, and I have no chance," he moaned. "Why?"

The next fall, Ricardo showed up for class with plucked eyebrows. His moods swung wildly from giddiness to guilt. He blamed himself for not graduating and he feared his mother would send him back to El Salvador. He called Jessica one night in tears. She told Ricardo a lot of illegals were able to obtain identification cards: You start with a driver's license and use that to get a Social Security number, and so on. She offered to accompany him to an immigration attorney. And while she was at it, she insisted he see a therapist. He agreed, then skipped the first session. A solution seemed at hand when President Reagan signed the new immigration law in early November 1986, offering amnesty to people who had entered the United States without papers before 1982, people like Ricardo. But the law wouldn't matter if Ricardo's mother, terrified at what America had done to her little one, deported him herself.

A few weeks later, Ricardo stopped by a *Seward World* meeting in the English office. He motioned Jessica into the hall and withdrew a snapshot from his wallet. The photograph showed Ricardo dressed as a woman, cheeks powdered and lips painted, hair hidden by a wig, legs obscured by a long, flouncy gown. Ricardo hung on the arm of a man in formal wear. They were evidently a couple bound for a stylish affair. Ricardo gazed at Jessica excitedly, gauging if, after everything else, he still could shock the one who accepted him, wound the one who supported him. He was smiling and he was pushing her away.

Christmas came and presents filled the Enriquez apartment. Ricardo helped his mother string ornaments on the tree. But then he wanted to go out dancing, and Eduardo demanded he stay, at least until midnight, at least until Christmas was over. They argued and Ricardo ran. In the next few weeks, he tried to make amends, helping his mother shop on a Sunday, then cooking plantains for Eduardo. As the brothers ate, Ricardo said again to Eduardo that he was afraid he would never go to college. Eduardo advised him to pray to God, the same God who had steered them safely to America.

Three days later, on January 7, 1987, a young cousin of the brothers entered their apartment at noon. She hated the bathroom in her elementary school, which was across the street, and so she always used the Enriquezes'. It smelled nice. She was the first person to see Ricardo's body, hanging.

On the day of his funeral, Jessica did not cry. That was strange for someone who cries often and for far lesser tragedies. She saw Mrs. Enriquez in her black mourning shawl, an ancient aura about her. She introduced herself to Eduardo, who said, "Oh, yes, I heard so much about you." A man in his mid-twenties, discreetly identifying himself as Ricardo's lover, told her the same thing. Then Jessica gazed on the seventeen-year-old boy in the open casket, and still no tears flowed.

"Seeing this young kid laid out," she says now, leaving the sentence unfinished. "So many people there. He never felt like there were that many people there for him when he was alive. And after he was dead, it was too late." She halts again. "I remember thinking that when you're dead, you're dead. The only way you can be remembered is by your impact on other people. While they're alive and while you are."

*   *   *

"Folks," Jessica says to the crowd around the table. "It has been—let's see—four weeks since we began working separately from the beginning journalism class. So I need either four articles or a combination of articles and rewrites totaling four."

She taps her fingers on one pile of handwritten articles, all by Rosie Sanchez. She has been the pleasant surprise. When Denise Simone discovered that Rosie enjoyed drawing, she mentioned that the Brooklyn Museum was giving a show by the black artist Jacob Lawrence. Rosie not only visited the exhibit but reviewed it for *Seward World.*

"See this?" Jessica says to the rest, lifting up the articles by her thumb and index finger. "Miss Efficiency." She returns the articles to the tabletop. "What about the rest of you?"

Everyone cringes except Rosie, who blushes.

"This Friday I want everything you owe me." She lets the reality penetrate. "Should we have an article about the Howard Beach trial? That's been going on. Should we have an article about Bess Myerson and corruption in the city? We can always use profiles. Anybody want to do Miss Kowadlo? Any new movies since last year we ought to review?"

She inhales. What a day. What a term. She is rapidly exhausting her inducements, having gradually boosted the bounty from donuts to bagels and cream cheese to today's homemade cranberry walnut loaf. She knows time is passing because now the days are shorter and the sky outside the office window is purple-blue at seven-fifteen as she waits for her reporters. She exhales. She will deal with everyone except Rosie one at a time.

"Helen." She swivels to face the girl in the pink down coat. "Your article was not bad. But do you remember where you put quotation marks?" She writes a sentence for Helen. "Now, which words is she saying?" Helen points. "Right. You put quotation marks around the words that come out of her mouth." Jessica reaches into Big Black. "And take one of these." Helen cradles her *Seward World* press card in a nest of two palms.

"Gregg." He is dropping a chunk of cranberry bread into his mouth in the manner of an emperor accepting grapes from his concubine. "Do you have your rap music article?"

"I'm not really done yet," he says, showering crumbs across the table. Rosie and Aracelis scrunch their noses.

"Not done? You've promised it to me three times already. How many times are you going to stand me up?" Jessica spots Rick Rowley in the office, eating a muffin. "You have Gregg in English? Right? Has he done his work for you?"

Rick pulls out his marking book, runs his pencil across a column and nods yes. He pats Gregg on the back.

"Then how come you won't work for me?" Jessica asks. "How come journalism comes last?" She throws up her arm, Job inveighing against the Almighty. "That's what I want to know."

"It takes so much time to think what I want to write. Every time I'm writing something I remember something I left out."

This is a shameless appeal to Jessica's missionary instinct, and a wholly successful one. She draws her chair close to Gregg at the corner of the table.

"That's all right," she says softly. "It's important to get your ideas down on paper. Then if you decide you forgot something—the Sugar Hill Gang or Grandmaster Flash—you can add it later. So . . ." Now she turns on the grouchy tone. ". . . I want that rap article. I feel like I've got to pull it out of your head."

Gregg waits for Jessica to turn her attention elsewhere. No such luck. He wriggles in his seat, hoisting up the hood of his sweatshirt.

"And where are your notes for Operation Pressure Point?"

"I don't have them with me."

"Gre-e-e-e-egg." She pauses. "Don't tell me they're too heavy."

"No." He laughs. "I just don't carry my notes around with me. I got 'em at home. In a memo book."

"Do you remember anything?"

"Yeah. The newspapers talk about what a good job the cops did. And it *was* better at first. But now I see dealers back on the street."

"As openly as before?" Jessica asks.

"No. They got a little more protection, but they're still out there. Never gonna get rid of them."

Jessica checks her watch. The bell rings. She hastily dispenses press cards. "Aracelis and Moonie, I'll talk to you tomorrow. Gregg, why don't we go to the library third period." She pauses. "Lydia, after eighth."

By the time of Lydia's appointment, Jessica has read and reread the girl's article about the Mets. Something disturbed her from the first glance, all the knowing flourishes of baseball jargon and then the use of *fait accomplis* misspelled as "fate accomplished." She showed the piece to Bruce, who agreed that Lydia possessed quite some understanding of the sport. Jessica was willing to grant Lydia that much, for many Dominicans, boys and girls, follow the Mets assiduously in tribute to the team's Dominican shortstop, Rafael Santana. But "fate accomplished" afforded no easy explanation. And last spring, Lydia had written a remarkably sophisticated article on beauty tips, which she seemed to have cribbed from a women's magazine.

"How did you write this article?" Jessica asks now, as gently as possible.

"I watched every game," Lydia says, her voice slow and deep. "I watched all the games."

"Did you read any sportswriters?"

"Not really."

"The thing about this—and it happened before—is I have the sense this isn't all yours." Her face sagging with disappointment, Jessica drags her fingers lightly across the article. Lydia places her backpack on the table, the zipper clanking softly on the varnish.

"Because I used some fancy words?"

This is what Jessica had feared, that Lydia would see the issue not as plagiarism but as racism, the unstated assumption that a Hispanic could not write well on her own. The moment demands diplomacy.

"Partly." Jessica waits for a reaction; none comes. "I want you to stretch yourself. And I want you to do research." Lydia twists sideways in her chair, rests her head on her backpack. "The problem is, once you start using someone else's language without quoting, it's plagiarism."

Jessica drops her head to the tabletop so she can meet Lydia eye to eye.

"It's like if you quote Howard Cosell. It's OK if someone says it better than you can. Just quote them." Her hands hang in the air, the index fingers curled like quotation marks. She slowly withdraws them. "But this article is *your* analysis. And I get the sense that you're so thoughtful, so intelligent, that you get impatient that you don't have the words to say what's in your mind."

The chance to confess without penalty hovers in the air between teacher and student. In seconds, it vanishes, unclaimed. Only now does Jessica notice the bustle around them, teachers carrying away piles of books, kids cadging hall passes. Lydia rises and picks her way through the crowd and into the hallway.

Jessica hates the way she feels. Accusing someone of plagiarism is like saying, "You're not smart enough," and her whole grail is "You *are* smart enough." What if she was somehow wrong? Maybe she's lost Lydia's trust for good. What did she gain then? Still, "fate accomplished." And the beauty article. Jessica can't unknow what she knows.

She returns Lydia's article to the manila folder marked "To Be Edited" and slides the folder into Big Black. Tonight she will begin typing stories to be taken to the printer. The Jacob Lawrence review and Aracelis's college article are fine, and from last spring's unpublished articles Jessica has resurrected a profile of Ian Ponman, a popular bilingual instructor, and an essay about what makes a good teacher, which will be accompanied by a ballot for Seward Park's best. But there's no way Operation Pressure Point will be done in time, and the alcoholism article needs reconstructive surgery. That leaves fashion tips and horoscopes and purloined sportswriting. That leaves a certain sense of futility, even failure.

*   *   *

Two weeks into October, with its copy finally set in type, *Seward World* crashes to a halt, thanks to the Board of Education. Along with every other high school newspaper adviser in the city, Jessica has been summoned to a meeting at which the board is going to announce a new policy requiring that all 116 public high schools have their papers produced at one of five approved printers; *Seward World's* is not among them. The board considers this policy to be a reasonable compromise, for the previous year it demanded that every high school use a single printer—every high school in a city of 303 square miles, in a city of islands and peninsulas and bridges and tunnels that conspire against efficient travel.

It was all the fault of a computer, a new computer that compiled accounts for the board's Bureau of Supplies. The computer discovered that a few printers were earning more than $15,000 annually on school newspapers, exceeding the state's limit for competitive bidding. That each adviser selected each printer individually did not matter to the computer, since the money that paid the shops ultimately flowed from one source, the Board of Education. Why human reason did not mitigate mechanical judgment has been the subject of much speculation among the advisers.

Jessica managed to evade last year's edict by finding a loophole in the standard contract and soliciting a set of bids that finally favored her longtime printer, Harold Steinberg. He represents to her all those things a competitive bid cannot assay—interest, flexibility, personal loyalty. It was Harold who taught Jessica layout and production, who inspected the articles for crimes against grammar, who suggested alternatives for uninviting headlines. He took Seward Park's student journalists as seriously as Jessica did, discussing their articles about AIDS and homelessness with her and insisting on seeing photos of the Kennedy award presentation.

At a more pragmatic level, Harold's shop, Official Press, is a ten-minute subway ride from Seward Park, so Jessica can dispatch her students there in free periods and stop by herself on the way home. The shop produces only three high school newspapers, so it can lavish attention on each enterprise. And best of all, Harold has silently shouldered *Seward World*'s deficits, hiding the red ink from his own bosses, two Koreans who depend on Harold's command of English, just as Jessica hides it from her administrators.

But as Jessica trudges into board headquarters for the October 14 meeting, dragging Big Black like a temperamental terrier, she knows she needs another loophole. Even if she finds it, she doubts she can complete the first issue by Thanksgiving, as she had planned. And meanwhile, the board still owes her forty-three dollars in expenses from her trip with Salome Junco to the Kennedy awards, some six months ago. Why can't the genius computer do something about *that?*

Forty teachers are scattered throughout the conference room, some sitting on folding chairs, some leaning against long tables in the back. Jessica saves the seat next to hers for Laura Miller, the newspaper adviser at A. Philip Randolph High School in Manhattan. Laura is a cousin of Ed Vernoff, a social studies teacher at Seward Park, and she has recently returned to her native New York after twenty years of teaching in England. Laura is still trying to recover from her experience at the board's hiring hall, where one receptionist asked, "England? That's a foreign country, isn't it?" Ed thought she could use a Sherpa this afternoon.

As Jessica pores over a thick volume of contract specifications, Laura settles beside her. "How does it look?" she whispers.

"It's, like, ridiculous," Jessica mutters.

A man and a woman sit at a long folding table in the front of the room. The man, Jules Feldman, is deputy administrator of the board's Bureau of Supplies. His balding head is fringed with curly brown hair, and his face has a certain hangdog quality, the slumped muscles and dull eyes one sees in longtime commuters. One of his hands, beneath the table, nervously taps his leg. Feldman's assignment is to explain board policy to those bound to resent it. Next to him is Vera Winitch, a plump lady in a red jacket. She is the newspaper adviser at Cardozo High School in Queens and president of the city's Scholastic Press Association. Her presence on the dais is designed to prevent a riot.

"We would just as soon have everyone do their own thing and save the headaches," Feldman says, trying the friendly approach. "But this is the law. Our role is to give you as many options as possible . . ."

"One printer in Manhattan," Jessica hisses to Laura.

". . . and what you should be aware of is that we are *your* representative."

"Not mine."

Feldman identifies the five chosen printers and begins listing their prices for special services, such as converting articles into type from computer diskettes.

"Hard or soft?" one teacher asks. "Five and a quarter or three and a half?"

Feldman lifts his eyes from the contract before him. "I want you to understand something," he says, laying his forearms wearily on the tabletop. "I know nothing about printing. I can only read what's on this page." He turns his palms upward in a gesture of appeal. "We're trying to maximize your options."

Jessica uses a momentary squall of laughter to slip out of the room and find a telephone booth. She calls Harold to ask if he had been invited to bid on the contract. Yes, he says, but he never responded. How was his small shop going to print every high school paper in Manhattan? That's one loophole sealed.

As Jessica sneaks back into the room, a teacher leaning against the rear wall is speaking. "Last year, a lot of the advisers looked for ways to get around this, and I have a funny feeling it'll happen again this year. What would happen if a school said, 'Screw these five. I'll use advertising money that doesn't go through the board to pay. And I'll use any printer I like.'"

"I will say that would not be in conformance with the law," Feldman replies, frowning. "You run your own risks with that. Any audit could turn you up. If you want to run that risk you'll be personally responsible."

Jessica imagines herself in jail. The English Teacher of Alcatraz. She exhales, the air exiting her throat with a dry gargling noise that is her standard expression of exasperation. Then she rises, holding the meeting announcement in her right hand and jabbing at it with her left.

"What I don't understand about this law," she says, her New Jersey accent hardening, "is that all the literary magazines must've spent more than $15,000 on a printer and it doesn't apply to them."

"If we receive information that we have this same situation with other publications or proms or school rings, we will deal with it," Feldman says.

"Thanks, Jessica," Vera Winitch adds with prim sarcasm.

The second loophole has been closed. But Jessica refuses to retreat. "I have another question," she says, picking her way through an obstacle course of chairs and approaching the front table. "Since the reason this came up is you said a few printers were cleaning up . . ." Feldman nods. "Since the reason is that the board thought it was being ripped off by these big printers . . ." Feldman nods again. "I have a printer I've used for a long time who actually cares about how the paper looks." Now it is the other teachers who nod. Feldman narrows his eyes, awaiting the angle. "If I can get my printer to underbid the Manhattan printer, can I still use him?"

"Can you bid anything out now?" Feldman says, making certain he understands. Jessica nods. "The answer is no."

"They're a small printing company," Jessica persists. "Maybe that's why we get such good service. They can't handle all the high schools in Manhattan. Maybe that's why they didn't bid. Why can't they bid now?"

"The bidding is closed. We can't do anything."

A teacher with red hair and wire rim glasses jumps to his feet. "I don't understand the advantage," he says. "If you're on a tight budget and you have only one printer to use, then what's the advantage? If I can find a cheaper printer, what's the advantage of this contract?"

"The advantage," Feldman answers, "is that it's legal."

"If this woman," the teacher says, indicating Jessica, "can find a better place . . ."

"She can't do it within the law," Feldman interrupts. For the first time anger flashes. Even a deputy administrator has his limit.

"That doesn't make sense," the teacher shoots back.

"The law doesn't always have to make sense," Feldman says. He moves his hand in an easy outward arc, like a driver divesting himself of an empty beer can. Teachers turn to their neighbors, wide eyes meeting wide eyes. The room has a static buzz about it. "The law is the law," he adds gravely. "That's why the Bureau of Supplies is there." He pauses. "Fortunately or unfortunately."

One adviser protests, telling Feldman that his old printer promised to employ several of his students. Another says that her principal insists the newspaper be printed on glossy stock, which is not covered by the new contract. A third says that she gets only $800 a year in student activity funds, which each high school receives from the board in a lump sum and then divides as it sees fit between sports teams, clubs, and activities. How can she possibly use the same printer as a colleague who gets $4,000 a year?

"I know it ain't good," Vera Winitch says, "but it's better than last year. I don't like this, but the Bureau of Supplies and Jules Feldman worked hard on this." She says the real blame belongs to the legislature, not the board. Does anyone want to lobby for changes in the competitive bidding law? Only a few teachers raise their hands. The rest stamp out of the room, lugging tote bags of homework and cursing with each step.

Jessica and Laura remain seated in the near-empty room. Jessica leans forward, arms resting on thighs, hands dangling, eyes facing the floor.

"I don't think I can weasel out of it."

"People talk about England," Laura says. "But New York has bureaucracy taped." The word is the British equivalent of "licked." "I have never seen anything like this in my entire professional career. The only thing I've ever seen to compare to this is the Mexican postal system." She pauses. "Which is appalling."

"It's, like, ridiculous," Jessica says. She makes the gargling noise and stands to leave, vanquished.

Then she decides to appeal to Feldman one final time, personally. Last year she escaped the one-printer rule by showing that *Seward World* had slightly different dimensions than those specified in the contract. She is reluctant to try the same scam twice, but it is the only scam left.

"You can only get your own bids," Feldman tells her, "if it's a *significant* difference." He is a tired man ready to go home. It is not an easy job being The Other.

Jessica returns to Laura.

"You have a ruler?"

Laura produces one.

Jessica reaches into Big Black for last June's *Seward World*. She spreads it across an empty chair and starts to measure, counting by quarter-inches.

"What are you doing, Jess?" asks another adviser, in the soft voice of an asylum attendant addressing a benign lunatic.

"Looking for loopholes."

4

Built to Fail

On Saturday morning October 17, the auditorium of Martin Luther King, Jr., High School on Manhattan's Upper West Side throbs with the frenzy of a flea market. Three dozen booths stretch across the stage, into the orchestra pit, and up the aisles, dispensing balloons, calendars, banners, and cupcakes to throngs of children and parents. This event is the Board of Education's annual High School Fair, ostensibly the occasion for junior high school students to peruse the wares of the various institutions they can attend, but more importantly the physical and material manifestation of a system in which certain schools are engineered for success and others, like Seward Park, for failure.

While most of the schools against which it must compete for pupils enjoy admissions tests, newer facilities, special programs, and attendance caps, Seward Park and the other traditional, neighborhood high schools must answer the door for whomever knocks. So fierce and frustrating is the rivalry at the fair that arguments routinely start over the position of booths and space for wall displays. The rare white family who wanders into the maelstrom will find itself virtually attacked by touts. "Civilized warfare," as one veteran puts it.

At center stage, besieged by suitors, rests the booth for Stuyvesant High School, renowned for its excellence in science and mathematics. Elsewhere in the auditorium, "education option" (or magnet) schools show off their goods, from fabric for Fashion Design to silkscreens for

Graphic Communications to dental plates for Mabel Dean Bacon. The Seward Park station, placed at the farthest corner of the room, can offer only pins, bumper stickers, and back issues of *Seward World*. There is not enough money even for the embossed pencils Seward Park had last year.

"Look at this," Jessica Siegel mutters as she arrives for her late-morning shift and surveys the scene. "Every kind of huckster thing. Every kind of shtick. It's like Forty-second Street. 'Free girls!'" She turns to Susan Chan, a guidance counselor who is ending her stint. "I don't mind competing, but what does having the best handouts have to do with giving a good education?"

"Kids still think we're the school of last resort," Susan says. "We don't have an admissions test. We lack the drama of, 'Do I get in?' We take kids who start out way below grade level in their skills and bring them up to where they aren't so far behind. How are you supposed to sell that?"

Daisy Severino and Sharrone Usher, two seniors who are assisting at the booth, are trying to answer precisely that question. Both girls commute nearly three hours daily between their homes in the Bronx and the Lower East Side, where they formerly lived, because they feel so strongly about attending Seward Park. But Daisy also remembers that when her younger sisters expressed a desire to follow her path, their junior high school counselors tried to dissuade them. One of the chief ways a junior high in New York establishes a reputation is by placing its brightest pupils in the most selective high schools, leaving those like Seward Park with the leftovers.

"It's been a highly rewarding experience," Daisy says, practicing her sales pitch.

"Can it," Sharrone says.

"But that's what you've got to tell these people."

"You think they're gonna believe it?"

Why, indeed, would anyone believe it? The disdain for Seward Park and the Lower East Side was not some recent and lightly held belief, of which people could be readily disabused. It was decades, and in some respects almost two centuries, old. It derived as much from a national ambivalence toward immigrants and poor people as from the specific and troubled history of public education in New York. These forces, entrenched and immense, defined the battles that students like Daisy Severino and Sharrone Usher, counselors like Susan Chan, and teachers like Jessica Siegel fought every single day.

*　　*　　*

The Lower East Side began its march to notoriety with an accident of topography. In southern Manhattan, near the present-day site of the Criminal Courts building on Centre Street, the land sagged into a marsh and a pond known as the Collect. Tanneries had sprung up around the Collect in the late 1700s, the better to dispose of carcasses, and the resulting stench and disease drove the wealthier residents uptown. So, too, did the tendency of structures to sink into the swampy soil, even after the Collect was drained and filled in 1808. A sanitary inspector for the city put it plainly: This land was "undesirable for a good class of population."

Its inheritors were, by one concise description, "freed slaves and hapless immigrants," predominantly Irish peasants fleeing the potato famine and the land-enclosure movement. They named their neighborhood Five Points for the corners created by its main intersection, since little about the area justified its prior title, Paradise Square. Forty-five thousand people lived in a square quarter-mile, piling two dozen to a room in cellars, backyard tenements, and abandoned mansions. One converted brewery was the original "Den of Thieves," and an adjacent passageway earned the monicker "Murderers' Alley."

By 1850, 26 percent of the population of New York (133,000 of 513,000) had been born in Ireland, and in Five Points, where Gaelic sometimes seemed the mother tongue, the proportion hovered closer to 70 percent. Congested and miserable, many of the immigrants sought identity in gangs, thieving and brawling and more rarely killing as troops of the Shirt Tails and the Plug Uglies, the Forty Thieves and the Dead Rabbits. But many more Irish immigrants submitted to the harsh doctrine of legal employ, the men toiling as manual laborers for fifty cents a day, the women hiring themselves out as maids for one dollar a week. As one newspaper of the time noted, "There are several sorts of power working at the fabric of this Republic—water power, steam power and Irish power. The last works hardest of all."

Still, the surrounding city saw what it always would see on the Lower East Side—an alien menace, teeming. Matthew Hale Smith wrote of the Irish poor: "Their homes are in the dens and stews of the city, where thieves, vagabonds and gamblers dwell. With the early light of morning they are driven from their vile homes to pick rags and cinders, collect bones and steal. They fill the galleries of the low

theater, they are familiar with every form of wickedness and crime."
As for education, Smith remarked that the children of Five Points
were "too dirty, too ragged and carry too much vermin about them to
be admitted to the public schools."

Wretched and oppressed as the early immigrants on the Lower East
Side were, their lot appeared enviable to millions of Eastern European
Jews, afflicted by poverty, conscription, and pogroms. From 1880 to
1924, when the adoption of immigration quotas stanched the flow,
two million Jews reached America. Talmudic scholars and illiterate
peasants, lumber dealers and innkeepers, minstrels and factory
owners, they poured into the Lower East Side, forming a Yiddish-
speaking city within a city, with its own newspapers and magazines,
banks and synagogues, nursing homes and mutual aid societies. Adjacent quarters swarmed with Italians, Greeks, Chinese, Germans,
Irish, and blacks, transforming southeastern Manhattan into what
Abraham Cahan dubbed "the metropolis of the ghettoes of the
world."

Barely recovered from steerage, Jews shoved themselves into sunless tenements, three or four families to a floor, six or seven floors to a
building, by their desperation raising the population density on some
blocks to 968 people per acre, the highest in the world save for
Bombay. "The architecture," Arnold Bennett wrote, "seems to sweat
humanity at every window and door." The nascent middle-class aside,
most turn-of-the-century Jewish immigrants held menial jobs. Some
25,000 peddlers sold pots, socks, pans, shoes, pickles, shirts, tools,
seltzer, sweet potatoes, and Indian nuts. Another 200,000 Jews
worked in garment factories, many of them owned by the more prosperous and assimilated German "uptown Jews," none of them protected by child-labor and occupational-safety laws until after 146 girls
and women perished in the 1911 Triangle Shirtwaist Company fire.

Articles about "the Jewish problem," a staple of New York journalism, identified Eastern European immigrants as "ignorant," "primitive," and "the dregs of society." The novelist Henry James wrote of
the Lower East Side in *The American Scene:* "It was like being at the
bottom of some vast aquarium surrounded by innumerable fish with
overdeveloped proboscis bumping together . . . Here was multiplication with a vengeance." German Jews contributed to the lexicon of
bigotry with *kike,* their slur against Eastern European Jews whose
name often ended in "ky."

There was real and bitter debate on whether these inferiors could be saved, or whether America needed to be saved from them. The nativists triumphed when Congress passed the Johnson-Reed Act of 1924, restricting immigration by 75 percent, establishing quotas based on national origins, and vowing to preserve "the racial preponderance of the basic strain of our people." But more progressive minds prevailed on the issue of education. Major cities needed compulsory schooling, at least on the elementary level, for the same reason they needed professional police forces—to regulate the rabble and so protect themselves. Teaching the poor, by this thinking, had no intrinsic merit; it justified itself only as a balance wheel, a vast threshing machine.

"Our task," wrote Elwood P. Cubberly, the leading education historian of the early twentieth century, "is to break up these . . . [ethnic] settlements, to assimilate and amalgamate these people as part of our American race, and to implant in their children, so far as can be done, the Anglo-Saxon conception of righteousness, law and order, and popular government, and to awaken in them a reverence for our democratic institutions and for those things in our national life which we as a people hold to be of abiding worth." A New York state senator conveyed the theory more succinctly: "They will be elevated and lifted out of the swamp into which they were born and brought up."

The children of the Lower East Side were taught hygiene, etiquette, and patriotism; they were expected to master serving manners and carry clean handkerchiefs. As if deliberately to defame the Jewish heritage of most pupils, each school day opened with a recitation of the Lord's Prayer, a New Testament invocation, and often proceeded in home economics to handling meat and milk together, a violation of kosher dietary laws. Textbooks of the period presented all ethnic and racial minorities—except the English, Scots, Germans, and Scandinavians—in various shades of debauchery, larceny, and sloth. Reality was not the battlefield; perception was, particularly the perception of foreignness.

However the elementary schools performed in assimilating immigrants, they showed severe problems in educating them. Overcrowded schools turned away 1,100 eligible children in 1900, while relegating 70,000 others to part-time classes. (One of the single most glutted buildings, P.S. 137, occupied what is now Seward Park's site.) Forty percent of the city's pupils lagged behind their grade level, and, according to a 1913 survey, only one-third of those entering the first grade graduated from the eighth. Not that the attrition troubled most educators. Industrial jobs and apprenticeships awaited the Lower East Side's dropouts, especially in the booming Brownsville district in Brooklyn. Teachers saw students' failures, David B. Tyack wrote, "not as a reflection of their own inabilities as instructors, but as evidence of the students' personal and moral recalcitrance."

Even for those who did manage it, elementary school graduation held a certain finality. In her unsentimental memoir, *A Wider World*, Kate Simon recalled receiving a rose and an ice-cream cone for the occasion, because "in the houses of immigrants . . . eight years in elementary school meant a long and broad education." In a 1910 tally, only 6,000 of the 191,000 Jewish pupils in New York were attending high school.

Larger aspirations, in any case, were irrelevant before the turn of the century. New York, a city of nearly 3.4 million, did not have a single public high school. The wellborn went to private academies, the future priests to parochial institutions, and all the rest to work. The concept of free secondary education had to be imported from Brooklyn, then a separate city, and it was not until 1897 that New York inaugurated its first public high school, Boys High School, soon to be followed by Girls High School and Mixed High School. Public in name only, these schools served a small, select population and attracted a faculty from the Ivy League, the Little Three, and other private colleges.

William H. Maxwell, the superintendent of schools and a Scottish immigrant himself, did promise a free education to every elementary school graduate, even as he opined that the handful of existing high schools could meet the demand for the next fifty years. His prediction seemed sound enough, considering that less than 5 percent of the city's students were enrolled in high schools and that those institutions were deliberately situated far from the crowded immigrant ghettoes. Maxwell, unfortunately, had not reckoned on the subway.

Once the Interborough Rapid Transit lines opened in 1904, the most impoverished immigrant could reach any of the three new high schools for a few cents. Enrollment in high schools citywide soared from 6,556 in 1898 to 63,000 in 1914, with well over half the elementary school alumni taking up Maxwell's offer. Some people, it seemed, just didn't know their place. So Maxwell tried to bring the appropriate place to them. He erected two vocational high schools, Manual Training for boys and Washington Irving for girls, on the northern border of the Lower East Side. No less an authority than

Elwood P. Cubberly, after all, had urged educators to divest themselves of "the exceedingly democratic idea that all are equal, and that our society is devoid of classes."

But even the system of trade and academic schools soon proved inadequate. As New York's population ballooned toward 5.6 million in 1920, virtually every high school in the city burst its bounds, stacking 40 or 60 pupils in a class and cleaving its schedule into dual sessions. The battle had been lost. Neighborhoods would get their own high schools, even a neighborhood as disparaged as the Lower East Side. Seward Park rose on the block formerly occupied by six tenements, a court house, Alimony Jail, and the famously overburdened P.S. 137.

The optimism that the new school embodied was the qualified optimism that the masses could be remade slightly, into what the historian Stephan F. Brumberg called "an enlightened yeomanry." But years later, through the distorting lens of memory, Seward Park's graduates would remember it as exemplary, the equal of any other. They would form not one but several alumni groups, so they could gather and tell themselves how much different, how much better, Seward Park had been in their time than in the present. And it was against that imagined past, rather than the real one, that Jessica Siegel and her colleagues would be judged and invariably found wanting.

"In the legend," the historian Diane Ravitch wrote,

> the public schools had successfully educated the children of poor immigrants; in the legend, some children fared better than others, but the difference was individual merit, rather than any variation among national groups. The poor record of New York schools in educating blacks and Puerto Ricans seemed to indicate either that those groups had unprecedented cultural deficiencies or that the schools were racist and/or educationally bankrupt in comparison to the greatness of former days. The legend of success supported this analysis, but the legend itself was not true.

*   *   *

That lesson began to be learned, and the modern history of New York's public schools began to be written, in an obscure corner of Brooklyn in 1967. A smoldering conflict over community control of ghetto schools burst into open war between school and neighborhood, union and parent, black and white. Beginning with several dozen firings and reassignments, within months the dispute ignited three teachers' strikes that sundered the tenuous partnership in New York classrooms between Jewish teachers and black and Puerto Rican pupils. In its aftermath, the city adopted a hodgepodge of local and centralized school management, frustrating all, satisfying none, anticipating a great deal of the current chaos.

Central control had first come to New York in 1896, when legislation replaced the ward school boards, most in the thrall of Tammany Hall, with a civil service of professional educators. And for a time, it worked. From the enactment of immigration restrictions in 1924 through the Great Depression and World War II, New York managed to achieve, by its own skewed standards, stability. The children and grandchildren of immigrants formed a solid English-speaking lower middle class and sent their children to public schools, creating the closest thing to a demonstrably golden era.

But then the war ended, the soldiers marched to college on the GI bill, and Robert Moses laid down the freeways and threw up the bridges that unlocked suburbia to city dwellers. Jim Crow drove blacks into northern cities, and the demise of sugar plantations pushed Puerto Ricans to the mainland. During the 1950s, New York City lost 800,000 whites and gained 700,000 blacks and Puerto Ricans. Schools tilted from 80 percent white to 80 percent nonwhite in the time an incoming class of freshmen proceeded to graduation, and, more important, the disparities that had long existed between schools in affluent and impoverished districts took on a sharply racial cast.

New York's increasing number of segregated schools suffered from a higher turnover, poorer maintenance, and greener faculties than did their integrated counterparts. The reading levels of nonwhite students, poor at the dawn of the 1960s, fell further as the decade unfolded, despite a doubling of school aid and a one-third increase in the teaching force. By 1966, 45 percent of nonwhite sixth graders performed below the state benchmark for minimum competency; in some neighborhoods, the figure topped 75 percent. Only 4 of 860 principals, meanwhile, were black. And from the time the United Federation of Teachers (UFT) won collective bargaining rights in 1961, under the aggressive leadership of Albert Shanker, the process of firing incompetent teachers became so expensive and cumbersome as to be virtually impossible. In the first five years of UFT coverage, the city board managed to dismiss only 12 of 55,000 teachers.

From the late 1940s, black leaders had consistently campaigned for mandatory busing or rezoning to restore racial balance, and so, they believed, to improve education for minorities. But by the time the city got serious about integration some twenty years later, many prominent blacks did not want it. "We must no longer pursue the myth that integrated education is equated with quality education," Livingston Wingate, a Harlem antipoverty activist, argued in 1966. Blacks and Puerto Ricans had to run their own schools. They, not the city board and not the teachers' union, had to possess the right to hire and fire. The white man, having stalled and stammered through a generation of impending disaster, could not be trusted.

The shift in direction to decentralization largely reflected the path of the national civil rights movement. The common cause between blacks and white liberals, especially Jews, had been eroding rapidly as the civil rights movement veered from dismantling the legal apparatus of segregation in the South to undoing the residential, vocational, and ideological divisions in the North. For all the burning crosses and sawed-off shotguns that Dixie brandished, it proved, finally, more capable of compromise than did the Union. It was no coincidence that as community control superseded desegregation as the goal of New York's blacks, Stokely Carmichael was chanting "Black Power!" and dismissing integration as "a subterfuge for the maintenance of white supremacy."

In the spring of 1967, as riots loomed in Newark and Detroit, the New York City Board of Education offered to create several experimental districts to test community control. The state legislature subsequently mandated Mayor John Lindsay to develop a plan, and Lindsay turned to McGeorge Bundy of the Ford Foundation to draw up the details. The foundation, in turn, earmarked $135,000 for establishing three trial districts, one in Harlem, one on the Lower East Side, and one in the Ocean Hill–Brownsville section of Brooklyn. Few New Yorkers had previously heard of Ocean Hill, which one journalist described as "a no-man's land between two no-man's lands," Bedford-Stuyvesant to the north and Brownsville to the south.

There was a certain irony to the selection of Ocean Hill, for the district's staff was more racially and ethnically mixed than that of the system at large, and teachers had marched beside parents only months earlier to demand a new principal for one of the neighborhood schools. But trouble began within weeks of the election of the Ocean Hill community school board in August 1967, and from start to finish, the key issue remained the same: Did the community or the union and the city board control the hiring, firing, and transfer of educators? The Ocean Hill board threatened to close all its schools unless it could appoint new principals, preferably blacks and Puerto Ricans. The city board tried to defuse the crisis by creating a new position of "demonstration principal." The Ocean Hill board immediately offered the post to Herman Ferguson, a principal in Queens who had been arrested two months earlier in a plot to assassinate two moderate black leaders, Whitney Young and Roy Wilkins.

The faculty in Ocean Hill, like many in the city, broke largely into two racial camps. When the UFT struck in September 1967 over such issues as higher wages and smaller classes, teachers expected support in the ghettos. Instead, parents picketed the picketers, seizing on the union's demand for more latitude in disciplining "disruptive" students as racism in disguise. In Ocean Hill, the African-American Teachers Association urged its members to continue working. The walkout ended after two weeks, but the tension persisted. Students began asking questions like, "Do you hate us?" and "Are you trying to steal from us?"

With the situation already so volatile, the administrator of the Ocean Hill district, Rhody McCoy, terminated fourteen white teachers and five white principals on May 8, ordering them to report to the Board of Education for reassignment. The union told the nineteen Ocean Hill educators to return to their schools, and crowds blocked their entrance; the union called two separate strikes in the district, and while most whites complied, the vast majority of their black colleagues crossed the picket line. The next fall, the discord spread across the city, as the UFT called three strikes, the last one idling one million students for more than a month. Ocean Hill suffered the most mayhem, with its schools surrounded by screaming parents, the parents surrounded by heavily armed police, the atmosphere one of insurrection, martial law, and racial hatred. As one teacher recalls: "We had the Jewish Defense League out there. We had Mark Rudd with the S.D.S. It was a Who's Who of fanatics."

Beneath the venom lay not only the disillusion and recriminations of the former civil rights coalition, but the myth of which Diane Ravitch wrote, the myth of New York's extraordinary public schools. Because blacks believed that the schools had raised the European immigrants, they asked why the schools were failing them. Because Jews believed that European immigrants had thrived in public schools, they asked why blacks faltered so badly. Neither side recognized an important

truth. Jewish immigrants had arrived in America with urban backgrounds and industrial skills, as well as a tradition of community-
supported religious scholarship. Blacks from the rural South shared
more with the Irish and Italian tenant farmers, whose children
dropped out of New York's schools in droves. Beyond all that, as
former slaves, blacks faced discrimination more pernicious and more
complete than that known by any ethnic white group. And blacks, like
Puerto Ricans, flocked to New York just as the industrial economy
that had elevated even unlettered immigrants from poverty was lurch-
ing into permanent decline. But the various antagonists in Ocean Hill
chose to ignore such factors. It was simpler to bow to the myth, and to
rail against its broken promise.

The decentralization war stilled in 1968, and one year later the state
legislature enacted a decentralization law. It divided the city into
thirty-one local districts (later increased to thirty-two), covering all
elementary, junior high, and intermediate schools, while requiring
high schools to report directly to boroughwide superintendents, who,
in turn, would answer to the board headquarters. This was a political
solution in the guise of an educational reform, offering the appearance of increased parental involvement while preserving the UFT's
power and endowing the city with an unwieldy combination of central and community management. The first school board elections
drew only 22 percent of eligible voters—with only 4 percent casting
ballots in Ocean Hill—and the figure has languished near the single
digits ever since. Rather than representing a public interest, many of
the community school boards kowtow to the political clubhouse,
generating patronage, nepotism, and waste in the finest Tammany
Hall tradition. At one point years later, ten of the thirty-two community school boards were simultaneously under separate criminal
investigation.

Fully 1,832 teachers and principals resigned in 1968, five times the
normal number. Violence against teachers, often with racial over-
tones, spread from Ocean Hill throughout the city. New York City lost
$7.8 billion in money spent in the local economy during the last and
longest of the three teachers' strikes. The UFT sacrificed its image as
an enlightened, progressive union—Woody Allen would joke in the
film *Sleeper* that the world was destroyed when Albert Shanker got
hold of a nuclear bomb—and black advocates of community control
alienated most of their white supporters. The ethnic middle class fled
Brooklyn, Queens, and the Bronx, and the Manhattan intelligentsia

swallowed its liberal platitudes while sending its progeny to private schools.

Whatever escaped injury in the decentralization war fell victim seven years later to New York's near-bankruptcy. With the city on the verge of defaulting on $11 billion in debts, the financial rescue operation included cutting 14,500 teaching jobs, halting construction virtually in midgirder of thirteen schools, and eliminating both free tuition and open admissions at the City University, the institution that had accurately styled itself "the poor man's Harvard." The money spent per public school pupil dropped by 16 percent in real dollars in the five years immediately after the fiscal crisis, and the city slashed by nearly one-quarter the portion of its budget given to the system. With layoffs made by seniority, the average age of a city teacher soared from twenty-eight in 1973 to forty-one in 1978. Young teachers, once enthusiastic, found other jobs or simply turned sour. When the city tried in 1978 to hire back 2,300 of the teachers who had been released, it had to contact 9,000 before enough consented to return. An entire generation of teachers had been, in essence, eradicated.

Even as the fiscal crisis pared down the city schools, it contributed to the long-term social problems that, inevitably, the schools would be asked to address. The 85,000 layoffs in a municipal workforce of 333,000 struck especially hard at blacks and Hispanics, who were "last hired, first fired," plunging an incipient middle class into poverty and onto public assistance. With New York's basic welfare grant frozen from 1974 to 1981, two national fuel shortages drove the cost of living up by 68 percent. The city ceased construction of middle-income housing while the Reagan Administration throttled federal funding for low-income housing, and suddenly the homeless numbered in the tens of thousands. Factory jobs that had supported families died off or left the city, while the burgeoning service economy failed to fill the gap either in numbers or wages. An epidemic of crack use made people almost sentimental for the days when heroin was the worst drug available. In a frightening way, New York was stretching itself to extremes. The two fastest-growing types of households in the city became the one living beneath the poverty level and the one earning more than $120,000 a year. And the fastest-growing group of poor people were children, nearly four in ten by 1984, a total of about 700,000 in New York City, or a population larger than that of Pittsburgh, Boston, or Denver.

The institution most immediately responsible for those children, the Board of Education, appeared least capable of helping them. No one disputed that any public body overseeing a $5.3 billion budget, 950,000 pupils, 110,000 staff members, and 1,000 schools faced daunting responsibilities. But the board's failures seemed practically willful. As a construction agency, the board blundered through fourteen years of building LaGuardia High School in Manhattan. As a labor negotiator, it bargained and signed a contract giving custodians more money and more autonomy than principals. As a recruiter of teachers, it dissuaded applicants with plodding and insensitive treatment, even as the city faced the need to replace two-thirds of its 62,000 teachers by 1993. The Board of Examiners, the subagency charged with testing and licensing educators, itself had a $6 million budget, a permanent staff of 114, and scores of paid consultants—and still routinely went years without offering certain examinations and months more in grading them.

So entrenched and ossified was the board's bureaucracy that when Dr. Richard R. Green became chancellor in early 1988, he discovered that nobody knew exactly how many people worked in central headquarters. (It was later determined that there were 6,447 staff members.) The nine appointed board members served largely as tokens of various racial, ethnic, partisan, religious, and labor constituencies. A series of chancellors, five in the 1980s alone, and each one an educator of merit, repeatedly failed to streamline the bureaucracy and withstand the political crosswinds. And each time the position became vacant again, the board found it more and more difficult to find anyone who wanted it.

The undeniable message was that public education no longer mattered to New York. Certain Cassandras, led by the investment banker Felix Rohatyn, warned that, as an international capital, New York could not tolerate inferior public schools. But New York had tolerated them and a housing crisis and a loss of meaningful jobs even as it had resuscitated itself from the fiscal crisis. More than anything, the school system was reminiscent of the mansions that had once lined the Collect and then been abandoned by owners fleeing the aroma of decay. It was like the husk of something, the shell, an eyesore inhabited by squatters and scavengers.

*   *   *

All through the first months of 1983, Noel Kriftcher had heard the rumors. The moratorium on school construction was ending, and

Stuyvesant High School was getting a new building. Stuyvesant would leave its home on the Lower East Side, about twenty blocks north of Seward Park, for tonier surroundings, reportedly near Wall Street. Stuyvesant, after all, had produced two Nobel laureates and more than a hundred winners of the Westinghouse Talent Search, a prestigious national science contest; Stuyvesant also happened to be the only high school in Manhattan with a majority of white students.

If the original building was an octogenarian unsuitable for the academic elite, it looked like a dream to Dr. Kriftcher. Seward Park was, by some measures, the most overcrowded high school in New York, peaking at 180 percent of capacity. Freshmen and sophomores were consigned to the annex, a former elementary school with peeling paint, scores of broken windows, a gymnasium interrupted by structural columns, and asbestos insulation so frayed that fibers of the carcinogen drifted into offices and classrooms. Dr. Kriftcher remembered when a college professor moved to Manhattan and a mutual friend recommended Seward Park as a high school for her daughter. He showed the mother around the main building, and she seemed impressed. Then he added that it was only fair that the professor should know her child would attend the annex for two years. The mother walked to the building, took one look at the exterior, and found the nearest telephone booth. "I'm going to try Humanities," she told Dr. Kriftcher, referring to another Manhattan high school. "I couldn't subject my kid to a year in *that* place."

So Dr. Kriftcher wrote a little letter in June 1983 to a highly placed education official, offering to take over Stuyvesant's old building for Seward Park's freshmen and sophomores once a new Stuyvesant was ready. Nearly four years passed without any formal reply to his letter. Then, one morning, he opened his newspaper to see an announcement that the city would spend up to $100 million erecting a new home for Stuyvesant in Battery Park City, a luxury residential and shopping complex beside the financial district. The new building would rise eleven stories above the street and would feature twelve state-of-the-art laboratories, classrooms equipped with computers and fiber optics, five gymnasiums, and an Olympic-size pool, all of it linked by escalators. The project was deemed so important that the construction was being entrusted to a special state agency, the Battery Park City Authority, rather than to the Board of Education.

Once again, Dr. Kriftcher let fly. "We are willing to accept overcrowding because in a perverse way it indicates a measure of community confidence in the school," he wrote to top education officials. "We are willing to accept administrative schizophrenia despite the burden which having two buildings places upon staff and students who are seeking a single identity. But we should not have to accept a physical environment which symbolically and actually says to youngsters, 'You are just not important.'" The latest rumor was that the Koch administration had promised Stuyvesant's building to the agency that administered municipal hospitals. Seward Park, it appeared, was not deemed worthy of wearing Stuyvesant's hand-me-downs.

The slight was no oversight; it was the very design of the state, the city, and the Board of Education. In the aftermath of the battle of Ocean Hill and the 1975 fiscal crisis, New York's public schools resembled nothing so much as themselves fifty or seventy-five years earlier. Analysts pronounced themselves baffled at the contradictions in a school system that produced one-third of the nation's semifinalists in the Westinghouse Talent Search and simultaneously lost 80 percent of the pupils in some high schools before graduation. Any battlefield medic knew the answer was simple: Triage. Triage is the process—and the principle—of separating the casualties and concentrating efforts on those who are most likely to survive. In fact, the New York public school system was a case of triage within triage—first the city schools versus those elsewhere in the state and, second, those city schools like Stuyvesant that were given the right to select the most skilled students versus those like Seward Park that were obliged to cleanse the great unwashed.

When the New York State Legislature was apportioning $7.3 billion in school aid for the 1987–88 year, the year now dawning, the politicians discovered that New York City might be receiving a larger increase than they had intended. No matter that the city schools harbored 80 percent of all state students with limited proficiency in English, 63 percent of those from impoverished families, 61 percent of those reading below minimum standards, and 54 percent of the handicapped. No, fair was fair. So the legislators struck upon a formula in which each New York pupil was counted as ninety-four one-hundredths of each pupil elsewhere in the state. Some New Yorkers made rueful jokes about the "Ivory soap solution," and others recalled the Constitution's calibration that a slave should be counted as three-fifths of a free person. Indeed, the legislature's arithmetic had provided a perfect symbol of scorn: Financially or otherwise, New York City schoolchildren counted for less.

Almost any statistic supported the same conclusion. The amount of state money spent on a pupil in the city lagged 17 percent behind the amount granted a pupil outside the city—$2,574 to $3,014. City schools received 32.6 percent of state school aid while educating 36.6 percent of the state's students. Alone among the municipalities in New York State, the city had no right to levy taxes for schools. Of 715 school districts statewide, the city's was one of only 15 without the "hold-harmless" provision to protect it from a cut in state aid because of declining enrollment. And enrollment in the city had declined by 100,000 after Ocean Hill and the near-bankruptcy. When school aid to suburban districts was imperiled, parents lobbied, wheedled, and bullied their legislators because in the suburbs, the mayor, the banker, and the real estate agent sent their children to public schools. When New York's schoolchildren were being whittled down to 94 percent of themselves, one wondered how often the telephone rang for Gotham's legislative delegation. Not one member of the Board of Education, not one citywide elected official, had children in the public schools. The mayor and council members themselves had been tightening the civic pursestrings for education. How could they complain when Albany followed their cue?

The difference in the state aid the city received for 1987–88 and the state aid it deserved—numerically, not to say morally—came to $450 million. What did $450 million mean? It meant that two in five high schools operated at more than 110 percent of capacity. It meant that the ratio of high school students to guidance counselors topped 600 to 1, double the rate outside the city. It meant that a junior high school pupil had an average of twenty minutes during an entire *year* to discuss the choice of high schools with a guidance counselor. It meant that 90 percent of the elementary school students had no library available to them. The prophecy fulfilled itself. When the state Department of Education identified the most troubled schools in the state, 90 percent of them, including Seward Park, were in New York City. Yet money to remedy the woes went disproportionately to the handful of afflicted schools outside the city. State curriculum specialists did not visit city schools because, as they later confessed to auditors from Comptroller Edward Regan's office, "the problems were too great for their visits to make a difference."

And in New York City itself, the landscape was anything but level, with its tiers of specialty, magnet, and neighborhood high schools. A team of educators, exploring a similar configuration in Chicago, dubbed it "the new improved sorting machine," and it undeniably worked. Of the four most selective schools in New York, Stuyvesant, Bronx Science, and Brooklyn Tech screen applicants by rigorous examinations, while Performing Arts, the inspiration for the film *Fame,* winnows according to auditions.* These schools remain 46 to 58 percent white within a system that is only 22 percent white, and hundreds of their students have reentered the public system from the private system to avail themselves of a superior education, cost free. Of the remaining seventy-seven academic high schools, fifty-six are permitted by the board to offer "education option" programs and to choose pupils either on a boroughwide or districtwide basis, adhering to a formula that reserves 25 percent of the seats for those reading above grade level, 50 percent for those reading at grade level, and 25 percent for those reading below grade level.† What appears to be an equitable plan is anything but one, for nearly three-quarters of the incoming freshmen in the city read below grade level. So the cream, however little of it there may be, is duly skimmed, and the residue is poured into twenty-one neighborhood high schools, expecting the worst and, all too often, finding it.

Although the Board of Education has tried to narrow the gap, municipal funds still flow more generously to selective schools than to neighborhood schools—$1,795 per pupil versus $1,631 as of 1985. A collection of ten selective schools, together serving 6 percent of the city's high school students, gleans 18 percent of the funds for special programs. Yet the neighborhood schools have the most truants, the most immigrants, the most special education cases—the most students, in other words, requiring special help.

Seward Park is one of only four high schools in Manhattan without either an admissions test or a selective "education option" program. Its nearest neighbors, Murray Bergtraum and Norman Thomas, have new buildings, special business programs, and limits on enrollment. At Humanities High School, another competitor, a specially recruited faculty requires a student body capped at 1,500 to study Shakespeare

---

*Music & Art, merged in 1985 with Performing Arts as Fiorello LaGuardia High School of Music & Art and Performing Arts, selects by portfolio and performance.
†The proportions were later changed to 16, 68, and 16 percent, respectively.

and complete a community-service project. Teachers at Stuyvesant, much to the bitter amusement of their peers at Seward Park, demand extra pay for all the letters of recommendation they must write for college-bound seniors. Geography condemns Seward Park two ways. Academically, it draws students from junior high and intermediate schools in which about 55 percent of the pupils read below grade level even before the best of them are siphoned off by selective schools. Culturally, it draws students from a neighborhood that continues to receive new immigrants in almost unparalleled numbers.

As a result, Seward Park in the 1987–88 school year was to test the English aptitude of 1,337 students who were likely to be entitled to bilingual education, to serve the 1,112 who proved eligible, and to spend nearly $1.5 million in the process. Each immigrant to arrive during the year—"over the counter," in Seward Park slang—was interviewed personally by Helen Cohen, the assistant principal for guidance services, and then evaluated by a half-dozen departmental chairpersons, a process consuming as much as a week. The challenge was heightened by the shifting nature of the newcomers. In the 1980s, relatively well-educated Chinese who were reared in Hong Kong and Taiwan and Puerto Ricans who arrived from the island with some English ability were being supplanted by rural peasants from the Dominican Republic and the People's Republic of China, most of whom were poorly schooled and some of whom were illiterate even in their native tongues. And while the Chinese and Spanish bilingual programs justifiably boasted of how many of their students won admissions to college—nearly 90 percent of the Chinese—the failure rates in bilingual science, mathematics, and social studies courses more than doubled over seven years.

Teachers like Jessica Siegel encountered another, less visible side effect of bilingual education in the person of the student who, under federal rules, had to be "labbed out" of the program for scoring above the twentieth percentile on a standardized English test and yet foundered in a completely English class.* Strong spirit and a pocket dictionary could painstakingly produce reading comprehension, but writing and speaking proved more recalcitrant. The gap between different skills appeared even in Shawn Gerety's advanced placement English class, in which eight of the twenty-one students were born overseas and fourteen of twenty-one spoke a language other than

*New York State later raised the cut-off to the fortieth percentile.

English at home. The same pupils who were capable of reading and understanding texts as demanding as *Heart of Darkness* and *Sons and Lovers* leapfrogged illogically in their writing from past to present, singular to plural. They were still abiding by the rules of Chinese, a language with no verb tenses and nouns that swing from singular to plural based on context alone.

The tension between Old World and New World informs even the most minute and subtle actions. A social studies teacher, assigned to decorate a hallway bulletin board, posts tourist photographs of Leningrad. Within a week, a student tears off the plastic covering, gouges out several of the pictures, and writes in black magic marker, "Afghanistan for White Rusky Subjugation. Infidels!" The older brother of a pupil, summoned to explain why he beats the boy for receiving poor grades, tells a guidance counselor matter-of-factly, "That's the way we do it in Yemen." A student in a bilingual English class writes in his journal: "Right now I am listening to the radio and I am thinking about what am I going to do in Christmas Eve. I guess I'll be sleeping because I have no Friends to give presents or cousins, uncles or aunts to give presents. They are in my native country Guatemala. I guess this Christmas, I'll be very sad."

The surpassing irony of Seward Park and institutions like it, then, is that the "neighborhood school"—once the rallying cry of a white middle class that was indignant at integration—has become the catchbasin for poor black, Hispanic, and Asian children in the late 1980s. These children are the waste products of the new improved sorting machine. The weight of history and the miracle of modern social engineering conspire for disaster, and yet when education critics, social scientists, and newspaper editors stumble upon it, they act as if they had discovered a startling scandal. But there is another way to conceive of Seward Park and its ilk. In a school built for failure, anything short of failure qualifies as a kind of success.

*   *   *

The High School Fair proceeds through the late morning. Having made no converts yet, Jessica turns her attention to a father and daughter.

"Seward's a good place to get a general education," she says.

"She wants to specialize in drama."

"We have a drama class."

"Well, thank you," he says, wandering away.

"That's one I didn't convince," she sighs.

Two girls ask about computer courses.

"We have a lot of 'em," Jessica says, hastily skimming a list of classes. "And you can go up to AP calculus." They turn to leave. "Want a bumper sticker?"

A mother arrives. She says her father went to Seward Park and adored it, but she hears it's overcrowded these days.

"People vote with their feet," Jessica says. "And you don't have to worry about us closing."

As the woman departs, Jessica checks her watch. It is noon. Her shift is over. She grabs her coat and bag, taps Daisy Severino on the shoulder, and says almost plaintively, "Knock 'em dead."

Method
Teaching

JESSICA SIEGEL HAS arrived at the shank of the semester. She has finished her lessons in note taking, composition, and autobiography. She has passed the holiday interruptions of Rosh Hashanah, Yom Kippur, and Columbus Day, settling into a sequence of five-day class weeks. She has zipped her summer clothes into plastic garment bags and arranged her winter plumage in the closet beside her bed. And today she will begin teaching American literature to students who are often new to America and just as often indifferent to literature.

Rain falls from low, creased clouds as Jessica pushes a metal cart of textbooks into Room 336, where her English classes meet. Heat hisses from two blue-gray radiators, and the air above them dances like a desert mirage. Jessica opens a window to moderate the blast, and when she looks down on Grand Street, she can see only one or two skeletal poplars, reddening with the season. The coming of hard, deep fall on the Lower East Side is better signaled by the foliage on Orchard Street, the cold-weather coats newly hung outside storefronts, strung low enough for eyeballing and too high for shoplifting. Among Seward Park's fashionable, the summery "Surf Club" jersey has given way to the Troop Jacket, a Korean-made variation on the traditional letter jacket, affixed with a fictitious school name and ornamented with embroidery enough to busy a score of seamstresses. The students wear them outside and they wear them inside, unbuttoned and dropped to the elbows, for they distrust Seward Park's boiler or its lockers or both.

Jessica notices that graffiti is building up within the classroom. The chalk signature of a certain "ae" slashes across her corkboard display, while "Redjack" marks a door. Like every other teacher, Jessica recently received from Helen Cohen a graffiti bulletin, with samples from Seward Park's most prolific scribes and a plea that she advise the proper authorities if she identifies offending handiwork on any tests or notebooks. Such sleuthing does not rank highly among Jessica's priorities. She consults her watch and writes on the blackboard, "Journal Topic: Why Did My Relatives Come to This Country?"

By now, Jessica can characterize her classes as classes, as collective personalities. Journalism is a disaster. She rushes through a huddle with her six advanced students and then faces a mutinous crew of beginners. They are so accustomed to Seward Park's standard desks, bolted in place facing front, that sitting in a room with normal chairs and computer terminals elicits the third grader in them all. She turns her head and they launch so many paper planes the room needs an air traffic controller. The Lower East Side class with Bruce, usually a source of satisfaction, is a misery of truancy and listlessness. Twice already, Jessica has had to dispense spot quizzes when she could not deliver her lesson because not a single student had done the preparatory reading. And the reading is rarely more than five pages overnight.

Jessica's salvation is second-period English 7. Wilfredo Ayala, José Santiago, and Lun Cheung all impressed her with their autobiographies. But as with *Seward World,* the class's real mainstays are Dominican girls, their teased hair and tight jeans belying restive minds. Aracelis Collado, wise and dependable, Jessica knows from the newspaper. Raquel Tamares, only sixteen years old as a senior, possesses an adult's emotional depth. And Addie Severino, insecure about her own substantial abilities next to those of her older sister, Daisy, seems almost an embodiment of Jessica's younger self. At the same time, of course, almost half the class is in danger of failing, and one Chinese boy is running a lucrative football betting pool, collecting $20 bills every Monday morning, cutting the next three days, and appearing on Friday with the coming weekend's odds. Jessica cringes, especially when she sees José Santiago, husband and father, paying his debt.

First-period English 7, despite the absences that always plague an early-morning class, is not at all bad. Mary Tam, surely the smartest kid in the group, attends only infrequently and speaks hesitantly when she does. In her stead, the engines are two boys with little in common but eccentricity. Angel Fuster, *Seward World*'s business manager, is as sensitive and witty as he is short, which is to say very. Jessica had to howl the other day when he dashed into class late, a pair of pajama bottoms wound around his neck Charles Aznavour style. Ottavio Johnson is quite Angel's opposite, a wide, hulking member of Seward Park's weight-lifting club, the Dog Brothers. The willful child of an Italian-black marriage, Ottavio is bright and aware but something of a sophist, awarding himself nicknames like "The Lion" and "$E = mc^2$." He dropped Jessica's journalism class because he cared little for revising what he considered his perfect prose, but he had no choice but to stick with English 7, a requirement for graduation, and he gradually came to respect the teacher who refused to indulge his act.

Jessica turns from the board and sees both boys in their seats. Angel has left the pajamas home this morning and wears his usual leather jacket unadorned. Ottavio, his pectorals almost bursting a Gold's Gym T-shirt, inhales a breakfast of Doritos and orange soda. Jessica allows him to dine during class because she knows he travels an hour each morning from the Inwood neighborhood at Manhattan's northern tip; she just wishes he would discover one or two of the major food groups. About fifteen other students trickle in, meaning that half the class has yet to arrive. In other words, the norm.

She turns sideways, pointing with her left hand to the board and with her right hand toward the class. "Well," she says, "why *did* your family come to America? Manny?"

"It was for a better life."

"Luis?"

"To find a better job?"

"Mike?"

"To live with their relatives."

"They have relatives in other places, too," Jessica says, right hand on her hip in a posture of challenge. "Why here?"

"Better life."

"Mary?" She is here today.

"I'm here alone," she says, eyes averted. "I came to study."

Snickering surrounds her.

"Steve?"

"So me and my brothers could have advantages they never had."

"Now," Jessica says, "suppose we went back to the fifteen hundreds, sixteen hundreds, seventeen hundreds." She raises the forefinger of her right hand. "What would be some of the reasons those people came here?"

"To get away from their political system."

"To make money."

"Is that true?" Jessica asks.

"They came looking for gold," Angel says.

"Ottavio?"

"They came as slaves."

Jessica crosses her arms and nods. Only Ottavio would have come up with that answer. For all his bullshit, he really thinks, and he really knows his own history.

"The point I'm trying to make," Jessica says, "is that most of us came here by choice." Ottavio flings up his hand like a first grader in need of a bathroom pass until Jessica adds, "With the exception of slaves." He subsides. "Most of us came for a reason. Including my grandparents."

"The potato famine," Ottavio shouts.

"Wrong ethnic group," Jessica says. "That's the Irish. I'm Jewish." She moves to the blackboard and writes the words "New World."

"What does that suggest to you?"

"A change."

"Absolutely new to them."

"New *World*," Jessica says emphatically. "Not New *Land*." She swivels on her heels to face a student who has not yet contributed. "Roberto?"

"Um."

Jessica waits.

"You know."

Jessica plants her feet, leans back, and grabs the rope in a pantomime tug-of-war. "Why do I feel I gotta pull this outta you?" she says. The class laughs and Roberto blushes.

"They came here to find a lot of space," he ventures. "They could have bigger farms."

"What else? 'New World.' Those are important words."

"Starting fresh."

"Totally different."

Jessica grins in triumph. Her tug-of-war is not only with Roberto. It is with the class, and it is with the subject. American literature is not accounting or metal shop or any of the more practical courses Seward Park offers. American literature does not indicate a vocation or promise its master a livelihood. Part of Jessica does not believe she can ask teenagers with very real financial worries to embrace the abstract of scholarship for scholarship's sake. Part of Jessica believes that embrace is an absolute necessity. She seeks to identify the element in a poem or story or novel that may touch a student's life in 1987 on the Lower East Side, and then to exploit that connection, luring the student through character and narrative ultimately into art.

"Relevance" was a favored term among the young educators of the 1960s, but "relevance" came to mean teaching only material reflective of daily reality. It condescended to a student, particularly an inner-city student, assuming one could recognize only the image in the mirror. Jessica, in contrast, taught more by the theatrical principles of Constantin Stanislavski, the Russian director who held that an actor has to plumb his or her past and there discover an emotional analog to inform the fictive character. For want of a more descriptive term, Stanislavski's theories became known as "The Method." What happens this morning in Room 336 is not dissimilar. Jessica does not preach the doctrine of American literature as "important" or "valuable," because value and import are best discovered along the way. Instead, she reminds her students that as immigrants of the 1980s, they may share some common feelings with immigrants of the 1680s, if only the desire to tell one's tale. Call her style "Method Teaching."

Up to this point, all the reading assignments have come in the form of rexos. To the delight, no doubt, of the two dozen teachers with whom she shares one duplicating machine, Jessica now dispenses texts. The book is an anthology of American literature, from Indian narratives to contemporary poetry, that was edited by two high school teachers from suburban Chicago. Each copy weighs four pounds and spans 944 pages; many copies carry such marginalia as "Breakfast Club 87—Philip, Gil, Jhon, Paul, Street." A few students heft the book in their hands like a general-store grocer weighing a chunk of cheddar, and they groan. One advantage of doling out rexos is that no assignment intimidates by dimension alone; there is no disguising this slab of verbiage, nearly two inches thick.

Jessica riffles the pages, as if exploring it for the first time. "Some people think no American literature existed before seventeen seventy-six," she says with calculated nonchalance. "Any ideas why?"

"No America."

"So if you were walking down Grand Street in sixteen-eighty and asked someone what they were, what would they say?

"British."

"Dutch."

"Irish."

"French."

"Puerto Rican."

"Little too early," Jessica says, laughing. "But there *was* writing before seventeen seventy-six. American literature didn't just emerge. We're going to discover the kind of writing there was before there was an America at all."

She writes the numeral "1" on the board and to its right the word "Indians."

"Did the Indians have a literature?"

There is silence.

"Why not?"

"They didn't write."

"Why not?"

"No pens."

"The Indian tribe is small. They talk a lot."

"You know those Indians," Jessica says, rolling her eyes in mock exasperation. "Can't shut 'em up."

"I meant they pass it orally."

"Good thinking, folks," Jessica says. "I'm impressed."

She proceeds through the next few categories—explorers with their adventure yarns, settlers with their reports to the crown, religious leaders with their sermons and parables, slaves with their fables and songs and autobiographies. This lesson is working well until a voice issues from the intercom.

"Attention, attention, this is Mr. Levine. In three minutes, we will have a fire drill. Please move in an orderly fashion into your stairwell."

Jessica sits and drops her chin into her palm.

"We have to go on this?" Angel asks.

"No," Jessica says sourly. "We can stay and burn up."

Three clangs resound, and the students follow Jessica into the hall and down the nearest stairwell. They linger for several minutes, with Jessica impatiently jostling a pen, until three more clangs order the class back into Room 336.

"Next time," one student says, plopping into his seat, "I'd rather fry."

Jessica twists the comment to her own end. "So you don't like the fire drill," she says, linking hands behind her back and beginning to pace. "What else don't you like? If you could change one thing about this school, what would you change?"

"This book."

"So you want to change it. What could you do?"

"PTA meeting."

"Petition."

"Steve?" Jessica says. She hears the rustle of a newspaper being crudely folded and stashed beneath a desktop. A distracted voice says, "I like the book."

"Angel?" He looks up. He is chewing on a toothpick. "You were the one who hated the book."

"No, Miss Siegel. That was Elvin."

"Elvin?"

"It was Angel."

Ottavio raises his hand and says, "Advertise."

"What do you mean, advertise?" Jessica says.

"You don't like something, you advertise to tell people how bad it is."

"You *convince*," Jessica says. She sits on the front corner of her desk. "You write a letter to Miss Jon. You write a letter to the *Seward World*. That great paper. Of which I happen to be adviser." She stands. "You *write*."

She loops the lesson back to the slaves. She asks why they depended so heavily on oral tradition.

"They weren't taught to write."

"Why?" Jessica asks.

"They didn't go to school."

"So you can only learn to read or write in school? You're giving us teachers too much credit."

"The white people," Angel says. "They wouldn't teach the slaves to read and write."

"Right," Jessica says, nodding assent. "In fact, there were laws against it." She leans forward, hovering over the students in the front row. "Because if you know how to read and write, what do you have?" She waits a beat. "You have power."

*   *   *

Lugging a black tote bag, Angel Fuster walks into the English office to the waiting Jessica. "This," he announces, dropping the bag to thudding effect, "is The Entity." The Entity bulges with college catalogues, admissions forms, and financial aid applications. Angel has tried to tame The Entity by donating some of its contents to his pet hamsters "so they can make little hamster houses," but even in slightly diminished form, it haunts his slumber, sprouting legs and baring teeth and chasing him around the room until he jolts awake. And daylight does nothing to temper his trepidation about college. He calls it "the 'C' word."

Angel knows that he goofed off for too many terms, and the proof shows in his 75 average. A lot of teachers consider him a "get-over," a dissembler who devotes more energy to avoiding assignments than he would have spent in completing them. Being a good student would be easy, Angel claims, but it would be boring. He would rather pass a hygiene course on manufactured sympathy, telling the teacher his girlfriend is pregnant and refusing to have an abortion, and soliciting excused absences for imaginary visits to Planned Parenthood. "Angel," says Bonnie Kowadlo, a business teacher who became one of his mentors, "could sell tuxedos to penguins."

"Getting over," however, has a second connotation, at least on ghetto streets. It means sustaining yourself or your family by whatever methods necessary. From age twelve, Angel has worked clandestinely to augment his divorced mother's welfare check, beginning by handing out leaflets for a supermarket at ten dollars a day, seven days a week. When welfare authorities learned of a later job, flipping hamburgers for minimum wage at McDonald's, they reduced his mother's aid. Deception and survival, then, commingle in Angel's morality, and as much as he desires success on his own merits, he doubts his ability to achieve it. Angel feels uneasy both in his extended family, where relatives ridicule his spotty Spanish, and in the larger white world. A suburban girl once refused to shake his hand on the podium of a statewide conference of Distributive Education Clubs of America (DECA) chapters, and when he gave her the finger in reply, he was nearly ousted from the organization. Bonnie Kowadlo found him alone that night, convulsed in sobs, more despondent than she had ever seen any child.

Jessica pulls out chairs for herself and Angel, and they commence disemboweling The Entity, organ by organ.

"Eugene Lang College," Jessica says, grasping a folder. "You don't want to stay in New York, do you?"

"No." He pauses. "Just in case."

"LaGuardia Community College, out. College of Staten Island, out. Hofstra, in. Cornell." Jessica faces Angel. "Let's get real."

"OK," Angel says. "Out."

"Marine Corps, out."

"They sent me free socks."

"Give 'em to a teacher for extra credit."

She resumes the digging, and the two piles grow, blocking the path of anyone entering the office. Emma Jon is the first who tries to pass. She gazes critically at the two paper mounds rising from the linoleum. Then she looks at Jessica, expecting an explanation when none is forthcoming.

"Did you type that letter for me?" Emma asks.

"Not yet. I'll do it before I leave."

"All right."

Irritation infuses Emma's voice, but Jessica is so engaged with Angel she seems not to notice. Or not to care. She continues dividing the college materials like a croupier.

"Bryn Mawr?"

"What's the problem?" Angel asks.

"It's a girls' school."

"Good odds."

"Fordham," Jessica sputters through laughter. "Do they have dorms? Yes? OK. Syracuse, in."

"I have dreams about Syracuse." says Angel, suddenly quite serious. "I'm driving in a jeep with the top down."

"I thought it'd be a red convertible," Jessica says.

"Snows too much up there. It's snowing in my dream. And this girl's at my side, and we're driving past this bell building."

Angel takes the glossy brochure from Jessica's hand and points to the photograph of Crouse College, a classroom building with a pipe organ and tower chimes. Then he opens the front of his leather jacket to display a T-shirt.

"Orange," he says. "Just like Syracuse." His eyes brighten. "I oughta wear this when I do my videotape."

"Videotape?"

"My videotape. Paint my room orange. Put on a suit. Stand in front of a bunch of trophies. 'I've wanted to go to Syracuse ever since I was a lad.'"

"Gimme a break."

But Angel is not done. He retrieves the Manhattan telephone book from atop a file cabinet and races through the pages, seeking the listing for the Young Democrats.

"I thought I could join up," he explains to Jessica. "Not do a lot. Just put down on my application, 'Longstanding member of Young Democrats.'"

"Angel," Jessica says, sliding from soprano to baritone across two elongated syllables. "You don't need hype."

"It couldn't hurt." He continues paging through the book. " 'Young Democrats of Chinatown,'" he pronounces in triumph. "Angel Ying Fuster."

Jessica suppresses a laugh, and when she recovers she suggests that Angel see Hal Pockriss. Hal is a guidance counselor assigned to College Discovery, a program providing special classes and extra counseling for students who lag more than two years below grade level in basic skills but have demonstrated reliable attendance and healthy study habits—in all ways, the antithesis of Angel. But Hal is also one of Jessica's fellow travelers in placing underachievers in college, and he is her friend. As Jessica dials Hal's extension, Angel moves from his chair to the long work table. He scribbles on a piece of scrap paper the numeral "4" and the letter "H." Jessica, by now off the phone, asks Angel what the 4 and the H mean. Angel's not planning to join the 4-H Club—at least as far as she knows. He explains. Four years at Syracuse, majoring in political science, and then law school at Harvard. He is not joking.

"Then I open up my practice," he says, "and I come back to Seward to start the Angel Fuster College Fund. Because I know that after I leave, there'll be someone else here like me."

"You can do that, Angel," Jessica says, drawing close. "You're the kind of person who really thinks about things, and asks questions. If you'd only trust that."

Angel stares at the floor, uncomfortable with the praise.

"Let's face it," he says. "I fucked up. I'd rather say I got a seventy-five because I was in Young Democrats than say I got a seventy-five because I had to go to work every night. If I was a college admissions officer, I wouldn't let me in. It's like the guy said, 'I wouldn't want to join any club that would have me as a member.'"

Jessica lowers her head, forcing Angel's eyes to meet her own. In social encounters, her eyes often roam and dodge. In school, they aim and fasten like a staple gun.

"If you want to get into Syracuse," she says, "you can start by revising your autobiography. You can go to see Mr. Pockriss. We'll make a time. You've got a lot going for you, Angel. You're in DECA. You're the business manager of the paper."

"And I'm a long-standing member of the Young Democrats of Chinatown."

"Enough with the hype, Angel," Jessica warns. "Remember: I'm your bullshit detector." Now she grins. "What would you do without me?"

"That's what I'm worried about."

*   *   *

Jessica rubs the sleep from her eyes as her second-period students write. The journal topic asks, "What Is Your Favorite Possession? Why?" This personal inquiry will serve as the preface to her lesson on Anne Bradstreet's poem, "Upon the Burning of Our House." Jessica plants her palms on her cheekbones and massages each closed eye with three fingers. She has been satisfied with the literature classes thus far—two on the Indians, two on the European explorers—but bearded adventurers and braves in headdress are familiar figures from popular culture. How is Jessica supposed to enthrall three dozen city kids with the self-lacerating verse of a seventeenth-century religious fanatic? She thinks of what Denise Simone always says: "We have to compete with sex, drugs, rock 'n' roll, and MTV."

Seeing the pens halt, Jessica solicits the students' answers, and a list spills across the blackboard. Walkman, guitar, cat, teddy bear, gold coin, T-shirt collection, self-confidence, a happy family.

"My guns," someone shouts.

"I don't want to think about what caliber or how many," Jessica says. Experience has taught her how to disarm a heckler with humor or indifference. Jessica is no naif when it comes to street violence or its potential inside Seward Park, but in her nine years at the school she has never once been threatened. The most dangerous kids on the Lower East Side do not bother attending school to study Anne Bradstreet or anything else.

"Now," Jessica says, "imagine how you'd feel if it went up in flames." No one answers. "Your favorite thing, up in flames." Again, silence. She sees something in the third row. "Harry, what's that? Do your physics homework in physics." She frowns with real dejection.

"What a slow class. Tomorrow I'm gonna bring orange juice to wake you all up. You've got to get a little more energized."

Point made, Jessica moves to the next stage of the lesson, reading the poem aloud. She stands erect, stiff as a schoolgirl in a spelling bee, and her voice issues flatly. The dry delivery is deliberate, because she leans harder on the words when she reaches the two key stanzas:

> Here stood that trunk, and there that chest,
> There lay that store I counted best.
> My pleasant things in ashes lie,
> And them behold no more shall I.
> Under thy roof no guest shall sit,
> Nor at thy table eat a bit.
>
> No pleasant tale shall e'er be told,
> Nor things recounted done of old.
> No candle e'er shall shine in thee,
> Nor bridegroom's voice e'er heard shall be.
> In silence ever shall thou lie.
> Adieu, adieu, all's vanity.

"So what's Anne Bradstreet's first response?"

"Scared," Aracelis says.

"Does anyone know what it's like to be in a fire?" Jessica asks. "Anyone ever been in one?"

A number of hands rise. Arson is distressingly common in the neighborhood, but no one responds to Jessica's tacit request for details. She decides the subject is too personal and returns to the text.

"So she's made it out alive. Standing in the cold. Seeing everything burned up. What's her first thought?"

"Her belongings," says Addie. "She's mourning for everything she lost."

"Just think," Jessica says, opening her palms in a gesture of appeal. "You're standing there. Everything's lost. But your family survived. What are you thinking?" A hand shoots up. "Aracelis?"

"Thank God."

"*Thank God*," Jessica repeats firmly. "We're all safe. 'And when I could no longer look, I blest His name that gave and took.'" She closes the book, her forefinger marking the page. "Then what? Raquel?"

"She starts to feel bad about losing her things."

"How do we know?"

Following her finger across the smooth page, Raquel reads, and as she does Jessica writes on the board the various belongings mentioned in the poem. Trunk, chest, and table appear beside Walkman, guitar, and teddy bear, making the point for Jessica.

"So she's getting sad about these possessions," Jessica says, turning again toward the class. "But what else? Wilfredo?"

"Her memories."

"Think about losing what you care about," Jessica says, now erasing the two lists from the board. "Your records. Your stereo. Your bike. They can be replaced. Anne Bradstreet can build another house. Like Wilfredo said, it's the memories of that house. It's the way everyone hung around the kitchen telling stories. That's why she's bummed out. But then she changes gears again. 'Adieu, adieu, all's vanity.' What does 'adieu' mean?"

" 'Goodbye,' " Raquel says.

"See, all the French you took came in handy. What about 'vanity'?"

"Prince's old girlfriend."

"That lady who turns the cards on 'Wheel of Fortune.' "

"The things you don't have to have," says Raquel, unruffled, "but that you want to have."

"Anybody else?" Jessica asks. She rarely settles for one answer, because that lets thirty students, timid or unprepared, hide behind an outspoken four or five. It is the quiet ones who she presses hardest to trust their own judgments, to search beyond easy answers. "C'mon. 'Vanity.' Hint: 'Vain.' "

A Chinese boy named Alex Tang extends his arm, which Jessica takes as a hopeful sign. She had Alex in the Lower East Side class last year, and remembers him as a sharp, irreverent kid strangely committed to failure. She has been trying to draw him out all term, from the very first day, when she asked him what he looked for in a blind date. Maybe her efforts are finally succeeding.

"Just concerned with your looks," Alex says.

"Suddenly she's calling all these dear possessions 'vanity.' Just wipes them all away." Jessica drags her hand across an imaginary slate. "And if you look further in the poem, she uses three metaphors for her possessions. Anyone know what they are?" She waits. "Anyone know two?" She waits again. "One?"

" 'Dunghill mists,' " Raquel says softly.

"What's a dunghill?" Jessica asks, scanning the room. "Roberto knows, I can tell. Maribel knows, too. I can see her smiling. It's a hill of what?" She fixes on Truman Chang, an honor society member doing dishonorable work for Jessica. He wears a T-shirt of the heavy metal star Ozzy Osborne swinging a cross-ax. Scatology ought to be his sort of subject.

"I don't know how to say it," Truman says, unexpectedly avoiding the chance to outrage. "It's, um, waste."

" 'Waste,' " Jessica says. "That's a nice word."

"Doo-doo?" Truman offers.

"It's a pile of shit," Jessica says, and the room explodes with laughter and shock, almost drowning out the bell.

As coincidence has it, Jessica commences her first period class the following morning on the subject of dunghill mist. Once again, her blunt definition delights some and appalls a few. Either way, the snoozers awake.

"My God," whispers a girl in the front row, touching thumb and index finger to forehead. "I went to Catholic school last year."

"Eunice can't believe a Puritan lady would talk like this," Jessica tells the rest of the class. "What's that saying?"

"She's showing how much she loves her possessions," Angel says.

"*Loves?* That's why she compares them to *shit?*"

"But it's like if you lose your bike," Angel argues. "Once it's gone, you think, 'I didn't care that much about it.' "

Jessica locks arms behind her back and paces the horizon of the room. Her contemplation is affected, but the performance has a purpose. Angel challenged her, intelligently and specifically, and by weighing his dissent she wants to encourage more. For most of these students, hearing a teacher admit error is rarer than hearing a teacher say "shit."

"So Angel thinks she's putting it on," Jessica says as she strides. "Think about how that works with the stanza before. 'Adieu, adieu, all's vanity.' Elvin?"

"Her stuff don't mean anything."

"Why?"

"Because she don't have it anymore."

"What are her feelings now? She's gone through all these changes. First she's happy to be alive. Then she thinks . . ."

"Rotten," someone calls.

"Worthless."

"Useless," Jessica says, and then she reads aloud the final stanza of the poem:

> A price so vast as is unknown
> Yet by His gift is made thine own;
> There's wealth enough, I need no more,
> Farewell my pelf, farewell my store.
> The world no longer let me love,
> My hope and treasure lies above.

"What's she saying there?" Jessica asks the class.

"That her stuff is priceless," Mike says.

"Priceless? She says, 'Farewell my pelf.' What does the book say 'pelf' means?"

Mike and the rest find the footnote, which defines the archaism as "Wealth or money looked upon with contempt."

"If it's priceless," Jessica says, "why the contempt?"

A girl in glasses and a ponytail raises her hand. On the first day of class, she had seated herself in the front right corner of the room. The front declared her dutiful intents, the corner her timorous instincts. Jessica nearly needs her Delaney card to remember the girl's name is Donna.

"She wants to go to heaven," Donna says.

"Good thinking, Donna," Jessica says, certain to honor the girl by name. "And what does that tell us about a Puritan's view of life? This is a short poem, but it can tell us a lot about what's in here." She taps her temple. "What does being a Puritan mean?"

"Someone who's clean."

"Kind of," Jessica says affably. "What else?" She leans against the corner where the south wall and the blackboard intersect, pretending the patience of a police interrogator. The class outlasts her. "Folks," she says, "maybe you slept through American History One, but you can make some connections. I know you think English is English and history is history and they're separate parts of your notebook and blah, blah, blah. But they're connected. See if you can fit the pieces together." She moves to her desk. "Why did the Puritans come here?"

"For their religion."

"They were persecuted by the Church of England."

"Awright," Jessica exults. "Ten steps forward. They thought the

Church of England was too lax. They wanted to purify it. What were their rules like?"

"Strict. *Stone* strict."

"Like?"

"No drinking. No smoking. No premarital sex."

"Oh, man," someone moans, and the class laughs.

Jessica, though, believes that the Puritan injunctions are not so distant from her students' lives as they may like to think. She feels the gravitational tug of Catholicism every time the subject of abortion arises. And where the Catholic Church has ebbed, particularly in the Hispanic community, Protestant evangelical denominations have begun to thrive. Inside trendy teenage cynicism, faith persists, promising explanation for the inexplicable and comfort for the unendurable.

"The main purpose for people on earth," Angel says, "is to get prepared for the afterlife."

"Absolutely," Jessica affirms. "And how could that philosophy come in handy in the New World?"

"The New World," Angel says, "is rough."

* * *

Jessica's battle to keep Wilfredo Ayala begins during first-period English 7. Tom Borelli, the acting coordinator of the Program Office, appears at the door of Room 336 with the names of four students, all of whom are being shunted into an eighth-period English 7 class and assigned a first-period typing course they probably neither want nor need. An agreement between the Board of Education and the United Federation of Teachers, designed to help faculty and students, limits the size of a high school class to 34. In a school like Seward Park, too large to begin with and constantly adding "over-the-counter" enrollees, a class that falls within the limit in September often exceeds it by October. The Program Office, charged with the unenviable task of organizing 3,500 students' schedules, then undertakes a process called "equalization," whirling about kids like cards in an immense game of three-card monte. All the effort amounts to exchanging the intolerable situation of overcrowded classes for the intolerable situation of upheaving students in midterm. But it placates union watchdogs, board bureaucrats, and state auditors.

Losing those four kids from the first-period class bothered Jessica, especially hearing one say in parting, "I really liked your class." So when Borelli's assistant turns up at the second period session asking for Wilfredo Ayala, she refuses to surrender him. Wilfredo is a muscular, big-shouldered boy, like Ottavio Johnson one of the Dog Brothers, but Jessica physically bars his exit. "They told me to go to the other class," he says with resignation. She shakes her head and says, "Just stay here."

In Wilfredo's rejiggered schedule, he would be taking English 7 with Lavinia Rausch, a disciplinarian generally loathed by her pupils. A steady stream of students, students who delight most other teachers, have landed in the English office this fall for violating Rausch's various rules. She provoked an otherwise docile Chinese girl into a shoving match. A Chinese boy once lamented to Steve Anderson, "Mrs. Rausch for English. Third time. Much unlucky." A self-possessed student, Jessica figures, can always survive an uninspiring instructor. Wilfredo, though, is someone on the brink, only beginning to treat his life seriously, and for all his brawn quite vulnerable.

Image normally means little to Jessica, but she can hardly miss a fastidious quality in Wilfredo. His handwriting displays the clean lines and precise corners of a draftsman's. He carries himself with a correct, soft-spoken manner that obviously serves him well in his part-time job at a Wall Street law office. While other boys maintain a stable of five or ten pairs of basketball sneakers, Wilfredo sticks with one set of white Nikes, which he launders religiously. Jessica feels certain Wilfredo is capable of far more than the 71 average he has compiled so far at Seward Park.

In his autobiography, Wilfredo said he regretted his former indifference toward school, but such admissions in Jessica's experience are not unusual. Where he separated himself, and struck her, was in the depth of his contrition, in his desire not for improvement as much as redemption. "When I look around me," Wilfredo wrote, "I see a lot of people around the neighborhood, and a couple of family members, wishing, Oh, how they should've gone to school, how they should've gotten a good education, how they could have made something out of themselves. Basically they go through life with a whole bunch of 'What if's.' At that point, I said to myself, 'Hey, self, you don't want to be a 'what if' person. Go to school. Get a good education. Have a future to look forward to. And let the world know you want to succeed in life.'"

Jessica does not know exactly what underlies those words, and Wilfredo is not the type of young man to volunteer intimacies. His parents, who left Puerto Rico for the promise of better employment in New York, are disabled, jobless, and dependent on relief. Of his older siblings, one brother works as a hospital aide and another as a parking-lot attendant, while his sister quit her accounting job to care for her children after her husband left. None of them failed, Wilfredo feels, but neither did they fully realize their possibilities.

In junior high school, when raging hormones transformed many of his classmates into fledgling hoodlums, Wilfredo remained a solid, serious student. It was when he entered Seward Park that he began to drift, cutting class two or three periods a day, once going an entire term without submitting a single piece of homework. Because Wilfredo was such a quiet, polite boy, not the sort to draw attention to himself, his absences generally went unnoticed. And once he felt it mattered little to his teachers whether he appeared or not, he vanished even more frequently. Sometimes he lounged outside the Ludlow Street bodega, and sometimes he strolled back to his apartment in the LaGuardia Houses, a subsidized project. When his parents scolded him, he ignored them. With the $150 a week he was making on his job, he was already supporting himself, and moving beyond the orbit of their influence.

Midway through his junior year, Wilfredo started to awaken. He told his guidance counselor that he wanted to attend Baruch College, a branch of the City University of New York, and that he had ambitions of becoming a doctor. The counselor said that with Wilfredo's 65 average he'd be lucky to get into a junior college, much less Baruch and then medical school. Wilfredo wanted something better than his siblings had, and he wanted to get out of the neighborhood, especially since the arrival of crack. The couple next door were addicts, supporting their habits by renting the premises to fellow smokers, and obliviously allowing their baby to wander into the Ayala apartment. "All raggedy," Wilfredo remembered. "Like a Cabbage Patch doll."

Wilfredo pulled his average above 70 by the end of his junior year, but he still took a few too many sabbaticals, often joined by two friends from the LaGuardia Houses. Then, in the summer before his senior year, both the friends were jumped by members of Here To Chill in a disagreement about a girl. Here To Chill continued threatening the two boys during the school year, until they deemed it wiser to transfer to another high school, Julia Richman. Their departure had two very different effects on Wilfredo. Without their company, cutting class wasn't nearly as much fun. And the spectacle of seeing them strong-armed out of Seward Park made him obstinate about staying. What he couldn't understand was why this Miss Siegel, who hardly knew him, should care. Teachers before her had never missed him when he was gone, and now she was refusing to let him go. "She saw something in me," Wilfredo would say months later, "that I didn't see in myself."

Jessica commences her campaign with a visit to the Program Office. She locates Tom Borelli amid computer terminals and bound volumes of printouts, a harried man.

"Tom," she says, "I want to . . ."

"No."

"You didn't even hear what I'm asking."

"It's about putting kids back who've been equalized out." He raises his eyebrows. "Right?"

"Not kids," Jessica says. "One kid. I really like him. I don't mind having him in class."

"Thirty-four in a class. That's the rule."

"Even if the teacher doesn't mind? Even if the teacher requests it?"

"That's the rule," Tom repeats. "What happens if the auditors come?"

"That rule has no connection to human needs," Jessica says. "I connect to this kid, and he connects to me." She brakes her accelerating anger, careful not to alienate a potential ally. "I'll take the extra kid. I'll give you a requisition in writing. You can show them."

"No. They may change the rule in two years. Then we can do it."

Tom's best isn't good enough for Jessica. In two years, Wilfredo Ayala might be parking cars. Jessica goes to Helen Cohen; Helen says she cannot intercede, but advises Jessica to talk to Emma Jon; Emma says she sympathizes, but she cannot override Tom. Jessica heads back to the Program Office, and there she runs into Larry Schwartz. Larry splits his time between programming and teaching English, and he is a friend who shares Jessica's passions for theater and baking. He also represents, at this moment, her final line of appeal. She tells him about Wilfredo.

"Oh, yeah," Larry says, "he's a great kid."

"He's changed a lot," adds Veda Luftig, an aide in the Program Office.

"So what do I do?" Jessica asks Larry. "I'm concerned about this kid sitting in my class."

"He's still sitting there, isn't he?"

"Yeah," Jessica says, "but what happens?"

"Nothing happens," Larry says. He presses his palms together and beams beatifically. "Wilfredo sits there and you teach him and you give him a grade." He points to a computer terminal. "And I put it in."

*   *   *

Jonathan Edwards, Tom Paine, Washington Irving, William Cullen Bryant, and Herman Melville all visit Room 336 as the weeks pass. The Great Awakening and the American Revolution come and go as rapidly as fruit flies or crocuses, and the Republic launches into the building of railroads and sailing ships and cities. A one-term survey of American literature is by nature an exercise in time-lapse photography, and Jessica is racing to reach the Civil War by Christmas, leaving January for the twentieth century. This Monday morning, well into November, she is embarking on Walt Whitman, although all her students know is that they are being asked to write in their journals whether they would prefer living in the country or in the city. But then, most of them realize by now that no question from Miss Siegel can be considered innocent because she always wants an answer.

"The city," says Maribel Mendez.

"Why?"

"That's where I grew up."

"Raquel?"

"City. More quick and advanced."

"José?"

"The country."

"Why?"

"I could have rabbits."

"So what's the argument for each?" Jessica asks. She smooths a rose-print blouse over a matching skirt as she waits. "I want you to think about them. Because the next couple of people we'll read were writing at the same time the cities were growing up. We're going to look at Thoreau in a couple of days. But right now we want to ask how Walt Whitman communicates his feelings about New York."

She commences a brief biography of Whitman, and without using the word, she paints him as a populist. In his homage to bustle and clamor and diversity, Whitman's vision of New York encompasses and enlarges Jessica's vision of New York; his poems throb with the same energy as the Red Grooms paintings Jessica so savors. With all the bums, drugs, and gangs in the New York of her students, she wants to remind them that it is, too, a city of magic.

Jessica hands out a rexo she typed early this morning of Whitman's poem "Mannahatta." The ragged edges of the verses instantly distinguish "Mannahatta" from the straight boundaries of Bradstreet's writing. What strikes many of the students, no doubt, as Jessica's sloppy daybreak typing is, in fact, one of the objects of her lesson. Suspecting the confusion free verse can cause, Jessica recites the first few lines herself:

> I was asking for something specific and perfect for my city,
> Whereupon lo! upsprang the aboriginal name.
>
> Now I see what there is in a name, a word, liquid, sane,
>   unruly, musical, self-sufficient, . . .

Then she asks for someone to finish. José and Raquel both volunteer, and José, gallant, defers. His chivalry is fortunate, because Raquel speaks poetry with ease and affection, and her throaty, Spanish-tinged voice glides through Whitman's tongue-twisting encomium. Whether anyone else understands equally well is the question.

"How does Whitman describe New York?" Jessica asks. "Julio?" She sees a head turned sideways on a desktop. "You awake?"

"Big time," he mutters.

"What do you mean?"

"Big time."

"Julio, you make me feel like I'm pulling teeth," she says, and her eyes trawl. "Truman?"

"Crowded streets."

"What else? Elizabeth?"

"A lot of immigrants are coming."

"How do we know?"

" 'Immigrants arriving, fifteen or twenty thousand in a week.' "

"Better," Jessica says. "Lun?"

"Talks about ships."

"Remember," Jessica says, "New York used to be a big seaport. They didn't just build South Street Seaport to put in all the shops." There is laughter. The Seaport, a short walk from Seward Park, is a favorite weekend hangout.

Jessica rests her chin on her fisted hand in a pose of inquiry. "So what's Whitman's attitude about New York?" she asks. "Which side of the argument would he come down on?"

"He loves it," says José, legs sprawling into the aisle. "He says, 'It's my city.'"

Moving from student to student, Jessica elicits examples easily, for "Mannahatta" is nothing if not a litany of praises, the "I ♥ New York" campaign of its era. That takes care of content, which for a few of Jessica's colleagues is destination enough in a literature lesson. For her, the harder part of the class lies ahead, the journey from the concrete of narrative to the abstract of style. She begins by rereading the first lines of the poem. Then she asks, "Where does the name 'Mannahatta' come from?"

"Indians," Lun says.

"Whitman says that name's 'specific and perfect' for his city. Why?" No answer comes. "Read those three lines." She taps her copy of the rexo. "It's down there in purple and white." She waits again. "Take a stab at it. Paulette? Addie? Joanna?"

This silence is not affected. The students are stymied. Jessica asks them to consider the difference between "Mannahatta" and "New York." But the onomatopeia, the jazz of language, eludes their grasp. Jessica decides to drop the point for the moment, intending to circle back to it by another route.

"What do you notice about the form of the poem?"

"It's like a paragraph," Jose says.

"Not exactly. But you're on the right track. Explain it more."

"It looks like a story."

"No stanzas," adds Harry.

"What's a stanza?" José whispers to him.

"What else do you notice?" Jessica persists.

"No rhyme," Aracelis says.

"And?"

"It's boring."

Jessica laughs easily, then slides back into the lesson.

"In other words, as José and Harry were suggesting, it's one continuous sentence." She pulls back behind her desk. "Now, the poetry you usually read in school has rhyme. And what goes with rhyme? I'll give you a clue." She marches across the room stiff as a wooden soldier in *The Nutcracker Suite*. "Da-dum, da-dum, da-dum." She executes an about-face. "Da-dum, da-dum, da-dum." At ease. "What's that called?"

"Beat," Jose says.

"Beat," Jessica confirms. "Or meter."

She draws an equation on the board: "No rhyme + no meter = free verse."

"Think about how this poem is constantly moving, constantly changing," she says. "It doesn't stop anywhere." She pauses. "Like New York City." She pauses again, letting the syllogism register. "You can see how Whitman gets across the feeling of New York. Not only from the words he chooses, but from the form he chooses. What he called"—she taps the board—"free verse."

*   *   *

Ben Dachs calls Jessica at home a few nights later. She is glad to hear from him and at the same time a bit suspicious. Somewhere amid the small talk, he asks Jessica how she's been getting along with Emma, and then it dawns on her that Ben is subtly sounding an alarm. Emma is Ben's successor as well as his friend, and it only makes sense that she would confide in him about her friction with Jessica. Jessica appreciates Ben's gesture toward diplomacy, but she rues its necessity. The problems with Emma are clearly more serious than she had gauged.

They are, in fact, utterly fundamental. Jessica earns an additional $800 a year for her work with *Seward World,* but for years she has wanted to trade the money for an additional free period—a dispensation known as a "point-two" because it relieves a teacher of two-tenths of the daily class load. She pled her case most mightily to Ben when he was chairman, and he frankly believed it a lost cause. Some faculty members received point-twos under the union contract, Ben knew, while the remainder were given by Dr. Kriftcher to teachers with administrative appointments. Ben could not imagine Dr. Kriftcher giving Jessica a point-two and setting a precedent for all the coaches and advisers who, like her, receive cash stipends rather than lighter loads.

Yet Ben saw all the dim mornings and dusky afternoons that Jessica poured into *Seward World,* and he could reckon by her reddened eyes and raw nerves how many midnights and weekends. So he engineered a little subterfuge. He won a point-two for the position of assistant chair, claiming there was a surfeit of clerical work for any one person, and he appointed Jessica. Then he gave a paraprofessional most of the clerical work and Jessica the free period for *Seward World.* But then Ben went to Beach Channel, and everything changed.

Ben had been a chairman tenured in his position and secure of his faculty's adoration. He was magnanimous because it was his nature and he was magnanimous because he could afford to be. Emma Jon replaced him under the shakiest circumstances. After teaching in New York's public school system for sixteen years, she now had one term to prove she deserved to rise up the ladder. Even if she erased every doubt, it might not matter, because Ben himself was on a one-term probationary appointment at Beach Channel and if the Board of Education did not make his posting permanent, he was entitled to return as Seward Park's English chairman, displacing Emma. It was a recipe for anxiety, and if the brimming ashtray and phalanx of Pepsi cans on her desktop were any indication, then Emma was anxious, indeed.

She clearly had neither the obligation nor the intention of abiding by Ben's sub rosa contract with Jessica; she wanted the assistant chairperson to do the assistant chairperson's work. Under the close scrutiny of her probation, Emma also needed to demonstrate she could manage a disobedient employee.

Jessica understood her duties; she also understood that on her personal agenda they ranked below the editing sessions and student conferences that filled her free periods. What Emma wanted done now Jessica was willing to do later.

All through the fall, they engaged in a war of wills. Jessica would huddle with Gregg Gross about a rap article, and Emma would assign her to distribute attendance registers to the rest of the English teachers. Jessica would catch Ottavio Johnson up on material he missed while absent, and Emma would tell her to inventory the audiovisual equipment. Moonie Ali would merely enter the English office asking for Jessica, and Emma would commandeer the girl to collect the attendance registers.

Bruce Baskind happened to be in the office on that occasion. He waited until Emma left for the afternoon and he listened as Jessica cursed in frustration. Then he told her what he thought: She would never get a point-two for *Seward World* because anyone who knew her knew she would sustain her standards for the paper without one, even if the effort sent her home exhausted and tearful. There was truth there, a truth Jessica herself harbored, and to hear it spoken was to hear it shouted. What makes it hurt even more deeply is that Jessica has just spent the better part of a month finding a loophole in the Board of Education's printing specifications and sliding a special dispensation for her longtime shop past some bureaucrat too inexperienced to know never to say yes. It was a triumph, a triumph nobody else saw or cared to see.

Emma is not an evil person or a narrow one. She is literate and intelligent and committed enough to have stayed in the New York schools while thousands of teachers fled. And for Jessica, that is precisely the rub. Ben was the exception; Emma is closer to the rule.

*   *   *

Jessica returns to Room 336 the morning after Ben's telephone call. She returns for the 140 mysteries and surprises she encounters every day, for faces and voices that have yet to explain themselves, and for the possibility they still might. She returns because she always returns. Fire drills and equalization and point-twos notwithstanding, when Jessica closes the door, the other world disappears, and only her world remains.

This morning should be better than most, for the first issue of *Seward World,* produced by Harold Steinberg of Official Press, is being delivered. In the hour before classes begin, a van disgorges 5,000 copies, separated into bundles of 250, each girdled by black plastic ribbon. Jessica called all six advanced journalism students the night before, but only Rosie Sanchez and Helen Moy are here to help. Two tiny bodies, they hoist the bundles one by one onto a dolly in the lobby, then wrestle the loaded dolly like a stubborn mule down the hall and into the Teachers Work Room. There they stand on tiptoes to stuff thirty or thirty-five newspapers in the mailbox of each homeroom teacher. Rosie and Helen labor erratically, stopping again and again to admire their articles. They plant their palms on the dolly and gape down at the open pages of *Seward World,* transfixed. Jessica just keeps muzzle-loading bundles into mailboxes. Her own excitement has been dampened—by the battle with the board and the delay it caused, by the meager turnout of her students this morning. She always tells them *Seward World* is *their* newspaper, but is she telling the truth?

It is a rainy, misty, unseasonably warm day. Through the windows, Jessica can see teachers approaching, their forms becoming clear in the gauzy air. She can see kids gathering outside the bodega and the plumbing-supply store. She starts to tingle.

"Congratulations," says Chris McKenna, an English teacher, as she enters the room.

"Late," Jessica says. "I feel like it was a ten-month pregnancy. Or eleven."

Bruce Baskind follows after Chris, beads of rain sliding down his black leather coat.

"Looks like a C-section to me," he puts in.

Janet Soffer, a music teacher, reaches for her mail.

"An article about you here," Jessica says.

She hands Janet an entire bundle. Janet gets as far as the door, then returns. She doesn't have a homeroom.

"Here, Jess. I only need a couple."

Jessica waves her off.

"Keep 'em. For your mother."

They laugh.

An English as a Second Language teacher, Ian Ponman, punches the clock, and Jessica unfolds a paper, open to the story about him. The time nears eight. Jessica dashes to the elevator with an armload of papers. In the waiting line, she meets Bob McMillan, the basketball coach, and she shows him an article on the team's prospects. She is genuinely proud of *Seward World,* but she is also playing the ward healer, doling out thermal potholders and holiday fowl.

Then, on the elevator, a teacher named Audrey Hyde moves beside Jessica.

"Have you got any flack from the paper?" she whispers.

"What flack?" Jessica asks, louder than she had intended. "I just stuck 'em in the mailboxes."

"Oh, my God," Audrey says. "I just ran into Judy Goldman and I have a headache from the screaming. 'It's unprofessional we have a survey. It's unprofessional.'"

Another teacher, Rita Ralph, overhears the conversation.

"That's right," she says. "Judy's on the warpath."

Jessica winces. Judy Goldman, as the UFT chapter chairperson at Seward Park, runs the union in the school, and so wields substantial influence. She is not an enemy to be desired. From what Audrey tells her, Jessica surmises that Judy objected to the article entitled "What Makes A Great Teacher?" and the accompanying ballot for Seward Park's best. Both seemed innocent enough to Jessica, especially considering that every June seniors voted for graduation marshals from among the faculty. Later in the day, Jessica hears secondhand, but reliably, that Judy complained directly to Dr. Kriftcher. The principal,

Jessica is informed, suggested that if Judy had a beef she might consider writing a letter to the editor.

Even with the principal's tacit support, Jessica frets. Judy Goldman could press for her to be sent to the annex. A few English teachers have been complaining for years that Jessica, Denise Simone, and Shawn Gerety, all of whom teach electives of their own design to juniors and seniors, never have to leave the main building. They could, if they choose, file a union grievance. Emma Jon, as an interim department chairwoman, is in no position to battle with Judy. Judy is instrumental in the Teachers Choice program, which gives teachers money to purchase their own supplies. Judy has, as the kids say, juice.

After school, Jessica confides her fears to Louise Grollman.

"My advice?" Louise says. Jessica nods. "Screw it."

Jessica grins and hugs Louise. She searches the coat closet for a small, lidded cardboard container, cuts a slit in the top, and covers the rest with brown paper. She writes on the front in large letters, "VOTE FOR SEWARD'S BEST TEACHER!!!" Then she places the ballot box atop the file cabinet directly inside the English Department door, a place where no student or teacher or union leader could miss it.

The House at the Edge of the World

D AVE PATTERSON SLOWS when he spots the Christmas tree. He is walking along West Twenty-third Street on a morning two months before Christmas, and suddenly here is this green plastic pine in a showcase window. The tree is decorated with ceramic angels and snowmen in tartan top hats. A few feet farther, in another window, Dave finds a dozen yuletide sculptures, all featuring Emmett Kelly's melancholy clown as Santa Claus. In one pose, Santa reclines on the carpet in front of a fireplace, balancing a blond girl and her teddy bear on his knees. A small brass plaque provides the title of the piece, "Spirit of Xmas II," and the information that it was manufactured in Taiwan. The third and final window contains a doll in wedding lace and a sign directing viewers to the building's Fifth Avenue entrance, with the enticement, "Christmas Is Just Around the Corner."

The Prince George Hotel, Dave Patterson's destination, is just around the corner, too. Dave moves five blocks up Fifth Avenue, past the china and crystal shops, past the German tourists posing for snapshots beneath the elm trees of Madison Square Park. When he turns east toward Madison Avenue, he catches the scent of marijuana and sees the torn black awning with the faded crest of the Prince George. Above it loom two flagless flagpoles and a dozen stories of amber bricks, darkened like old snow by decades of auto exhaust. In one of the large lobby windows hangs a sign futilely ordering "NO LOITERING." A yellow school bus pulls away from the entrance, leaving in its wake a score of indifferent mothers and their truant children. One woman in a cheap quilted ski jacket reads a comic book. Her son sits on a standpipe, aiming a toy gun. When Dave passes before him, the boy pulls the trigger. Teenagers in baseball caps and sweatpants amble up and down the block, wearing out their sneakers going nowhere.

Dave is searching for a boy named Darnell Reese, who has not been coming to school. Dave is Seward Park's school-neighborhood worker—its truant officer, in lay lexicon. When a Seward Park student starts accumulating absences, the school undertakes various efforts to lure him back. First an automatic telephone, known as a TelSol, is rigged to ring the student's home at 6:30 A.M. with a tape-recorded admonition. That failing, a postcard of concern is mailed to the family. If the card goes unheeded, it is followed by a registered letter of escalating alarm. When none of these methods conjures the child, the school dispatches Dave Patterson, its last resort.

Dave is a fifty-five-year-old black man who looks a decade younger, a bit fleshy on the outside but firm and strong within, like a linebacker several years into retirement. This morning, he wears a houndstooth check hat and a coffee trenchcoat, unbuttoned to reveal a navy blazer, gray flannel slacks, and a powder blue shirt with striped tie and collar bar. Vanity is not the point, and Dave earns only two-thirds of a teacher's salary, which hardly allows for indulgence. Dave dresses well because he knows that he may be the only responsible, working male in the lives of these children. In the course of a year, he traces an average of 350 youngsters, youngsters so troubled or disaffected that they do not even bother coming to Seward Park so they can cut class. He lists on a legal pad each one's name, homeroom, address, and telephone number, and to these he adds such details as "English Abs 7 times," "Letter sent," or "Missing 2 mos." He carries in a coat pocket the telephone numbers for AIDS-Info, Alcoholics Anonymous, Crack Hotline, the Victim Services Agency, and twenty-five other outposts of assistance. Already this morning Dave has made two visits, the first to the mother of a sixteen-year-old girl who ran away from home during the summer and is still missing, and the second to a seventeen-year-old boy who disappeared from school about two weeks ago. The truant himself answered the door wearing a fur coat, all but announcing his entry into the narcotics trade. The legal pad tells Dave that his next assignment, Darnell Reese, is a sixteen-year-old freshman who attended Seward Park for precisely two days this fall.

Entering the lobby, Dave threads his way between five police officers. He must present himself and declare his intentions at a guard station, which is surrounded by plexiglass to protect the protectors. Sometimes Dave has difficulty getting past the desk, but this time, when he shows his Seward Park identification card, a guard smiles. "Hey man, I went there," he says, giving Dave a soul shake. "Ten years ago. All them gangs and stuff." After Dave signs the logbook and heads for the elevator, the guard calls to him, "You be careful, now. Watch yourself."

There are three elevators for the 459 families in the thirteen-story building. One is broken. The second is stuck between the fourth and fifth floors. The last takes ten minutes to reach the ground floor. Dave glances around the lobby. He notices the bas-relief on the portals and the light fixtures shaped like tapers and the curved wooden bar in what had once been a cocktail lounge. "This used to be a fabulous place in the old days," he says. Indeed it was, with its wing chairs and marble tables and ceiling murals, with the towering seventeenth-century clock that had once belonged to King James I of England. They came, the buyers from Bismarck and Jefferson City, choosing from the bounty of the toy industry's nearby showrooms and thrilling, no doubt, to their expense-account adventure in Gotham. In a promotional brochure issued in 1976, the Prince George promised "to achieve the look, the mood, and the atmosphere that few remember and even fewer will forget."

The present clientele, homeless families, would no doubt concur. Dave can feel them gathering around him. He can hear them. A pregnant Puerto Rican woman argues in Spanish, shifting into English only long enough to say, "A thousand dollars for this fuckin' hotel." Her son, who appears to be twelve or thirteen, sucks his thumb. Two black brothers huddle together, one of them suckling on a formula bottle filled with sugar water. Their mother wears a T-shirt saying, "Save the Next Generation." A young man of about twenty, strapping in his Adidas sweatsuit, pile drives his girlfriend into the wall. He reaches with a free hand for a pay telephone and begins beating her with the receiver. No one intercedes, for nothing is unusual.

When the elevator arrives, a dozen passengers shove into space enough for half as many. "You got too many people in there," one of those left outside shouts. "You gonna get stuck if the Lord don't help you." The elevator crawls upward, and at the first stop the door spends thirty seconds opening. Rap music and children's cries echo down the dim hallway. Sweat beads on Dave's temples. Jaw muscles rise as he chews two sticks of gum, trying to escape into the repetition. "Press eight," hollers a voice outside. "Press eight." Dave rolls down his eyes to see a little girl doodling on a patient discharge form from Bellevue Hospital. At the twelfth floor, he debarks.

He follows the hall southward. The walls are yellow except where white primer, which has been applied to cover graffiti, has, in turn, been tattooed with a new set of spray-paint flourishes. The ceiling panels sag; the exit sign hangs like a loose tooth by one bolt. Around a corner, Dave finds Room 1221, the temporary home of Darnell Reese.

A middle-aged woman with spindly limbs and an unkempt Afro answers Dave's knock. She regards the stranger through bleary eyes, struggling to bring the form into focus. A faint aura of alcohol surrounds her.

Dave introduces himself. The woman says she is Ruth Reese, Darnell's mother. Dave asks if he can see the boy. Ruth shuts the door. While she is gone, Dave considers her eyes and her haggard frame and her boozy breath. Normally he can turn a mother into his ally, make even a tough kid blush at disappointing her. This time he is skeptical. Ruth may be more the problem than the solution.

A moment later a boy emerges. He is thin, too thin, all knobby bones and stringy veins. He wears cuffed blue shorts, a too-large pair of Nikes, and a baggy fashion shirt printed with the word "Workout." His two front teeth are covered by full gold caps, the sort sold by jewelers, not dentists.

"I was just gettin' up," Darnell says in a low, phlegmy voice. "I was still sleepin'."

Darnell moves woozily past Dave and into the hall, slumping against the wall like a grain sack on a freight dock.

His mother stands in the half-open door. Dave uses the moment to glimpse into their quarters for whatever clues it might offer. The room is dark, the only light emanating from a fuzzy television picture. A fan stands on a table. A couple of inflatable dolls bob from the ceiling, one of which bears the words, "Hug Me."

"Miss Reese," Dave says, "you know he's been out of school for awhile." He waits for an acknowledgment. None comes. "I wanna know why."

She stares balefully at her son.

"You wanna tell him the truth?"

Darnell closes his eyes.

"You wanna tell him where you goin'?"

"I been at a friend's house," Darnell mumbles. "O. B.'s house."

"I been sendin' him to school," Ruth insists to Dave, "but he ain't been goin'."

She retreats into the room and reemerges with a Seward Park attendance card indicating that Darnell went to class twice. Dave suspects what that means: Darnell showed up just long enough to grab a few textbooks, so his mother could prove to the welfare caseworker she was sending her boy to school. That way, she would still get money for him twice a month on her check.

"I understand," Dave says to Ruth. He drags a handkerchief across his forehead and then fingers the attendance card. "But this is no good. You know this is no good." Ruth rocks her head as if witnessing in church. "I want to know if you can come in to school. To see me. Talk about Darnell."

"I got to go over to the welfare this week," she says. "And I got to see my daughter."

"How 'bout next week? Next Monday?"

Ruth does not answer, so Dave turns to the boy.

"How old are you, Darnell?"

"Sixteen."

"Darnell," he says, pushing forward to corner the boy's evasive eyes. "You're sixteen years old. You're not coming to school. And that's a problem. You're sixteen. You're almost a man. But you got to do better than this." He pivots to face the mother, but speaks loudly enough for Darnell to listen. "Maybe Darnell doesn't feel well. Maybe he has a lot of depression. I won't be too hard on him now." He returns to the boy. "So come in tomorrow." He tugs paternally on Darnell's sleeve. The boy nods slowly. Dave arranges a formal appointment for the mother and son at 10 A.M. He slides his clipboard under his arm. "You don't come in tomorrow, I'll have to be tougher."

He waits for the elevator, thinking about Darnell and his mother, thinking about gold teeth and glassy eyes. He asks himself, *What's the situation here? What can I do?* He reaches for strength. He is always reaching for strength, because the nature of his job is that successes are so few, so limited, so fleeting. A woman walks toward Dave, trailing a shopping cart and an empty Hefty bag, ready to root through Fifth Avenue's refuse for nickel-deposit bottles. The housing projects are no prize, but this hotel devastates Dave. He drifts again into his thoughts of the Reeses, wondering, *Where did it all begin with these two?*

*   *   *

Holidays held a particular importance in the Reese family. Darnell was born on Christmas Day 1970, and on Valentine's Day 1985, a fire destroyed the last apartment the Reeses could truly call their own, rendering them refugees in their own city and ultimately delivering them to the doorstep of the Prince George Hotel. Their odyssey— anything but atypical of the 5,200 homeless families in New York City and of the hundreds of thousands nationwide—could be reconstructed by tracing a paper trail that stretched from agency to agency to agency, each one encountering the family at a more desperate juncture.

The Reeses first went on public assistance in 1970, when Ruth became pregnant with Darnell. Unlike many welfare mothers, she was legally married, but her husband, Nate, was a diabetic who had lost his right hand in an automobile accident many years earlier. Three years after Darnell's birth, Ruth and Nate had their only other child, Annie. They lived on one floor of a three-family house in the Fort Greene section of Brooklyn, for which they paid $190 a month. Their foothold was tenuous already, and the earth beneath them was beginning to quake.

As it entered the 1980s, New York City was experiencing an unparalleled explosion in housing costs, brought on by a confluence of factors. In the wake of New York's flirtation with bankruptcy in 1975, real estate lost its usual luster, threatening the city with large-scale disinvestment. The Koch administration attacked the problem with an extensive program of tax abatements for constructing both residential and commercial buildings, many of them marketed toward the affluent, assuming, in a version of Ronald Reagan's "trickle-down" economics, that aiding the richest citizens would ultimately aid the poorest. When even the mayor's generous sensibilities were offended—as when developer Donald Trump demanded a multi-million-dollar tax break to erect an upscale shopping center named for himself next to Tiffany's on Fifth Avenue—the courts granted tax relief. Thousands of rental apartments, meanwhile, were falling out of circulation because of arson, abandonment, eviction, and conversion to cooperatives. And the combination of Wall Street's long bull market and a steady influx of anxious foreign wealth produced customers who were willing to pay substantial sums to rent or own. All told, the city lost 57,000 units of rental housing from 1978 to 1987, and the monthly cost for what was left rose nearly 10 percent faster than inflation. The vacancy rate, only 2.95 percent to begin with, tightened to 2.46, and less than that in low-income neighborhoods.

What did this have to do with a family in Brooklyn? While Manhattan was the epicenter of the real-estate boom, the tremors rippled into New Jersey and the outlying boroughs. The same young professionals who were pushed out of Manhattan by rents only the wealthy could afford flocked to working-class ethnic neighborhoods beyond the island, where they drove up prices and drove out longtime residents. Fort Greene was one of Brooklyn's most promising candidates for gentrification, a national historic district notable for its brownstones and row houses, home to the renowned Brooklyn Academy of Music, and situated only fifteen minutes by subway from Manhattan's offices and nightlife. It was common for a realtor to offer a six-figure sum for an unrepaired building, sight unseen. The *Village Voice,* the favored reading of urban pioneers, advertised apartments for $450 a month or more, twice their price five years earlier. For property owners who had long endured negligible returns, who had resisted the temptations of abandonment and arson, here was the prospect of deliverance, of bonanza.

In early 1984, the Reeses's landlord arbitrarily doubled their rent to $380. The quid pro quo was a standard and legal strategy for forcing out tenants in small buildings—municipal law regulated rents only in those with six or more units—and it was decidedly more genteel than such documented maneuvers as stanching heat and hot water, loosing pit bulls in the hallways, or inviting crack addicts to squat in vacant units. True, a landlord who was inclined toward such schemes might find himself a defendant in housing court, but if he prevailed in the war of attrition, he carried off a handsome prize indeed. He could slather on some plaster, lay down some linoleum, and peddle the "newly renovated" apartment to a young professional at "market value"—meaning half what similar space would fetch in Manhattan and twice what anyone in Fort Greene could scrape together. An especially enterprising landlord could oust almost all the tenants and sell the building, for a residential property was most lucrative when it was least occupied and thus least fettered by laws protecting renters.

The Reeses surrendered without a fight and moved in April 1984 to a five-room, $325-a-month apartment Nate's mother located through her landlord. Ruth remembers being concerned about the exposed wiring in the building, but she was hardly in a position to be particular. As it was, the higher rent strained the family's finances, for at a time of dizzying escalation in housing costs, New York City paid a maximum rental allowance of $270 a month for welfare clients. Using $55 of their basic grant for rent, the Reeses were left each month with $203 in public aid and $198 in food stamps. They did not buy the eyeglasses that teachers told them Darnell needed. They periodically had their gas and electricity cut off for nonpayment. Dunned for a utility debt of $408, Ruth Reese explained that she had used the money to buy her children clothing. Yet the welfare department by law would have paid the money if Ruth or Nate had submitted the overdue bill. This instance of their apparent indifference to rescue was not isolated. When the Reeses overlooked a recertification hearing, they forfeited their existing Medicaid coverage. They nearly lost their public aid on several occasions after missing evaluation meetings with their caseworker. Even by slum standards, the Reese family presented a portrait of almost total dysfunction. But Darnell and Annie went most mornings to the neighborhood school, and Ruth and Nate counted friends and relatives within walking distance. The family clung to a semblance of stability, if only compared to what would follow.

On February 14, 1985, a fire caused by faulty wiring razed the Reese's building, destroying their apartment and incinerating all their possessions. The Reeses spent three days in a city-run shelter, then a week at the Prince George, where at that time the Red Cross was leasing one floor for emergency housing. For nearly five months thereafter, the Reeses lived with friends, two entire families cramming into a three-room apartment that was snug for one. Kicked out by their hosts, the Reeses encamped with other friends, until they were friends no more. This living arrangement was becoming increasingly common in New York, for the Reagan administration had throttled funding for building new subsidized housing, and the wait for space in the city's existing projects was an average of eighteen years. "Couch people," was the phrase for people like the Reeses, or "the hidden homeless," and they were said to number nearly 200,000.

At midnight on July 13, 1985, Ruth and Nate and their children straggled into a twenty-four hour crisis center in Fort Greene, pleading for a place to stay. "Couple states they have worn out their welcome," an intake worker noted in her report. The emergency office sent the Reeses to one family shelter, which sent them to a second, which sent them back to the emergency office. The shelters would not accept the family because Ruth had recently contracted tuberculosis, a disease that had been nearly eradicated until homelessness gave the contagion a constituency. The family was placed in the Prince George Hotel, at a cost to the city of $1,780 a month, enough for a luxury two-bedroom apartment. As the Reeses and 28,000 other homeless people were languishing in shelters and welfare hotels, more than 70,000 apartments remained vacant in New York, half of them being "warehoused" by landlords and speculators to inflate rental costs artificially.

The Prince George, its mercantile trade in decline for years, had been only too happy to become a welfare hotel. The hotel's management first approached the New York City Human Resources Administration in 1984, but the agency declined in the face of opposition by neighborhood groups, economic-development officials, and the owners of adjacent properties. The streets surrounding the Prince George already contained four welfare hotels—the Madison, the Latham, the Le Marquis, and the Martinique—and to add another would concentrate two-thirds of the city's homeless families in a five-block zone. But by July 1985, the shortage of shelter for homeless families had grown so acute that the Human Resources Administration swallowed its misgivings and contracted with the Prince George. A hotel never designed for permanent occupancy suddenly swelled with homeless families; rooms built for lone salesmen instantly accommodated mothers and children. The Prince George, in fact, became the largest welfare hotel in the city, housing 459 families with 800 children old enough to attend school. Whether they actually did so was another matter entirely.

At the best, a devoted parent would lock her children in the room from the moment they got home from school until the moment they left in the morning. If the stench and the shrieks were not too bad, the children could even do their homework and get some sleep. "I felt sad living there," one Seward Park student who spent thirteen months in the Prince George told me. "Because everybody had a home but I didn't. I didn't want anybody to know where I lived. If they asked, I said the Bronx. It'd really bother me on my birthday. How you gonna have a birthday party in a place like that?"

The effects, of course, far exceed embarassment. The diseases of the Prince George are the diseases of the destitute—asthma, scabies, impetigo, iron deficiency, lice infestation. Mothers trade diapers for drugs, and addicts steal clothing donated by department stores. The upraised fist is the favored method of child rearing. In March 1988, one resident of the hotel beat to death his girlfriend's three-year-old daughter, who had been his partner in panhandling. And in the perverse triumph of a horrific system, the tenants of the Prince George and similar hotels often found it difficult to leave when they finally got the chance. "Hell has become a familiar cocoon," Robert M. Hayes, the city's leading advocate for the homeless, told *The New York Times.* "It's a subtle, more insidious harm that has been done than just living with rats and broken pipes."

An array of public and private agencies operated in and around the Prince George, offering residents services from pediatric medicine to indoor basketball. The Board of Education also installed an office in the hotel, making its failure to serve homeless children all the more striking. No one who has visited the Prince George could miss the fact that dozens, even hundreds, of children wander the lobby, the hallways, and the streets outside all day long, clearly at the expense of study. Andrea Berne, a nurse who served the Prince George in 1985 and 1986, tried fifty times, over a period of months, to alert the Board of Education to the problem, but not once did she receive a response. Across the city, almost half the 6,000 homeless children of school age could not be accounted for either by the central board or the community school districts.* The board inexplicably withdrew from a program that would cross reference its computer records of school enrollments with the Human Resources Administration's computer records of homeless families' addresses. Disgusted by the decision, the board's ombudsman for homeless children resigned. The youngsters, meanwhile, continued to migrate from shelter to shelter, hotel to hotel, school to school, dropping out at a rate exceeding 70 percent.

Darnell Reese was a case in point. He was never a good student, even by the measures of an elementary school that was less than mediocre, but once his family became homeless, it defied credulity to call him a student at all. From kindergarten through sixth grade, Darnell attended the same school, P.S. 56 in central Brooklyn, repeating the second and third grades and striking his teachers as "easily discouraged." The school called in Ruth for several conferences and placed Darnell in special programs for slow students. As a fourteen-

---

*It is estimated that of the approximately 600,000 homeless children of school age nationally, 200,000 do not attend school.

year-old sixth grader in early 1984, only months before his family became homeless, Darnell was reading at third-grade level. His mathematics ability, tested one year earlier, placed him in the lowest 6 percent of his peers nationally. If school frustrated Darnell, it was no wonder; but at least he showed up.

In September 1984, Darnell started seventh grade at I.S. 320 in Brooklyn. It was one of the worst junior high schools in the city in terms of reading scores and it was forty-five minutes away from Darnell's new home in the Prince George. A motivated student might not have minded the distance, but Darnell was not such a student. After missing 158 of 185 days in the 1984–85 school year, he was held back. He shifted in the fall of 1985 to J.H.S. 25, a Manhattan school only marginally better than I.S. 320 but located closer to the hotel. His attendance improved to the point that he missed 102 days of school. Not only were a number of teachers, counselors, and principals aware of Darnell's chronic truancy, so were the welfare authorities. During a 1985 recertification procedure, Ruth informed her caseworker in writing that Darnell was not going to school regularly. She repeated the admission, again in writing, a few months later. There is no indication that either the Human Resources Administration or the Board of Education brought any pressure on Ruth and Nate to send their son to school. Nor did anyone from any school contact them personally until the day Dave Patterson arrived.

Instead, Darnell joined the eighth-grade class of J.H.S. 25 in September 1986. He appeared for class only forty-five days the entire year and failed every subject, although on his final report card he somehow earned a handwritten "good" in the category of conduct. After twelve years of public education, Darnell had the skills of a fourth or fifth grader, at best, and an academic history fragmented almost beyond recognition. His scholastic records were spread among three different schools. He had two different student identification numbers. Some documents showed he had a sister, others did not. He had never taken a half-dozen of the required examinations in reading and mathematics. There was no proof that he had ever been vaccinated against polio, measles, mumps, and rubella. But he was sixteen years old, and a high school in New York must admit any pupil of that age, however abominable his preparation. So J.H.S. 25 promoted Darnell into the ninth grade, making their problem Seward Park's problem, and finally Dave Patterson's.

*   *   *

Two weeks after his initial visit, Dave Patterson returns to the Prince George. The deli near the hotel, he notices, does a brisk business in paper cups filled with ice cubes, because tenants cannot keep kitchen appliances in their rooms. The air reeks of griddle grease and deep-fryer fat from the coffee shop where tenants buy their meals. A thin, twitchy man coughs, then slaps palms with a passerby. That was a crack deal, the seller retrieving a vial he had secreted inside his mouth, then exchanging drugs for dollars. The transaction had doubt-lessly been preceded by hand signals flashed at a safe distance, an action no more disturbing to the untrained eye than a third-base coach giving the bunt sign. Dave's eye is anything but untrained. Crack explains to him why on a street thick with stunted, malnourished children, a street suitable for Cairo or Manila, he also sees Aprica strollers, Oleg Cassini jeans, and three young men installing a solid-gold license-plate frame on a Cadillac. Dave wishes he were not so familiar with the symptoms. He has devoted his life to attaining the middle class, and now the same plague has hit his own neighborhood in Queens, transforming neat frame houses into narcotics factories and paramilitary fortresses, threatening courtroom witnesses and nosy neighbors with assassination. And Dave does not even drink.

He retraces his path through the lobby, up to the twelfth floor, and around the corner to Darnell Reese's room. This time, a man in a green shirt and a religious medal answers the knock. He identifies himself as Darnell's father, Nate, and offers Dave his left hand. The right ends short of the wrist in a stump. Dave explains his business, and Nate walks to the room next door to get his wife. She appears in a housecoat.

"Now, Mrs. Reese," Dave says, "you remember me?" She sways on her feet. "I was here on the twentieth of last month? We made an appointment?" Now she faintly nods. "And you never came in."

"I had to go to the welfare."

"You put us through some hell of a stuff," Dave says, his voice rising in pitch, like a soul singer arching into a falsetto. "And now Darnell hasn't been to school."

"Darnell ain't been to school?"

"Darnell hasn't been to school," Dave says gravely. "You told me faithfully. Now when can we expect you to come in?"

"Today we got the furniture to pick up."

Dave looks past her and into the room. A new walnut wall unit is already there. But he does not comment on its presence.

"I know, I know," he says. "I don't want to put you through all the time and energy."

"Time and emergy," Ruth says, her mouth uncooperative. "I know 'bout that."

Dave decides it is time to threaten subtly. He hates playing the heavy. His gift is to be tough without being hard, and usually he gets the best results by playing the surrogate father, warm and forgiving. But that stance failed once already.

"I don't want trouble for you." He waits an extra beat. "I can cause trouble for you." He touches two fingers to his brow. "But that's not nice."

"We movin' anyhow," the father says.

"Where you movin'?" Dave asks. "Brooklyn?" He imagines Darnell lost again. Another borough, another room, another school not to attend.

"I been trying to get to Brooklyn," Ruth says. "They sendin' me to the Bronx."

"What about Darnell? He here?"

Ruth enters the family's room. She shakes the form under the sheets until a brown head pokes out, snaillike. Darnell has been sleeping in gray sweatpants and a black T-shirt. He shambles out into the hall, even more stuporous than he was last time. Dave faces him squarely, places his hands on Darnell's shoulders in a priestly way.

"What happened, man?" he says, again in his falsetto range. "You gonna make me be hard on you?"

Darnell wriggles out of Dave's hold and lists against the wall. He says nothing, and Dave looks at Darnell's mother. He didn't want it to come to this.

"If we put the Bureau of Child Welfare on you," he says, "you could be here till Doomsday."

"I been tellin' him that," Nate says, lifting his good arm in menace. "He leave here like he's goin' to school, and I don't know where he go."

Dave wishes he were surprised. He figures that seven of every ten parents he sees have lost control of their children or stopped caring much about them. He's met alcoholic parents, junkie parents, crackhead parents, parents imprisoned by illiteracy, parents afraid of being beaten by their own kids. He cannot believe these people started out so badly, but this is how they are when he enters their lives, and he has nowhere near enough time to chart the geometry of each descent. So he turns back to Darnell.

"When can we talk, Darnell?" The boy's head sags. His eyelids droop. His mouth moves soundlessly. "You don't wanna talk now, we can talk on the phone."

"Monday," Darnell whispers.

"The ninth," Dave says, thumbing his calendar. "That's too long. How 'bout tomorrow?" Darnell stands silently. "You call me?" No response. "Can I have a shake on that?" Again. "Look me in the eye, Darnell." Dave's voice stiffens. "Look me in the eye." He waits until Darnell tentatively lifts one lid, as if peeling back a blind to check the morning weather. "Shake?"

Dave thrusts out his right hand, spreading his fingers wide, like a pianist stretching for a difficult chord. The hand hangs in the air for a long time, untaken, almost disembodied. Finally Darnell offers a limp grip.

"You heard," Nate says to his son. "It's up to you. Or we gonna be left in this room with no check."

Dave excuses himself and heads for the elevator. He pumps the button for ten minutes before surrendering and shouting, "Twelve." He wants to get out of this place. He is pretty sure he smelled liquor again on Ruth. He thinks of crack dealers driving Cadillacs and mothers carrying french fries and cups of ice. These are the poles of Darnell's world. "Can't even look you in the eye," Dave sighs. "You know he's gonna rip somebody off. You know he's gonna be in trouble." The boy's been to school two days all term, and the only thing Ruth or Nate worry about is losing some welfare money.

Walking back to the subway, passing the Christmas displays, Dave comes to a large crowd. The people are arrayed in a semicircle in front of the white-columned building that houses the Hasbro toy company. They are watching a movie being shot, chattering and pointing and pleading for autographs. Normally, Dave would not join them, but just now he needs some diversion. He stands at the back of the crowd, tall enough to see into the cleared central area. It is hard to tell what this movie might be about, because the director is between takes at the moment. The only clue is the movie's title, *Big,* which is stitched on the satin jackets worn by cast and crew alike. It is the story of a thirteen-year-old boy who is magically metamorphosed into an adult, filling out a man's frame while retaining the carefree zest of a child. Darnell Reese's dilemma is rather the opposite.

*   *   *

Dave Patterson works in an office that he has decorated with reasons to believe. He cultivates a tiny African violet in a wax cup. A room divider sports a small cloth dog, a Mardi Gras mask, and a fuzzy Polaroid snapshot of Dave with two students, whose names he has written in pencil on the white border. Nearby hangs a certificate with the silhouette of a child running through tall grass and the legend, "Outstanding In Your Field." When Dave received the award, he slid it inside a plastic bag and sealed the open seam so the colors would not fade. Elsewhere on the wall, at eye level, Dave has placed a prayer card with a painting of Jesus Christ and these words:

> Be Thankful Always!
> Be Giving Always!
> Be Forgiving Always!
> Be Self-Helpful Always!
> Be Faith-Full Always!

One afternoon, during the period he was pursuing Darnell Reese, Dave discovered me cataloguing the contents of his office. I commented on their rather emphatic tone. "You got to psych yourself up," Dave explained. "If not, you fall apart. There's so much bad to look at. You *have* to look for the good." He stopped, wincing at an old ache. "Because I don't need to be put down. I been put down all my life. Comin' up black."

Dave was born August 8, 1933, in Columbia, South Carolina, not far from the Army base where his father earned his livelihood constructing barracks. His earliest childhood, with games of tag and Aunt Maybelle's banana pudding, had an ill-fated innocence out of William Faulkner. The black neighborhood of Columbia was called Waverly, and Dave did not appreciate the meanness beyond its borders until as a boy of ten he heard you could make two dollars a day caddying at the local golf course. Dave did not make much of traveling to the course because it was near the base, a familiar place. But as he rode his bicycle across the racial line that severs every Southern town, the white children showered him with rocks, and when he sought safety at a corner filling station, the pump boy told him, "Get out of here, nigger."

Brand that it was, blackness alone did not account for the depth of

Dave's pains, for the unyielding sense of himself as an outsider. His family left the South when Dave was ten, following his father's transfer to New York, leaving Strom Thurmond's South Carolina for Langston Hughes's Harlem. Dave loved the vegetable vendors and the Garveyite orators and the snowy hills of Central Park. And he tried to accommodate himself to the big-city hustle, to filching milk off morning doorsteps and hurtling the turnstile for a subway to Times Square. He tried, but it felt wrong to him, "standing on the bad corner, not having enough clothes, trying to act tough when you weren't." It felt wrong to be snubbed by other blacks, for having nappy hair and ebony skin when cachet required a lye conk and high-yaller tones.

For the rest of Dave's youth, he trailed his father from post to post, crossing the Mason-Dixon Line from Harlem to North Carolina to Bedford-Stuyvesant to Columbia, too country for the city, too city for the country. He felt excluded even from his father's love, a love he saw bestowed on his brother Lloyd, the patriarch's namesake. Dave knew only a military man's discipline, the rules and curfews that never applied equally to Lloyd. "It made me feel that I had to be accepted more by other people," Dave says, "because I didn't feel I was accepted by my father."

Dave found only more exclusion when he enlisted in the Army after graduating from high school in 1952. The military was newly integrated, which is to say integrated in statute but not in spirit, and during Dave's service in Korea, he made the mistake of courting a young woman who was white. As it happened, the woman had also captured the eye of a white private from Kentucky. One night in the enlisted men's club, Dave saw a glass of beer flying toward his head, from the direction of the Kentuckian. He dodged the glass, and he dodged the ax handle that followed it, but he could not escape the guttural cry, "You black motherfucker." Dave eventually won the friendship of his foe, but the incident, like so many incidents before it, hardened in him the conviction that as a black man he would never be accepted. Years later, he would not tell his children of the rocks and the catcalls because he wanted to spare them his hurts, and because he knew that when he remembered he would want to cry.

Adrift in the world, Dave longed for his own righteous place, and with it his identity. After his discharge from the military, he worked as a credit interviewer for Gimbels department store and then drove a limousine in partnership with a friend. The friend held a second job as a teacher's aide at Seward Park, and he mentioned that a similar position was open. Dave took the job in 1969, forgot about the limousine, and never left. Along the way, his first marriage ended and his three children grew up and left home. He wed a second time, busied himself with his Masonic lodge, and taught in a high school equivalency program four nights a week. But after nineteen years, his work at Seward Park still gripped him, and Darnell Reese, another outsider, another sojourner, gripped him most especially.

"You give these kids a part of yourself," Dave says. "You think about the times you were comin' up, the knocks you received, the money you didn't have. And you see these kids and say, How can I help them? Now that I've made it above water where I can breathe." He turns from the general to the specific. "A kid like Darnell Reese, he's like a blind dog in a meathouse, don't know which way to run. And I know somewhere down the line is a jail waiting for him if he doesn't make the right turn. And it makes my soul feel good that I can say that I *gave* something just like I *received* something."

*   *   *

Joggers swaddled in sweatclothes stagger up the East River promenade and into the pitiless north wind of February. On the far shore, steam rises in crooked columns from factories and tenements. A pale disc of sun beats without effect against the icy windows of Dave Patterson's car. Crossing the Willis Avenue Bridge from Manhattan into the Bronx, Dave squints at the Newport cigarettes billboard, which tells him the time is 9:11 A.M. and the temperature is sixteen degrees. His Buick Electra has run for six years and 100,000 miles, serving him well on days colder than this, but as a man who does not wholly trust the temporal world and its pleasures, Dave has bedecked the dashboard with two crucifixes and a dried frond from Palm Sunday 1987.

It is one day short of three months since he last saw Darnell Reese. The boy never returned to Seward Park, as he had told Dave he would. He did call Dave one day, confiding that he often stayed out all night and that he had "court problems," which he did not specify. The fact that Darnell had contacted him at all gave Dave some hope. "The kid's gotta need *somebody*," he said to Florence Buschke, his office mate and the coordinator of Seward Park's drop-out prevention program. "In your life, you're wanderin' and wanderin' and wanderin'. Got to stop somewhere. Got to get some rest."

But again, Darnell broke his promise to attend school, and again,

Dave fell into a funk. A few weeks ago, he learned that the entire Reese family had been moved in December from the Prince George to a city-owned apartment in the South Bronx. The destination tempered Dave's joy at the escape. Jimmy Carter had established the South Bronx as a national symbol of urban despair with his presidential visit to the rubbish and weeds of Charlotte Street, and even to the hardened souls of the Lower East Side, the South Bronx seemed a distant and frightful place. Darnell, Dave believed, would soon be a statistic. So he cleared his calendar for one morning and one final chance.

Dave's car is cozy, with heat from the vents and jazz on the stereo and the ersatz bouquet of twenty air fresheners shaped like tiny evergreens. If only the atmosphere outside were so easily enhanced. Dave bounces down the chunky asphalt of Southern Boulevard, its stores closed off by cinderblocks, the cinderblocks battered loose by junkies seeking sanctuary, the evolutionary cycle of slum life repeating itself block after block after block. The wind hurls garbage against a chain-link fence, and a charred couch sits in a vacant lot. The windows of abandoned apartments are covered at municipal expense with plastic decals of drawn curtains and blooming geraniums. Anyone driving fast enough might accept the deception.

Dave is driving slowly, consulting a street map spread across the passenger seat, peering into the mass of lines and letters for Kelly Street, where the Reeses now live at number 1021. The 1000 block begins north of Westchester Avenue and ends at a T-intersection with Intervale Avenue. Dave coasts carefully up the street, but he can find no building marked 1021. When he stops to ask directions from a group of men, they scatter like cockroaches from a flashlight. Junkies, probably, waiting to score. Why else would anybody be standing still, and sweating no less, on a sixteen-degree day?

One Hispanic woman, her head wound mummylike with a blue wool scarf, remains on the curb. Dave rolls down his window and asks, "Did a Reese family move in here recently?" She moves a gloved hand back and forth across her face, repeating, "No English. No English."

A man wearing thermal underwear and a St. Louis Cardinals hat emerges from an adjacent basement. Dave judges him to be the super of the building. He might know.

"Reese?" Dave calls. The man shrugs. "Black family. Been here about two months. Two kids, two adults." The man shrugs again.

Dave now stares down the block. Only a handful of houses stand, three on the west side and two on the east, masonry mesas on a rubble plain. Wild dogs prowl the gutters, sniffing the frozen garbage for food. A moraine of splintered furniture spills across an empty lot, and on its slopes rest bald tires, broken televisions, and mattresses slashed open to their spring skeletons. In his rear-view mirror, Dave can see the junkies returning to their stoop, satisfied that he is not a "narc." They draw near the fire one has built in an oil drum, thrusting cracked hands toward the heat. Up ahead, at the corner of Intervale, a car is burning. Dave watches the flames curl from the chassis around the doors and onto the vinyl roof before resolving into wind-whipped coils of oily smoke.

There seems nothing more to do. Dave starts the engine and pulls away from the curb. He turns right on Intervale and right again on a street named Tiffany. Across a field of broken bricks, he looks for the last time at the 1000 block of Kelly Street, with smoke twirling and wild dogs circling and junkies sweating and shivering and waiting, waiting, waiting. This is the edge of the world. This is the edge of the world, and the Reese family has slipped off the edge. A nonexistent address. Dave cannot deny that there is something grimly appropriate.

He stops at the corner of Westchester Avenue, in the shadow of a dirty steel subway trestle, waiting for traffic to pass so he can cross the four lanes. At the horizon, cars whizz down the Bruckner Expressway and toward Manhattan. Dave could be back at Seward Park in twenty minutes. Instead of crossing, he turns right on Westchester and right again on Kelly, as if 1021 might burst from the earth to reward his diligence. All Dave finds is a building numbered 1029, a five-story tenement with windows missing and bedsheets rippling in the wind and improbably gaudy aquamarine paint. *1029. 1021.* It wouldn't be the first time someone gave Dave the wrong address.

He shoves aside the reinforced steel front door and strides into the chilly first-floor hallway. A young man in an official-looking blue coat sits at the foot of the stairwell.

"Reese?" Dave asks.

The young man consults a list of tenants.

"'partment Two A."

Dave ascends the stairs. The walls are stripped bare, and the ceiling droops here and there. Shallow pools of urine collect on marble steps. As Dave huffs up the second flight, the cold frosts his breath. Still, he thinks to himself, *This is Christmas compared to the Prince George.*

Ruth Reese answers the door. She wears a green housecoat and blue puffy slippers. Nate has on a hospital gown. At the base of the living room wall stand two empty pints of E & J Brandy and five empty liters of Midnight Dragon malt liquor. But Ruth is clear eyed for a change, smiling at her familiar visitor. Dave notices the plastic tile floor, the lamp and television, the shoe rack laden with dolls and stuffed animals, the trappings of a real home. There is a Mardi Gras mask on the wall, very much like the one in Dave's office, and beneath it hangs a portrait of Darnell from sixth grade. He is wearing a blue suit and he is smiling. Dave spots another photograph, this one of Ruth and Nate toasting with a quart of beer.

"Our last night," Ruth explains.

"At the hotel," Nate adds.

Dave removes his coat, folds it across his lap, and sits on a kitchen chair. He is buying time, waiting for Darnell's entrance. The doors to both bedrooms are open. The household seems to be awake.

"Where's Darnell?" he finally says.

"At the Prince George," Ruth answers.

"He doesn't stay here with you?"

"That's over now," Ruth says. She reaches for a cigarette and a lighter. "They was gonna take him off my check."

Dave leans forward, his arms resting on his thighs. Where are the words? He straightens up, takes off his glasses, wipes them free of condensation.

"He's a young man," he says. "He's leanin' in the wrong direction, the wrong path. If he keeps hangin' around there, he could go away for a long time."

"Darnell do what he wanna do."

There is silence.

"I want you to have Darnell call me," Dave says. "I'll meet him halfway. *Three-quarters* of the way. I want to do something for him."

"Don't you worry," Ruth says, as if Dave is the one who needs help. "He'll call you Monday. That'll be one call he makes."

"He comes down to school, I'll give him carfare back." Dave digs into his pocket. "Here's two quarters so he can call."

He hands Ruth the coins. He unfolds his coat. He thinks how every time he's seen the Reeses, every single time he asks for Darnell to call or come to school, they say he'll do it on Monday. Never today or tomorrow. Monday is the polite lie. Monday is the delusion that things change.

"If he can come in," Dave says, slipping his left arm into a sleeve, then his right. "We can take him to see Helen Cohen."

He pauses. He realizes they have no idea who Helen Cohen is. He needs a different appeal, but he has used just about every appeal he knows.

"I believe in miracles," he says at last.

He waits for an answer that does not come. He looks at the Reeses and imagines their son, still at the Prince George, doing God knows what.

"Don't you believe in miracles?" he asks.

Ruth smokes her cigarette.

"Sometimes?"

7

Raccoon Badge

W̲ʜᴇɴ ᴊᴇssɪᴄᴀ sɪᴇɢᴇʟ writes the word "Aim" on the blackboard of Room 336, the woman in the far left corner shudders. The woman is Harriet Stein, an English teacher now nearing the end of her first term, and she shudders because "Aim" is the word she saw in her nightmare. The word was floating in the air, daring her, mocking her, challenging her, for it is the word that by Board of Education edict must begin every single lesson in every single school in New York City. No matter how long Harriet works, no matter how hard, she feels herself slipping off the pace, scrambling with an overloaded backpack toward another classroom and another thirty-four students and another "Aim," the tyrant of her days.

Harriet has not slept well all semester. She pushes herself to bed at midnight and wakes at five-thirty, electrified by worry. She has not seen some friends in months, and when she does, she asks them to massage her sore neck and tells them only partly in jest, "I want to be a secretary." For the first time in eight years, she has no relationship, and little time and energy for one if she did. On Friday nights, when she would normally enjoy dancing or a dinner party, she deposits herself at a classical music concert to be solitarily soothed. The next morning brings the emotional hangover Harriet remembers her mother calling "The Saturday Awfuls." Sunday she starts dreading Monday, when she steps on the treadmill again.

The problem is not the job. Harriet turned down offers from high schools in two suburbs on the mere chance of working at Seward Park. Her parents thought she was crazy to forsake a certain paycheck for a chancey one, and her professors at Columbia University's Teachers College thought she was crazy for favoring the city system. All of them had ignored the clues. Before entering graduate school, Harriet had counseled patients in a women's health center and done casework with victims of marital rape. Her moral compass could point her in no direction other than toward teaching the children of poverty. She understood affluent kids had problems; she just felt they needed her less desperately to solve them. And her months at Seward Park, however arduous, have only confirmed her thinking.

No, the problem is not the job itself. The problem is the conditions of the job. Harriet teaches five classes a day, three sections of a required course in British literature and two sections of an elective in mystery and adventure, burdening her with 170 students. She oversees a homeroom of an additional 34 youngsters, and she assists Helen Cohen in the guidance office during one of her nominally free periods. One of Harriet's friends from graduate school teaches in Scarsdale, one of the wealthiest communities in the state, where she has four classes of twenty pupils each. Another teaches in New Rochelle, Harriet's hometown, and has his own classroom with a little library and a closet for his running shoes and shaving kit. These friends are in more of a dancing mood on Friday nights.

Harriet did not receive her schedule until the first day of school, and she had to slap together her courses on the basis of whatever books the English department happened to stock. She is still learning how to write lesson plans, and she is still learning how to modulate her manner between too strict and too soft. When she failed a boy in one of her British literature classes, he calmly informed her, "You're Number One on my hit list." Harriet did not take seriously the physical threat, but she suffered to realize that a student saw her as the enemy. How many others agreed?

So badly had Harriet wanted to become a superior teacher that she had paid $300 a credit to attend the renowned Teachers College, more than three times the rate at the City University. Far from feeling superior, however, she has been discovering all term how many of her professors' pronouncements are useless in a real classroom, at least a real classroom on the Lower East Side. For instance, why didn't somebody tell her about beginning lessons with an aim? Didn't Teachers College expect that a few of its students would work in New

York? Harriet considered transferring to City University until she found she would forfeit most of her Columbia credits. Life can wield few tortures worse than educational methods courses the second time around.

The frustration reminds Harriet of studying cello as a teenager. She spent her first three years under one teacher, then switched to an instructor who required that she position her hands in a different way. Suddenly she didn't know what to do with her hands, hands she had trusted, and the more she practiced the new method the worse she sounded.

One day after school, she sent a letter confessing her depression to a favorite undergraduate professor, attaching to it a paper she had written for Teachers College about his influence upon her. The professor's response arrived a few weeks later. He recalled his own early years of teaching, when he made so many mistakes he feared he had caused "permanent brain damage" to his pupils, and he advised her not to be so hard on herself. She had done the right thing with her life, he wanted her to know. "The profession needs bright, concerned people, and we're lucky to have you," he wrote. "There are very few things that are exciting to do, that contribute to society, that exercise the heart and refurbish the soul and that bring home the bacon. We're very, very lucky people." Harriet laid down the letter and cried for two hours.

She does not lack for advice at Seward Park. The question is what to save and what to discard; the question is what combination of tiles constitutes the mosaic of classroom persona. Emma Jon told Harriet not to worry about assigning students seats, because they would bridle at the imposition. Rick Rowley explained his system of giving a numerical grade to each pupil in each class on each day. Steve Anderson suggested Harriet seek out Jessica, who had been his "buddy teacher" last year, and Jessica herself extended an open invitation. Harriet admired how students flocked to Jessica during free periods and after school, and she telephoned Jessica at home a few times. Still, she demurred at approaching her in school. Jessica always looked so busy, so immersed, so, so—what was the word Harriet invented?— *scurried.* Did this dervish ever relax over a cup of coffee? But, really, the fault was shared. Harriet's own schedule afforded little freedom for observing other teachers. It was a bit late to register for swimming lessons when you were already in the pool drowning.

Yesterday afternoon, though, Harriet collected herself enough to ask Jessica if she could watch this morning's lesson. Jessica said fine, and with good reason. Harriet would be attending the second period section of English 7, Jessica's best class, and the lesson would cover "Passage from Africa," an excerpt from a slave narrative entitled "The Life of Olaudah Equiano, or Gustavas Vassa, the African." Jessica could not say the Equiano lesson was one of her favorites, because her favorites, in hindsight, were whatever worked with a given class, but it was doubtlessly one of her most striking. Equiano was carried off from his Ibo tribe in 1756, at age eleven. He survived the Middle Passage and toiled for ten years in Barbados, Virginia, and Pennsylvania before buying his freedom and moving to England, where he devoted himself to antislavery agitation and writing his autobiography. Jessica first read a portion of his account in a social studies anthology, and only later learned that Equiano's story was one of the most famous in slave literature.

Jessica hardly suffered from hubris, but she liked to think that "Passage from Africa" was one piece of literature she taught at a collegiate level of complexity. Her lesson united history and literature and it forced students to penetrate past the text to the subtext. Most important, her lesson celebrated the power of language and ideas, the power of prose crafted in 1789 to stun children nearly two centuries later.

As Jessica finishes jotting the aim on the blackboard — "How Does 'Passage from Africa' Reveal How Racial Attitudes Are Established?" — Harriet reaches into her backpack for a blue ballpoint and a pad of binder paper. She wears a navy skirt hemmed at mid-calf and a black-and-blue flowered wool sweater. The attire is typical of her subdued style, as typical as her small voice and her doe eyes. Uncertain of her footing in Seward Park, she treads lightly. Jessica, in contrast, appears to have been assembled in a Third World bazaar.

"Yesterday," she says to the class, "I had you write about your pets. How many of you have pets?"

A few hands rise.

"Lun, what do you have?"

"Two cats and a dog."

"Wilfredo?"

"A parakeet."

"My little brother," someone shouts.

Harriet writes a note about the atmosphere. Kids talk without raising their hands, yet classmates respect whomever has the floor.

"For anyone who ever had a pet or has one now," Jessica continues, "what do you have to do?" She tosses her curls, rolls her eyes. "*Oy vei.* Feed it. Wash it. Clean up." She unscrews her face. "But how would you feel if it died?"

"Sad," José Santiago says.

"Upset."

"I'd kill myself."

"You're laughing about it," Jessica says, planting her palms on her hips. "But think about the love and affection you have for your pets. And now think about how the slaves were treated." She frees her hands to hang at her side and walks to the front of the desk. "What I want to get at is how it's possible for a group of human beings to treat another group of human beings worse than we treat our pets."

Harriet writes another note. Jessica was pretty forceful, pretty direct, while she is generally reluctant to state her opinions. Maybe she edits herself too harshly and cheats the classes out of important contexts. She scribbles a small question mark in the margin.

"Equiano was in Africa," Jessica continues. "He was eleven years old. Ran around. Played. Just like a regular kid. Then he got caught. And on this ship to America, a process took place. A reeducation process. And when he got off, he was a slave."

Jessica turns to the board. She draws a trapezoid to represent the United States, then sketches a vague shape several feet to the right.

"What's that, a pork chop?" someone calls.

"Africa," Jessica answers. "Now you know why I'm not an art teacher."

She charts a line connecting pork chop to trapezoid, approximating the route of the Middle Passage.

"Anyone got an idea how many Africans were brought here as slaves?"

"Two million," José says.

"Raquel, what do you think?"

"Two million."

"Joanna?"

"A lot."

Harriet notes that Jessica will call on a student who has not raised a hand, while she usually sticks with volunteers. She worries about intimidating a student by forcing him or her to speak. But it seems to work for Jessica. Harriet places a second question mark in the margin.

As Harriet writes, Jessica scowls. Nobody wants to take a risk.

Nobody except Ottavio Johnson, who got to school late and is cutting his second-period class to catch up on what he missed in first-period English 7. Ottavio waves his hand wildly, like a hitchhiker who has just caught sight of the first car in an hour.

"Twenty million," he calls.

Jessica nods. That Ottavio knew surprises her not at all.

"Historians differ on this," she tells the class, "but the estimates are ten million to twenty million." A hush settles over the room. "And how many survived?"

"Half," Ottavio shouts.

"Half," Jessica confirms. "And I think Equiano gives us clues why."

She retrieves from the desktop a copy of *Living World History,* a social studies textbook, and finds page 547, marked by a torn strip of paper. Then she passes the open book to Lisa Carerra, the first girl in the left row, as it begins its voyage through thirty-four pairs of hands. Page 547 contains a diagram of a slave ship, showing oval shapes arrayed for maximal volume on a single deck. In the dispassionate blueprint, the shapes could represent logs or cigars. Only the small lines, indicating the shackles at neck, wrist, and ankle, suggest that the cargo is human. The book moves slowly up and down the aisles. As it does, Jessica asks a girl named Cindy James to read aloud one paragraph from the rexo:

At last, when the ship we were in had got all her cargo, they made ready with fearful noises, and we were all put under the deck, so that we could not see how they managed the vessel. The stench of the hold while we were on the coast was so intolerably loathsome that it was dangerous to remain there for any time, and some of us were permitted to stay on the deck for fresh air. Now that the whole ship's cargo was confined together, it became absolutely pestilential. The closeness of the place, and the heat of the climate, added to the number in the ship which was so crowded that each had scarcely room to turn himself, almost suffocated us. This produced copious perspirations, so that the air soon became unfit for respiration from a variety of loathsome smells, and brought on a sickness among the slaves of which many died, thus falling victim to the improvident avarice, as I may call it, of their purchasers. This wretched situation was again aggravated by the galling of the chains, now become insupportable, and the filth of the necessary tubs, in which the children often fell, and were almost suffocated. The shrieks of the women and the groans of the dying rendered the whole a scene of horror almost inconceivable.

There is a long silence, a silence Jessica has learned to expect.

"So what was it like under there?" she asks with deliberate detachment.

"Horrible."

"How?"

"Hot."

"Stinky."

"That's an understatement," Jessica says.

"Crowded."

"Again, an understatement," she says. Impatient, she switches strategy. "I asked you to look for the meaning of words in context. What about when Equiano talks about the slaves 'falling victim to the improvident avarice . . . of their purchasers'?"

No one answers. Jessica writes the phrase "improvident avarice" on the board. Still, there is silence. Jessica calls on Addie Severino, one of her strongest students, but Addie says nothing.

"Lun," Jessica declares. "I saw the wheels turning."

"Means the slave traders were so greedy they killed off their own slaves."

"Obviously, Lun looked up some words," Jessica says approvingly. "Now, there's a part where Equiano describes himself being beaten. Why?"

"Because he wouldn't eat," Ottavio says.

"Why would they beat him for that?" Jessica asks with feigned innocence. "Why would they care?"

"He's a dollar sign," Ottavio answers.

"A dollar sign," Jessica repeats, glad to borrow the metaphor. "When they saw a slave, that's all they saw. A healthy kid, $2,000. Thin and scrawny, $500. And there's another part where Equiano tells about a slave being beaten to death. Can you figure out why?"

"For trying to escape?" someone offers.

"In a way," Jessica says, tilting her head and squinting as if reckoning a promontory on the horizon. "But he's in the middle of the ocean. Where's he gonna go?"

"He wants to kill himself."

"And that *is* a kind of escape," Jessica says. She extends her right palm in a comforting, approving gesture, then fists the hand except for one pointed finger of inquiry. "But what do they care if he's gonna kill himself? Either way, he's a dead slave. They still lose that much money. So why beat him to death?"

This is a seminal question, and Jessica will not wait for volunteers. She conscripts Wilfredo Ayala.

"To make him an example so there won't be mass suicide."

"Maybe. But why? Addie?"

"Because they preferred death to slavery."

"To get the point across," says a boy named Julio Valentin.

"What's the point?"

"To make a threat so no one else will try suicide."

"But the slave's still dead," Jessica says. She shifts gears. "Think of it this way: What rights do you have as a slave? Aracelis?"

"As a slave, you have no rights."

Harriet thinks what a clean answer that was. How'd she know what to say? She adds a note and a question mark to the lengthening list on her pad.

"Right," Jessica says to Aracelis. "On a slave ship you couldn't decide where to sleep, what to eat, when to go to the bathroom. What's left? José?"

"No rights."

"No," Jessica says with uncharacteristic oomph. "There's one right left. What is it? Aracelis?"

"The right to live or die."

Again, Harriet is struck. How'd she pull that answer out? Was it Jessica? Or the girl? Or the lesson? If it was the lesson, is that good or bad?

"The perfect slave is the person with no choices," Jessica says in summation. "The person who's had that last right taken away. The right to decide whether to continue breathing or not."

Jessica lets her words linger. She scans the faces assembled before her. How many of them believe they have choices? How many are willing to surrender the choices they have? She stresses that point about the perfect slave, hoping some will grasp its relevance to their own lives. But you hardly ever know. You look in someone's eyes, you see the light ignite, you wonder how long the flame will flicker. You wonder if you made any difference at all. Harriet, sitting in the back, must know the feeling.

The moment passes. Jessica proceeds to another incident, the beating of a white sailor by the ship's officers. Arms wag, voices compete. It is a good day, a good day to be seen, one of those days when Jessica stands in front like a silver disco globe, catching light from one direction and shooting it out in another, just turning and shining and turning and shining. The bell rings and Jessica talks through it. Some of the students rise, but many remain seated, listening and perhaps learning.

Harriet writes a note about the kids staying seated. It is the last note on her pad. She is not sure what she learned by watching. She has questions without answers, and she cannot tell how much the answers might help. Jessica's style is not her style, and yet something here provokes her, something Teachers College could never teach. Harriet asks Jessica if she can see her after school. Then she shoulders her backpack and skims across the linoleum toward her own class, looking altogether scurried.

*   *   *

The mathematics teacher was a gray, rumpled man, lumbering toward the retirement that lay mere weeks ahead. Governing on the principle of lethargy, he issued his students the same tests time and time again. His was a torpor so encompassing that he ignored the old sandwiches rotting in his desk and roused himself only to engage a few young girls in a grotesque parody of flirtation.

It was May 1978, and Jessica Siegel had just joined the staff of Seward Park High School as a paraprofessional. As a newcomer, she was dispatched immediately to the annex, the old man, and the remedial math class. Perhaps all anybody intended was that Jessica help see this disaster to a quiet conclusion. The teacher was a short-timer and the kids were losers and before long both would be gone. But the events offended her, and they equally offended a boy named George Vega. George was a tall, thin sophomore with a nasty wit, a fast temper, and a finely honed sense of injustice. If his classmates had given up, on their teacher and on themselves, then George refused to surrender. Asked to take the same test he had taken and passed once or twice already, he bellowed his protest. Out into the hall he was cast by the teacher, and out into the hall Jessica pursued.

She calmed him, promised to help him, and penetrated the armor of his rage. George ultimately told her of his parents' failed marriage, of his father's visits to beat his mother, of the night it fell to him to summon the police. Jessica had barely a notion how to teach someone, much less someone as wounded as George, and the math teacher was the last person inclined to enlighten her, but the boy had touched the organs she trusted most, her ear and her heart. So she brought George to a guidance counselor named Hal Pockriss, who was known for his personal touch, and together the three cut a deal: Jessica would tutor George in math, and Hal would counsel him on behavior. George passed the remedial course and passed the Regents examination and eventually won admission to college. Jessica could tell herself that summer she had won one small victory, and that alone justified returning in the fall.

It was accidental that she had landed at Seward Park at all, and when she looked back over her path, she felt as if she were regarding a line of footprints impressed by an impostor. Jessica had left Liberation News Service in 1974 bound for an imprecise destination dubbed "the real world," taking temporary jobs as a secretary and asking little more than a paycheck that covered the rent. In the aftermath of Vietnam and Watergate, it was a time for the children of the 1960s to lick their wounds and count their losses, to contemplate abrupt endings, to ponder the consequences before seizing the day.

Then, one Sunday in 1976, Jessica attended a wedding where she met a social worker from Covenant House, a residence for troubled teenagers. Jessica asked if there were any jobs available, and a month later she was called with an offer to become a secretary to the social work staff. Each teenager with an appointment for counseling had to check in first at Jessica's desk, and the procession included children of junkies, victims of incest, hustlers and runaways, and a pair of transvestites unbuttoned to their bras. Jessica discovered she enjoyed them, enjoyed their humor and their vigor and their potential. She chatted with them at her desk and she visited them in their group homes, often bringing a cheesecake or a pumpkin pie.

She might never have left Covenant House had she not learned that at a salary of $8,350 annually, she was making $150 less than the organization's other secretaries. The principle mattered, and so did the money; $150 was almost one month's rent. So when her superiors pleaded poverty, Jessica resolved to leave. Another secretary had a sister who worked as a paraprofessional at Seward Park and earned about $9,000 for the ten-month school year. Jessica placed her application, made the first of many visits to the Board of Education's hiring hall, and waited. Two months later, she was given the job.

The paraprofessional program had been designed as a way for schools to hire neighborhood parents as classroom aides, but Rubin Maloff, then the principal at Seward Park, had adroitly adapted it into a recruiting vehicle. He made a point of signing on young people with a college education, with degrees in history and literature and philosophy, and he counted on at least a few of them deciding in time to teach. The problem was that these bright young aides, a good number of them graduates of dissident politics, tended to view the teachers they assisted as enemies to be resisted rather than as models to be emulated. Jessica's encounter with the remedial math teacher suggested many of the reasons why.

But in September 1978, Jessica was placed in the main building instead of the annex, and she was paired with a social studies teacher named Lanni Tama. In Lanni, Jessica saw a twelve-year veteran of undimmed enthusiasm, and in Jessica, Lanni saw intellect and energy, abundant if undirected. Lanni habitually sought to teach Seward Park's experimental classes, and that fall she was working in a special reading program emphasizing individual instruction. Instead of delegating Jessica the clerical chores, as many teachers did with their aides, Lanni essentially shared the class with her. They tutored together. They marked papers together. They met with parents together. They ate lunch together.

Lunch was important. The Seward Park faculty cafeteria was more than a collection of long formica tables; it was a collection of world views. There was a table for talk of investments and there was a table for whispers of discos and there were lots of tables for bitching and moaning. Lanni Tama sat at a table for teachers who cared about teaching—not Pollyannas, to be sure, but realists who believed in possibility. Teaching is a solitary task, and so lunch was the one time of the day when the believers could share ideas, trade theories, and reinforce in one another the very ethos of believing.

The woman at the table who impressed Jessica most was Hannah Hess, an English teacher of stocky build and owlish eyes. She was a German Jew whose family had escaped the Nazi regime in 1939 and reached the expatriate colony in Manhattan's Washington Heights district by way of Ecuador. As a girl of six, unable to speak a word of English, Hannah had entered the New York public schools, and as a woman of twenty-three, she had become a teacher in the same system. She had lived the legend of immigrants and schools and success, but she had lived long enough to question it. For when Hannah left teaching in 1962 to raise her three children, she began to learn precisely how resistant a public school could be to dismissing incompetents and accepting innovation. Her awakening reached its peak during the 1968 teachers' strikes, when she joined a group of parents in keeping open their neighborhood elementary school. To the United

Federation of Teachers, that act branded Hannah a traitor, and even when she resumed teaching after a twelve-year hiatus, she faced a spiritual blacklist. The union could not deny Hannah a job, but some of its supporters could conspire to make her job miserable. During Hannah's first year at Seward Park, various colleagues ignored her in conversation, slammed doors in her face, and refused to lend her change for a pay telephone. When her car was ticketed by mistake in a school parking zone, an administrator declined to verify for the Traffic Court that she indeed taught at Seward Park. Hannah outlasted the petty harassment, but she never forgot it, and the experience gave her a special empathy for the outsider.

Hannah invited Jessica to watch her teach. In the English office afterward, she talked to Jessica about the children in the class. When Passover arrived, Hannah welcomed Jessica to her family's seder. Their conversations over the months gradually moved from the purely educational to the political and the personal, and for the first time at Seward Park, Jessica trusted someone enough to confide her radical past, a past she had feared might cost her her job. Hannah was, if anything, relieved. She knew the lonely lot of the freethinker, and she appreciated the company out on Seward Park's left wing.

To Hannah and Lanni and the rest of the lunch table, it was obvious that Jessica should become a teacher. Jessica had the mind and she had the soul and she had a frightening capacity for labor, for "working herself to a frazzle and thinking she should be working herself to two frazzles," as Hannah put it. The campaign required a lot of tuna and yogurt and coffee and cajoling, but eventually Jessica agreed to try. She refused to begin immediately with a temporary license, but she consented to taking the English licensing exam and to entering Teachers College while remaining a paraprofessional. There was so much Jessica needed to know, and Teachers College, with its international reputation, seemed the place to learn it. Hannah knew better. The only classes she had cut as an undergraduate at Hunter College were in education, and her graduate studies at Fordham University had taught her "zip." There were only two ways anyone really learned how to teach, by teaching and by watching others teach. Learning how to teach was not an academic process as much as a tribal rite, a secret passed from elder to child, atavistic as charting the stars or planting the maize.

But Jessica had her plan: She would go to Teachers College and learn to teach reading. Reading classes were small, reading instruction was individual. A reading class was a theater built for a thespian with stage fright. If only Jessica had been able to stay awake during her reading-education classes at Teachers College. So little in her courses struck her as practical. The professors could not be bothered with subjects as pedestrian as writing a lesson plan. The students marched toward graduation blithely unaware of anything as fundamental as New York City's licensing system.

Jessica doubled her course load to graduate in time for the reading-license exam in fall 1980. In her final, frantic semester, she took the single memorable class of graduate school, "Arts and American Education," from Professor Maxine Greene. Greene was a presence, a self-deprecating wit whose craggy voice and constant cigarette reminded Jessica of Lillian Hellman. Whereas her colleagues rode the rut of narrow theory, Greene uncoiled skeins of ideas, spanning education, painting, fiction, and politics. "What's going on?" Jessica could hear some of the younger students mutter during the reveries. "This is too fast." But Jessica thrilled to the pace. She learned from Maxine Greene the texts she someday would teach her own students — *The Great Gatsby* and "Bartleby the Scrivener" — but what was more important, she learned the way she would teach them, by "showing the connections between things."

Her master's degree completed, Jessica entered her third full year at Seward Park as an overeducated paraprofessional. It was then, in September 1980, that events overtook her cautious design. One of the teachers of Spanish bilingual social studies died of a heart attack only a few weeks into the term. As a search was mounted for a successor, his classes were placed in the receivership of a substitute, whose pedagogy consisted of perusing *The New York Times* while his flock ran wild. Jessica heard the whooping from an adjacent classroom, and when she peered in the door she saw the anarchy. She hurried to the social studies office and described the scene to Stan Carter, the department chairman.

They were Seward Park's odd couple, Stan a combat Marine veteran still strapping in his fifties, and Jessica, a bundle of self-doubt and bright colors. "The sixties are over," he would tease her, and she would laugh, because she sensed the affection behind the barb. Like Hannah Hess and Lanni Tama, Stan judged Jessica to be teacher material, and now she would have her chance. He told her to assign homework to the chaotic class. How could you give homework, Jessica asked, without teaching a lesson? And how could you teach a lesson to a class of recent immigrants from a textbook written at twelfth grade level? The only solution, as Jessica saw it, was to create and teach a lesson of her own. So she did.

Then she taught a second and a third. An aide could not officially lead a class alone, so Stan hired another substitute to sit in the room. A few weeks later, he located a fully licensed Spanish bilingual history teacher, and relieved Jessica, but the new man proved so poor that Stan fired him and restored Jessica to the lectern. By now, she had received her temporary license, so she took over the deceased teacher's entire load—four sections of bilingual social studies and one section of World History II.

She felt herself sinking in quicksand. She did not speak Spanish. She had never taught. She had never even studied much history. What caused World War I? She would find out the night before informing her classes. Stan lent Jessica some of his lesson plans, as did a teacher named Maureen Lonergan, but working from another's outline was like wearing a stranger's shoes. The classes, sensing Jessica's inexperience, burst into blizzards of spitballs and invective. Jessica asked Hannah for advice on discipline, and Hannah said, "Just give them the beady eye." The beady eye worked better for a veteran than a beginner, and soon Jessica was back to the same plaints: "Turn around! Stop tickling her! No, you can't go to the bathroom. Sit down! Leave the window alone! Where's your homework?"

Stan scheduled his first formal observation, and of all Jessica's classes, he chose to watch World History II, her worst. The room brimmed with thirty-four brigands, "repeaters" who had failed the course from one to three times already. They had bedeviled Jessica daily with fake passes, profane answers, and sundry roughhousing, and they had delighted in their demonism. Jessica was terrified to smile; she marshaled all her strength just to dam her tears until the end of the day. But the November morning Stan Carter swaggered through the door, a redwood on legs, her tormentors fell silent. It was not fear of Stan that had hushed them, it was the fear he had come to fire Ms. Siegel. Jessica taught a lesson on Renaissance artists, and to her amazement, hands rose and inquiries filled the air. Grace was all. Stan left the room with five minutes remaining in the period, and the second the door closed behind him, a voice shouted, "Now we can get back to normal." As paper balls cross-hatched the air before her, Jessica ventured her first laugh of the term.

Not long after, Jessica received word she had passed the English licensing exam she dimly recalled having taken two years earlier; the Board of Examiners was operating at its customary crawl. She reported to the English Department chairman, Lew Saperstein, a man she distrusted utterly. When Jessica had been Lanni Tama's aide, Saperstein had tried to commandeer her as his personal file clerk. She resisted, and he bullied: "You can follow my orders, or I can get you fired." While Saperstein had relented, his threat still rung in Jessica's ears, for now, as a new teacher, she was most vulnerable to caprice.

Saperstein first offered Jessica several sections of English 8. The course, world literature for second-semester seniors, was usually awarded as a plum to a skilled veteran. Jessica, fearing its scope beyond her abilities, wavered.

"OK," Saperstein said. "English Four. The annex."

Jessica sobbed. English 4 was a course in oral communication for first-semester sophomores. Public speaking mortified her, and the annex was the annex, a dismal old academy far from Hannah and Stan, Jessica's mainstays.

"But no one will bother you," Saperstein said.

Suddenly Jessica realized Saperstein had been trying to mend fences. He would send her to the Outback, and she would be left alone. She could falter in sublime isolation. Saperstein had designed his own office so that a phalanx of filing cabinets guarded him from all petitioners, and he had appropriated a diminutive paraprofessional as his factotum. As far as Jessica could tell, not being bothered was, to Saperstein, the highest plane of existence.

"But I *want* to be bothered," Jessica pleaded.

The spring term of 1981 was her worst ever. Now that she finally had a career, she was failing at it. She asked Hannah what she should teach, and Hannah said, "Anything you want." She asked Hannah what to choose as an aim for a lesson, and Hannah said, "Anything you find interesting." What Hannah was saying was, "Trust yourself," but what Jessica heard was, "You're on your own, kid." As for Saperstein, after observing Jessica teaching a typically disastrous class, he assured her, "I won't write it up." Ignoring her faults, Jessica realized, was his idea of helping.

"Jessica was overwhelmed," Hannah Hess recalls. "She probably spent seven hours on every paper she read. Would go home with a humongous stack of paper every night. Would plan a lesson and if it didn't work would be beside herself. And she was always convinced everyone else was doing something better than her. She'd say, 'X is a better teacher than I am,' and I'd say, 'Have you ever seen X teach?' and Jessica would say, 'No.' I'd say, 'So how do you know X is better?' and Jessica would say, 'X said so.'"

As much as Hannah knew Jessica was foundering, as deeply as she sensed Jessica was suffering, as many times as she watched Jessica slink home for her nightly cry, she had no doubts about her protégée. "I knew Jessica wouldn't quit because Jessica's not a quitter," Hannah says. "Jessica couldn't walk away from something she felt she'd failed. She could only walk away from a success."

One day late in the spring term, Jessica was summoned to the main building. There, she and the rest of the English teachers were introduced to Ben Dachs, a hulking man with a full brown beard who would become their chairman in the fall. Lew Saperstein had been nudged toward a transfer; he would leave Seward Park for—it was only appropriate—the Board of Examiners. Neither Ben nor Jessica knew much about the other. Canadian born and American educated, Ben was coming from Edward R. Murrow High School, a magnet school in Brooklyn, where he had taught English, advised the yearbook, directed plays, and coordinated a writing program. Jessica was less than a year out of the paraprofessional ranks, and Ben assumed she had gained her teaching position less by merit than by patronage. Here, he thought, was a case of a corrupt system taking care of its own.

Early in September 1981, he began to change his mind. Jessica warmed to Ben for returning her to the main building, and for rearranging the office furniture so he faced teachers instead of hiding from them, as had his predecessor. Ben installed a work table and a magazine rack and a chair beside his desk for personal chats.

Jessica planted herself in that chair at the first opportunity and poured out all the frustration of the previous year.

"I'm really glad you're here," she said. "I need someone like you. I'm overwhelmed and underconfident. I never got any help from Saperstein. I want to learn how to be a good teacher. I need to know so many things. I want to learn from you."

Then she exploded into tears.

Ben could not have wished for more. He was an accomplished educator tiring of the classroom. Oh, he still enjoyed teaching well enough, but he had gotten too good at it. Ben played poker and bet the horses because he loved risk and challenge; effortless triumph held no satisfaction. He had sought a chairmanship because he believed that in teaching teachers, he could find that spark, that serendipity he called "the 'Aha' effect." And now, in Jessica, he had the consummate pupil, intellect in search of form and insecurity in search of fealty.

Over the weeks, Ben advised Jessica on constructing lessons, framing questions, and planning curriculum, but he never intended that counsel alone would suffice. Midway through the term, he taught his English 8 class a series of lessons on *Hamlet*. He typed a schedule of dates and topics and issued the faculty an invitation with only one caveat: whoever saw him teach had to provide him with a critique of the lesson. The school buzzed. There was substantial debate in Seward Park about whether inner-city kids could understand *Hamlet*, much less enjoy it, and here was an untenured chairman teaching Shakespeare as nakedly as a stripper. Even before Jessica made it to Ben's classroom, word was racing through school: The new guy took some old newspapers, whirled the sheets into a hat and a sword, leapt onto the desktop, and started teaching from there. Jessica sat in on nothing quite so dramatic, but she was dazzled by Ben's personal alchemy of entertainment and education. He orated. He inquired. He told shaggy-dog stories. He physically shaped students into armies and courts.

Jessica trod through a story or poem line by line, following elaborately scripted lesson plans that dragged on for days. The idea of fibbing a little to invigorate a class seemed as illicit as perjury. She was a public servant; she was a bore; she was a raisin and Ben was a great juicy grape. Yet Jessica had a restless mind, and she had a motherly warmth, and Ben considered that combination all too rare. The first time he observed her, he noted that thirty-one of her thirty-four pupils had turned out for a first-period class on a bitter, blustery December Friday. They were voting with their feet. And when Ben inspected several students' notebooks, he saw they were comprehending. He cushioned his criticism of Jessica's stiff style with plenty of praise. "You are your own toughest critic," Ben wrote after that class. "Lighten up on yourself and you will see that this was a fine lesson that needed only some finer tuning."

The more Jessica trusted Ben, the safer she felt loosening the standard lesson. Teaching under his stewardship, she would later say, "was like flying with a net." If she recognized that she could never be a stemwinder, a classroom natural, then she realized she could infuse literature with her humor and her values. "You want kids to love literature," Ben often told her, "not just the piece you're teaching." Outside class, he encouraged her to chaperone field trips and to advise

Seward World. He lobbied for approval of the Lower East Side course she had designed with Bruce Baskind.

Ben was not the only one to notice Jessica's metamorphosis. One day in spring 1986, he said to her, "That was *some* letter." She asked, "What letter?" Ben withdrew it from his desk:

Mr. Robert Mastruzzi, Superintendent
Manhattan High Schools
Martin Luther King, Jr. High School
122 Amsterdam Avenue
New York, New York 10023

Dear Mr. Mastruzzi:

My nominee for Teacher of the Year for 1985–86 is Jessica Siegel. Ms. Siegel, it should be noted, began her career in education as an educational assistant and now has become an excellent role model for colleagues and students.

Jessica Siegel is a teacher of English, but this describes her as well as daVinci might be described were we to call him a medical illustrator. She serves as advisor to our newspaper, *Seward World,* and has overseen expansion of this publication to four issues annually. In addition, recent recognition by the Robert F. Kennedy Foundation and the Columbia Press Association gives testimony to the effectiveness of her guidance and leadership. Further, together with a superb colleague, Bruce Baskind, she has created a humanities course which focuses on the Lower East Side and its history of immigration, which has earned the plaudits of New York University in the form of financial backing for her research and curriculum development, in addition to their enthusiastic encomiums.

Ms. Siegel is a creative self-starter who commits herself wholeheartedly to professional activities. She attends evening and weekend functions which we sponsor, strives constantly to improve her classroom performance, and involves herself in a myriad of activities which contribute to a viable school environment. I nominate her for your consideration.

Sincerely,
Noel N. Kriftcher
Principal

Jessica did not win the boroughwide award, and she wondered why she had to learn of her nomination secondhand. But she carried home a plaque as a distinguished also-ran, and she dined at a four-star restaurant as Bruce Baskind's guest. By now, Hannah Hess had left Seward Park to become chairwoman of the English Department at Chelsea Vocational High School. Ben, feeling his familiar craving for new terrain, was quietly surveying the city for a principal's position. Jessica was the veteran. At the start of the 1986–87 school year, Ben's last at Seward Park, he appointed her the "buddy teacher" for a newcomer named Steve Anderson. Steve called Jessica every single night for months, with desperate pleas for aid in writing lessons and tips on buying grade books, and each time Jessica answered she indulged in a private pleasure: She knew something; she had something to share.

When Ben departed Seward Park in September 1987 to become principal of Beach Channel High School, he could view Jessica as perhaps his greatest single success. He had always maintained that a teacher did not have to be born, that a teacher could be trained. His sole regret was that he had trained Jessica rather too well. Her skills were high, with standards to match. She held *Seward World* to a professional benchmark. Never did she deny a student in need. He saw in her pride and assurance, and he saw in her exhaustion and heartbreak. And he, more than most, had helped engineer this benign Frankenstein, nourishing to students and colleagues, damaging only to herself.

*   *   *

A pale blue sky, sunless in the late afternoon, hangs above the housing project, outside the English office window. The north wind drives newspapers down Essex Street like tufts of sagebrush. In the hours near noon, the day had achieved a hint of warmth, but Harriet and Jessica, seated at the long table, know only the chill that shoved them toward Seward Park this morning and that will hasten them home tonight. It is past four on a Friday, and they have the office to themselves. A tousled morning *Times* and two empty cans of Diet Pepsi sit on the table, the daily detritus. Jessica opens her Delaney book and places a pen above her right ear. Harriet lays down her purse and backpack and pushes aside a pile of homework to clear room for her notes from Jessica's morning class.

That they are tired is a given. The proof is in their eyes. These eyes, forced to shine for students all day and all week, take on the dull cast of a stagnant pond. On the flesh beneath them, dark lines fan toward the cheeks. Each woman has two—no, three—sets of lines, each tinted the purple of a bruise, each etched deeply as detail in terra-cotta. Bruce Baskind has a name for this condition: The raccoon badge of honor. It is true that insomnia or a new baby or a long commute could cause the same symptoms, but the raccoon badge is the medal of the devoted teacher, the teacher up late reading essays, the teacher up early decorating a classroom, the teacher still in school as Friday's firmament darkens.

"Do you give them journal questions every day?" Harriet asks.

"Yes," Jessica says. "Ben and I used to argue about it. He thought they were a waste of time. But I disagree. It's important kids get their ideas on paper."

"I think that's important," Harriet seconds. "It tells them you're interested in what they have to say. And . . . ," she yawns and briefly loses the thought, "that writing can teach someone."

"It's also—and with the autobiographies, too—that they want me to know things," Jessica says. "Sometimes it's like, 'You read it yet? You read it yet?' They want you to know."

The clatter of a custodian emptying garbage cans interrupts.

"The thing I noticed the most, and the comparison depressed me, is you don't have a chatter problem," Harriet says. She frowns. Her voice is solemn. She might have been speaking of a terminal disease.

"You oughta see my journalism class," Jessica says. "They're hanging from the chandeliers. Sometimes it's just the combination of kids."

"But what makes it different? This class seemed to attend on you so closely."

Jessica brushes a few stray curls clear of her eyes.

"It may not help you to hear this," she says, "but it's a matter of putting in the years, getting the confidence in yourself." She pauses. "But I still have days. I had to really yell at my journalism class the other day. They were being really obnoxious. There's one girl who's had a chip on her shoulder, and the other kids got pulled in by it, and I had to scream at them."

"What do you say? 'Don't do it.'"

Jessica explains. The class was posing in a hallway for its yearbook portrait. Only five minutes remained in the period. An argument broke out because no one wanted to kneel in the front row; the floor dust would ruin their clothes. Now only thirty seconds were left. It was all so bratty that Jessica snapped. It was a privilege to be in the journalism class, a privilege to be on the *Seward World* staff. Anybody who disagreed could get out of the picture. Then, sure enough, they all shut up and posed.

As Jessica finishes her account, Denise Simone enters the room. She has just locked up the College Discovery office for the weekend, as usual having had to shoo home a couple of kids, and she is recruiting company for Mexican food and margaritas. From the pieces of conversation she heard on her way in, she knows a rapid exit is unlikely, and so she takes a seat and listens. Beneath her ringlets of raven hair, she wears the raccoon badge.

"You know that bad class I had?" Harriet asks. Jessica nods. "I still have it. That kid Louie hates me. I know it. I talked to him once. I said, 'What don't you like about me?' 'I dunno.' I said, 'Pretend I'm a friend.' 'You're boring.'"

"What do *you* think?" Jessica says.

"I don't have a clue."

"C'mon," Jessica says in taxi-driver tones. "Could it be because you're young? Or he's attracted to you?"

"I can't tell," Harriet says, seemingly embarrassed at the notion. "There's just this tension."

"Well, he isn't gonna tell you," Jessica says. Then her voice softens. "He may not understand it himself."

"I moved him to the back of the room, and things seem better," Harriet says, reassuring herself more than Jessica.

Denise unbuttons her wool overcoat. At age twenty-nine, it has not been many years since she shook with the same anxiety. If anything, she had it worse, for early in her teaching career she landed in Brooklyn's Prospect Heights High School, where eight teachers were attacked by students in her first two weeks on the job. Having aspired to teach since she led classes for a Chatty Cathy doll in her kitchen, Denise almost resigned amid the bloodletting. Only a transfer to Edward R. Murrow High School convinced her to continue.

"Have you tried calling parents?" she asks Harriet. "Once you call the parents of your five worst kids, the next day they come in and say—" she affects a dull, sullen voice—" 'Man, she called my mother.' Then the whole class straightens up."

Harriet acknowledges she has not called Louie's parents. It is too extreme a step. She wants a resolution within the classroom. She is striving for a style that is "firm *and* nice."

"How about writing a guidance referral," Denise says. "Maybe the kid's having problems at home. With his mother. Or his girlfriend."

"So, uh, what's a guidance referral?" Harriet asks sheepishly.

"You have to find out first who his guidance counselor is," Jessica says. "I hope it's Nancy Wackstein. She can do anything."

Harriet makes a note. Jessica returns to the prevailing topic.

"So what can I say?" She turns her palms toward the ceiling. "It's a terrible thing to say. But it's a matter of time. My first few terms were bananas."

She tells Harriet about teaching Spanish bilingual history without knowing either Spanish or history. She tells Harriet about the "repeater" class of World History II. Harriet taps her foot rapidly. She pinches her pen between thumb and forefinger.

"So why'd it change?" she asks.

"Experience."

"But if you have to get from this point to that point, how can you get there quicker?"

"I think you're smarter than I was," Jessica says, "and more mature."

"How old were you when you started teaching?"

"Let's see . . . thirty."

"So *you* were more mature."

Age is a pointless cul-de-sac. Denise suggests that Harriet chose several strong teachers to observe regularly.

"I keep saying I'm going to," she answers, "but so much of my time gets eaten up."

"You're trying to learn so many things," Jessica says. "Delaney cards. Lunch books. Transportation passes. How to write a pink slip. What note to accept. What note not to accept. Those are things that will fall into place."

"You may just be hard on yourself," Denise adds. "Your kids seem to like you." She smiles. "My first year teaching, I used to come home so nuts I had to keep a bottle of blackberry brandy in my room. I'd have to come home, take a shot, and veg out in front of the TV."

"And if I had to write a new lesson plan every day, I'd go crazy," Jessica says. "You can spend two hours on a great creative idea, then it doesn't work on the kids. You bomb and you feel everything that goes with that."

The office is silent. The sky over the housing project, blue not so long ago, is coal black. Clouds stifle the stars. The only lights on the eastern horizon are bulbs burning in the kitchens of the housing project. The building itself fades into the evening, leaving the electric pinpricks afloat in an inner-city constellation.

"Shall we go?" Denise asks.

Jessica and Harriet agree they shall. The destination is a restaurant in the East Village, not far away. Denise and Harriet plan to return to school after dinner for a dance. Jessica will pass. Everything lately seems to remind her how spent she is. A former student visits her and recommends a vacation at Club Med. The Dominican girls on *Seward World* offer her a "fashion makeover." The rexo she typed for English 7 early this morning, listing possible choices for the required book report, is studded with mistakes. *Maes Agee, Last of the Mohegans, To Kill A Nocking Bird.* She needs sleep more than a high school dance.

"So you think I should just wait it out?" Harriet asks Jessica as the three women walk down the deserted hall.

"It's alright to freak out," Jessica says. "I remember people telling me I'd stop crying after a few years, and that's no good to hear. It's like a teenager with acne. The last thing you want is for your mother to say, 'Just wait a few years and you'll be beautiful.'"

8

The Ever
Waveless Sea

Whats a luxury?" Jessica Siegel asks her second period English class one blustery November morning, beginning a lesson on *Walden*.

"Something that costs a lot of money. Like a new car."

"Something that makes you feel good."

"All right," she says, "and what's a necessity?"

"Something you need."

"We all agree?" She surveys the nodding heads. "OK. What are examples?"

Hands rise like August grain.

"Pizza."

"McDonald's."

"Rap music."

"Sex."

"With condoms," someone interrupts.

Jessica spies the boy in the seat beside the window, straining to attract her. He stretches his right hand toward the ceiling, and the cuff of his gray sweater slips down his thin arm. His head leans against his upraised arm, as if providing ballast. Jessica remembers his name, See Wai Mui, and she remembers from his autobiography that he grew up poor in rural China. She remembers in particular one phrase that lifted from the clutter of his English—"the cold life of my childhood." Before Jessica learned even that minimum about See Wai Mui, she had reckoned him a newcomer of modest means. His hair was roughly cut and fell in the irregular slope of a mushroom cap. He wore the same beige sweatpants and smudged sneakers almost every day, and this morning's gray sweater had only recently replaced a blue hooded sweatshirt. He carried his books in a nylon bag, its zipper handle stamped with the word "HERS," to which he appeared oblivious. It could have been a hand-me-down or it could have been a throwaway.

"See Wai?" Jessica says.

"Sea Weed?" mimics the bully who sits beside him.

"The necessity," See Wai says, undeterred by the titters. "The necessity." He often begins with such declarations. "The necessity, they are compass, matches, knife."

"You live in the woods?" the bully sneers.

Jessica regards See Wai. It is for her a moment of pure recognition. The discussion had been light and jokey, a short course in conspicuous consumption, and then he shifted into the most pragmatic terms possible. When Jessica asked, "What's a necessity?" others heard a setup and delivered a punch line. See Wai heard a practical inquiry, grounded in Thoreau's text: What does a man require to survive? *Here must be someone,* Jessica thinks, *who knows.*

*   *   *

In bare yards set off by bamboo stakes, chickens circled madly, squawking, straining for flight. On concrete streets, dogs whimpered and howled. The animal cries bounced off the gray brick houses, noise building on noise, echo on echo, swirling into a cacophany of chaos. Mui See Wai, seven years old, raced across the alleys and down the lanes, uncertain where to run, uncertain what to run from, certain only of his own terror. His mother chased but she could not catch him. Sweating and panting, she shouted ahead to a neighbor to grab the child and hold him fast. She gathered See Wai into her arms and carried him home, and then he saw that the first floor was empty, stripped to its stone floor. The family's belongings, the few things their own, the cooking pots and the cotton quilts and the altar to the household gods, all had been moved to the second and topmost floor. Their four children now collected, See Wai's parents locked the house and fled for a cave in the mountains. The flood waters were washing down the valley, descending on the village of Yong He Li.

The family huddled in the cave for ten days. When they returned to Yong He Li, the water still stood thigh high, making the village an archipelago of brick and mortar islands. See Wai and his friends, as yet innocent of the flood's consequences, merrily swam from house to house. More enterprising elders sold fish they caught and vegetables they had hoarded. The flood waters drained slowly toward the sea, dragging off uprooted trees and leaving behind a dark frosting of mud. It was late fall 1976, harvest season in southeastern China, and the rice crop was ruined. The worst time of See Wai's life was about to begin.

Even before the flood, the Mui family had been the poorest in the village, too poor to buy firewood, too poor to eat pork, too poor to send See Wai to school. Now there would be little food for at least four months, until the new crop matured, until the next New Year's gift arrived from See Wai's uncle in America. The Muis, six in all, ceased eating breakfast, took only a watery soup for lunch, and rationed their little rice for dinner. Already indebted to their neighbors, the family could not afford food on the black market, so See Wai's mother, Sau Ling, begged potatoes from her relatives and his father, Let Keung, fished by moonlight, when the farm labor was done. Still, there was never enough. "I starving," See Wai would remember more than a decade later. "The stomach is crouching. I hear it make noise. The feeling is out of breath. I want to sleep all the time. If I sleep, I forget I am hungry."

Gradually, life returned to the deprivation that passed for normal. Let Keung and Sau Ling rose before dawn and traveled the ten miles to Gold Pig Mountain, where they chopped the day's wood. By the time the rooster's call awakened See Wai, his mother was in the kitchen, cooking rice soup on a stone hearth. The two older children, Fon Wai and May Fong, headed for school, but See Wai spent his days in the fields. Although education was free, school supplies cost one dollar a year for each child, and every two hands writing at a desk were two fewer hands picking rice or raising pigs and adding to the paltry family purse. So See Wai walked barefoot along the narrow paddy walls, carrying a bucket and a hoe, and gazed back across the dirt road at the children bounding toward the South Ocean School, some in the bright nylon sweatsuits their overseas relatives sent, some in the red neckerchiefs the principal awarded for excellence.

During the few lulls in the fields, See Wai would steal to the school, hunching outside the classrooms to hear his friends singing "Red Flag" and reciting bits of English: "car" and "gun" and "jeep" and "rubber." An old man in Yong He Li taught See Wai how to add on an abacus, and a teenager drew him alphabet characters. Burn as he did for a more formal education, See Wai never pressed his parents, working instead with that stoicism the Chinese call "eating bitterness."

He irrigated the fields bucket by bucket. He tended the village cow. He cut and husked cane and lashed together forty stalks at a time for the float downriver to the sugar refinery. Three times each year, he girded for the rice harvest, the hardest toil of all. As Sau Ling cut the rice stalks, See Wai bundled them, and they worked as long as there was sun and often longer, squatting on their haunches hour by hour, feet fighting the paddy mud's suction every single step.

When the crop was in and the paddies were bare, Sau Ling beseeched the gods. She arranged an offering of rice balls and vegetables and knelt before the altar and uttered the prayers she had known all her life. Behind the altar, on the brick wall of the living room, hung strips of red paper with gold lettering, and one of them read, "If your home is prosperous, your wishes will come true."

The Muis' home was not prosperous and the Muis' wishes went unanswered. The family earned more than one hundred dollars only in the best years, and invariably owed money to neighbors. See Wai received an allowance of less than one cent a month, enough to buy only a marble or two. But the summer harvest of 1978 was a bountiful one for all the villagers, and the Mui family was able to sell its pig for thirty-five dollars in a newly reopened private market. Let Keung decided he could afford one luxury, and that September, when See Wai normally would have been planting lotus, he attended school for the first time in his life. He was two weeks shy of his ninth birthday.

See Wai wore his only good clothes, the clothes he closeted between holidays, a white button-down shirt and matching olive pants and Mao jacket. He rode through the morning fog on the handlebars of his father's bicycle, and when he heard the class president blow the assembly trumpet and saw the students form lines, he thought they looked as impressive as the People's Liberation Army. See Wai's class had thirty-five children, arrayed in pairs on seats like sawhorses before wooden desks as dark and grainy as weathered fences. Four bare bulbs lit the room and on the front wall an electric clock ticked, the first clock See Wai had ever seen. He sang the national anthem that morning, and he learned to write the three characters of his name, and he memorized the proverb that said, "Starting out, going forward."

As the year ended, See Wai took the all-day examination for promotion into the second grade. He had not studied much because he had done well in class and he preferred to play hide-and-seek and to swim in the irrigation ditch on spring afternoons. He failed the test and carried home his report card, crying and wondering how he would tell his mother. She turned from the hearth and saw him sitting in the threshold and asked what was the matter. For a moment he considered lying, saying another boy had beaten him, but he confessed. "I work so hard for you, and you do this to me," she shouted. "You really disappoint me." He saw himself as a beggar, wandering down the road with a broken bowl, and his tears poured in torrents. Then his mother came to him, as she had come to him on the day of the flood, and gathered him into her apron. "Don't worry," she whispered. "Don't worry. Next time, you do better. Next time, you will study."

The dream Let Keung and Sau Ling held for their children, the dream of freedom from the fields and the seasons and the tyranny of want, depended on Mui Dap Sing, Let Keung's brother in New York. As relations warmed between China and America in the 1970s, the Muis' hopes rose that Beijing would allow emigration for the first time since 1949. Dap Sing could sponsor them; he was a rich man—all Americans were rich. Let Keung had heard stories of gold floors and diamond windows and seven-foot white men with big red mustaches. See Wai asked Mui Chin Da, the wisest man in the village, and Chin Da confirmed that it was all true. "Living in America," he told See Wai, "is living in heaven." But by 1980, after seven years of trying, the Muis were no closer to the visa of their wishes. Their lives, it seemed certain, were to be lived not in heaven but on earth.

*　　*　　*

For 140 years before Let Keung set his sights on America, the Chinese of Taishan County had shared the identical aspiration. Taishan is a mere sliver of China—3,200 square miles in a nation of 3,692,244 square miles, fewer than a million people in a nation of more than a billion—yet it is the ancestral home of half the Chinese-American population. As of 1988, 950,000 people lived in Taishan, but one million Taishanese lived overseas. The 200 residents of Yong He Li claimed 800 relatives in the United States.

The reasons for this remarkable tradition of emigration are complex, muddled by both time and legend, but what is undeniable is that Taishan was, for centuries, peopled beyond its ability to feed itself. The words *tai* and *shan* translate as "plateau" and "mountain," and, in fact, only 40 percent of the county's land is flat and suitable for rice, bananas, and other staples. And although starvation threatened great regions of China, offering other Chinese the same incentive for flight as it did the Taishanese, what made Taishan so singular as a cradle of immigrants was the Ever Waveless Sea, as the locals named the portion of the Pacific Ocean that lapped against their coast.

The Ever Waveless Sea brought with it ships under foreign flags and carried away those same vessels with the first Chinese to dare the three-month, seven-thousand-mile passage to San Francisco. The mere act of leaving China could have cost those pioneers their lives, for under Manchu law anyone caught fleeing without imperial imprimatur was to be decapitated. Those who safely boarded the ships learned that *the Ever Waveless Sea* was a term freighted with irony, for the calm waters off Taishan soon roiled with swells and currents and typhoons, and California greeted the arrivals with institutional bigotry and vigilante violence. A certain number of the early Chinese immigrants, however, survived every danger to mine their fortunes in the Gold Rush of 1849, and their letters back to Taishan spoke of America as *Gum San,* the Gold Mountain. Long after the gold fields were exhausted, long after exclusion laws and coolie labor should have tarnished the appeal of America, *Gum San* retained its luster.

Men like See Wai's uncle formed the "bachelor society" of American Chinatowns, living womanless in dormitories and tenements, laboring in laundries and restaurants and factories, and sending back to China the dollars they would have spent bringing their families across the ocean, had they been permitted like all other immigrants to do so. A total of $14.6 million from overseas relatives flowed into China in 1946 alone, and probably half that came to rest in Taishan. With decades of donations from expatriates, the tiny county paved roads, lit streets, built a railroad, and opened what is still the most selective high school in the region. A new profession arose around the villager who could write letters to American relatives on behalf of illiterate peasants.

Then, for the decade beginning in 1966, the Cultural Revolution swept through Taishan, along with the rest of China. Families were prohibited from accepting the largesse of their overseas relatives. Private farm plots, which produced 25 percent of family income, were abolished, and high agricultural production was deemed proof of "inattention to Chairman Mao's new campaign," as a scholarly study of one Guangdong village noted. Education essentially halted for half a generation. China's vitally important birth control campaign similarly collapsed, creating a population boom during an agricultural bust. When the political whirlwind subsided in the late 1970s with Mao's death and the arrest of the Gang of Four, Taishan reckoned itself no better off than it had been at liberation in 1949. Per capita income averaged about $8.50 a month. Roads and houses crumbled under thirty years of neglect. High tension towers strode across the farm fields, delivering power to households that could not afford what few consumer appliances were being manufactured. In an age of mechanization, agriculture remained the endeavor of humans and animals, and both toiled as beasts.

When China threw wide its doors to the West in the 1980s, an economic revolution transformed Taishan, which was included in one of the special economic zones designed to profit most under free-market policies. Beauty parlors and coffee shops sprung up in the county seat of Taicheng. Private factories and three-story mansions rose along the main roads. Young people of means studied English on weekdays and danced in discos on weekends. It was a remarkable time, a buoyant and hopeful and even dizzying time, but it was a time that arrived too late for Mui See Wai.

*   *   *

The letter came on January 15, 1980. The letter bore the red star of officialdom. Let Keung opened the envelope and looked at the characters and said nothing, for he had never learned to read. He prevailed upon a neighbor to read the letter to him, and the neighbor did, and then the neighbor said the letter was clearly a fake. Let Keung's family was the poorest in all Yong He Li. How could they possibly be going to the Gold Mountain?

But Let Keung's very name meant "determined," and he knew that his patience, his seven years of patience, had been rewarded. Seven days later, he left for Hong Kong, where he could make money for his family's passage to New York. He found work arranging flowers for funeral processions, and he earned more in his first month than he had in the previous year in China. Within six weeks, Let Keung could afford to bring his family to Hong Kong, and so they bade farewell to the village of their ancestors and their gods. The Muis packed what they could carry and parted with the rest, abandoning Let Keung's farm clothes on the bedroom floor, See Wai's baby bonnet in a wicker trunk, and the altar against the cold stone wall. So many villagers were leaving Yong He Li for the United States that the house would remain empty and undisturbed for years to come, the tableau of a family who had vanished in haste and with no intention of returning.

For a boy who had traveled outside Taishan only once before in his life, the twinkling nighttime necklace of Hong Kong was magical and magnificent and frightening beyond words. See Wai clung to Sau Ling beside their mountain of suitcases and waited for his father to rescue them. He gaped at the neon signs and shuddered at the street racket and wondered if a bandit would rob him, for he had been warned about the big, evil city. The Muis spent their first night with relatives, kinship cushioning their shock, but by the next dusk they were on their own, several miles up the Kowloon peninsula from the Hong Kong that tourists plied. The family of six squeezed into a two-room apartment that cost forty-five dollars a month, sharing a kitchen and bathroom with their landlord. Factories lined the streets, four or five or ten to a building, factories that stamped buttons, sewed clothes, cut steel, and retread tires. In one of those anonymous workshops, Sau Ling stitched dresses and in another Let Keung pressed jeans and in a third Fon Wai and May Fong assembled plastic toys, eating enough bitterness to buy six airplane tickets to New York.

As for See Wai, he became a surrogate son to the landlord and his wife, who had only daughters. They fed him lucky candy, presented him with an embroidered pillow, and, most important, secured him a seat in the nearest public school. See Wai needed all the education he could get, for he was ten years old and barely literate in his own language, much less in the English of his new, chosen land.

*   *   *

The Mui family reached New York on July 5, 1980, in the depressingly familiar condition of debt. All the money they had made in Hong Kong, the money that seemed so abundant by the standards of Taishan, had amounted to a pittance in American dollars. In the end, Dap Sing had paid for their airplane tickets, had rented them an apartment, and had arranged factory jobs so they could reimburse him promptly. For all the sights that thrilled See Wai, for all the sports cars and skyscrapers that equaled the villagers' stories, when it came to toil, the new life resembled the old.

Home did not have gold floors and diamond windows. Home was a three-room apartment with falling plaster, cracked walls, and a bathtub in the kitchen. See Wai slept with Fon Wai in a single bunk in a dark, airless bedroom, its sole window covered by wood slats and nailed shut against intruders. The apartment was on the second floor of a six-story brick building on the northern rim of Chinatown and it shivered with the endless din of trucks grinding toward the Williamsburg Bridge. No sooner did the landlord meet the Muis then he raised their rent from $200 to $300 a month. As a Chinese himself, he could size them up by their coarse accents and sun-browned skins as newcomers, peasants, hardly the sort to object. If anything, these farmers owed *him* a favor. Only because the landlord knew Dap Sing had he not charged the Muis the usual $5,000 bribe known as "key money."

See Wai entered P.S. 130 in September 1980, equipped with his parents' advice to dress drably and say little. He was a *sang sau,* "one without experience," and he would do best to listen and obey. But even wordlessly, See Wai unsettled the school, for he was an eleven-year-old with fewer than two years of formal education. Academically, he belonged in the second grade, socially in the sixth. The school compromised by placing him in a fifth-grade class for English as a Second Language, and there he learned the alphabet and the family members and the different types of transportation. He carried with him a small thick book entitled *A New Essential English–Chinese Dictionary,* and he thumbed it until the shine was gone from the jade green cover. With its definitions from "a" to "zoology," with its charts of tenses and conjugations, the book served as See Wai's Rosetta stone.

As it had in China, however, free education exacted a hidden price. Each day after school, See Wai hurried down Canal Street to work beside his parents in a garment factory owned by a cousin and her husband. It was an oppressive place, a single square room with flaking paint and swirling lint and drifts of cardboard cartons and machines whining like a chorus of dental drills. Bent forward on a metal stool, Sau Ling stitched until her eyes burned and her back throbbed, and then she stitched more. Let Keung pressed the finished garments, sheathed them in cellophane, and arranged them on metal racks. It was common to find children in the factory, some simply collecting there because Chinatown had a dire shortage of day care, and many more laboring because on garment factory wages, making the rent was a family-wide campaign. Sau Ling worked seventy-two hours a week, and even with See Wai assisting her for twenty hours, they brought home a total of $200 on the piecework pay scale. Only when his shift ended at 10 P.M. could See Wai begin the normal task of an eleven-year-old, doing his homework.

Gradually, the Muis hardened their hold on America. Let Keung repaid his brother and then pulled himself, Sau Ling, and See Wai out of the garment factory, infuriated at how his cousins, his blood, had abused them. He worked as a cook and then a noodle maker, and with Sau Ling's income from a new factory job, he saved enough money by 1984 to open a sidewalk vegetable stall, his own tiny version of the Chinese-American dream. Through the sixth and seventh grades, See Wai had his afternoons and evenings free for study. He won a school prize for his sketch of a Taishan landscape and wrote simple poems and essays to improve his English. He taped his drawings and writings over the holes in his bedroom wall. Sometimes See Wai dreamed of China, but the dreams were not sentimental; in one, he stumbled upon snakes while hiking through a forest and in another, he returned to Yong He Li to find the village deserted. He was trying to become an American now, and the more the intricacies of language defied him, the more he relied on the external emblems of belonging. On the small portable television in the kitchen, he watched "The Little Rascals." When he posed for his graduation portrait in junior high school, he affected a Beatlesque moptop. At about the same time, he and his sisters took part in an informal ritual of renaming themselves, a common moment of passage for the children of Chinatown. As an older cousin read a list of American names, each of the three Muis chose one. May Fong took Christine; So Fong selected Cindy; and, finally, See Wai, "Calm Famous," set aside the brand of his birth for the prosaic alias of Andy.

*   *   *

The Chinatown that was home to See Wai and hundreds of other Seward Park students contradicted not only the Chinese vision of *Gum San* but the American image of an ethnic idyll, peopled by industrious parents and their scholarly children. Industry and scholarship certainly abounded in Chinatown, but so did youth gangs, sweatshops, and tuberculosis. The stereotype of Chinese Americans, or more broadly Asian Americans, as the "model minority" left little room for the realities of life in New York's fastest-growing ghetto.

To conceive of the seismic changes in Chinatown, one must understand that as recently as 1960, some city planners were predicting the neighborhood's demise and suggesting its demolition in an "urban renewal" scheme. Chinatown, after all, still occupied the same six-block zone it had since the late 1800s, and its population in all those years had never exceeded 15,000. Separated from their families by exclusion laws, heartsick in their "bachelor society," Chinese immigrants from 1909 until 1943 departed the United States in twice the numbers they entered. "War Bride" legislation permitted more women to enter the country, but not nearly enough to balance a male-female ratio that had at times topped thirty to one.

But with the 1965 immigration reforms, Chinatown was reborn, its population booming to 150,000 in one generation, and the neighborhood itself swelling from its six-block core to encompass forty blocks of Lower Manhattan, from the Brooklyn Bridge in the southeast to SoHo in the northwest. The vestiges of "bachelor society" vanished amid an explosion of families, and the traditional Taishanese dominance was diluted with the arrival of immigrants from Hong Kong, Taiwan, all corners of the People's Republic, and such way stations as Canada, Cuba, Indonesia, and Jamaica. Fissures divided speakers of Mandarin and speakers of Cantonese, followers of communism and followers of nationalism, factory owners and factory workers, while Chinatown's various newspapers argued "every point of view from the Gang of Four to the restoration of the Manchu Dynasty," as Professor James Shenton of Columbia University once observed.

The most unifying factor in Chinatown was, unfortunately, its subsistence economy. Despite such prominent Chinese-American successes as the architect I. M. Pei and the computer executive An Wang, the new immigrants typically had more in common with Let Keung and Sau Ling. The 1980 census found that 55 percent of New York's Chinese spoke no English and 71 percent had not completed high school. Six of every ten families staked their lives on two industries, food and textiles. A waiter generally earned $200 a month in base pay, predicated on a sixty-hour week without overtime, medical care, or job security, and a seamstress could expect to bring home $500 a month for similar hours and similar conditions, her lot softened only by a union health care plan. Even the youngest girls referred to themselves as *yee chong ah mo,* "garment factory old woman."

Chinatown's poverty coexisted with Chinatown's plenty, for at the same time that peasants were thronging into one small, discrete sector of Manhattan, desperate for any bed and any job, Asian investors fleeing the forthcoming Communist assumption of Hong Kong were sowing their millions in the same soil. Only two banks served Chinatown in 1940, but there was business enough for twenty-seven in 1986, and they tallied assets above $2 billion. The money made Chinatown, if not the golden mountain, then at least the golden ghetto, a study in staggering contrasts, with high-tech shopping arcades rising beside turn-of-the-century tenements where tuberculosis raged at almost twice the national rate. While the waiters and seamstresses saved toward opening their own small restaurant or factory, the neighborhood's soaring rents, narrow profits, and vicious competition felled such businesses at the rate of two a week. The days of buying a dream for $25,000 were over in Chinatown.

The single uncomplicated success of Chinatown, it appeared, was its youth. In 1985, when Asian-American children made up but 5.5 percent of the city's public school populace, they accounted for about 30 percent of the students in the most selective academic high schools—Bronx Science, Brooklyn Tech, and Stuyvesant. From there, the immigrants marched off to Harvard, the Massachusetts Institute of Technology, and the University of Chicago, brandishing 1,400-point scores on the Scholastic Achievement Test and Westinghouse Talent Search plaques. The very personification of the Asian-American superstudent was a boy named Chi Luu, an ethnic Chinese who escaped Vietnam by boat, reached New York in his teens, and graduated from City College in 1984 as the valedictorian. The explanation of such achievements struck many as simple: Chinese culture venerated scholarship, as it had since Confucius, and children of superior character excelled, as they always had in America.

All the accolades were grounded in truth, but there was more than one truth at work in the Chinese-American experience. A poll of Chinese immigrant children conducted by author and academic Betty Lee Sung in 1987 found that while three-quarters believed they could succeed in America if they tried, an almost comparable majority said they were *not* better off in this country. The dichotomy derived, in part, from the shifting nature of Chinese immigrants. Students like See Wai, rural peasants unschooled in English and barely literate in their own tongue, were supplanting the urban, educated elite of Hong Kong and Taiwan in New York's classrooms. Nearly half the pupils in See Wai's elementary school required bilingual courses, and a 1984 study found that only 28 percent of the elementary school pupils in Chinatown were reading at grade level, compared to 55 percent of their peers citywide. One-third of the neighborhood's teenagers worked at least twenty hours a week. The combination of the need to learn a bewildering new language and to contribute to the family coffers drove the failure and dropout rates for Chinese-American children steadily higher. And whenever a student grew disaffected, a youth gang stood ready to recruit him for its protection and extortion rackets and to pay him as much in a week as his father made in a month. The promising candidate who demurred at gang membership often had a change of heart after being beaten by his suitors.

The degree to which many Chinese-American students surmounted the obstacles and mastered their schoolwork reflected cultural factors, but not necessarily those most widely assumed. The process of learning the 1,000 ideograms required for basic literacy in their own language heightened the ability of Chinese immigrants to memorize material. Their particular skill in science and mathematics had much to do with the limited role English plays in quantitative subjects. The Chinese-American affinity for such courses, and at Seward Park for the business curriculum as well, gave lie to the legend of Confucian scholarship. The major reason the ancient Chinese hurled themselves into study for the imperial examinations, the major reason their ancestors in New York crammed for tests in chemistry and computer science, was that achievement promised employment and employment promised upward mobility. What the Chinese immigrants shared with the Jewish immigrants who had once slept in the same tenements and sat in the same schoolrooms and slaved in the same sweatshops was not a religious belief in Education, the god on the wall of the Seward Park auditorium. What they shared was the pragmatic judgment of a landless people with a diasporic past that one could survive best by one's wits, for they were the single possession no despot could plunder.

*   *   *

See Wai wanted to avoid Seward Park High School. His friends had told him, "It's all ESL, low grades on exams, lots of gangsters." His friends scared him, but they did not completely sway him. Then See Wai set eyes on the annex for the first time—"so old, so boring"—and made his decision. He would apply to Brooklyn Tech. He failed the admissions examination for Brooklyn Tech on his first try, and never got a second chance because his subway stalled on the way to the test. He reluctantly remanded himself to Seward Park in September 1985.

It was a painful year. The Mui family had bought a small home in the Flushing section of Queens, and See Wai was commuting more than two hours a day. When he gave a wrong answer in class, the other kids laughed at his error; when he gave the right answer, they laughed at his accent. He withdrew into himself, offering little and expecting less, and few teachers bothered to engage him because everyone knew how timid those Chinese were. See Wai felt accepted only in his Chinese course and gravitated toward the comfort of his own tongue, reading and writing Mandarin and falling further behind in English. Free hours were a rarity in any case. Let Keung had abandoned his vegetable stall after six months, when his landlord raised the monthly rent from $1,000 to $1,400 for a refrigerator and patch of pavement. Now he was back in the noodle factory on the graveyard shift and was having trouble making the mortgage payments in Flushing. So See Wai returned to work twenty hours a week, first as a foot messenger, then as a bus boy, and finally as a cook, never earning more than $3.45 an hour. "Just 'Patience, patience,' like Confucius say," he recalls. "Until you explode."

See Wai's filial duties only started with work. He served, in many ways, as his parents' portal to the outside world, writing their letters to relatives in China, addressing their Christmas cards to friends in New York, translating the words of cashiers and traffic cops. When a utility bill claimed the Muis owed $800, See Wai battled the company down to the correct figure of $300. As limited as his English was, it was the most fluent in the family. He felt pride, he felt strain, and he felt things he had no words to express. Some Sundays he rode the subway to Rockaway, a spit of sand jutting into the Atlantic, and he fished from a pier and had time to think. He thought of his father, skin coated with noodle flour, asleep on his feet when he walked through the door, and he thought of his mother, hands gnarled from sewing, pieces piled beside her even at home. He wondered when the struggle would cease. Sometimes he blamed America, where "you have to be talented *and* sneaky," and sometimes he blamed himself. He could not learn English fast enough, he could not earn grades high enough, and he could not imagine going away to college and leaving his parents to fend for themselves. When he saw the bums asleep on the subway, when he saw the beggars tottering through traffic, he saw a fate he feared was his own.

Yet there remained in See Wai an unconquered spirit, and it led him to a class called Arguing Issues, a most unlikely destination, indeed. Denise Simone, the College Discovery coordinator, had designed the public-speaking course, and of the 300 students she had taught over the years, no more than a half-dozen had been Chinese. Even now, in See Wai's junior year, neither she nor Hal Pockriss had noticed much that was distinctive about him, much that would suggest why he would defy the odds. His name was Andy and he looked like a teddy bear and he kept company with a few short, silent Chinese boys, the practical sort who wanted to major in business. For the first three weeks, See Wai contributed little, for the mocking laughs he had endured at the annex still sounded in his memory. Gradually, he risked a comment or two, and eventually it came time for the final exam, a one-on-one debate judged by the class. Denise paired See Wai against a girl, similarly soft spoken and foreign born, and assigned them the topic of gun control. Then she sat back in shock as the teddy bear dismembered the girl more in the manner of a grizzly. One of the Hispanic students turned to Denise and uttered admiringly, "That *Chino,* man, what happened to *him?*"

No one was quite sure, but the effects were obvious. See Wai had Lavinia Rausch for English the next term, and she ordered him out of class one day for talking during her lesson. She had been speaking too swiftly for him to follow, so he had asked a classmate to decipher her words, and he felt shameful enough to be lost without being punished, as well. When he tried to explain, Rausch cut him off. So See Wai began skipping her class, and his guidance counselor, Hal Pockriss, summoned him for a conference. He wasn't cutting, See Wai insisted. He had been wronged and he had declared a boycott and he would not return without an apology, the consequences be damned. Officially, Hal could not condone the absences, whatever See Wai called them, but privately he applauded the boy's spunk.

If only spunk alone sufficed. See Wai's average stood in the seventies, and he had yet to pass the Regents Competency Test in writing, which was required for graduation. In his bedroom at night, he wrote essays to inspire himself, essays with titles like "Facing the Problem," "Chance of a Lifetime," and "Hope is the Lighthouse of the Heart." He remembered a fable he had heard as a child in China: A young man wishes to apprentice himself to a master carpenter and travels many *li* to the master's workshop, only to be turned away. He pleads for instruction and again is dismissed. But he refuses to leave, and the master carpenter consents to teach the young man his craft, continuing the lessons until the apprentice himself becomes a master. The parable provided solace, but not a solution. See Wai wrote and thought in Chinese, and that was the problem. His interests were history and literature, not mathematics and science, so he could not hide his flawed English behind formulas and equations. He agonized over English, bending syllables like soft wire and handling idioms like hot coals. He circled certain words in his dictionary and introduced them into class discussion, even if it took three tries to transform *pozmonus* into *parsimonious*. When he went to the public library in Chinatown, he forced himself clear of the Chinese-language stacks and withdrew books in English, reading their most mystifying passages ten or twenty times until he thought he understood. See Wai's ally was his sister So Fong, the youngest child in the family and the most easily adapted to English. After she noticed See Wai reading *The Pearl* for a Seward Park assignment, she bought him an armload of John Steinbeck paperbacks, hoping to wean him from the Chinese novels he favored.

See Wai placed the books in his bedroom, on a shelf beneath a photograph of Hong Kong and a poster of Don Mattingly, the star first baseman of the New York Yankees. It was through the Yankees, appropriately enough, that See Wai finally found acceptance as an American. The same classmates who once snickered at his accent now conferred with him on the condition of the Yankee bullpen. When Bruce Baskind taught a lesson on methods of Americanization, See Wai offered his answer unprompted: "Baseball." He might have mentioned cars, too, because he was taking driver's education. See Wai had a bit of a dilemma in that his taste for speed exceeded his ability to control it, and during one lesson he nearly ran down a school crossing guard, who proceeded to curse him in Spanish. The driving teacher, a protective fellow, insulted the guard first and only then turned to his student and shouted, "See Wai, what the fuck are you doing?" Then they laughed and turned the corner and when they pulled alongside Seward Park at the end of class, See Wai thanked his teacher and told him what any New York teenager would have: "That was *fresh*."

The more secure See Wai felt as an American, the more passionate he grew about reclaiming his past. There were not many pieces to which he could cling, so far from his village, across the Ever Waveless Sea, but there was the matter of names. All the school knew him as Andy, and some people pronounced it as if calling a cute pet. So back in September, on his first day in English 7, he had taken his Delaney card and written "See Wai." It was the only name by which Jessica Siegel would know him.

*   *   *

On a Friday afternoon, a few weeks after the *Walden* lesson, See Wai sits in the English office with Jessica. She has come to depend on his outspoken nature in class, and she has sensed enough of his humanity to recommend him for the Pathfinders program at University Settlement. This is their most private discussion yet, and See Wai is plainly ill at ease. He sits only inches from Jessica, but his eyes fix straight ahead on a cabinet and his fingers toy with the zipper of his book bag.

"So where were you thinking about going to college?" she asks.

"John Jay. Or Stony Brook. I don't want to go away from home."

"Stony Brook *is* away," Jessica says.

"But not far. I can come home."

"You're right," she says, nodding. "It's about two hours. You can take the train." Stony Brook, though, specializes in sciences. It's the wrong place for See Wai, Jessica is certain. She has her own plan in mind. "You know," she resumes innocently, "New Paltz is about two hours by bus."

"Bus? You mean I can live there?"

"They have dormitories."

"Dormitories," See Wai says. "Yes."

Jessica briefly explains the state's Educational Opportunity Program, under which students from poor households can be admitted to New York colleges with grades that otherwise would be too low. The program's premise is that the marks do not reflect the student's true intelligence because in low-income families, children must work in the after-school hours when more affluent peers can study. From what Jessica recalls of See Wai's autobiography, he is the ideal EOP applicant. But she needs to be certain he qualifies.

"How much does your family make?"

"Ten thousand."

"How many people?"

"Six."

"So," she says, making a note, "financial aid is no problem."

"No problem," See Wai repeats softly.

"I know you're worried about your average, See Wai. What is it?"

His eyes trace the edge of the file cabinet down to the linoleum tile.

"Not so good. Seventy-seven."

"Seventy-seven!" Jessica shouts. See Wai dips his head, assuming Jessica is incredulous, when in fact she is delirious. She got Sammy Ryan and Vinnie Mickles and their 69 averages into New Paltz. "You're practically ready for Harvard!"

Although they laugh, the eyes he raises to hers are plaintive.

"I got a lot of thinking," he says. "Questions and answers." He pauses. "But people say too much thinking is crazy."

"What's crazy about thinking?"

"People say, 'You're a wimp.'"

"A wimp? What do they think you ought to be doing? Lifting weights?"

"Having a party."

Jessica straightens in her chair, looses a heavy sigh.

"It's important to have a party sometimes, See Wai. But you're the kind of person who'll really do well in college. You're an independent thinker. You're stimulated by ideas. You're not afraid to ask questions. I have this feeling, boom, you're going to blossom in college. You'll do just fine." She pauses. "You're doing great in my class." A thought stops her again. "How're you doing in your others?"

"Not bad," he says. "But my mind works in Chinese. Sometimes I can't think of the words in English."

One of Jessica's *Seward World* photographers enters the office to drop off an envelope of finished prints. See Wai averts his eyes, and his limbs almost visibly contract. Only after the photographer leaves does he resume form and speech.

"I need to be better with English. I need to read more books in English. I'm lazy."

"Of course, it'd be good to read more," Jessica says, laying one arm atop her desk. "But you also need a break. It's OK to watch TV sometimes."

"I don't watch TV."

"What do you do?"

"I write poetry and compositions." His eyes glisten for a second, then his gaze goes opaque. "Sometimes I feel like I'm writing baby stuff."

"Well, I can tell you like writing by the way you write," Jessica says. "And if you want help with your college applications, I can help you."

"Thank you, Miss Siegel."

"But I think you'll do fine."

She inhales and thinks, and in that moment See Wai hoists his book bag and rises to leave. He is walking out the office door when she says, more to herself than to him, "See Wai, you're amazing."

9

Liquid Paper

WHEN SHE RETURNS to the English office from the Lower East Side class, Jessica Siegel does not take her customary chair. Instead she settles heavily on the desk and drops her feet onto the seat, heels striking hardwood. She reaches to her mail slot and begins opening letters, ripping a ragged wound across each envelope. She stops after four or five, strewing the papers in the arc of an open fan, and plunges her chin deeply into her palm. Curling a few fingers over her bottom lip, she stares at the wall, four feet straight ahead.

Bruce Baskind leans against the portal and waits for a safe moment to approach.

"I think that was a great lesson," he says.

"I think it was a shit lesson."

"Jessica, it was great," Bruce insists. He shuffles his feet a bit in unease. "The kids were shit today."

"Bruce, as you always say, you can't blame the kids."

Her disgust hangs in the air. Bruce fidgets again, rubs together his hands.

"C'mon," he says, "let's get lunch. Get outta here for awhile. We can talk about this some other time."

"I don't want to talk about it."

Bruce backs out of the doorway and retreats down the hall. Jessica remains sitting, sphinxlike on the desk, only her thumb and forefinger moving, one assaulting the other, grating. She does not want to talk about it. She cannot help but think about it. After all these years, she tells herself, it is still no fun to bomb.

She could feel herself out of rhythm this morning, feel her synapses misfiring like old spark plugs. She managed to muddle through two sections of English 7, but in the Lower East Side class, her dejection caught up with her. She had barely begun her lesson when a noisy shoving match in the hallway interrupted. Then she found that, all too typically, only three or four students had bothered reading the two pages of homework. She had given so many pop quizzes already in the term that the prospect of another zero in the grade book terrified no one, so she had no choice but to wait ten minutes while everyone did the assignment, and then to plod through the material banality by banality. As she was asking a question, Bruce saw a boy in the middle row, dozing.

"What's the matter with you, Peter?" he shouted, interrupting the lesson and directing all attention to the startled student.

"I'm bored."

"You know something? You wanna know a secret? You're not the most exciting person who ever lived." The class hooted. "You reap what you sow. You take out what you put in. An interesting person wouldn't be bored."

Now Peter had been dared. Bruce had "dissed" him, as Seward Park students put it, shown disrespect. The code of conduct required that the boy strike back or lose face.

"Tellin' me you're not bored?" he challenged Bruce.

"No."

Peter smirked, and to ensure that everyone saw, he swiveled his head broadly as a harbor beacon. Then he tilted his face down toward the desktop, until it lay flat against his unopened notebook.

"Peter," Jessica said, "sit up."

In affected increments, he complied. But at the next pause in Jessica's lesson, he unleashed an audible, aggressive yawn. And in that instant, all Jessica's experience counted for nothing. The muscles in her face went slack, as if she had been told of the death of someone dear. Her cheeks reddened. Her eyes watered. And the bell rang before she could even attempt to rally.

What was it that had unhinged her so? Jessica had caught students sleeping in her classes before, and she had caught them reading newspapers and passing love notes and finishing biology homework, unashamed in their affronts. The process had required years, but she had learned how to "snap" on them, making humor her most effective discipline. And she thought she had learned not to take juvenile defiance so personally.

Cerebrally, intellectually, Jessica could remind herself of the miserable odds she faced in an unselective, overcrowded, neighborhood school. Jessica the evangelist preached dreams and horizons, a profession instead of a trade, college instead of the military; but Jessica the educator read the tests and homework and too often saw skills sufficient only for bicycle messengers and short-order cooks. Just the other day, she asked a girl in the Lower East Side class, one of the better students, to read aloud. She found herself shuddering as the girl stumbled on words as simple as "crooked," "content," and "hamlet," shuddering not only for that girl in that moment, but for the many, many similar instances.

Yet Jessica had understood all those problems from the beginning, accepted them as the givens. What troubled her more deeply, and more often, was watching children sink to the occasion. Sure, lots of teachers in lots of schools hollered themselves hoarse pestering kids about doing homework and getting to class on time. Sure, students everywhere extracted a singular delight from submitting the same book report on *Animal Farm* to as many English teachers as possible. But at Seward Park, Jessica saw diseases more debilitating than sloth or deceit—an acceptance of inadequacy, a passive pitch into failure. On the first day of every term, she explains the school rule that five unexcused absences in a marking period guarantees a failing grade, and still cutting is a plague. If the rationale isn't warm weather, it's cold weather; if it's not the first period, it's the last period; if it's not Monday, it's Friday. The same faces return to her class two or three terms in a row, smiling faces, faces of houseguests who do not realize they have overstayed their invitation.

And many of those who do not fail settle for such a meager measure of success. It is rare for a student to argue about a grade with Jessica, the way students at elite high schools routinely dicker over the difference between an 88 and a 91. When Jessica returns tests, the question she hears classmates asking one another is not, "What'd you get?" but "Did you pass?" Passing is sufficient; passing is enough. When Jessica upbraided a boy in English 7 for missing an assignment, he quite candidly answered, "Today's not my homework day. I do homework every Wednesday." He had calculated that by turning in homework one day of every five he could just skid through the obstacle course, and since he was a senior, his hypothesis had been proved by empirical testing. A few years ago, Ben Dachs developed a series of lessons entitled "Essays Made Easy" to help his teachers improve their students' expository writing skills. The lessons imparted a basic outline for a four-paragraph essay—a thesis, two supporting examples, and a conclusion. The ironic result was that Seward Park students seized on the lessons as proof that an essay *should be no longer* than four paragraphs.

What have these students learned? What have they mastered? They have learned the uses of image. They have mastered mirrors. Who has taught them? In part, their teachers. They understand from experience that if you show up (most of the time), hand in homework (every so often), and keep quiet (this is paramount), you will receive your 65 and be permitted to shuffle on toward a diploma and a mortarboard. Appearance is all. Sometimes Bruce Baskind will deliberately write notes on the blackboard that contradict the material in his lesson, waiting for someone to rise in protest, and too often, the class will obediently record the errata. But let Bruce or Jessica misspell a word and listen to the watchdogs bay. "How about the content?" Jessica pled one time. She received only silence in response. It was a foolish question because any student knows that what is important is not comprehending the material; what is important is taking notes so the teacher can see you taking notes; what is important is less being a student than resembling one. The kids call the technique "brain checking," the mental equivalent of racking a coat when you enter a restaurant. For Jessica, the prevailing metaphor is Liquid Paper. So many Seward Park students carry Liquid Paper that a visitor might think he or she had wandered by mistake into the sort of secretarial academy that advertises in matchbooks. The gifted carry Liquid Paper; the dim carry Liquid Paper; the gang members carry Liquid Paper, stowing it along with their beepers and knives. Jessica hands out a test. It contains two essay questions, plenty of work for a forty-minute period. She looks across the room, sees two or three kids applying Liquid Paper to their prose as gingerly as debutantes painting their nails.

"Just cross out!" she shouts.

"But I want it to be neat," comes the answer.

"I don't care! I'm interested in your ideas."

How many times can you insist before you bore even yourself? A good teacher doesn't fall out of bed one morning as a burned-out case. A good teacher is ground down to mediocrity over weeks and months and years, and a good teacher who tries to resist learns that the millstone is an implacable adversary. But when the time comes to assign blame, Jessica cannot point the accusing finger. When a class turns churlish, as it did this morning, Bruce decries the system and the students. Jessica judges only herself.

She left the English office—too many inquiring eyes—and has come to hide in the auditorium. Two dozen tardy students linger in the rear rows, waiting for the sixth-period bell. Jessica slumps in Row E, surrounded by empty seats, tears sliding down her cheeks. Sydney Sidner, Bruce's assistant in the drama class, trots down the aisle to retrieve a scarf she left on the stage. She spots Jessica, begins to say hello, fixes on the red eyes and the rolling tears, and shrinks away, embarrassed and bewildered.

"When I teach, I need a script," Jessica had told me earlier. "I can ad lib if I have a script. I can't do it without one. I get nervous. I forget where I'm going. My lesson plan today was not great. I just didn't have the energy to riff off of it, to try to joke and open up the kids. And so it was like bomb after bomb after bomb. A comedian bombing continuously. Sometimes you can be like Johnny Carson, laugh about it. 'Boy, am I bombing!' 'What's with everyone today? You coming off a hard night?' It's a Pirandello way of commenting on the action—'This *is* a play, you know.' Rather than let the ball hit the ground, you catch it and send it off in another direction. And *that's* rhythm. That's real rhythm. If you don't have enough energy or you're not quick on your feet, you can't come through. You can't catch the ball.

"Obviously, you develop a certain amount of thick skin, to let the typical teenage stuff about 'It's boring' wash off you. But, ultimately, your ego is on the line. Your identity is on the line. What do I do for a living? I'm a teacher. And so if you get negativism or disinterest or hostility from the class, then that's really a blow. That's a comment on my whole being. I don't know if I'm more vulnerable than other people, but I get my self-worth from this job. And if I'm bombing, then I criticize myself. Am I too loose? Am I too disorganized? Am I pushing myself hard enough? Have I done the same lessons so many times that I'm stale? There are teachers who never do the same lesson two terms in a row. There are teachers who are constantly trying new things, being innovative." She lifted her brows then. "What can I say? I'm tired."

* * *

She is tired, but everyone is tired. The long trek to Christmas is almost finished, and the nearer the caravan draws to the oasis, the more onerous seems each day's march. Jessica's colleagues will feast and toast and revel and return in January at least somewhat renewed. But her exhaustion exceeds the physical; it is a condition of the spirit. She gives so much; she gives too much; she gives as she has given since childhood, compulsively, relentlessly, and at her own expense, until her soul is windblown topsoil, a spent strip mine. Yet there is something more, something specific to this morning, something specific to herself and Bruce Baskind, who for many years had been the finest of friends at Seward Park.

She could conjure the moment in 1980 when she had first seen Bruce, robust and bearded, standing in a stairwell wearing jeans, a flannel shirt, and a leather vest. The gold band on his left hand precluded anything beyond friendship, but within that boundary, they filled all the spaces. Bruce was substituting then to earn tuition money for his doctoral studies, and Jessica was about to be hurled by coincidence into her inauguration as a teacher. From Bruce's attire alone, Jessica could tell he was an ally, flaunting the same counterculture credentials she was then trying to obscure. From the earliest chats, Bruce could tell she was a true believer, in ghetto children and in him. He considered himself a misfit by nature and a dissident by choice, and his cool reception by the history department had done nothing to alter his opinion. In Jessica, he found someone at last who did not condescend to his questions with the weary refrain, "When you're a regular teacher, you'll understand." She shared ideas about curriculum and she sat beside him at the school play; she invited him and his wife to a party at her apartment, and when they turned her down in shyness, he saw that she was genuinely hurt.

The next year Bruce was a fleeting presence, spending most of his time wrestling with his dissertation, still intending to make his life at the collegiate lectern. But the scholar's road proved slow and lonely, and at its end Bruce saw few prospects. He returned to Seward Park in September 1983, ostensibly to replenish his purse, actually to become consumed by the challenges of a slum school. "The more obvious it became that I wanted to teach at Seward," he would say later, "the more obvious it was that Jessica was someone important to be next to."

They ate lunch many days at the Grand Street Dairy, a kosher restaurant fifty feet from the school, and talked often of their common interest in ethnic studies and their mutual frustration with the forced separation between courses in history and literature. "Like satellites," Bruce would grouse. "Like satellites." Over one particular cup of coffee, inspiration struck. They would create a class together and teach it in tandem—a course that would explore the ethnic identities of the Lower East Side from the precolonial Indians to the present-day Hispanics and Chinese. Jessica always looked back on that encounter as an old movie flickering in black and white, as Judy Garland and Mickey Rooney shouting excitedly, "Why don't we do the show right here in the garage!"

Ben Dachs and Noel Kriftcher endorsed the idea, and New York University granted Bruce and Jessica $1,000 for research. They spent the summer of 1983 combing through college libraries, specialty collections, community archives, and small-press book fairs, and they emerged on Labor Day with an entire curriculum. For the final project, each student was required to produce the oral history of a parent or elder, and each June these testimonies were typed, duplicated, and bound under the title, *Our Lives, Our Stories, Our Neighborhood*. Few things made Jessica feel prouder, of her students and of her profession.

For all their collaboration, however, Jessica often felt like a student of Bruce's, especially when it came to means. Bruce was so loose, tossing chalk at soporific students, spinning lessons from blues songs and sepia photographs, spouting racial stereotypes the better to knock them down. It was history as taught by Lenny Bruce, and if Jessica could not reinvent herself as a stand-up comic, then she could surely evolve into a superior second banana.

Maybe that was part of why she and Bruce had begun to drift apart. How could Jessica—the very word troubled her—compete? Lenny Bruce always adored jazz, and there was much of the jazz musician in Bruce. Bruce could improvise. He could perform. Dared by the spotlight, he thrived like a natural. Jessica was more akin to the ultimate technician or the ultimate fan, sitting up late with Charlie Parker records, transcribing solos with the turntable slowed to sixteen, practicing and slaving over each arpeggio, finally mounting the bandstand on open-mike night, only to go dumb when the pianist changed key. Perhaps Bruce's native talents disguised substantial technique, and perhaps even Charlie Parker once scuttled offstage ahead of a well-aimed cymbal. All Jessica knew was how she felt.

And the feeling was not all of it. Part of the tension was political.

Bruce assailed "The System," outside Seward Park and within, while Jessica busied herself with the classrooms at hand. Part of the tension was pedagogical. Bruce was striving toward education without authority, with the drama course as his laboratory, while Jessica counted herself content to push pupils from behind. Part of the tension was style. As devoted as Bruce was to his students inside school, he protected from them the private life that Jessica surrendered. One day last year, coming upon Jessica surrounded by pupils, this one soliciting a college recommendation letter, that one delivering a *Seward World* article, a third asking advice on writing essays, Bruce had first called her "Saint Jessica." As he repeated the nickname in the succeeding months, it sounded a variety of chords, occasionally affectionate, often punitive. "Saint Jessica" was no joke to its inspiration.

The differences dividing Bruce and Jessica might not have told had they not shared the Lower East Side class, particularly during this term, with enrollment low and enthusiasm absent. Professionals always, Mickey and Judy for public consumption, Bruce and Jessica put on a good show, stirring discussion at silent times, swapping the badges of good cop and bad. And they socialized a bit, eating hamburgers in SoHo, treating former students to a Robert Cray concert, celebrating Jessica's birthday with silly hats and homemade gumbo. But mostly, they separated after class, and even inside their common room, a certain polite distance could be observed. They resembled a divorced couple who are forced by finance to continue inhabiting their marital rooms and become ever more estranged for the unwanted intimacy.

*   *   *

The agenda for the English Department meeting contains twenty-one items, but the focus of all this day's attention is the fourth, Teachers' Choice. Teachers' Choice is a new program begun by the Board of Education at the behest of the United Federation of Teachers. Instead of a school's administration ordering supplies, the traditional arrangement, each teacher now is alloted $40 per class to spend on materials. The spectrum of selections fills two entire catalogues, ranging from trombone mouthpieces to spermatozoa slides, from claves to coffeepots, and from hacksaw blades to silica sand to the more mundane paper, chalk, and seating charts.

The union has depicted the adoption of Teachers' Choice as a triumph of "teacher empowerment," its current rallying cry. In fact, by letting every individual submit a wish list, by removing central supervision, the program threatens to leave schools without enough paper to last the year or to create a chaos of hoarding and rationing like something out of postwar Vienna. The faculty at Seward Park already has agreed to set aside $14,000 of the school's $39,870 in Teachers' Choice funds for paper. The remaining $25,870 is being spent department by department. For certain departments, like science and fine arts, the catalogues offer specific equipment for specific needs; but in the English department, among others, the subject does not dictate an obvious choice, and so that choice amounts to a statement of the department's educational philosophy, an answer in dollars and cents to the question, "What is important?"

For weeks, the battle lines have been forming. The surface of life in the English office has remained entirely civil, but the undercurrent has had about it something secretive, even conspiratorial. Conversations have stopped or shifted direction, depending on who has entered the room. Telephone calls to the annex have transpired furtively, in whispers.

One faction in the department compiled a $2,169 order for four video cassette recorders; two televisions; two television carts; and, as if in a concession to the antiquated notion of written communication, one electric typewriter. The department already had one VCR and one television, but, so the reasoning went, these appliances could not meet the demands of thirty English teachers. The question of why teachers of English would rely so heavily on a visual medium was never broached. This faction's most persuasive argument was its leadership. One general was Judy Goldman, a reading teacher who served as the UFT chapter chairwoman at Seward Park and, as such, wielded more power in school than anyone except the principal. The other general was Emma Jon, the interim department chairwoman, whose permanent appointment rested, in part, on not antagonizing the union.

As far as Jessica could tell, the second faction consisted of herself. She was on a crusade for a copying machine, a crusade of both selfish and altruistic ends, and she had found one for $3,000, within the department's means. The handful of copying machines in Seward Park labored for the central administration, and a teacher could use them only with special permission or, in Jessica's case, the connivance of a friendly secretary. Without regular access to this standard piece of modern office equipment, a teacher had only three choices in developing curriculum—relying on texts already in stock, typing material on rexos, or paying for high-quality duplication out of pocket. Jessica had wearied of them all. Depending on the existing stock guaranteed the repetition of material from other classes. Using rexos allowed flexibility but wasted hours. Every time Jessica taught her lesson on Equiano, for instance, she had to type two 8½-by-14-inch stencils and print seventy copies of each on the rexo machine. And it was a blessed day when that contraption could turn out seventy copies of passing legibility. As for the third option, it was simply not viable on a teacher's income. Jessica had decided a few months ago to add August Wilson's drama *Fences* to her English 7 course and asked Emma if the school could buy seventy copies of the published playscript for a total of about $425. The answer was no because money was tight, and so Jessica paid a copy shop to clone seventy playscripts from the one she already owned. The price came to $79.67, one day's take-home pay almost to the penny. And if Jessica could tolerate such an expense only rarely, then her colleagues with families and mortgages could not even conceive of it. A fellow English teacher, Rick Rowley, had the sensible idea of spending his Teachers' Choice money on copies of *Julius Caesar* and *Inherit the Wind,* so he could teach both plays. Then he discovered that amid the solar-powered calculators, electric pencil sharpeners, and Christmas wrapping foil, the Teachers' Choice catalogues included not one piece of literature.

Jessica's campaign was not simply for a copying machine, it was against more televisions and VCRs, for she saw in her classes not minds in need of more visual stimulation but minds stunted by a surfeit of it. When she collected book reports each term, she invariably uncovered several cribbed off celluloid. There had been an especially telling moment in the English office a few weeks earlier, when Harriet Stein was running a video cassette while one of Jessica's students, Francisco Ramirez, was taking a makeup test. Francisco heard British accents and asked Harriet what she was watching; she told him it was *Macbeth.* "We had to do that play the *hard* way," he remarked without irony. "We had to *read* it." Harriet was, in fact, using the film to augment reading assignments, but, as Francisco's presumption indicated, Seward Park did not lack for teachers who were ready to employ an electronic baby-sitter. In the recent past, one teacher had shown so many movies that he was nicknamed "RKO."

The day's debate, though, promised to tread on more than educational ground. Judy Goldman, hearing of Jessica's proposal, had already been warning teachers that the UFT opposed purchasing copiers this year because maintenance was not covered in their cost. So Jessica found herself taking on the union, and that was a daunting task. She could recite by memory the specifications of her favorite copier and she had gathered estimates for service, but every time she argued her cause, it seemed, her listener would reply, "Well, Judy says . . ."

The UFT did not exactly run the city school system, but the system could not function without the union's assent; in microcosm, the same held true for each individual school. Fewer than thirty years after first gaining collective bargaining rights, the UFT boasted 93,000 members and a $36 million annual budget. It spent about $700,000 yearly on legislative elections, guaranteeing it a powerful voice in Albany, and another $150,000 on local school board contests in New York. Candidates who were endorsed and aided by the union held 94 percent of the seats in the city's thirty-two community school districts. Between the language of the contract and legal assistance, the union protected its classroom constituency so fiercely that from April 1979 to September 1988, only 31 tenured teachers from a work force of about 60,000 were fired.

Yet there was persistent criticism from teachers themselves, especially younger teachers, that the union did not speak on their behalf. Entering the 1987–88 academic year, the UFT had successfully pressed for a new transfer plan allowing any tenured teacher to dislodge an untenured colleague teaching the same subject in a different school. This system provided a disincentive for principals and department chairs to train their new teachers, their Harriet Steins, whom they might lose anyway, and it threatened to funnel the greenest conscripts into the most treacherous and demanding schools, worsening an already appalling attrition rate. Even teachers who endorsed union policy often found its manner wanting. When the UFT in September 1987 signed its new contract with the Board of Education, which featured a top salary of $50,000, a social studies teacher from Seward Park went to union headquarters to request a copy of the document. He recounted what happened next: "First they tell me, 'We don't have a copy.' Then it's, 'No, we couldn't give you one if we had it.' It was like, 'Get out of here, man!' I went home and told my wife, 'This is like dealing with the Board of Ed.' And she said, 'I think they send them to the same school for bureaucrats.'"

Within Seward Park, one heard similar mutterings. One common complaint was that Judy Goldman, the woman charged with representing the faculty's interests, spent fewer than ninety minutes a day in the classroom. She was relieved from one class each term as chapter chairwoman, under the terms of the union contract, and relieved from two others as the school's reading coordinator. Those dispensations left her to teach two sections of reading, in which homework was generally minimal and enrollment was limited to twenty by federal regulation. Judy Goldman, then, saw four or five more students all day than most teachers saw in a single period. And while she enjoyed frequent, personal, and apparently amicable contacts with Dr. Kriftcher and Jules Levine, the assistant principal for administration, she did not regularly communicate, even by writing, to her teacher constituents. But for all the grumbling about Judy, no one was willing to run against her in the annual union election or to apply for her position as reading coordinator, and few teachers sought even the informal kind of confrontation that Jessica was inviting on Teachers' Choice.

Judy sits in the far right corner of Room 323 when the English department meeting opens. A box of cookies moves up and down the aisles, followed by a list of prices and specifications for the televisions, VCRs, carts, and electric typewriter. Officially, Emma Jon leads the meeting, but as soon as she arrives at the topic of Teachers' Choice, Judy issues the union's warning against buying a copier without service included. The school is planning to purchase a new copier for Jules Levine, Judy continues, and Jules has promised to permit teachers to use it. If not, there is always next year. Emma then resumes. Unless anyone has an objection, she says, the electronic equipment will be ordered.

A short woman with thick glasses and frizzy black hair raises her hand. She is Lois Stavsky, who teaches in the drop-out prevention program at the annex. Why does the department want to buy televisions and VCRs, she asks, when such appliances are currently being stolen from the annex? A total of three VCRs had vanished in the preceding eighteen months, along with cash, radios, blank video cassettes, and student transportation passes. In no case had there been a sign of forced entry, and on one occasion, the motion alarm inside the school had been conveniently switched off for the evening. An inside job, in other words.

The security problem has been rectified, Emma assures Lois, and the teachers accept her word without elaboration. (The truth is that the annex robberies remain unsolved.) The matter is settled. The English Department will join the Global Village.

Jessica waves her hand wildly, but Emma does not react. Only after proceeding to the next item on the agenda, concerning exams, does she acknowledge her.

"Can we go back to Teachers' Choice?" Jessica asks.

Groans fill the air.

"We have four thousand other things," Emma says.

"Well, I have some ideas that may be different from other people," Jessica says. Before giving up on a copier this year, she wants to know *exactly* how much time English teachers will get on Jules Levine's new machine. And will he put his pledge in writing? Because no one needs a copying machine more than an English teacher.

"There will have to be some limitations," Emma says. "We have to be realistic."

"I'm not talking about Xeroxing three-hundred-page novels," Jessica says. "But I have a feeling any schoolwide policy won't give us enough copies."

Now Judy Goldman rises. All eyes rest upon her. She is a wide, thick woman and she crosses her forearms and plants her feet firmly.

"I think Jessica is absolutely right," she begins cannily. "I don't trust Jules Levine. We already have a heavy-duty copier in Dr. Kriftcher's office, and you see, on a day like today, he's out, the door's locked, we can't use it." She pauses. "But that's besides the point."

Jessica wonders how. To her, access is precisely the point. And Dr. Kriftcher's copier, except for special cases, is off limits.

"Instead of buying a low-volume copier now," Judy says, "wait another year. We've done without one for so long already." She turns to her left to face Jessica. "I don't know if that makes you feel better."

Jessica shakes her head no.

"I looked it up," she says, consulting her own notes from the Teachers' Choice catalogues. "There's a $3,000 machine."

"But it's not high volume," says Sonny Whynman, a teacher at the annex.

"Fourteen thousand copies a month," Jessica answers. She sifts through her papers for the maintenance estimates. She finds the sheet, runs her finger down the margin, and readies to speak.

Before she can, Emma Jon again invokes the subject of exams. Teachers' Choice is part of the past. There has been little real discussion and no vote. Jessica has been buffaloed, made to play the blowhard and then scorned for being one. She sits down, rubbing together thumb and forefinger. A few teachers still glare at her or sigh deeply in annoyance. Perhaps they worry that the meeting now will exceed forty minutes and will delay briefly their departure for home. Perhaps they do not like the friction.

Emma moves briskly through the remainder of the agenda and concludes the meeting with several minutes to spare. As the teachers slide into their winter coats and make for the hallway and the time clock, a man with a mustache, chin whiskers and horn-rim glasses approaches Jessica. It is Mark Fischweicher, a new teacher whom Jessica barely knows. Mark leans over and tells her he thought she was right. He straightens as if to leave, then bends down again. He is sorry, he adds, that he didn't say so when it might have mattered.*

The next morning Jessica awakens at 4 A.M. to type on a stencil an essay about Christmas in a Puerto Rican household. When she runs off the copies two hours later in the English office, the ink spreads irregularly, forming zebra stripes of deep purple and palest blue. And when she passes out the rexos to the Lower East Side class, the first boy to receive one complains, "I can't read this thing. How come you don't make Xeroxes?" Jessica laughs ruefully and says sotto voce, "Ask my department."

*   *   *

Jessica's friend Ilene Kantrov was in town yesterday. They dined together on homemade cioppino and after the meal, they talked. Ilene taught at the college level before taking her current job in an educational consulting firm, and she counts among her colleagues a number of former public school teachers. What was the matter with the system, she asked rhetorically, that it drove away such gifted people? What was this bureaucracy that cannibalized the creative minds in its midst? Jessica had to be honest. She could not really respond to Ilene's observations because she did not buy Ilene's premise. She spoke instead about Ben Dachs and Hannah Hess, excellent teachers who not only stayed in the system but rose through its ranks. If you worked for sensitive people, if you worked around them, you could spend your career in the trenches, and more or less gladly. The landscape was not nearly so inhospitable as outsiders were led to believe.

*After I attended this meeting, I was barred from several subsequent English Department meetings. This action was taken, I was told, at the request of Judy Goldman.

The words sound saccharine to Jessica this afternoon. They echo in her memory in tones of childish naïveté. They ridicule her.

The problems started during the seventh period, when the librarian evicted Jessica's advanced journalism students, culminating weeks of conflict. The six then repaired to the English office, pleasing Emma Jon not at all. Jessica saw their unexpected assembly from her classroom across the hall and left the beginning journalism class on its own recognizance—a decision fraught with risk—long enough to discover what had gone wrong and to instruct the advanced students to return at the ninth period.

The copy deadline for the second issue of *Seward World* was drawing near, and as usual, all was confusion. Harold Steinberg had slipped on an icy sidewalk a week earlier, landing him in the hospital with a broken hip. Deprived of their English-speaking front man, the Korean owners of Official Press could barely converse with Jessica. Meanwhile, where was Gregg Gross's article about Operation Pressure Point? It had to appear in the next issue to be eligible for the Robert F. Kennedy Award, and Jessica believed that only the prospect of a national prize would keep Gregg committed to school. He had told her once that none of the boys in his extended family had graduated high school on time, and the tradition distressed her.

Earlier in the term, Jessica would have called a *Seward World* meeting for 7:15 A.M., but she was tired of the no-shows, tired of baking for six and serving two. The ninth period was the only other option. But when the students arrived, and for a change they all did, Emma was sitting down with a second-year teacher named Frances Mayer to deliver an observation report. Emma wanted privacy, and Frances deserved privacy. A *Seward World* staff conference would afford none.

Because only half the student body has classes past eighth period, there were actually a few free classrooms, so Emma sent Jessica and her staff around the corner to Room 325. Gregg Gross was across the street buying soda, and Jessica asked Emma to send him to the room when he returned. Then, as Jessica led her itinerants to their next shelter, Emma asked her if she had typed a particular letter to a textbook company.

"I'm meeting with my students now," Jessica said. "I'll do it after. It'll take a minute."

She turned to leave, then stopped at the sound of Emma's voice.

"But Jessica," the chairwoman said, "you have an assignment to this department."

"Every free period today I've had kids to see. I haven't had lunch today."

Jessica's words fluttered, ragged and forlorn. Emma clasped her hands on the desktop. Frances, a reluctant witness, stared at a bookcase.

"You have to choose a period each day to do your work for the department," Emma said.

"I don't have a separate class for advanced journalism. I tried seeing them at seven in the morning. I need to—"

Emma interrupted, her voice shearing Jessica's own.

"You have certain responsibilities to discharge." She paused. "You choose a period when you can discharge them."

The air fell still. *An assignment to this department . . . responsibilities to discharge.* In that small room, in the narrow space between Emma and Jessica, the very molecules vibrated.

Then Jessica withdrew—out the door, down the hall, and around the corner, feeling sullied and low. She knew she put the department's chores at the bottom of her list. But she knew she always got them done. The letter she was supposed to write was to order new journalism books, so why wouldn't she get it written? But this wasn't a matter of who was right and who was wrong. She hated the sensation of losing her temper, slipping out of control. "The System" was distant, and often, so was the principal. But your chairperson was close. Your chairperson could make your life miserable. Was she making an enemy? Was she setting herself up to be screwed? She had to watch her words. But between nagging the kids, hassling with the printer, and glancing over her shoulder for Judy Goldman, she had so few reserves to call upon. She didn't hate Emma, and she didn't think Emma hated her. They had friends in common—Ben, Hannah—yet they clashed constantly, like two chemicals whose valences could never join in compound.

So she sits now in Room 325 thinking about last night's Pollyanna propaganda. Gregg has not reappeared from his soda run, and Jessica sends Lydia Pagan to the English office. Sure enough, he is there. No one told him the staff meeting had been moved. After Gregg opens his soda, he dips into a bookbag and unearths his article on Operation Pressure Point, finished at last. A couple of periods ago, Jessica would have cheered. Now she can barely strike a glimmer. She slides the article into a folder and puts a checkmark beside "Oper. Press. Pt." on the assignment list and asks herself, *Who the fuck needs this shit?*

*   *   *

After Jessica exited the English office, the room was not left entirely to Emma Jon and Frances Mayer. Seated at the work table were Linda Rothman and one of her students, a slender Chinese girl with a shy smile. Linda was skimming *The New York Times* as the girl was reading compositions and jotting marginal comments such as "Sloppy!"

Theirs was a partnership that had proceeded, with certain variations, all term long. It was not unusual for teachers at Seward Park to enlist favorite pupils to aid in clerical chores. Such an arrangement lightened the teacher's awesome load and provided the student with recognition and approval. Linda Rothman, however, had stretched the formula substantially. Generally, she would give her chosen girl a stack of multiple choice tests and an answer key. Then she would relax as the girl proceeded, paper by paper, marking the errors, tabulating the score, and recording it in Linda's grade book. Subsequently, Linda let the girl read and rate short answers on tests. And now the girl had graduated to evaluating her peers' expository writing.

Asked why the girl was doing what appeared to be a teacher's job, Linda responded, "I have a headache from reading four million of these."

Yet that headache did not prevent her from perusing *The Times.*

"If I assign a composition and there are fifteen questions to answer and someone only answers seven, she can count as well as I can."

Unprompted, Linda volunteered still more information. The girl had not yet passed her minimum-competency test in reading and by grading papers and compositions, she was gaining valuable practice in identifying grammatical errors.

The logic was startling. Here was a girl who was unable to satisfy a reading test scaled at the eleventh-grade level, now vested with the responsibility of educating her classmates. Here was a teacher who was unashamed of abusing a student's desire to please, so unashamed, in fact, that she practiced this abuse within a few feet of the department chairwoman.

These events would make sense only months later, when Sonny Whynman told me a story about his maiden teaching job, some twenty-five years earlier. Sonny had entered the classroom on the first day to find his charges shooting craps. He wrote his name on the blackboard and asked the students to be seated. "Listen, man," one of them said. "You don't bother us, we don't bother you. You sit up there, read the paper, take your course so you can make more money. And we'll have our game." Sonny was stunned, less by the effrontery than by its sophistication; the kid understood most new teachers were in the process of finishing graduate school and would receive a pay raise when they did so. He insisted a second time the kids sit. The boy looked up from his dice and in a tone more of concern than of condemnation said to Sonny, "You a dumb motherfucker."

Put more genteelly, the point was this: When the students loafed, as students were wont to do, the teacher could loaf; when the students "got over," the teacher could "get over." Far from all did, but the option was always available. In a ghetto school, it was the rare student who demanded to be educated rather than merely promoted. In an immigrant slum, it was the rare parent who inspected the syllabus, the homework assignments, and the graded tests. Not being summoned by the school was sufficient proof that one's child was doing well, and even when the school did invite them for Open School Night, the turnout was paltry. Teachers who had 150 pupils were fortunate to see 20 or 25 parents.

The symbiosis was not always as obvious as a teacher deploying a pupil as an unpaid assistant, but it could be found in many guises in Seward Park. It was there when an English teacher issued multiple-choice and short-answer tests rather than requiring and, in turn, having to read essays. It was there when a social studies teacher provided an essay question as unchallenging as "Give two examples of FDR's 'good will' toward the American people." It was there when one of Jessica's English 7 students proudly proferred her the term paper about the Vietnam War for which a history teacher had awarded him a 95. Jessica was impressed the boy had read a 471-page tome for the paper and that he had typed a 7-page response to the reading. Yet the most glaring barbarisms went uncorrected — "The book Vietnam mainly tells about why we was there" — and the teacher's entire commentary consisted of, "You did an excellent job summarizing the book and most of all your reaction to it." In the short term, the 95 buoyed the boy's confidence; in the long term, which Jessica hoped would include college, it set him up for a dizzying fall.

It set up Jessica for one as well. Inside the door of her classroom, she set standards, and since she had joined Lanni Tama at the lunch table years earlier, she had surrounded herself with colleagues—Hannah, Ben, Bruce, Harriet, Denise, Steve, and Shawn—who set standards in their own domains. The list could go on; there was no lack of dedicated souls. And it was seductive to imagine they defined the atmosphere, for they coalesced around one another, at the work table in early mornings and late afternoons, in the gymnasium and auditorium for basketball games and talent shows, over "T.G.I.F." cocktails at the bar near Tompkins Square Park. But as many as wore the raccoon badge, there were many more whose decoration was the "2:15" imprinted diurnally on their time cards. Maybe the 2:15 crowd never saw teaching as anything other than a safe harbor in the civil service, comparable to delivering mail or filling potholes. Stripped to the minimum, after all, the working conditions were cozy: 6 hours and 20 minutes a day and 185 days a year until the pension kicked in. Lynn Yellin, a young history teacher, told me about one of her former colleagues in Kennedy High School in the Bronx, who stacked old papers against a wall, marked in ascending strata "Weekend," "Vacation," and "Retirement." Some of the clock-punchers must have begun with admirable intentions; they must have enjoyed the camaraderie and occasionally even the kids. But they would not sacrifice their personal time to the cause; rather than quit, rather than surrender the health insurance and free summers, they chose to cut corners, to scale back from full essays to one-paragraph answers to mere phrases to multiple-choice circles and true-false slashes—to replace, in essence, the scribbles and cross-outs of endeavor with the Liquid Paper of image.

Jessica saw the world in gray tones, but she saw her own life in polarities of black and white. She could not slacken her standards. But neither could she abide them. She could not revive herself the way Hannah, Ben, and the rest of the true believers apparently could. How did they do it? What on earth was *their* secret?

*   *   *

The idea has been dogging her for a month: Maybe she should quit. So much has weighed upon her these past weeks, distance from Bruce, friction with Emma, battles against Judy, quests for a copying machine and a class that does its reading. None by itself may be a decisive force, but each offers one more disincentive to stay, especially when added to the unending work and unfulfilled ambitions that are the constants of Jessica's life.

She can remember the day the notion of leaving first insinuated itself into her thoughts, November fourteenth, a Saturday. She had set aside that afternoon and all the following day to lay out the first edition of *Seward World* with her staff, but after all her harassing of the kids and the printer to meet their respective deadlines, the galley proofs had not been completed in time. For a minute, she luxuriated in relief. And then she realized she had been liberated only to undertake the rest of her work. She unzipped Big Black and lit a desk lamp and swore to herself, "There has to be a better life than this."

The moment had its antecedent, an antecedent that was Jessica's secret. Midway through the 1985–86 school year, her fifth as a teacher, she had applied to the Columbia University Graduate School of Journalism. Of her friends at Seward Park, only Bruce knew of the decision. The larger part of her choice was to escape the unrelenting work load, but journalism itself exerted an attraction. She had been grooming Sue Lee and Ricardo Enriquez that fall, imbuing them with her style of socially conscious reporting, and the process had re-awakened her best memories of Liberation News Service. She imagined herself an athlete who had retired to coaching, insisting that coaching alone would suffice, only through coaching to taste new sweat, to feel soft muscles hardening, to crave the field of play once again.

Columbia's journalism school did not quite concur. A letter in April 1986 informed Jessica she had been placed on the waiting list. She wrote a letter reiterating her reporting experience and her misgivings about teaching. She pled her case by telephone to a dean. And on June 5, three weeks before the end of the year at Seward Park, she received notice of her admission.

Only then did the gravity of leaving teaching truly seize her. She considered the rootless quality of the reporter's life and compared it to the home she had fashioned at Seward Park. She wondered whether at thirty-seven she still possessed the unquestioning ambition "to compete against the twenty-three year olds who'd walk over their grandmothers to get jobs." And she had to admit that her work at Seward Park was not yet complete. She and Bruce had a publisher who was interested in a collection of oral histories from the Lower East Side class. She had just discovered a diffident junior named Sammy Ryan, for whom she alone prophesied a future. One night her brother Steve told her, "A *lot* of people work as teachers for four or five years and move on." He meant to offer balm for a difficult decision already made, but instead, his words acted to change Jessica's mind. When she thought of talented teachers who left after a few years, she thought of people incapable of commitment, harvesters of experience for its own sake, tourists indulging in a savory bit of slumming. She wrote to Columbia on August 22, 1986, to forfeit her admission, and two weeks later she returned to Seward Park, where only Bruce knew how unlikely, how remarkable, her return was.

There was a bizarre postscript to the entire episode. For years, a woman named Judy Seigel had lived next door to Jessica; each occasionally received the other's mail and forwarded the misplaced letter in person. It developed that Judy had a daughter named Jessica who was in her early twenties and that Jessica Seigel had applied to the Columbia journalism school at the same time as had her neighbor and namesake. The two joked that only one would be admitted because there obviously was a quota. In the end, however, both of them were accepted. And as Jessica Siegel declined the call, Jessica Seigel heeded it. By now, December 1987, almost two years later, she has graduated and begun working as a reporter—an alter ego whose path suddenly, starkly, calls into question Jessica the teacher's own.

10

Friends

AN ATOLL SURROUNDED by a sea of hurried humanity, Bruce Baskind's drama students huddle beside a brick pillar in Pennsylvania Station. It is 9 A.M. on a Wednesday, well into Christmas shopping season, a time when the commuter tide is at its height. Men in wing tips and lined trench coats and women wearing aerobics shoes and carrying pumps ascend from platforms and swarm down corridors and clamor toward offices and jobs. The process and the place, to them oppressively familiar, reduce the teenagers to a state of silent fascination. The students' eyes dart from video monitors flashing information in red and green to machines spewing tickets for mysterious destinations to stores selling eyeglasses and oil paintings and oat bran muffins. Barely reconciled to these environs, they are bound in moments for a setting more alien still, a private school in a suburb called Locust Valley.

With Bruce across the floor buying tickets, the Seward Park ensemble numbers seven. Sydney Sidner, an aspiring director, and Julia Halperin, a college student, assist Bruce as unpaid volunteers. Angel Fuster, Moonie Ali, Luis Almonte, and Robert Mateo are among twenty students taking the course in History through Drama. Ivan Abreu is a friend whom Angel convinced to cut school and join the expedition.

Last spring, the first edition of the drama class performed an original play about immigration, entitled (with Bruce's weakness for the leaden pun) *José, Can You See?* Bruce suggested to this fall's students a show about working, which they greeted with a collective yawn. Challenged by Bruce to offer an alternative, they opted for a play about Seward Park, and what has been evolving is a caustic, accusatory canvas of students and teachers locked in a cycle of mutual lethargy. The working title is *School?*

Today's field trip has one official purpose, an inspection of the Friends Academy, a century-old institution affiliated with the Quaker denomination. Bruce wants his students to see how Friends Academy involves its own in operating the school, according each an equal say with teachers and administrators at a weekly meeting. He wants them to see the facilities and conditions that affluence can attain. He wants them, quite clearly, to draw critical comparisons to Seward Park. Although Bruce has tried to run his drama course as an experiment in democratic education, an alternative to the force-feeding of concepts like "patriotism" and "upward mobility" he decries in the traditional classroom, he is so passionate a man and so convincing an orator that his own instruction can verge on a type of indoctrination. His students are developing the play's themes through discussions and improvisations and they are scripting the scenes with help from Julia and Sydney, but they are also parroting a political vocabulary of "dependency" and "under-development" supplied by him.

Beyond Bruce's designs for the day, others exist. One of the deans at Friends Academy is Ron Baskind, Bruce's younger brother. Largely at Ron's behest, the school has courted Bruce for a teaching position. Bruce would not be surprised to receive another entreaty today, and given his frustrations with Seward Park and the Board of Education, he cannot predict how he might react. For his students, meanwhile, the visit to Friends Academy will foreshadow the culture shock they are bound to experience at college. As diverse and compressed as New York City is, as much as Seward Park students browse beside well-born children in Greenwich Village and South Street Seaport, as much as their separate spheres intersect in the popular culture of Air Jordan sneakers and U2 concerts, most have lived a perversely sheltered life. Money, class, and race surround them, but rarely do they cut and bruise directly. Seward Park's students populate a subcity in which minorities are the majority, in which any college is a good college, in which weekend homes and seaside summers are so far from reality they are not even fantasies.

Trying to crack the tension he senses among his classmates, Angel points out a commuter in a pin-striped suit and herringbone over-coat. "That guy's from New Jersey," he says, New Jersey connoting to him not tract houses and chemical plants but moneyed mansions. Then he indicates a black teenager, a messenger he reckons, wearing a leather bomber jacket atop ill-fitting cuffed trousers. "From Brooklyn, trying to be from New Jersey," Angel says. "Probably just got his GED."

Angel and the rest follow Bruce down a gray cement stairway and into the train. It is so different from the subway—clean floors, cushioned seats, luggage racks, nearly empty cars for this reverse commute. This kind of train, Angel imagines, could whisk you to a foreign country, with wine and caviar to ease the journey. And it is just the plain old Long Island Railroad.

Bruce asks how many students have ever set foot on Long Island.

"Once," Luis Almonte says. "I went fishing."

"North Shore or South?" Bruce asks.

"All I know's I couldn't see the land."

The train rumbles through a dark tunnel on its route to Queens. The Seward Park group spreads across four bench seats. Bruce steps into the aisle so he can talk to everyone at once. But for the missing blackboard, he could be in his classroom.

"What if I told you the part of Long Island where we're going used to be called the Gold Coast? What would you think?"

"Big houses, some farms, lots of grass," Angel says. "White people. No Puerto Ricans. Maybe some blacks."

"And what'll they be doing?" Bruce asks.

"Saying 'Massa' a lot," Angel says before dissolving into laughter. He regains his composure and adds, "And there might even be some at this school."

"Why?"

"To keep the government from bitching."

The train spurts from the tunnel and climbs a trestle above Queens. The first stop is Woodside, once a German and Irish neighborhood, now mostly Hispanic and Asian, but always a half-step between some poorer point of origin and a tract house on Long Island. A conductor maneuvers down the aisle on sea legs. A young, burly white man with brown hair and a drooping mustache, the conductor could be a Woodside expatriate, living with his wife and kids in Islip and returning to the old neighborhood only to visit his grandmother and watch cable sports in a bar with a satellite dish.

The conductor regards the group, punches their tickets, exhales wearily through his nostrils, and regards them again.

"What is there, some kinda party in Locust Valley?"

"Class trip," Bruce answers.

"Easier than working," the conductor snaps.

"We're going to see a school for rich kids," Bruce says, sensing a lesson in the making.

"Well, you chose the right place," the conductor says. The Gold Coast was historically home to families whose very names define wealth and privilege, to Morgans and Vanderbilts and Whitneys and Du Ponts. "Where you from?"

"The Lower East Side," Bruce says.

"Should I check my wallet?"

The conductor laughs at his own joke and swaggers to the rear of the car, where he sits down and opens a newspaper.

"What'd he say?" Angel asks Bruce.

" 'Should I check my wallet?' "

Angel grimaces and stares out the window. The blocky apartments of Woodside have given way to the mock Tudor stores of Forest Hills and to redbrick houses branching off from the trestle in diagonal rows. Bare elms line streets, and dry leaves spill across gutters and curbs. Angel's breath fogs the window, for outside it is perhaps twenty-five degrees.

When the train reaches Jamaica, Queens, the transfer hub for the railroad's numerous spurs, Bruce leads the group across the platform for the Locust Valley local. Angel waves to the conductor, who flashes a two-fingered salute in return. "Still got your wallet?" Angel asks with a deceptive smile. "You better check."

The local is populated only by the drama class and four black women bundled in cloth coats and knit hats. The women chirp in West Indian accents and carry plastic grocery bags in which they keep their uniforms and their sensible shoes. They are the maids, the cooks, the cleaning ladies, and often the surrogate mothers of the sort of children who attend Friends Academy. When their day is done, and the market bag is replaced by one from Bergdorf's, one found in a hall closet or under the sink, they travel back to their own neighborhoods and their own families to raise the sort of children who attend Seward Park. There is a wordless acknowledgment between the domestics and the teenagers, each group understanding that its passport for these precincts is merely temporary.

Bruce kneels on his seat and leans over the backrest to address the five students. He tells them that tuition at Friends Academy is $9,000 a year and that with an enrollment of 700, the school has fewer students in twelve grades, kindergarten, and preschool than Seward Park has in its senior class. He tells them about the weekly meeting and the teachers who live on campus. He tells them about the field-house and the cafeteria and the library and the theater. Then he mentions that Friends Academy may be seeking Seward Park kids for scholarships.

For Friends Academy is a private school with convictions quite beyond the expected noblesse oblige. Every student must perform public service, the youngest collecting cans for recycling, the oldest rehabilitating slum housing. About 18 percent of the academy's pupils are racial minorities, and more than half of them are receiving full or partial scholarships, which are tactfully called "financial help for those who are needy." In the school's introductory brochure, care has been taken to include in virtually every group photograph one or two black or Hispanic youngsters, striding across the campus or asking advice from a teacher. Nowhere in the brochure, however, is the precise price of tuition noted.

His brief description completed, Bruce offers some final advice. Any school, whether Friends Academy or Seward Park, is not only a collection of individuals but a social system. It is not enough to lampoon teachers and students without analyzing why they act how they act. As a way to anchor these abstractions, Bruce asks his students to keep three main questions in mind during today's visit: How are Friends Academy and Seward Park different? At which school do teachers work harder? And at which school are the students more dependent?

"There," Angel volunteers. "Because they're not just dependent on their teacher. It's their parents being rich. I gotta ride the subway. I gotta go to work. I come home starvin', and there's two pork chops on the table. One for me and one for my sister. I tell my mother, 'Diane's sleepin' over her friend's.' If she doesn't believe that, I cut some corners off her chop before she gets home." The others laugh knowingly. "These kids probably don't even have cockroaches at home. Got, I dunno, *tuxedo bugs.* All they gotta worry about is, Did Daddy's check come?"

No one else offers an opinion. Bruce's words have plunged the rest into thought, and so has the changing terrain outside the window—

houses with yards, fences, and patios; driveways with Volvos, Mercedes, and Jeeps; golf courses and tennis courts and parks groomed like velvet. Angel rises when he catches sight of horses, cantering through the dim sun in an exercise ring. When he sits, Ivan begins singing the John Mellencamp song "Pink Houses." As he reaches the chorus, Angel knows enough words to join.

> Oh, but ain't that America, for you and me
> Ain't that America, we're something to see, baby
> Ain't that America, home of the free
> Little pink houses for you and me

The Seward Park students and the black ladies exit together at Locust Valley. Angel turns to Ivan and says, "I bet there'll be a lot of blonds," but his joke barely relieves the anxiety.

The group awaits Ron Baskind beneath the terracotta tile roof of the train station. Across a small parking lot stand Le Papier Shoppe, Maison Posh, and Sign Of The Quail, each in a white brick row house with a green and yellow awning. Even the lumber store features a cream portico, green shutters, and red Christmas ribbons.

A bearish, red-haired man four years Bruce's junior, Ron arrives in a minibus bearing the Friends Academy crest. Already Angel is impressed and intimidated. A Seward Park class trip, today aside, means riding the subway. With this van, he thinks, you could cool out and get girls. The brief drive to Friends Academy skirts stone fences and colonial graveyards, and the campus is bounded by roads named Duck Pond and Piping Rock. As the group climbs out of the minibus, they can see several buildings. Most are brick, some older and some newer, one topped with turrets and a weather vane. Luis says that he's never seen a school like this except in the movie *Ferris Bueller's Day Off.* Bruce recognizes the white-shingled house where Ron has a three-bedroom apartment, subsidized by the academy, for $300 a month. "That's my bro's crib," he tells Julia and Sydney. Angel smells beef being grilled in the cafeteria. "You know they don't get government food here," he says.

Inside the main building, the Seward Park students are welcomed by the Friends Academy peers who will act as their guides for the day. One of them, true to Angel's prediction, is a tall, slender blond with green eyes. The second is a thin boy with glasses. "I'm really excited today," he says by way of introduction to the Seward Park students. "I just found out my best friend got into Harvard." On the wall behind the boy hangs a mathematics poster, which sets forth a problem of value per unit, using the example of a student's pearl necklace. Angel knows somebody with pearls, although he's pretty sure they're fake.

Actually, the Friends Academy kids dress less fancily than he expected, and that throws him. Their ties are loosened, their shirts are creased, their shoelaces are untied. Why would anybody with nice clothes try so hard to look like a slob? He spent all afternoon yesterday searching for something decent to wear, and he couldn't afford anything. He was left with his one formal jacket, a blue polyester blazer with DECA's insignia on the breast pocket, and he knew it would never measure up. So he decided this morning to carry the jacket over his arm, where nobody could feel the fabric or spot the patch, and to pretend he always went coatless on winter days. But what would happen to Moonie with her Bengali brass earrings? And Luis with his thin tie and gold crucifix? How many fingers would point their way?

The Seward Park group separates until lunch. Ron leads Bruce down a carpeted hallway, flanked by separate offices for each teacher, and into a faculty lounge with its own stove, couch, Xerox machine, electric typewriter, and personal computer. A homemade chocolate cake sits on a table. Then Bruce observes a sensitivity-training session that Ron moderates for sixteen junior high school students. Listening to them discuss the difference between sympathy and empathy, skimming their essays posted on the rear wall, Bruce judges that these twelve-year-olds command English more completely than do his seniors at Seward Park. "So many of our kids," he tells Ron afterward, "don't even know when to capitalize." That may be true, Ron replies, but many of his students lack the expressiveness and street wisdom and self-reliance of city children. They feel pressured to match their parents in status and income. They form their strongest bonds with their maids. They suffer socially for not having a car or the right car. Even coming from his brother, all this strikes Bruce as cold comfort indeed.

Separated from the rest, Julia and Sydney trawl slowly down hallways, suffused with sense-memory. From their own days as private school pupils, they recognize the oak desks, the classes seated in circles, the pets roaming the campus, the fancy-sloppy attire that so baffled Angel, the voice they overhear saying, "But I don't *know* if I want to go to Harvard early decision." All these touchstones remind Sydney how different she is from her drama students, no matter how devoted to them she is. Even after a year at Seward Park, she cannot decide whether to dress well and feel she is flaunting or dress shabbily and feel she is slumming. Living on Avenue C, she wonders whom she displaced.

As she and Julia wander, they peek into the admissions office. The woman at the desk meets their gaze and dashes into the hall with greetings. With her bobbed hair and glossed lips and high cheeks, she reminds Sydney of Maggie Smith. The woman indicates her office to Julia and Sydney and says, "This is where you'd be interviewed. Where I'd talk to you. Students such as yourselves." Then it dawns on them. The admissions officer had been alerted to the Seward Park visit and thought Julia and Sydney were students; in her haste, she could not register that she was encountering not two minority teenagers but two white women in their twenties. Sydney breaks the news.

"I'm so sorry," the admissions officer says. "I'm familiar with your kind of school. I started in the East End of Montreal and it was very much like the West End of Manhattan."

"Lower East Side," Julia amends. West End is an avenue on which playwrights and psychiatrists reside.

Undaunted, the admissions officer gathers up catalogues and school newspapers and passes them to the visitors. "You should be interested in this," she says, extracting a recent issue of the newspaper. "There's a poll about drug and alcohol use."

Sydney cannot remember if her private day school had scholarship students or any minorities. She recalls white faces, L. L. Bean turtlenecks, and Brooks Brothers oxfords. Only later does she think of a classmate named Beverly Simmons. Beverly was black and lived a few blocks from Sydney, and one afternoon invited Sydney into her home. The rooms were small and sparsely furnished, and in the kitchen stood a battered refrigerator, its door held fast by rope. She overheard Beverly asking her mother when the refrigerator would get fixed and her mother saying that there was no rush since it was rented, anyway. One of the last times Sydney saw Beverly was in the eighth-grade play, *The Boyfriend.* Sydney played the ingenue, and Beverly played the maid.

Angel, Ivan, and Luis, meanwhile, follow their blond guide through a series of classes. The kids in Spanish, Angel is shocked to realize, speak the language more correctly than he does. Only their accents are amiss, reminding Ivan of Frank Perdue. He laughs, and Angel and Luis join him, and they prolong the laughter deliberately. In the next class, mathematics, no such sarcasm is possible. Angel can follow the part about the quadratic equation, but once the teacher introduces the problem, involving a balloon that is blown sideways while it rises, he knows he is lost. And all he sees before him are eyes impatient for the next challenge.

"Oh, shit," Ivan whispers to Angel.

"We're gonna have to do this on the SAT," Angel says.

"Oh, man."

Then the three boys join Moonie and Robert at a student-faculty meeting. The setting is the Senior Lounge, a long room of easy chairs and window seats, and the topic is cafeteria cleanliness. Angel is amazed to find a student running the meeting and teachers having to raise their hands to be acknowledged. He served on the Consultative Council, an advisory group to Dr. Kriftcher, and it galled him that the principal always prevailed. Then again, the teachers seem to be carrying the day here, too. These kids, Angel thinks, could learn a few things from him. They don't know how to get over. They don't know how to get what they need. They don't know how to survive.

The assumptions, though, cut two ways. Occasionally, a Friends Academy student whispers and appraises the Seward Park students with suspicion, head drawn back, eyes flat, lips tight. More often there is a curiosity that is more lacerating for being so well intentioned.

As the visitors enter one classroom, a girl points to the floor and says, "Isn't it neat we have rugs?"

"Somebody get a camera," Angel answers with mock excitement. "I want a camera. I wanna get a picture of the rug." He takes satisfaction from seeing the girl blush with shame.

A boy says he is surprised that the Seward Park boys are wearing ties. Friends Academy has a code specifying proper attire, but he didn't think public school kids had to dress up.

"We just wear our spikes," Luis answers.

"And switchblades," Angel adds.

The five students locate Bruce, Julia, and Sydney in the cafeteria and draw tightly together, for this place humbles them more than does any class. The cafeteria is a large split-level space, all red bricks and smoked glass, reminiscent of a Vermont ski lodge. A student disc jockey spins rock records, and a toy train courses across the green felt of a Christmas display. Posters remind diners to save their cans for recycling. Students and faculty alike enjoy unlimited trips to the grill, the salad bar, the steam table, the sandwich board, and the bakery counter.

Angel bites into his hamburger, appreciating that it tastes like a real hamburger, not one of those skinny, slimy school patties. He envisions the beautiful blond who was his guide and all the other pretty girls he saw here in just an hour or two. He imagines them in the Ivy League, them in the executive office, them behind the wheel of a Mercedes. He ponders his own future and pictures himself managing a floor at Macy's or working in marketing, perhaps working for one of these kids. Going to the counter for two or three desserts, he tries to banish the thought. He seizes instead on the notion of these rich kids collecting cans. Angel cannot conceive of recycling as an environmental issue, only an economic one, and in his neighborhood nobody with any esteem would even consider the chore, five-cent deposit or no five-cent deposit. Collecting cans is the labor of the homeless and the drunken and the addicted, pawing through dumpsters with shopping carts at their side, New York City's caste of untouchables.

Still, Angel cannot help thinking that at Friends Academy, the Seward Park kids must appear about that desperate. His hosts must see him the same way he saw that messenger in Pennsylvania Station, vainly feigning class. It is too late, obviously, to change costume, but at least they can change voice. What must their hosts make of Luis's Dominican accent? And Mateo's street slur? And Moonie's Indian lilt? And the way she speaks so fast when she gets excited? From his travels for DECA, limited as they have been, Angel knows something of embarassment. He suggests to the others that they appoint a "designated talker," who will answer all questions the rest of the visit, and he is elected. But the victory and the plan prove moot. Bruce tells his students it is time to leave.

The one-twenty-eight local to New York wobbles and squeaks under gunmetal skies. Maybe the afternoon train is slower than the morning one, or maybe it only seems that way now that the anticipation is spent. The trip to Friends Academy has been a short trip, but then again quite long enough. Nobody says very much until Bruce asks what the students thought of the classes.

"Smaller than Seward," Robert says. "You work better."

"More freedom," Luis adds. "You don't have to ask permission to go to the bathroom. I was sayin' how our desks are nailed to the floor, we got no carpet, we got thirty kids in a class. And they, like, couldn't believe it. I said, 'Hey, that's life, you can't do nothin' about it.'"

Moonie mentions how Friends Academy was so safe that students left their backpacks unattended in the hall.

"That's 'cause they can afford to buy a hundred backpacks," Angel puts in. "Who'd need to steal one?"

The train rumbles toward the darkening horizon. The discussion withers. The most significant conversations now are of the internal variety.

Bruce thinks of Xerox machines and classes of ten. He tells himself he's a shmuck for staying at Seward Park, where he feels every obstacle is thrown in his path. How many times—three? four?—has his drama class been booted out of the auditorium in some scheduling snafu? He protests up the chain of command, like he's supposed to, and the same thing happens again. Yet he loves the kids and he loves the fight. The changes he seeks have already reached Friends Academy, and maybe they were there right from the start. If he took their offer, he would have nothing to battle. And more to the point, he would know he had given up.

Luis thinks about how money means everything. If his family had money, he wouldn't be working, and starting his schoolwork at nine-thirty each night. But tuition for one kid at Friends Academy amounts to what his father earns annually as a hotel housekeeper. He hears Julia and Sydney recounting their run-in with the admissions lady, hears them laughing at her folly, and he wonders where his life would be if Friends Academy had had a scholarship for him.

Angel has the same idea. *Damn,* he says to himself, *why didn't this happen when I was applying to high school?* Then the "4" and the "H" he'd scribbled in the English office a few weeks ago, four years at Syracuse followed by law school at Harvard, wouldn't seem like such an impossible aspiration. Then he might someday run a company instead of working for one. Then he might date a blond.

The train rattles across the railyard as it approaches Jamaica. Clouds crease and furrow overhead. The black ladies are not on the return train, and neither is the conductor. When the doors open, only Bruce departs, taking a shortcut to his apartment in Queens. "Later, Baskind," Angel calls to his back.

Then he returns to his thoughts, and the train slides into the tunnel. If he went to Friends Academy, he tells himself, maybe he'd be an asshole. Maybe he'd have strayed from his family. Maybe he wouldn't be friends with Ivan. And that's hard to imagine. The two are so close that when Angel knows only the melody of a song they both like, he can always depend on Ivan to supply the words. All day, for instance,

Angel's been trying to remember the last verse to "Pink Houses."
Now, rolling homeward, Ivan reminds him.

> Well, there's people and more people, what do they know
> Go to work in some high rise and vacation down at the Gulf of
>   Mexico
> And there's winners and there's losers, but they ain't no big deal
> Because the simple man, baby, pays for the thrills, the bills, the
>   pills that kill.

11

Month of
Somedays

DAY DAWNED ON a child's fantasy, a great snow that had fallen silently overnight, a storm that, better still, promised one day's reprieve from the return to school after Christmas vacation. Soft, wet flakes coated the trees of Sara Roosevelt Park and the baseball backstops along the East River and the arching rooftop girders of Seward Park High School. Four inches deep the frosting lay atop the cobblestones of Ludlow Street and the market stalls of Orchard, drifting to fill footprint and tire track, pothole and gutter. In the dim, tranquil morning, the city streets stood as dainty and charming as sugared sweets in a confectionery window.

Then came the decrees that there would be school and there would be work, and in moments the fanciful was rendered mundane. A slow line of cars skidded down the Williamsburg Bridge and onto Delancey Street, staining the snow with exhaust and shoving the dirty piles aside.

Marching toward the subway, the pedestrians drummed the flakes into silvery slush, while the legion of the homeless, driven into the stations underground, sought refuge on concrete platforms and wooden benches. "I'm not proud of this," said one, who had energy enough to ply a southbound train crowded with Seward Park students. "I'd rather work than beg." He wore a blue ski jacket, zipper broken and lining thin, and a bolt of burlap, wound around his waist like a sarong. "But I'd rather beg than freeze."

His was an appropriate prologue for the month ahead. On the streets outside Seward Park, January would bring the harshest cold spell in five years, killing six New Yorkers, one of them a newborn girl abandoned on a garbage heap. Inside the school, January would bring Regents examinations, RCT basic-skills tests, and the last round of term grades that any senior could include on a college application. For the seniors Jessica Siegel taught, and she taught nearly one hundred, January would determine, in large part, who moved forward, to college and career, and who remained behind, amid drugs and home-lessness and minimum-wage employment. "Someday" started now.

So they trudge across the wintry mess, girls in down, boys in leather, almost all bound around neck and ears by a *khaffiyeh*, the checkered headdress hawked by Palestinian and Senegalese peddlers. They stamp their snowy shoes and climb the stairs, trailing rock salt and wadded tissues. Above cowgirl boots, Jessica bundles herself into a puffy coat decorated with paisley swirls of purple and green. A man on the F train studies her and says knowingly, "Nineteen sixty-six."

The Monday morning syndrome is worse than ever in the wake of vacation and snowfall. A dozen bodies dot a classroom that accommo-dates thirty-four. The only excitement surrounds the settling of bets on college football bowl games and the professional playoffs. As she makes her third trip to the door to admit a straggler to English 7, Jessica says, "If I ever stop teaching, I could always be a doorman." Back at the lectern, by way of beginning, she touches both cheeks below her eyes.

"I'm sure you can see these bags down to the floor," she says.

"From what?" Ottavio Johnson asks.

"I only had three hours sleep last night. Can you figure out why?"

"There could be a few reasons," Ottavio says, winking, and both he and Jessica laugh.

The real one is that Jessica ended her holiday plowing through the most recent English test, and the results depressed her deeply—not only the scores of 30, 10 and 5, but her suspicion that some had passed by cheating on the few multiple-choice questions. And the test marks were hardly an aberration: Shortly before Christmas, Jessica had submitted her "predictive grades" for the semester, and almost half her pupils, even in the second-period class she savored, were career-ing toward failure. If a student could not meet *her* standards, stan-dards that were necessarily affected by empathy, Jessica could only wonder how they would fare with the officials in distant Albany who maintained the final authority on every single Regents examination, evaluating the South Bronx alongside Scarsdale.

"Let me say something about the test," Jessica announces before returning the papers. The class, knowing bad news awaits, wilts as one. "In general, they were lower than the last test. I don't know what it is. Some people are just not keeping up. And after all our work on writing essays, some of the people who have the most to say in class write down the first thing that comes to mind." She pauses. "I feel like a broken record on this: You have to back up what you say with evidence. You have to *prove it.*" The phrase is one of Bruce Baskind's favorites. "And I don't mean you say, 'On page thirty-one blah blah blah.' Put it in your own words. Go over your test before you hand it in. You can correct tenses, run-ons, sentence fragments. You know I'll always give you extra time to finish."

She taught a review lesson on essays last month, and she would like to teach another before the Regents, but there is no time. Jessica has barely enough periods left to complete *The Great Gatsby,* the one full-length novel she assigned during the term and the culmination of the course's exploration of the American Dream.

Nick Carraway may narrate the story, lead the journey, and voice the judgments at journey's end, but Jay Gatsby invariably serves as the surrogate for Jessica's students. Gatsby is perhaps *the* American dreamer, Horatio Alger with trace elements of Al Capone, a farm boy in search of fortune, position, and Daisy Buchanan, "the king's daughter, the golden girl." It requires no great leap for a class of new Americans and native-born outcasts to see a bit of Gatsby in themselves, their parents, and their friends. Geography and pigmentation may set them apart, but their aspirations are fundamentally Gatsby's, to transcend the bondage of birth and class, to attain a place among the prominent.

Over the years, Jessica has seen the same phrases recur in her students' journals and autobiographies, bromides repeated until they become mantras. *You've got to reach for the top. . . . You've got to keep at it. . . . If you try hard, you'll make it.* Popular culture presents her pupils with moral choices as clear cut as Rambo versus the Reds. Now comes Jay Gatsby, who wins their trust and admiration, charms city teenagers as he charmed West Egg society, and then confounds them with his criminal deceits, his ethical ambiguities. Is Gatsby good or bad? What's good or bad? Who decides? The lessons on *The Great Gatsby* animate Jessica's classroom as few others do, but when the day comes to discuss Fitzgerald's final chapters, his benediction on Gatsby's dream and America's, the silence can be funereal.

That day, though, is more than a week away. To this point, Jessica has spent one period on a social history of the 1920s, another on Nick Carraway's voice and role as narrator, and two others on the emerging characters of Daisy Buchanan, Gatsby's beloved; Tom Buchanan, her husband; Jordan Baker, Nick's lover; Myrtle Wilson, Tom's mistress; and George Wilson, her cuckolded husband. Today she begins peeling back the layers of Gatsby, and she starts by sketching on the blackboard the outline of a man's profile. Then she touches her chalk inside his head and draws a question mark.

"Who is Sherlock Holmes?"

"A great detective," says Rafael Guerrero, normally a quiet boy.

"Is he real?"

"No," says Harry Nieves, another introvert only now emerging. "He was invented."

"That's right," Jessica says. "He's fictional, but he seems so real a lot of people think he was an actual person." She remembers herself and her brother Norman creeping into an English chop house for a meeting of the Baker Street Irregulars, two children at a table of graybeards. "How did he solve crimes? How did he get clues?"

"With this," Rafael says, peering through an imaginary magnifying glass.

"He was observant," Harry adds.

"Observant," Jessica repeats, embossing the word as if lowering a seal onto warm wax. "There are crimes he solves because he analyzes cigarette ashes or can tell the make of a bicycle from its tracks. He was able to notice things nobody else noticed." She smiles. "And now I want you all to be Sherlock Holmeses and look at what we can learn about Gatsby from what he tells Nick." She pauses. "Who wants to read? Raquel? Page sixty-five. I want everyone to put on your hat and get out your pipe."

"Look here, old sport," he broke out surprisingly, "what's your opinion of me, anyhow?"

A little overwhelmed, I began the generalized evasions which that question deserves.

"Well, I'm going to tell you something about my life," he interrupted. "I don't want you to get a wrong idea of me from all these stories you hear."

So he was aware of the bizarre accusations that flavored conversation in his halls.

"I'll tell you God's truth." His right hand suddenly ordered divine retribution to stand by. "I am the son of some wealthy people in the Middle West—all dead now. I was brought up in America but educated at Oxford, because all my ancestors have been educated there for many years. It is a family tradition."

He looked at me sideways—and I knew why Jordan Baker had believed he was lying. He hurried the phrase "educated at Oxford," or swallowed it, or choked on it, as though it had bothered him before. And with this doubt, his whole statement fell to pieces, and I wondered if there wasn't something a little sinister about him, after all.

"What part of the Middle West?" I inquired casually.

"San Francisco."

"I see."

"My family all died and I came into a good deal of money."

His voice was solemn, as if the memory of that sudden extinction of a clan still haunted him. For a moment I suspected that he was pulling my leg, but a glance at him convinced me otherwise.

"After that I lived like a young rajah in all the capitals of Europe—Paris, London, Rome—collecting jewels, chiefly rubies, hunting big game, painting a little, things for myself only, and trying to forget something very sad that had happened to me long ago."

With an effort I managed to restrain my incredulous laughter. The very phrases were worn so threadbare that they evoked no image except that of a turbaned "character" leaking sawdust at every pore as he pursued a tiger through the Bois de Boulogne.

"Then came the war, old sport. It was a great relief, and I tried very hard to die, but I seemed to bear an enchanted life. I accepted a commission as first lieutenant when it began. In the Argonne Forest I took two machine-gun detachments so far forward that there was a half-mile gap on either side of us where the infantry couldn't advance. We stayed there two days and two nights, a hundred and thirty men with sixteen Lewis guns, and when the infantry came up at last they found the insignia of three German divisions among the piles of dead. I was promoted to be a major, and every allied government gave me a decoration—even Montenegro, little Montenegro down on the Adriatic Sea!"

Little Montenegro! He lifted up the words and nodded at them—with his smile. The smile comprehended Montenegro's troubled history and sympathized with the brave struggles of the Montenegrin people. It appreciated fully the chain of national circumstance which had elicited this tribute from Montenegro's warm little heart. My incredulity was submerged in fascination now; it was like skimming hastily through a dozen magazines.

"OK, Sherlock Holmeses," Jessica says, lowering her brow and pinching her chin between thumb and forefinger. "What do you find strange, odd, suspicious?"

"He looked at Nick sideways when he told him about Oxford."

"Anything else?"

"He left his sentences unfinished."

"Anything else odd?" A snowplow rumbles down Grand Street, its mechanical moan silencing Jessica. "Maribel? Joanna?"

"San Francisco," Julio Valentin replied rather cryptically.

"What about it?"

"It's on the West Coast."

Jessica pivots to the board and draws one of her standard trapezoidal maps of the United States. With the students, she locates San Francisco and the Midwest. Then she turns forward, soliciting again the perverse and the peculiar.

"He's telling Nick all these things and he hardly knows him," says Addie Severino.

"How his family died and he came into all this money," adds Harry.

"Again," Jessica says, spreading her arms like a scale. "Could happen. Could be true." She drops them to her side. "But looks kind of strange."

She starts to list the clues on the blackboard, next to the profile with the question mark. As she proceeds, Julio mentions Gatsby's military record.

"Anyone know how many people in a division?" she asks.

"A thousand," See Wai offers.

"Two thousand."

"Five thousand."

"Well, I didn't know, so I asked," Jessica says, gaveling the auction to a close. "I found out a German division in World War I had seven thousand to ten thousand men. And Gatsby held off three divisions with one hundred thirty men and sixteen Lewis guns?" She adds this to the list. "And what else? Raquel? Aracelis?" She raises one index finger like a wand. "Think about his life in Europe. 'I lived like a young rajah.' Does anyone know what a rajah is?"

"An Indian prince."

"Where do rubies come from?" She stops long enough to hear the murmurs of "India" and "Africa." "And he talks about hunting big game. In Paris and Rome?" No one bites at the bait, so she tries a more direct approach. "Is there much big game in New York?"

"Cockroaches and rats."

Another clue, the last for the moment, joins the litany. Jessica directs the inquiry to Gatsby's friend Meyer Wolfsheim, gambler, gangster, and rumored mastermind of the 1919 World Series fix. Next under the magnifying glass is Jordan Baker.

"Bad driver," volunteers See Wai, an expert on the subject.

"What does that say about her?"

"She's not responsible," See Wai says.

"Reckless," Wilfredo Ayala adds.

"And what else?"

"She's a golfer," said Cindy James, a tiny girl of infrequent attendance.

"Why does that matter?" Jessica asks.

"She cheats at it," Cindy answers.

"And what does Gatsby say to Nick? 'Miss Baker's a great sportswoman and would never do anything not right.'" Jessica leans on the corner of the desk and crosses her forearms in an interrogator's tableau. "What does that tell us about Gatsby?"

"That he's dumb."

"What's another way of saying that?"

"Stupid."

"That's not quite it," Jessica says delicately. "We're not talking about his IQ."

"Naive," Aracelis says.

"Gullible," Lun Cheung calls from his corner.

Jessica nods her head in affirmation and lightly bites her lip, as if tasting anew a remembered feast.

"Now you have to do what Holmes did," she says. "You continue on with the investigation and you test your theories."

Wilfredo rubs the wispy whiskers on his chin and says, "Elementary."

*   *   *

Gregg Gross's grandmother settled more than fifty years ago among the lettered avenues in the northeast corner of the Lower East Side. His mother was born there in 1947, and so, in 1970, was Gregg. The neighborhood was known as the East Village then, the tenements

shared by aging Jews and leftover hippies, the housing projects home
to blacks and Puerto Ricans grateful for their clean, well-lit rooms.
Gregg's grandmother still has a snapshot of foundations being poured
for the Jacob Riis Houses, a great event in the neighborhood, and
another of Gregg marching past the completed buildings in a Little
League parade. The East Village seemed fertile enough soil for raising
children, with a Catholic school down the block, basketball courts
and ballfields behind the projects, and little worse than some un-
sightly drunks by way of social deviance. Gregg remembers skirting
them on Avenue D, old men with gray stubble, playing dominoes on
milk-carton tables and tossing back rum and sweet wine. There was
little threatening about them, and even less that was appealing.

Now, as he completes the story of his neighborhood for *Seward
World*, Gregg resides in what police have dubbed "the retail drug
capital of America." It is the perfect Petri dish for culturing a narcotics industry, with abandoned buildings for transacting business and
vacant lots for surveilling cops and access to the Holland Tunnel and
the Williamsburg Bridge for customers' convenience. Drugs define
these streets and everything on them—the steel doors on dilapidated
buildings, the constant lines beside pay phones, the jet black Jeeps
with smoked-glass windows, the ubiquitous fencers of auto tires and
prescription pills, the immense spray-painted murals honoring the
young and the dead. They were the Gatsbys of Gregg's world, savvy
enough to thrive for awhile, striking enough to inspire pretenders,
self-made men in an era celebrating entrepreneurs.

Gregg sees their less romantic results when he walks to school each
morning. His route down Avenue B takes him past a marijuana
concession; a bodega and car service both fronting for cocaine
dealers; a shantytown thick with buyers and sellers of crack; a vacant
lot littered with empty vials and used needles; and, finally, where he
turns onto Houston Street, an assemblage of alcoholics, almost a
sentimental throwback to the neighborhood of his childhood. Here is
a community that cannibalizes its young, that desecrates its own
fleeting promise. Beer cans are heaved into community gardens. Elaborate murals espousing political ideals or racial pride are spattered
with brainless graffiti. "Hope = Demise," some cynic has scrawled
along East Ninth Street.

Few still call this area the East Village. First drugs provided it a new
identity as Alphabet City, an homage to Dodge City and the Wild
West. Then came the young bohemians with their art galleries and

sushi bars, and they elevated metaphor to a more sophisticated plane, replacing Alphabet City with Downtown Beirut. In their rituals of upper-middle-class rebellion, they made art of trash and graffiti and wrote stories about dabbling in hard drugs and prostitution, because otherwise life was so damn predictable. Downtown Beirut was for them the capital of the country of anomie. Gregg and his family felt more like the Beirutis of Lebanon, trapped in a war zone and ducking the bullets daily.

The transformation of this obscure bit of urban blight into a national symbol of narcotics could be traced in no small measure to a Kennedy. On the night of September 5, 1979, David A. Kennedy, the twenty-four-year-old son of Robert, was robbed of thirty dollars in a Harlem hotel. Kennedy's original account had two pedestrians waving down his car on West 116th Street and then forcing him into the Shelton Plaza Hotel. But as the police pressed their investigation, it became apparent that the hotel was a well-known marketplace for heroin and that Kennedy had entered altogether willingly to make a buy.* The prominent media coverage of his case sent a warning to whites about pursuing their drug tastes in the black ghetto. The East Village, which had seen heroin arrive in the latter years of the hippie movement, subsequently became the bazaar of choice. As a federal drug agent who made undercover buys in both neighborhoods explained: "When I went to Harlem to buy heroin, I felt uncomfortable. I had to keep my agents near me. You were going into a territory that was totally uncontrollable. You had to get out of the car alone, go into a building alone. As a white, you stuck out. On the Lower East Side, I could pull up in a car and a dealer would come to me. He gave me service. He was polite. 'What do you want?' 'Two bags.' 'Drive around the block.' And by the time I did, the kid was waiting with the dope."

Within a year of Kennedy's arrest, the drug culture first entered Gregg's life. There was the day he and his mother were leaving his aunt's apartment when suddenly two men raced down the street, one firing a pistol at the other. There was the day he was playing Pac-Man in a candy store and noticed people giving the cashier ten-dollar bills for little envelopes. "What are you doing there?" Gregg asked. "Sellin' weed," the cashier replied. Gregg was ten years old.

---

*Tragically, Kennedy never resolved his drug problem, dying in 1984 from an overdose of Demerol, Mellaril, and cocaine.

He had chanced upon not random miscreance but the contours of a burgeoning industry. In the early 1980s, drug gangs worked Alphabet City two or three to a block, each outfit a hierarchy of steerers, runners, carriers, packagers, and supervisors. Touts shouted brand names, hand-lettered signs offered needles for rent, and customers queued up as if for lottery tickets. With sales reaching $30,000 a day, each gang guaranteed the safety of its consumers, for as the Kennedy incident had shown, mugging was bad for business. When the police set up surveillance cameras, they filmed young mothers with strollers receiving complimentary tastes of cocaine as inducements to buy. Enforcement proved futile, for the city's force of narcotics officers had been slashed to 153 after the 1975 fiscal crisis, and the courts and prisons were chronically overwhelmed. It was not uncommon for a dealer to be arrested for the seventh or eighth time before his first case had even been heard.

The Koch administration sought to reverse this losing battle in one massive campaign, known as Operation Pressure Point. Unleashing 200 officers on January 19, 1984, the city abruptly shifted tactics from investigating high-level traffickers to attacking the street-level dealers who ruined life for the average citizen. Within seven weeks, the toll of arrests ran to 2,653; the seizures totaled 88,361 envelopes of heroin, 3,746 packets of cocaine, 9,628 pills, 1,759 hypodermic needles, 25 guns, one bomb, and $111,574.86 in cash; and armed robberies in the neighborhood had dropped by nearly half. Gentrification gathered such momentum along Avenues A and B, on the western fringe of Alphabet City, that one heroin shooting gallery was reinvented as luxury condominiums.

A few blocks east, however, the effects were far different. Ousted from their former habitations, Alphabet City's dealers thronged among the laundromats and Medicaid clinics on avenues C and D, and infiltrated the housing projects between Avenue D and the East River. It was in the months *after* Operation Pressure Point that Gregg first saw signs of cocaine. He was walking into a bodega to buy some potato chips, and the front door was blocked by a man's back. When the person turned, Gregg could see his badge. He retreated and asked a streetwise friend what had happened. A coke bust, he was told. Before long, arrests were part of the daily ritual. So were the cries of "Fila" and "Jordache" for crack, which first appeared in late 1985, during Gregg's sophomore year of high school. So were the shootings and slashings in transactions gone awry.

Not only had the dealers increased their presence in the neighborhood, they had adapted into a hardier, cannier, more ruthless breed. One gang sold $11 million of crack annually from "The Rock," a city-owned building on East Eleventh Street, and was thought to be responsible for nineteen murders in the vicinity. More than 150 arrests made little difference, and it took a court-ordered eviction and the actual sealing shut of five apartments to close the cabaret. Four blocks away, on East Seventh Street, two gangs established their own rudimentary government. They guarded against robberies and quieted noisy teenagers. They paid bail and legal fees for their employees. They treated the street to fireworks and roast pig on Independence Day, cleaning up afterward like thoughtful neighbors, and competed against each other in erecting the most elaborate decorations at Christmas. All they asked in return was free rein to sell cocaine, pounds of it. When one resident rose in opposition and began organizing tenants to oust dealers from their building, gang members beat him, broke his apartment windows, and stole and burned his car. Thus persuaded, the man resolved to live with his fellows in the spirit of harmony.

In 1988, New York City boosted its narcotics force to 1,100 officers and pumped $250 million into fighting drugs, with Alphabet City an area of special scrutiny. The Drug Enforcement Agency patrolled its streets so regularly that the locals coined the term "Fed Day" to announce the arrival of undercover agents in Chevys and Dodges. Yet no measure of manpower seemed sufficient. Violent crime, fed by drugs, soared across the city. Of 65,000 arrests for narcotics in New York in 1986, only 3,000 resulted in the criminal spending more than three days in jail. Seward Park students came to know the term "minimum wage" not only as the $3.35 hourly pay for legal jobs but also as the $100 daily that was guaranteed to beginners in the drug business. Youngsters were, in fact, preferred labor, for if arrested, they received lenient treatment as juveniles.

These were the kids Gregg knew. They were his friends and relatives, his neighbors and classmates, fifty or sixty all told. Maybe half managed to pull free, to direct themselves to the less flashy pursuits of an equivalency diploma and a cafeteria job. Others, like a buddy named Rodney, never got out. His story was, to Gregg, all too common—starting high school and finding new friends, cooler friends, friends who had friends who had stuff. Nobody worried much when Rodney was smoking pot and cutting class, not until he began rolling crack into his joints in what cognoscenti called a "woolah." Then he was through with the halfstep and addicted to crack alone, dwindling from pudgy proportions down to ribs and elbows and knees. Rodney's mother tried, without success, to talk him into entering a treatment program. He was arrested three times, twice beating the charge, once receiving probation. The last Gregg heard, Rodney had stolen his brother's VCR and television for drug money, and even at that he owed his dealers thousands of dollars. The word was he faced a death sentence if he didn't settle up soon.

When Gregg thinks of Rodney, he cannot help but judge. Rodney is weak. Rodney has no willpower. How much sympathy can you muster for someone who robs his own brother? But Gregg also remembers the Rodney he sat next to in school, the Rodney he played baseball with all summer. And then Gregg is not so sure what he thinks. Surrender is so available. When Gregg was a sophomore at Seward Park, arguing often with his sisters and tasting the thrill of independence, some friends introduced him to marijuana. One afternoon toward the end of the school year, in a park adjoining the annex, their hospitality extended to crack. A friend opened his palm to reveal a cellophane bag containing several beige pebbles, which looked to Gregg like bits of Camay soap.

"Try it," Gregg's friend said.

"Nah," Gregg answered.

"C'mon, man," that friend and others cooed. "Just a try."

They did not relent until Gregg was screaming, "Get away from me! Get away!"

The users who know Gregg now grant him the admiration due an abstinent among the debauched. But the rest of the merchants still reckon him as cash in their pockets, meaning crack in their pipes. Walking to school or the bus stop or his girlfriend's apartment, Gregg can expect a come-on every block or two. How many times can you just say no?

So writing about drugs in his neighborhood was not a difficult assignment for Gregg, at least in the conventional ways. Other than interviewing a police lieutenant, reading a history of narcotics, and looking through newspaper accounts of Operation Pressure Point, all tasks in which Jessica assisted, he had most of his information at hand. He spoke to his grandmother, his mother, his sister, his cousin, his teachers, his friends. Gregg's difficulties were those a more detached reporter would not have encountered. When he quoted sources, he had to obscure them behind more than pseudonyms. When he mentioned brand names, he had to cite out-of-date examples. People knew who sold what, and Gregg had no desire to identify dealers at his own peril. If he blurred some details, he preserved the depth, and in the end his intimacy was the strength of the piece. Others might write more stylishly, or with greater sweep, or more urgency, but Gregg knew the landscape as only a native son could. "Let me take you on a walk," his article began, "on the Lower East Side."

*   *   *

Four days since the resumption of classes, and less than a week before she must submit final grades for the term, Jessica reaches her lesson on Gatsby's fall. She has led her student Sherlocks through discussions of Gatsby's dream and Daisy's part in it, lingering especially over his memory of first kissing her and imagining the sidewalk on which they strolled lifting to "a secret place above the trees." The class's pursuit has frequently been fitful—one boy suggested that Gatsby was pining for a treehouse, another that Gatsby was gay because he refused so many willing women—but in the end, it has delivered results. By now, the sleuths of English 7 have unmasked Jay Gatsby as a bootlegger and an adulterer and, perhaps worst of all, the poseur whom Tom Buchanan calls "Mr. Nobody From Nowhere," James Gatz of North Dakota. At the same time, they have appreciated the purity of his love for Daisy, an infatuation as stubborn and senseless as any in a Harlequin paperback. When Jessica asked her students if Daisy would leave Tom for Gatsby, almost all swore she would. Only José Santiago, himself a husband and father, argued that sometimes security overrides passion. Knowing the romantic bent of her charges, Jessica yesterday issued an unusual warning with the nightly reading assignment: "Try not to get too upset." She felt obliged somehow to prepare them for the betrayal of Gatsby, the embodiment of upward mobility, by his lover.

Sitting among the students during the second period this morning is Emma Jon, notebook open before her, conducting a required observation of Jessica. Her presence should not have mattered to Jessica; 95 percent of the time she doesn't care who visits her room, because her intimate relationship is with the class. Whether she succeeds or fails, she measures herself by the class's reaction and she judges herself more harshly than would any superior. Yet because this is the first time Emma as chairwoman will watch Jessica teach and because of all the tension between them, Jessica wants to impress, partly as a way of reconciling. For the occasion, she has worn a sleek black dress set off by a silver necklace and matching earrings, as elegant an outfit as she owns. Still, she frets a bit because this lesson almost inevitably stuns a class into silence; to an observer, the quiet might appear to be the product of indifferent teaching.

"What's intuition?" Jessica asks the class.

"Like ESP," shoots back Julio. "You know something's going to happen."

"Now that you know what it is," Jessica answers, drawing both hands behind her back, "think about *The Great Gatsby* and how it ends. Could the ending have been foretold?" She pauses, but no answers come. "Do you remember what exactly the ending *is?*"

"I don't know," says the first voice. "I didn't read it."

Great, Jessica thinks to herself. *Fucking great.* She quickly calls on Addie, who obliges: "George Wilson kills Gatsby and then he kills himself." Jessica makes certain everyone has heard Addie's soft voice. Then she reads the paragraphs in which Nick describes coming upon the bodies.

"What I want to get at today," she says, closing the book and turning to write on the board, "is to what extent Gatsby's death is inevitable." With those words behind her in white chalk, like a scripture in Bible school, she again faces the class. "And what do we mean by inevitable? Aracelis?"

"Bound to happen."

"Knowing what we did about Wilson," Jessica continues, "what do we think he'd do?"

"That he'd go after Tom Buchanan," José says. "Because Tom was making it with his wife."

"Did he know it?"

"No," says Truman Chang, who Jessica recently moved forward from the seclusion of the last row. "He just knew it was a yellow car that killed his wife."

"He knew that clearly," Jessica acknowledges, beginning to pace. "But was the person driving the yellow car the person who had an affair with his wife?" She waits in vain. "Aracelis? Raquel? Addie? Lun?" Having played her best cards to no avail, she withdraws the question for another. She feels a nervous twinge at the stall. "What did Myrtle Wilson do when she saw the yellow car?"

Several students call in unison, "She ran to it."

"Right," Jessica says. "She *recognized* it." She pauses. "Why? We went over this yesterday."

"Because she saw Tom driving it that morning."

Jessica strides to the board and draws an arrow representing George Wilson's route, beginning on the left at a circle signifying his home, moving to the right into a circle marked "Tom's," and rising diagonally to a bull's-eye entitled "Gatsby's," in which Jessica inscribes an "X."

"And here's 'the holocaust,' as Nick calls it," she says, tapping the spot. She lets the word hang and descend before speaking again. "Could anything have intervened?"

"Daisy," says Lisa Carerra, a tall, tough girl who raced through the novel a week ahead of the class.

"What could she do?"

"Confess," Lisa says. "She hit Myrtle."

"What else?"

"Warn Gatsby," says See Wai.

"And why didn't she?"

"Careless," he declares so emphatically half the class swivels to stare.

"That's what Nick says," Jessica says with satisfaction. "Hang onto that." For months after, whenever she hears the word "careless," she will think of See Wai. "But why didn't she call him on the phone?"

"She couldn't."

"Why? She wasn't chained to the bed. She sent Wilson to kill the man who loved her."

"Because she was involved," See Wai says. "It was her fault."

"Right!" Jessica shouts. "She could've called him up, told him to run away, hide, go to"—she sneers—"New Jersey." It is a cheap joke but an effective one. When the laughter dies, she shifts from Fitzgerald's invention to her students' reality. "If you see someone running down the street with a knife or a gun and you don't warn people, what's your role?"

"Accomplice," Wilfredo says.

"And why do you think Gatsby stayed at home when Wilson came?"

"Because he was innocent," José says.

"What else?"

"He wanted to go to jail for Daisy," See Wai answers.

"And what else?"

"He was waiting for Daisy to call him." The voice is See Wai's again.

"And we know she didn't. So what does that make you think of Gatsby?"

"Determined."

"Foolish."

"Stupid."

"He might've been sick," José says, shifting his large legs into the aisle and reclining to expound. "But he wasn't stupid. He was in love like a teenager. And he had a dream and he wanted to act it out complete. I mean, Daisy told him she loved him."

Now the familiar silence suffuses the room. It provides Jessica with a moment to appreciate these students, to thank them. José hadn't even read the book as of yesterday, and today, he bursts with ideas. See Wai has been outspoken all term, but no piece of literature has similarly stirred him. Jessica has to marvel: A boy from peasant China swept up in a novel of the Roaring Twenties. Aracelis, pale and thin from a bout of bronchitis, came to school today in defiance of her doctor. In some ways, they saved her, as the World History repeaters had saved her before Stan Carter so many years ago. Yet this is different. This class could not have known the importance of Emma's presence. Oblivious to her, they did not perform. Their enthusiasm is more than well timed; it is real.

"I have a feeling you're quiet," she says softly, "because this ending is so sad. And I agree. I'd rather have a happy ending in a book. But *could* the ending be any different? Gatsby and Daisy get married. Church bells. Go off into the sunset. Could that happen? Knowing these people?" She flips open her palms, tilts her head. Then she reads Nick's comment about Gatsby's being worth more than "the whole rotten crowd."

"What do you think?"

"He was willing to go to jail for Daisy," Wilfredo says.

"It doesn't matter if he was a crook," Lun adds. "He was a genuine person. And genuine is genuine."

The bell sounds. As her students scatter, Jessica closes a binder on her lesson plan. When she looks up, Emma stands before her. She nods her head and says, "Very nice. Very, very nice."

*　　*　　*

Except for the mufflers and galoshes, the scene Bruce Baskind finds in the Board of Education's hiring hall could be the same one he left back in September. The same worn faces read the same dogeared newspapers from the same Channel Thirteen tote bags. The same school district map draws the same curious stares. The same bureaucrat presides with the same bonhomie: "You're not supposed to be *here!* You're supposed to be *there!*"

One mercy limits the misery. Today's visit to the numberless room on the sixth floor of 65 Court Street in Brooklyn should be Bruce's last. On this January afternoon, four years and seven months after he began teaching full time at Seward Park High School, he will be formally appointed to its faculty. Standing in line, he calculates the price he has paid and will continue to pay, for the board's leisure in scheduling and grading a social studies licensing exam and in officially assigning those who passed. The $500 he lost with his salary stalled since September at fourth-year level—one month's rent, to put it tangibly—cannot be recovered. Instead of having earned tenure a year and a half ago, he will not earn it for another three years. Instead of being eligible for a sabbatical in two and a half years, he will not be eligible for seven. Only now does the clock start ticking toward his pension.

A teacher behind Bruce hears him figuring aloud and lets slip a dry, rueful laugh. Bruce turns to meet her eyes and says, "I don't know whether to laugh or cry. I've been screwed so many ways." She nods knowingly. "I mean, what do these people know about what goes on in school? About the kids we teach. You think education is *their* guiding principle?" Again she nods. "I'll tell you what," Bruce whispers in mock conspiracy. "One of these days, we'll all get together and blow up this place. Start all over."

His rage need not wait so long for relief. Tonight, Bruce's drama class performs its satire on Seward Park, *School?*, bringing some balm to what, for him, has been a maddening term. He lost two weeks in October to hernia surgery and convalescence. Assemblies uprooted the drama class from the auditorium without warning a half-dozen times. Not until the last month have his students grasped any of the autonomy Bruce has offered them, and there is part of him that feels that if they bomb tonight, it may provide the most pungent lesson of all, for they would be the architects of their own disaster. But another part of him, the larger part, throbs with the intensity of an athlete on game day. Hadn't Bruce always said his two heroes were Phil Ochs and Mickey Mantle?

Bruce has called a rehearsal for 5 P.M. at the Henry Street Settlement, a few blocks east of Seward Park, where the play will be performed. But the only people on hand are his assistants, Sydney Sidner and Julia Halperin, and a lone pupil, Matthew Paoli. They enter the settlement's experimental theater, a rectangular room with cinder-block walls on three sides and a black curtain on the fourth. A few lights hang from girders, and ladders lean in the corners. Five burglar alarms can be counted. The stage, a bare floor with tape indicating a previous play's blocking, juts into the midst of 135 seats like water filling a wide, shallow pan. Distance is one luxury actors and audience will not share.

The next two students arrive, one of them, Benito Perez, fresh from Housing Court, where his mother is battling an eviction order. Three more follow, then two others. High-fives and soul shakes are exchanged. Lines are rehearsed, dance clubs discussed. Someone tunes a box to the "Hot Music" station. The drama class's one couple, Gerald Chan and Sophia Santana, appear and announce their engagement. Sophia lifts her left hand regally toward Sydney, the golden ring glinting. The bride-to-be is eighteen years old. Her fiancé, the same age, will enter the Marine Corps in July. Sydney presses her palms against her cheeks. Sophia stares at her with dark eyes wanting affirmation. Sydney says, "I'm just . . . I'm just . . ." She cannot speak her true thoughts, and a half-minute passes before she can control her shock enough to hug Sophia and wish her and Gerald luck. That, Sydney knows, they will need.

At 5:55 P.M. Bruce realizes he has forgotten the programs and runs back to school. At 6:20, the 5:00 rehearsal begins. At 6:30, Angel Fuster races into the theater, carrying torn, bloodied jeans to prove he was delayed by a motorcycle accident. At 6:50, the spectators start to arrive for the 7 P.M. curtain.

"Keep them out till we finish the run-through," Bruce tells Julia, who locks the door. Then he turns to his wife, Melicia, and says, "The crime of murder is the same if you kill one person or ten. I'll take 'em all out. Like potato chips."

Rehearsal ends at 7:40 P.M., and the door opens five minutes later. Half the seats fill with teachers, students, graduates, friends, and sundry hangers-on. It is an impressive turnout, all told, for a night of relentless wind and mercury in the teens.

School? begins with a scene of students awakening in their separate households. One buries himself under the blankets, another rushes out after having overslept, a third steals his little brother's lunch money, and a fourth convinces his father there is no school because of the holiday "Kosher Thursday," which draws the biggest laugh of all. This is followed by a rendering of Seward Park's real morning ritual—students producing their schedule cards for a security guard before being permitted inside the building—the twist being that while a cardless boy is turned away, a pretty girl without one is admitted. *School?* then enters a history class to lampoon "brain-checking," the campaign of sloth by which students reduce their teacher to writing notes on the blackboard. When one boy asks for the evening's homework, the rest mug him. "Like the Lower East Side class," Jessica whispers to Denise Simone, and they both laugh, as do most of the faculty in the audience. It is the students who turn mute before the scene's incisiveness. The next skit illustrates what Bruce calls "passive resistance" to education. One boy meanders into class late and without the required note, another argues about the location of his seat, and a third, played by Angel with pitch-perfect insincerity, diverts the teacher with questions about his high school days. By the time the teacher can launch into his lesson on the theory of evolution, the bell rings, ending the period. Jessica's eyes crinkle with amusement. The closing scene depicts Bruce's drama class, with its egalitarian ethos, as the preferred alternative. The play's version of the class, however, is a romanticized remembrance, omitting the absences, squabbles, and missed assignments that actually plagued it, right up to tonight's belated curtain.

Now, thirty-five minutes after it has taken to the stage, the cast assembles for a curtain call. The evening's drama, however, has yet to begin. It is time for questions and answers, an exercise for which Bruce equipped each viewer with a pencil and a blank page in the program. If the students can withstand inquiry, Bruce believes, they have not merely mimicked, but learned.

"Do you feel all teachers are like that?" Denise asks.

"No," Angel answers. "That's why we had some variations in the kinds of classes. One worked better than the others."

If a freer classroom with students sharing power is supposed to be the answer, Bruce's sister-in-law Meredith asks, how well would it work in courses like chemistry?

"The school wants to make us dependent," says Ralph Sorrino, a gangly boy with curly bangs. "We want to be independent." The diagnosis, verbatim, is Bruce's own.

"You can be that independent in a drama class," Denise volleys.

"Can you self-generate a biology class? 'Let's act out the theory of evolution.' From a teacher's standpoint, that might work if students did their homework, read the chapter. I try to teach a story and three students read it."

"Why you think they didn't read it?" Angel asks.

"A lot of it is apathy," Denise says. "So what would you have a teacher do?" She fixes her stare on the cast. "I have better things to do at night than read your homework. But I need to measure your knowledge, and I can't wait till the tests, because that's too late. Whether you know it or not, a lot of your teachers are as frustrated as you are. So how do you help me and how do I help you?"

"You have to stimulate us," Gerald says.

"You have to give us a reason why," Matthew puts in.

"How can we be stimulated," Benito adds, "when you're told not to think, that you have no power, that you can't make suggestions?"

As had Ralph's before him, Benito's words echo Bruce's own. And Benito, like Ralph, delivers the analysis less with a historian's detachment than with a teenager's temper.

By now, the room is abuzz with electricity, more than the play itself had generated. Whatever else can be said of the entertainment, it has provoked, and surely that was among Bruce's intents. So discomfited were his students by the acute self-criticism of their play, they have lashed back at any teacher in sight. The question is whether their aim, and in a sense Bruce's, has found its proper target. Seward Park's clock-punchers went home six hours ago. The teachers who ventured out on this bitter night—Denise, Jessica, Bob Campus of business, Carlton Schade of science, Leah Gitter of special education, Ted Auerbach and Jon Goldman of English as a Second Language—must feel some commitment. Several came to see a favorite student perform, largely because a parent could not or would not. But in a month of examinations, this is an evening for reversing roles. The graders are being graded, and the report card shows straight Fs.

When the questions cease, Bruce strides from a corner of the theater into the spotlight. As he opened the evening, he will close it. He wears jeans, running shoes, and a thermal underwear top, dark chest hair pushing out at the neck. He spreads his legs solidly on the ground, as if awaiting a punch. Every passion he has harbored about education, every idea he has floated at lunch tables and in subway cars, every indignity he has endured as student and teacher and promised never to forget, pours forth in a torrent.

"If you know kids at Seward," he says, "you know they're very smart, very bright. But in Seward, every student is told, 'Take off your coat,' 'Don't wear a hat,' 'You can't go to the bathroom now.' As if these kids don't know when they want to take a piss." His students hoot, whistle, shout him on. "What we need is to turn the school on its head. Give these kids a broom, and let's see what happens to graffiti. Let them run the cafeteria instead of the profiteers who make millions from cardboard hamburgers. Let them run a day-care center, and see how fast they want to become parents. I say, if you give people responsibility, they'll be responsible. If you give them no responsibility, forget it."

Jessica grabs a ride to Greenwich Village with Bob Campus and his wife. She asked no questions in the theater and says nothing now in the car. Denise was her voice, clear and direct, but vicarious speech permits no catharsis. As much as Jessica laughed at several of the skits, for there is no denying they were witty and well observed, a different reaction colors her retrospection. Where in *School?* was the conventional class that works, at least occasionally? Where was English 7, analyzing *The Great Gatsby* and enjoying it? She cannot believe that every time a kid asks a question it's a ploy; she cannot believe that she never stimulates, that she does not care. Was the cry she just heard, so full of condemnation, that of twenty students or of their teacher? Whatever its origin, the sound sends her home hurting. She cares rather too much.

*   *   *

On the morning after Emma's observation, the heaviest snow of the winter tumbles outside Room 336. The flakes twirl in whirlpools of white, cloaking the skyscrapers, muffling the clatter of traffic, forcing this most hurried of cities to slacken its pace. In English 7, it is a morning for summation, for contemplation, fine avocations for an inclement day. Gatsby is dead and buried, but it remains for Jessica and her students to define the meaning of his demise. "What's the American Dream?" she asks by way of both introduction and completion, for it is the same question with which months earlier she had begun English 7's exploration of literature.

"Money."

"Freedom."

"Happiness."

"Dusty Rhodes," says Truman.

"I don't understand," Jessica admits. *Dusty roads? Is he talking about the West? The frontier?* This, assuredly, was not in the lesson plan.

"He's a pro wrestler," Truman elaborates.

"Pro wrestling is the American Dream?"

"No," Truman says, brusque in enlightening the ignorant. "Dusty Rhodes. That's his nickname. 'The American Dream.'"

Still a bit baffled by Truman's contribution—maybe she should have left him in the last row—Jessica proceeds. She elicits from the class Gatsby's sources of wealth, bootlegging and selling stolen bonds, and reminds them of his partnership with Wolfsheim the gangster. Then she shifts the discussion to the daily regimen of self-improvement that Nick discovered among Gatsby's belongings. Finally, she recalls what Gatsby's father said of him, that he was "bound to get ahead."

"But, in fact," she says, placing hands on hips, "how did Gatsby end up?"

"Dead," José says.

"Alone," Wilfredo adds.

"Without his dream," Addie offers.

"And at *thirty*," Jessica underlines. "With just three people at his funeral." She pauses. "Why does he end up that way?"

"He got shot."

"I mean looking at the whole book."

"He chose the wrong girl."

"But if you can generalize," Jessica persists, "what's Fitzgerald saying about a poor person trying to move up?"

"If you get close," José says, "somebody'll take it away."

She sits on the corner of the desk, domestic in black corduroys and a purple jacket she wove herself. Opening the book, she could as easily be situated before a fireplace. She reads Fitzgerald's final paragraphs:

. . . I wandered down to the beach and sprawled out on the sand.

Most of the big shore places were closed now and there were hardly any lights except the shadowy, moving glow of a ferryboat across the Sound. And as the moon rose higher the inessential houses began to melt away until gradually I became aware of the old island here that flowered once for Dutch sailors' eyes—a fresh, green breast of the new world. Its vanished trees, the trees that had made way for Gatsby's house, had once pandered in whispers to the last and greatest of all human dreams; for a transitory enchanted moment man must have held his breath in the presence of this continent, compelled into an aesthetic contemplation he neither understood nor desired, face to face for the last time in history with something commensurate to his capacity for wonder.

And as I stood there brooding on the old, unknown world, I thought of Gatsby's wonder when he first picked out the green light at the end of Daisy's dock. He had come a long way to this blue lawn, and his dream must have seemed so close that he could hardly fail to grasp it. He did not know that it was already behind him, somewhere back in that vast obscurity beyond the city, where the dark fields of the republic rolled on under the night.

Gatsby believed in the green light, the orgiastic future that year by year recedes before us. It eluded us then, but that's no matter—tomorrow we will run faster, stretch out our arms farther. . . . And one fine morning—

So we beat on, boats against the current, borne back ceaselessly into the past.

"What was this island the sailors saw?"

"Manhattan," José answers.

"And what are they holding their breath about?"

"All the riches the land has," Addie says.

"The glamour of it," José adds.

Jessica reads again one phrase, "face to face for the last time in history with something commensurate to his capacity for wonder." The words ask their own question.

"He's talking about the Statue of Liberty," Lun says.

"Let's get our dates straight," Jessica cautions. "These are Dutch explorers. Think when the statue was built. What did they see in the New World?"

"Their dreams," Aracelis says in her raspy, ill voice. "A better chance for themselves." Finished, she coughs.

"A chance," Jessica says. "Even if they left Europe with just the shirt on their back. Here they can begin again. A poor man can get rich. You can change who you are." She pauses. "Fitzgerald talks about a 'fresh, green breast' of land. Remember Gatsby reaching out to the green light on Daisy's dock? How is that similar?"

"It's something he sees in front of him," Aracelis says. "Calling him."

Jessica again reads aloud the final paragraph, then asks, "What does this say about Fitzgerald's idea of the American Dream?"

"You have to work hard," See Wai says. "Toil."

"You have to struggle," Lun says. " 'Against the current.' "

"What do *you* think he meant?" José asks Jessica.

"I'll tell you in a minute."

"Well," José says, advancing unprompted, "I think he means that life's a bitch and then you die."

His words halt the class for a moment. The sound of snow crunching under a truck can be heard.

"Fitzgerald is saying that you can try," Addie says at last. "But . . ."

"But what?"

"But you can't succeed."

"It's nothing but a dream," Wilfredo says. "Something that isn't real. Something that doesn't come true."

The message is both devastating and unavoidable. Sensitive reading and sound reasoning were bound to bring a class of dreamers to this awakening.

"I think if Fitzgerald walked through the door," Jessica says, "he'd probably agree. He was very cynical. Look how Gatsby ended up. Even with intelligence and energy. He can't really advance from where he started in life." She lifts her brows a bit. "But that's not the only opinion. Next week, we'll read someone else's view on the American Dream." She dusts chalk off her hands. "And it's very different."

*   *   *

Officially, Jessica is home ill; unofficially, she is taking a "mental health day." She called in sick this morning, it is true, and she is spending the day in her apartment in jeans and a floppy sweater, a cup of coffee at her elbow, but far from relaxing, she is doing the hardest job she knows. She is playing God. By this time tomorrow, she will have issued final grades for 140 students, judgments that will propel some toward college and consign others to a fifth year of high school, judgments that will affect everyday matters, from athletic eligibility to parental affection.

She started before breakfast, pulling her leaf table away from the south wall and into the center of the living room. Papers surround her station like a moat—final tests on *The Great Gatsby,* galley proofs and blank dummies for *Seward World,* brochures on financial aid for college, Sunday's *News* and *Times* still unread on this Tuesday. She sets her grade book and two folders of English exams before her and opens a plastic garbage bag at her side. Her cat, Marmalade, wanders across the table, sniffing at jars of rubber cement, before stretching out beneath a desk lamp as if tanning under the Aruba sun.

Although it is midmorning, little daylight enters the apartment.

Cold gusts rattle the windows, and steam bumps through the radiator. The sounds of drill and motor seep into the room, incessant and dull, yet oddly as comforting to an urbanite as are crickets to a rustic. Against their background, Jessica taps red pen to white paper, turns pages with a leafy rustle, moves each completed test to a corner with the crisp hiss of a skater skimming ice. She turns sideways in her chair, draws her right leg onto the seat beneath her left, and falls into a rhythm as regular as that of the machinery outside.

Some grades are a pleasure to inscribe. In second-period English 7 alone, Jessica awards a 98 to Addie, a 96 to Aracelis, a 95 to Lun, a 90 to Raquel, an 85 to See Wai, an 85 to Wilfredo, and an 80 to José. A few others force Solomonic calculations. Angel, for instance, had test scores of 60, 75, 85, 79, 75, and an incomplete. He never submitted a revised autobiography. He handed in homework only eleven of twenty-eight times. In Jessica's first year as a teacher, Angel would have failed, period, because she required a standard that was quantifiable. Then Hannah Hess took her aside and asked her some questions. What's the point of failing someone simply to punish? What's the point of making someone go through the motions again? You fail someone, Jessica came to believe, only if they have something to gain in repeating the course, something to learn. So here is Angel, who is capable of superior work, no question about it, and who owes her one test and a rewritten autobiography. Yet his writing did improve. He did understand the literature. He did stir discussion with insight and wit. If she held him back, if she rubbed his nose in his inconsistency, would he benefit? Or would he just get bored? If anything, Angel needs the stimulation of different, more demanding material, not redundancy with rules. Jessica locates the tiny box in the far right column of her grade book and writes within it "65." To the right, in the space for "comment codes," she adds "14," which translates as, "Has the ability to do better."

For too many students, though, no such hairs need be split. Failure is obvious; failure is rampant. What most disturbs Jessica is that fewer fail because they work poorly than because they do not work at all. She forces her students to rewrite papers and to elaborate on tests. She permits them to linger over exams for as much time as they need to finish. Unlike many colleagues, she confers with every individual pupil before each report card is released. She met with 23 parents on Open School Night, more than all but 6 of Seward Park's 200 teachers, counselors, and chairs. And yet the failures mount—2 of 6 students in advanced journalism; 13 of 25 in beginning journalism; 22 of 35 in the Lower East Side class; 16 of 33 in first-period English 7; and 15 of 35 even in second-period English 7, the section that seemed so impressive. And when she tallies these failures, all 68 of them, she sees that 38 are due solely to absences. *They're hanging on by a thread,* she thinks, *and if the wind blows, that's it.* A few, particularly perceptive, can observe and evaluate their own self-destruction. Earlier this week, a girl in English 7 returned her copy of *The Great Gatsby* with a message tucked inside the cover.

> I know that you are probably mad at me, definitely disappointed in me, and you wouldn't want to hear from me at this point, but I really felt that I had to write this note. I'm really sorry that I let you down. I guess I wanted to reassure you that it had nothing to do with you personally. I failed on my own. You happen to be a very good and caring teacher and I appreciate what you did in trying to help me. I guess my will-power is hopeless, or rather non-existent. I hope that if you happen to be one of my teachers next term that we will meet on better terms and in a later period. I just wish that there were more teachers like you, who do make a difference.
> P.S. Your efforts are not futile (although they may seem so).

Placing the Fs into her grade book, Jessica cannot help but feel futile, and never more so than when she writes one on the line reserved for Tam, Mary. Everything Mary did she did with excellence, earning 100 on her autobiography, 95 on her book report on *Ethan Frome,* 90 on a test on Indian and Puritan literature, 90 on a surprise quiz on Thoreau. But that essentially was all she did. The grade book reveals that Mary missed every other examination and all but three of twenty-eight homework assignments. The Delaney card shows she skipped class twenty-four times and arrived late six others. *How can I pass her?* Jessica thinks. *How can I justify it?*

Yet Mary was among the smartest students Jessica had all term, and she was quite possibly the one with the hardest life. There was no forgetting her autobiography, with its intimations of suicide. She remembered, too, Open School Night, and the appearance first of a nun from Mary's group home and then of her adoptive father. He was an old man in a baggy blue suit and a dusty trench coat, bifocals slipping down his nose and age spots marring his parchment skin. He did not want to hear about Mary's talents and he did not want to hear about Mary's troubles. He wanted simply to know how Ms. Siegel would ensure that Mary passed. He wanted results. Now Jessica could see the threatening side, the fierce will of which his daughter had written. When she told him she could not promise to pass Mary, he picked up his umbrella and disappeared into the hall. She was glad he had not asked where Mary lived, because she would have refused to tell him.

And what was her part in Mary's miseries? What else could she have done? She had talked to Mary and telephoned Mary and steered Mary into the Pathfinders program at University Settlement, a mooring for her good heart. There had been times, a day here, a week there, when Mary seemed to be responding. But in the end, she had withdrawn more completely than ever. She had given Jessica nothing to engage, nothing but an empty seat in the first row, where emptiness could not be disguised. What Jessica feels this solitary afternoon is not blame, for Mary or herself, but sadness and exhaustion, the awesome helplessness of charging into the breakers and heaving the lifeline and watching the hand that could have grabbed it slip instead beneath the water's surface.

There are mysteries. There are mysteries a teacher can barely apprehend and an outsider rarely pauses to imagine. The other day, Jessica was having lunch with her Aunt Hilda, and the conversation turned to grading. "You have to have high standards," Hilda said. "Just because kids have lots of problems doesn't mean you let them off easy." Her point, to Jessica, was irrelevant. She sets high standards and the kids, for all their complaining, want them. But school lasts for only six hours a day—six hours that are powerfully affected by whatever happens in the other eighteen. A mother must go to the hospital and cannot speak English; the best job around gets off at midnight; somebody has to watch the baby. And for any of those reasons, or a dozen others a teacher may never know, a student misses class too many times to pass. Jessica does not invoke the exigencies of poverty and foreignness as an excuse, only as an appeal for help, help in the form of more counselors and smaller classes, starting in kindergarten. Anyone inside a school like Seward Park understands; it's just common sense. But the Fs Jessica gives, ironically enough, will only arm those who argue that all that is missing from inner-city education is character, on both sides of the desk.

As the hours pass in Jessica's apartment, she peels off her sweater to reveal a *Seward World* T-shirt. The noises of labor abate, and the footsteps in the corridor increase, for it is the time of homecoming. Darkness falls over the concrete courtyard, where only a few bulbs burn above the garbage cans. Jessica works until midnight, sleeps until 4 A.M., then finishes playing God in a nightgown and bare feet. With her grades filed, the term is essentially complete. But since the students have several more days of class before the week of Regents exams and minimum-competency tests, their teachers are obliged to continue teaching, and to pretend everyone's efforts are not super-fluous. On what is now Wednesday morning, Jessica need not pretend. She has a lesson guaranteed to grip.

*   *   *

"Aug. 28, 1963," Jessica writes on the blackboard. "March on Washington." She passes out a set of rexos and then reaches inside a record jacket for a black disk, warped with wear. After placing it on the record player, a portable antiquated enough for a sock hop, she hands Lisa Carerra the album jacket. It has a photograph of a black man at a podium with a crowd of thousands arrayed before him; to the right of the picture is a list of names: Roy Wilkins, A. Philip Randolph, Whitney Young, Jr., Walter Reuther, and Martin Luther King. Anyone unacquainted with the occasion it captures might judge the record from its cover to be a soul-music anthology.

The disk spins, wobbling like a tipsy hostess. The sound emerges, first the scratches etched by earlier needles, then a thunder of applause, and then a man's deep, rich voice, talking about his dream. Aracelis folds her hands solemnly, and sometimes her head jerks back in reflex to the power of the oratory. See Wai stares to the front of the room, as if expecting to find the speaker there. Raquel reads along on the rexo, mouthing a phrase now and again. Jon Goldman, passing in the hallway, pauses by the door to listen. Jessica leans against the pale blue radiator, thinking, remembering. Sun slants across her arms, for it is warm outdoors with January's first thaw.

"You know," Jessica says, lifting the needle, "we've followed the American Dream all through the class. We talked about Fitzgerald's view. Now we've heard Martin Luther King's. What's his dream?"

"No racism," Raquel says.

"Closer relations between people," See Wai says.

"Justice," Addie says.

Maribel Mendez raises her hand, and when Jessica calls on her, she reads aloud from the text: ". . . to work together, to play together, to struggle together, to go to jail together, to stand up for freedom together . . ."

"Going to jail together," Jessica repeats, tightening the aperture.

"That's an interesting image. What does he mean by that?" No one answers. "I've had people laugh at that line before. Nobody laughed here." She rereads the phrase. "What does he mean?"

"Was there a jail for blacks and a jail for whites?" José asks.

"No," Jessica says. "They put them all together in jail."

"A lot of blacks went to jail protesting for their rights," Aracelis volunteers. "And King wants the whites to stand with them."

"Right," Jessica says, pressing her palms together. "And he says, 'I *still* have a dream.' Why?"

"Because his dream hasn't come true," Wilfredo says.

"We haven't been following what we put down in the Constitution," Harry adds.

"Obviously," Jessica says. "Slavery was banned in 1863, and almost one hundred years later, blacks needed a civil rights movement just so people could use the same bathroom." She pauses. "What does that have to do with King talking about going to jail?"

"It looks to him like he's going to have trouble," Addie says.

"And what happens to him?"

"He dies," Rafael says.

"At home?"

"He got shot," Jose says.

"In 1968," Jessica resumes. "Almost twenty years ago. So why do we still listen to his words today?"

"Because what he talked about changing, it all happened," Rafael says.

"Because nothing changed," Julio shoots back.

"So what do other people think?"

"Howard Beach."

"But we all go to school together."

"People look at you funny."

"You're all right," Jessica says, glad to be dealt such complexity. "It's true that a black person in the South today doesn't have to use a different bathroom, a different water fountain, a different hotel. Yet there's still racism and injustice today." She drops her left elbow into her right palm. "When you were listening to the record, I noticed everyone was quiet. King's a powerful speaker, but even when I've had kids in class read the speech, it's the same way. This man has been dead and buried for twenty years. The fact his words still live tells us about the power of literature." She allows the thought to air. "Now, Fitzgerald and King never met." She waits for laughter, but nobody appreciates the irony. "I guarantee it." Still nothing. "They ran in different circles, I guess." She gives up on the comic interlude. "They both had ideas about the American Dream, and we know their views were in conflict. Who do you agree with?"

"Fitzgerald," says Joanna Chau. "There's no chance in this society."

"The dream doesn't work sometimes," See Wai seconds.

"It's some of both," José says. "I mean, King struggled and he accomplished a lot. But some of this racism stuff is still goin' around. I have a friend in the Army in Kentucky, and he says they still burn crosses down there."

"King," Raquel says. "Because he has a more optimistic dream. If you struggle you can make it."

"But King was like Gatsby," Harry argues. "He got killed for believing in his dream."

Aracelis, so composed most of the time, reddens. She hears the words as an assault on her own aspirations.

"Poor people can *accomplish* things," she insists, iron in her voice. "King made life better. Even if he didn't accomplish everything."

The last word arises from an unlikely source, a girl named Lynette Haines. A gifted writer, she rarely spoke aloud all term long. Even eye contact appeared to pain her, and she seemed often to desire nothing more than to vanish down the neck of her sweater. Jessica had seen Lynette one afternoon on a subway platform with her boyfriend, and the girl unclasped her beau's hand and blushed at being observed.

"King gives us hope," Lynette says, eyes set on her pencil tray. "He helps you struggle. Because we're all poor. Even if you have money, you're missing something. We're all missing something. And King says we have to try to find it."

Now it is Jessica's turn.

"I have a number of goals for this class," she says. "I want you to pass the Regents. I want you to appreciate American literature. And I want you to come to your own conclusions about things, to have confidence in your own abilities. In high school, teachers give you one answer. In college, you find out there are many answers, many interpretations. And you saw today that history and literature aren't separate. They're related. Everything's connected. You'll see that in college." In this moment, she can assume the impossible, that they will reach college, all of them. Without believing so, she could not have served any of them. "And it makes me feel good to see you finding that out. It makes me happy."

12

Castillo
de Jagua

THE SECOND EDITION of *Seward World* arrives during the week of Regents examinations, a most terrible time. With homerooms disbanded and test taking the only activity, Jessica and her staff have no choice but to stack the papers in Seward Park's central hallway, beneath a sign urging passersby to help themselves. The pile indeed diminishes as days pass, like a mound of birdseed eaten by an unseen flock, but on Friday afternoon, Jessica hauls a dozen unopened bundles into the English office, there to be stashed in file cabinets galore.

Its primitive distribution aside, the issue pleases her, far more than the first. The masthead carries the name of Rosie Sanchez as editor-in-chief, a testament to Rosie's prolific output and dependable nature. The center contains a four-color film advertisement, supplied and paid for by the agency Jessica had chastised back in September for offering only enticements to join the Army. Gregg Gross's article on drugs in Alphabet City occupies a full page, with photographs and enlarged quotations. Norman Wong, a favorite alumnus, contributed a report on a holiday visit by students and teachers to residents of a Brooklyn nursing home, while Sammy Martinez, a current pupil, completed an article about the "Seward Follies" talent show as he was mourning his father's death.

Then there is the story atop page 12, bearing the headline "Professional Sports—A Dream or a Fantasy?" It is a sobering piece of work, a well-researched warning to high school athletes who expect a career in the big leagues. The story was suggested by the same boy who wrote it, Carlos Pimentel, and instead of spouting the standard cautions in advice-column fashion, he employed irony and counterpoint, posing the youthful bravado of Seward Park athletes against the adult wisdom of such figures as Mark Jackson, the rookie guard of the New York Knicks, and George Vecsey, a sports columnist for *The New York Times*. For a seventeen year old and a journalistic novice, Carlos had approached them with a minimum of awe. But what struck Jessica most was the insight implicit in the piece, for Carlos is the star of Seward Park's basketball team, averaging twenty-eight points per game, the sort of boy usually most vulnerable to the very myths he demolished.

Carlos never intended to take beginning journalism, and considered, in fact, that he hated to write. It was his counselor, Hal Pockriss, who surreptitiously assigned him to the course. The first qualities Jessica saw in him were those everyone saw: twin dimples and feathery lashes from the child he was and long, stringy limbs for the man he would be. His charm was unaffected and his reputation unsullied, from basketball court to classroom to comic turns in school plays. Carlos seemed so much the paragon that few teachers dared ask for more, and yet his most offhand comments indicated the depth behind the dimples, at least to Jessica. On the third day of journalism class, she wrote on the board a favorite wisdom of Thomas Jefferson: "Were it left to me to decide whether we should have a government without newspapers, or newspapers without a government, I should not hesitate a moment to prefer the latter." She then asked the students why America needed its free press, and Carlos simply said, "Oliver North, 'I don't recall,'" an allusion to the Marine officer's selective memory in testifying before Congress about the Iran-Contra affair. A few weeks later, when it was Carlos's turn to suggest the daily journal topic, he solicited reactions to President Reagan's nomination of Appellate Judge Robert Bork to the Supreme Court. Whether or not Carlos enjoyed writing news, he clearly enjoyed reading it.

The writing came soon enough, anyway. First was a forecast for Seward Park's sporting teams, then the story for the current issue. Already in the works for the next edition is an article about military recruiting of high school students, a subject that inflames Jessica, a topic she could entrust only to one who shares her sentiments. Out of that miserable journalism class, Jessica can tell herself, she has discovered in Carlos one pearl. And in a school full of children wrestling society's demons, here is a boy who seems to have skirted them all.

*   *   *

Where other places, larger and more prosperous places, might have situated a town square, the hamlet of Boca de Mao in the Dominican Republic laid out its baseball diamond. The baseball field stretched from the sharecroppers' shacks to the sugarcane fields, just north of the irrigation ditch and the main road, an expanse of scrub grass with baselines worn into sandy soil and chickens pecking for worms in the outfield. Far beyond the longest home run hung the Septentrional mountains, and far behind the worst wild pitch rose the Central peaks, and it was these two ranges that demarked the Cibao valley, that drew down the rain that nourished the land that made life for the farmers secure enough to allow for baseball on Sunday.

There and then, Carlos's memories began, the memories of a magical boyhood. At the age of five, he was the first grandchild in his mother's extended family, and younger by eight years than the closest of the seven relatives with whom he shared a hut of thatched palm leaves and plantain tree bark. Too young for fieldwork, Carlos spent his days splashing in the waterfall on the Rio Mao and his nights nestling next to Daniel, his favorite uncle. In the warm darkness, he smelled the perfume of papaya and mango and lemon and he heard feet shuffling down the dusty lane, for evening was the time for visiting, when oil lamps flickered with welcome, making mean shacks glow like jack-o-lanterns. After each harvest, Carlos went with his family the two miles to Mao, a bustling burgh of 1,000, and in the central *zócalo,* he watched prize fights and listened to accordion and saxophone entwine in the bittersweet serenades of *bachata.*

Carlos did not know his father, it was true, and could not even remember his face, but others told him that Ramón Pimentel was in America, which meant he was a man of position and means. And the best chance for Carlos and herself ultimately to join him, as Bernandita Pimentel saw it, lay in leaving Boca de Mao for Santo Domingo, trading the sureness of the country for the possibility of the city. But when she carried Carlos out of paradise, 120 miles across the mountains, he could not comprehend. He was young and protected; his innocence was absolute.

The name of their new neighborhood was Villa Maria, and the houses along Calle Once, where Carlos and Bernandita lived with family friends, seemed appealing enough. The houses were painted peach and aqua and had little front porches set off by cinder-block fences and the finest featured wooden louvers and wrought-iron grilles. On the inside, though, they were airless and stifling and cramped, with two rooms for sleeping and one for both cooking and cleaning. And back behind the bright colors of calle Once snaked jagged dirt alleys, flanked by shacks of sheet metal and warped palm wood, their walls and roofs patched until nothing original remained. Gray water drained down gutters, past coconut husks and cardboard cartons and empty quarts of motor oil. Chickens fed in makeshift pens, and pigs and goats stood tethered to trees. Dogs ambled through the heat, trailing clouds of flies, and children tussled shirtless in the dust. When the children rose, it was hard to tell where the smudges ended and the blotches of disease and starvation began.

Most of the people in Villa Maria had come from the country, like Carlos and Bernandita, and they still lived like farm folk, only worse, for in the big city, sustenance had to be purchased, not picked off a tree. They hustled one way or another, lining up for day labor, running motorbike jitneys, vending limes or cigarettes or lottery tickets. Bernandita sewed in a garment factory, nine hours a day, six days a week, for eight dollars. Carlos lugged buckets of water from the community tap for five cents a trip and he raced other boys on bets, but because he was so young and frail he often fell in the effort, returning home bloody and broke. After church every Sunday, Bernandita spent two dollars on a purse or a pot or a pair of new shoes and then plied the streets selling chances in the informal raffle known as a *rifando*. On a good day, she ended her rounds with a profit of six dollars, enough for oatmeal and *plátanos* at breakfast, enough for pencils and notebooks in school. Carlos usually followed her from house to house, ashamed of his worn clothes and his skinny legs, taunted by the older kids who turned his nickname of Albi into a chant of "Al-bin-bin, Al-bin-bin," *bin-bin* being slang for penis.

Little in his childhood had prepared Carlos for the harsh tang of city life, and least of all for the cruelty of his own family. While his grandmother in Boca de Mao considered Carlos a gift from God, his grandfather in Santo Domingo deemed him the son of scandal. Ramón Pimentel had hauled trash before moving to America. And he had sired another son named Carlos by the woman he had left for Bernandita. And worst of all, he was a black man, a black man who had won the love of a woman with blond hair and green eyes, a woman whose father traced his lineage not to African slaves but to their Spanish masters.

Exhausted by her factory job and anguished at how poorly she could provide, Bernandita reluctantly surrendered her son to her father. Carlos lived in a fourth-floor apartment not far from the sea, and he received a gray uniform to wear to Catholic school. But fair-skinned classmates shunned him at play, and fair-skinned family shunned him at home. Carlos was left alone for ten hours at a time, left to watch television and dream of his mother and count the minutes until Sunday, when she would visit. He tried to escape into the routines of school, reciting the catechism and molding art clay, but whenever his grades or behavior displeased, the nuns informed his grandfather. Then the patriarch lashed the boy's back with belt and sandal, leaving him to sob wildly and to wonder what inside him could deserve such cruelty.

Alone in Villa Maria, unknown to Carlos, Bernandita plotted a path to America. She would travel illicitly, with too many risks for a child, but once in New York, she would send for her son. With dollars mailed by Ramón, Bernandita bought from a broker what she believed was a valid entry visa to the United States, or at least a sophisticated imitation. But on the day of her arrival, as Ramón waited in a newly rented apartment, immigration authorities unmasked the document as a forgery and ordered her returned to Santo Domingo. The bitterest bile of all was spending a single night on American soil, in detention at Kennedy Airport. Several months later and with another endowment from Ramón, Bernandita paid a coyote who promised to spirit her into America via Haiti. They traveled as far as a hotel in Port-au-Prince, from which her guide vanished along with her money. Together, the two failures cost $3,000, years of savings from Ramón's job as a nursing home porter. Ramón was down to his last $500, and determined to cut the final deal himself. He purchased a paper marriage to a Puerto Rican woman and, equipped with a green card, began assembling airfare to the Dominican Republic.

Meanwhile, Bernandita returned to reclaim Carlos, ending an eighteen-month separation. Together, they went back to Villa Maria, which seemed now so wonderful, and when the time came for bed, Bernandita brought Carlos inside the mosquito net and under the blanket to sleep beside her like a baby. Ramón, too, reappeared in his son's life, first through the toy planes and tanks he sent at Christmas and then in the flesh on a 1976 trip. He formally wed Bernandita, and

Calle Once rejoiced. Amid the celebration, Carlos sat in his father's lap and peered into a face whose darkness mirrored his own.

A year passed, enough time for the memory to fade in Carlos's mind, enough time for him to construct a world around only his mother and himself. Even when Bernandita told him in December 1977, "We're going to see your father," Carlos conceived of a brief visit. As friends and relatives said goodbye, he assured them, "Hey, I'll see you again." They told him, too, that he would be rich and ride in a limousine, and gradually their words wove with images he had obtained from "Kojak" and "Batman." He would live in a white mansion and drive his own go-kart. He would wear brand-new sneakers, eat chicken every day. New York would be an Eden to dash Villa Maria, to diminish even the memory of Boca de Mao.

Bernandita bought Carlos a white shirt, brown loafers, and a blue suit that was the first of his life. Then she draped a rosary around his neck. Their neighbors dispatched them with a final festival of *sancocho* stew and overproof rum and loud, throbbing merengue. When it was over, Bernandita and Carlos climbed into a taxi, their belongings in boxes tied fast with twine. As they headed toward the airport, Carlos gazed at his playmates one last time, and he saw alongside happiness, fleeting flickers of envy. "Why do you get to go," he would remember their eyes asking, "when we're still here, stuck in this shit?"

*   *   *

For a sovereign state occupied twice within fifty years by the United States, the Dominican Republic retained a remarkable capacity for either forgiving or forgetting. Such responses were the province not only of the dictators and conservative democrats whose power rested in American approval or of the bankers and businessmen whose profits depended on American investment, but of the tenant farmers, taxi drivers, and market clerks who after 1965 would form the bulk of the largest migration of foreign nationals to New York. Their affinity arose from the most fundamental self-interest: They had gone to America to survive, and for that survival, they were grateful.

As the first colony in the New World, the Dominican Republic long abided mixed emotions about colonialism. Having wrenched its independence first from Spain and then from Haitian invaders, the Dominicans in 1861 took the remarkable step of inviting back their former European rulers to run the nation. Four years later, a nationalistic rebellion sent the soldiers, clerics, and bureaucrats scurrying home to Castile, but left the Dominicans themselves torn between their contradictory desires for the chaotic freedom of democracy and the martial certainty of dictatorship. Coups, assassinations, looming bankruptcy, and virtual civil war characterized the next half-century of Dominican affairs, ending when the United States Marines surged ashore in 1916 to commence an eight-year occupation. With the republic's Congress suspended and its Supreme Court rendered powerless, Washington essentially operated the nation through a military governor. The occupation government evicted squatters and partitioned communal lands to open up vast sections of the fertile eastern plain to American-owned sugar plantations, creating a lasting resentment. Yet the imposed regime demonstrated a pragmatic side, too, improving public health, education, and communication; reducing foreign debt; installing a freely elected, if largely ceremonial, president; and creating a national guard to preserve order.

The national guard, unfortunately, visited upon its countrymen rather a surplus of order, in the person of Lieutenant Rafael Trujillo. Winning election as president in 1930 with more votes than the Dominican Republic had eligible voters, Trujillo possessed complete power until 1961. In the name of nationalism, he concentrated more than half the country's economy in the hands of himself, his family, and his closest cohorts, amassing a fortune estimated at $300 million to $1 billion. With control of the military and the secret police, he wielded censorship, imprisonment, and terror against dissidents. And because he shrewdly presented himself as the Western Hemisphere's "Foremost Anti-Communist," he enjoyed American largesse and protection.

At least he did until President John F. Kennedy decided that Trujillo's dictatorship was an incitement to Communist subversion and had intelligence operatives help assassinate the inconvenient despot. With Trujillo buried and his tight emigration restrictions obsolete, the flow of Dominicans into the United States quadrupled to 3,000 in a single year, 1962. American immigration laws of the time gave preference to professional people, so the early arrivals included many doctors, engineers, and intellectuals. For their poorer, less educated countrymen, hope resided in Juan Bosch, the liberal reformer elected president in 1962. But the military toppled him the next year, and the campaign of arrests and "disappearances" that followed struck many Dominicans as Trujillo revisited.

When left-wing "Constitutionalists" revolted in April 1965, the

Americans invaded. Battles raged in parts of the capital, and the graffiti of "Yanqui Go Home!" entered international political lexicon, yet the intervention did surprisingly little to damage America's reputation. The most severe fighting was contained by the U.S. Marines in several small sectors of Santo Domingo, and when the troops left eight months later, the Johnson Administration bestowed food, loans, and medical supplies. Thanks in large part to Fidel Castro and all he embodied, the Dominican Republic received more American aid per capita in the 1960s than any nation except South Vietnam.

Within a decade, foreign economists were hailing "the Dominican miracle," the creation of a stable mercantile class in a developing nation. But the boom in personal income and public works never reached the *campo* (the countryside). For all Carlos's halcyon memories of Cibao, unemployment and illiteracy were rampant and life expectancy was a decade shorter than in the cities. It was small wonder that so many Dominicans fled the fields. In a scenario reprised throughout the Third World, a nation whose population was 70 percent rural in 1960 reckoned itself 60 percent urban fewer than thirty years later. The population of Santo Domingo increased by half from 1970 to 1980, and the city sprawled into a crazyquilt of half-paved streets, abandoned foundations, and weedy plazas. With inflation approaching 100 percent and the currency devalued, the precarious middle class guarded its possessions with attack dogs and revolvers, while the poorest piled into hillside shanties of plywood and cardboard, roofs secured by bald tires and concrete chunks.

For all of them, as for the Pimentel family, the only solution seemed to reside in America. Everywhere was the name of the United States writ large—in imported television shows, in obsessive coverage of professional baseball, in trade and tourism, in the unceasing immigration. When the social scientist Glenn Hendricks studied a Cibao village for his book *The Dominican Diaspora,* he found that 85 percent of the households had immediate family in America. Half the daily mail originated *allá* ("up there"), and one-fifth contained money sent to support relatives. Computed nationally, the magnitude of overseas remittances was staggering—$600 billion to $800 billion annually in the late 1980s. All across Santo Domingo, signs advertised "Instituto Inglés," and clients abounded for the visa brokers called *tributarios.* More than 1 million Dominicans obtained tourist visas for the United States between 1966 and 1976 as a means of evading immigration quotas. Thousands more crammed into craft as small as canoes to cross the Mona Passage to Puerto Rico, risking death in the turbulent seventy-mile strait and arrest and deportation on the far shore. By the late 1980s, the romance surrounding America should have been tempered by testimony about sweatshops, poverty, and violence, and yet the pace of emigration only quickened. Nothing talked louder than money, and meager wages in Manhattan were a windfall in Mao. As a merengue song said of villagers in Cibao:

> Everyone who comes from there,
> This is what they believe.
> They think that dollar bills
> Are to be gathered up in Broadway.
> That is what they believe. . . .

* * *

As he watched the suitcases slide by on the Kennedy Airport carousel, Carlos thought he must be at some kind of show. The people around him viewed the luggage with respect and devotion, like the audiences for touring bands he remembered from Mao. It was only with prodding that Carlos plucked his own bags from the stage and staggered through customs and out into the terminal. Beyond the double doors waited a wall of anxious faces, and Bernandita told Carlos his father's was one. Carlos searched for a white man, for in America everyone was white, and he stiffened with confusion when a dark stranger strode forward to envelope him in a hug. Only belatedly, as the man draped a winter coat over his shoulders, did Carlos realize who indeed this brash fellow was.

The three Pimentels slid into a burgundy Cadillac owned and driven by Ramón's boss, and as they traced the contours of Brooklyn on their way to Manhattan, Carlos gaped at the lawns and the cars and the skyline. The Cadillac crossed Central Park, and Carlos warmed at the sight. *It's OK,* he told himself, *we're going to live on a farm.* Then the Cadillac emerged on a street of tall buildings, with uniformed men guarding brass doors, and proceeded past the grandeur for almost twenty blocks. Finally, it turned off Central Park West and up a hill flanked by old graystone tenements, coasting to a halt before a crowd of wellwishers, whose presence told Carlos that this thin, treeless street was his home. *"Ese el hijo de Ramón,"* he could hear some saying as he stepped onto the curb, *That's Ramón's son.*

Others waited in the fourth-floor apartment, with merengue and plátanos to ease the shock. But it was all too much, the whirl of trousers and hems, the hissing of steam heat, the flat Inca faces of Ecuadoran friends. People asked Carlos to dance, and he felt better when he did, but the happiness did not last. He wanted only to sleep with his mother beside him, to feel some security at his most insecure. Finally, the last guest said goodnight, and Bernandita walked Carlos to a folding bed in the living room.

"You're sleeping here," she said, and Carlos dutifully crawled under the covers. He replayed in his mind the phantasmagoria of the day, and he imagined how wonderful life could be in America, home of Batman and the Yankees. Bernandita reentered the room to ask her son, as she did every night, "Give me your blessings." He replied, "I give them." Then they reversed the ritual. She kissed Carlos's forehead, and he moved to the edge of the mattress, opening space for her. But she simply smoothed the covers over Carlos and walked toward Ramón's room.

"You're not going to sleep?" Carlos asked.

"Yes," she said. "I'm sleeping with your father."

She saw his eyes moisten and returned to his bedside. "Shhh, go to sleep," she said soothingly. "Tomorrow I take you to the park."

Then she vanished behind the bedroom door, and Carlos began to wail, eventually bringing Ramón. "Shut up," he shouted. "Fall asleep." Carlos thought to himself, *I hate this man.* He stared into the street lamp suspended moonlike outside the window, and after a time, snow started to fall, the first flakes Carlos had ever seen. He opened the window and stuck his hand into the storm and welled up with amazement. But the amazement was no match for the anger, and as he fell asleep alone, he swore, "I've got to leave."

*   *   *

In the playground, they called him a *Cibaeño,* the kids who were born in America or assimilated enough to claim it as their own. The noun literally stated a geographic fact, that Carlos was from Cibao, but in its colloquial connotation and its pointed enunciation, it branded him a hillbilly. The kids could hear Cibao in Carlos's accent, the high pitch and slurred words that were the Dominican equivalent of a redneck drawl. They could see Cibao in his *cabana* shirt, with its baggy cut and waist pockets. "You swim here?" someone taunted, for it was only the most destitute who dared the Mona Passage.

The bell, at last, rescued Carlos. He had imagined an American school along the lines of the Starship Enterprise on "Star Trek," and to his naive eyes, P.S. 145 did not disappoint. It was a fairly new building of yellow brick and orange panels, and the second-grade classroom overflowed with books and toys. The teacher called upon Carlos to write the numeral 4 on the blackboard, and to try to impress her he drew a tight triangle on a pole. "No, no," she reproved, replacing his geometric design with the casual, open-topped 4 Carlos normally scrawled, and he slunk back to his seat. In the cafeteria, he shuffled down the line with only one slice of bread, then returned for a hot dog, a mystery to him. Holding meat in his right fist and roll in his left, he hurried them down two-handedly, hoping that no one would see.

English confounded him, with its incongruous grammar and its devious diction, and even in a bilingual class, he needed to repeat himself three or four times to be understood. He pronounced "people" as "pay-oh-play" in the Spanish style, "yes" as "yez," and "is" as "ees," and when he erred too often, the teacher commanded him to write the troublesome word on the board one hundred times. One escape was art class, where he needed no language, where he could draw sports cars and Hercules and drift back to Cibao. The other was the bathroom, to which he repaired frequently to think and study and unscramble his brain. After months of futility, he earned 100 on a spelling test, proceeding without pause through "come" and "went" and "left." The teacher inscribed his name on the board, and "Carlos Pimentel" remained there in chalk for a full week, until the next test. He walked past it every morning, a war hero admiring his monument.

But with one swipe of the eraser, Carlos was returned to the familiar frustration. Every night before going to bed, he peppered Bernandita: "When we goin' back? When we goin' back? When we goin' back?" She promised him, "Soon," to lull him into slumber, and he dreamed dreams of baseball in Boca de Mao. But when morning light pierced the pane near his pillow, he knew he would be going no farther than school.

*   *   *

Unnoticed except by demographers, ethnologists, and fellow Hispanics, Dominicans thronged to New York by the hundreds of thousands after 1965, becoming the city's largest community of newcomers. The 1980 census counted 121,000, and the arrivals since then have amounted to 15,000 or 20,000 a year. But such figures took into account only those entering legally; the sub-rosa Dominican population ran in some estimates to 270,000. But because Dominicans were not identified as readily as were Chinese or Indians or Soviet Jews, because many Anglos could not tell the Dominicans apart from the Puerto Ricans among whom they settled, a massive population transplanted itself with deceptive quietude. How many New Yorkers knew that Dominicans had largely supplanted Puerto Ricans in running bodegas and car services? That merengue had replaced salsa as the Latin music of choice? That there was a Dominican Day parade and a Dominican channel on cable television? That all through the city, urban neighborhoods were being renamed for the Cibao villages?

As Dominican districts went, the portion of the Upper West Side known as Manhattan Valley was small and intense—a postage stamp, to alter William Faulkner, of alien soil. It spanned only the ten blocks north of 100th Street and the three west of Central Park, and it was tightly bounded by the park, Columbia University, Broadway, and several middle-income high-rises. Somehow 33,000 people crammed into its confines, a majority of them earning less than $10,000 a year in 1980.

Manhattan Valley had always been an anomaly amid affluence, but one that made perfect sense. When the lavish apartments on Riverside Drive and Central Park West were the domain of New York's WASP gentry, their Irish domestics packed the tenements of Manhattan Valley. When those choice addresses belonged to Jews in midcentury, the blacks and Puerto Ricans who cleaned their homes and reared their children rented the old Irish apartments. And when the first wave of Dominican migration started saturating Washington Heights, a mile uptown, the surplus followed the sound of Spanish into Manhattan Valley, where a six-bedroom apartment still could be had for one hundred dollars a month.

True to history, many Dominican women worked as nursemaids, and their husbands became doormen, porters, and supers. Others opened stores, and the streets of Manhattan Valley bristled with 300, from bakeries to travel agencies, from pharmacies to furniture showrooms. The largest single occupation, for the women especially, was in the garment industry, following the tradition of Irish and Germans and Swedes, of Jews and Italians, of blacks and Chinese and Puerto Ricans. The paychecks from even menial jobs supported families in the Dominican Republic and purchased the televisions and stereos to soften life in Manhattan. Even the industry's pattern of seasonal layoffs provided a perverse advantage, allowing Dominican workers to visit their homeland for extended periods without losing their jobs.

What neither salaries nor vacations could undermine, however, was the fierce emotional attachment of Dominicans to their nation's culture and affairs. A drive around Manhattan Valley found businesses named with homesick twinges—Cibao Barber, Quisqueya Tailor, La Perla Del Sur Grocery. Perhaps the most telling title belonged to an eatery not in Manhattan Valley but on the Lower East Side, two blocks north of Seward Park. The place called itself Castillo de Jagua. A *castillo* is a castle, and *jagua* is plantain tree bark, the stuff not of castles but of peasant huts, among them the one that was Carlos's first home. Castillo de Jagua spoke to a past both actual and invented, a past made only more alluring by the labors and dangers of another man's land.

Parents, at least, emigrated expecting to struggle, convincing themselves that the effort would be justified by better lives for their young. But children are impatient by nature, and children who are cut loose from traditional strictures and planted beside world-class opulence tend to be more restive than most. Not for them the slow roads of sewing machine or taxi meter or bilingual education, not when the highway to riches was paved with *perrico,* Spanish slang for cocaine. The same immigrant energy that enabled Dominicans to thrive in legitimate business also served them well selling drugs, for like the Italian and Jewish gangsters generations their senior, they found that the survival instinct rarely discriminated between sources of capital. Young captains of commerce returned to the republic, buying houses and discos and multiple cars, and their example instructed others in a new American dream. The Dominican drug dealer of the late 1980s was less often a frustrated greenhorn who saw scant options than an arrogant *arriviste,* bent on selling his share and retiring in luxury. Gangs staked out turfs up and down Manhattan, and murders mounted into the hundreds. These were not ordinary rubouts, either, for the preferred macho method was a point-blank blast to the face. The stereotype outside such neighborhoods as Manhattan Valley was that most Dominicans dealt drugs; the fear inside was that the minority who did would seduce one's child, either with cash or cocaine.

*   *   *

It was hot in the apartment, hotter even than in Villa Maria, and so Carlos went outside to sit on the stoop. A man walked past wearing a braided gold chain, so gaudy the grandmothers clucked, and quite suddenly, as he passed before Carlos, gunshots began to crackle. Carlos hid behind a concrete planter, tucked as tightly as an infant abed, and waited for the volley to cease. The target was gone, as were his attackers, and the sidewalk was free of blood. Someone peeked out the front door of the building and shouted to Carlos, "Is anything wrong?" He shrugged and replied, "No, it's all right." Then came other children, pointing to Carlos and with awe in their voices telling their playmates, "Ooh, he was there."

If Carlos did not yet recognize the import of the ambush, a few more years on the block would enlighten him. There was a type of brazen young man on 105th Street, he noticed, who enjoyed unpeeling a five dollar bill from a thick meaty roll and telling a boy, "Buy me a soda, keep the change." The same guys who had the money also carried little bags of green stuff. And they seemed to share an apartment with a slot beneath the peephole, through which green bills entered and green bags exited. "Marijuana," Carlos overheard.

One dealer bought firecrackers and beer for the block on the Fourth of July. Another erected a basketball backboard, which became the social center of the street. If a mother called out the window to her child, "Get me a can of green beans," one dealer or another would holler back, "Don't worry, I got it," and reach for his wad. Carlos's parents warned him to keep his distance, but he ignored their advice. The dealers had money and new clothes and big rings. The dealers had clout, what slum slang called "juice." How could a hillbilly, how could a Mama's boy, not want some juice of his own?

It was during the fifth grade that an older friend named Chi-Chi pulled Carlos to a corner of the schoolyard and lit up his first joint. "This make you feel real good," Chi-Chi promised, "like you walkin' on air." Carlos felt only a choking sensation, but he followed Chi-Chi's lead and acted dizzy and light. When Chi-Chi rasped, "This shit is good," Carlos dared not disagree. They became partners thereafter, sneaking into the movie house on Broadway to get high and "bug out," and obscuring the aroma with cologne Carlos stole from his father.

Carlos failed fifth grade and lost interest in the youth group and dance club that had made elementary school fun. By the time he reached sixth grade, he was getting high three or four times a day, beginning after breakfast, and carrying a carpet knife for protection and cachet. On warm weekends, he might jog three blocks to Riverside Park, hook up with his buddies, and steal some chains or a bike. Sometimes guilt nagged Carlos, and he vowed never to smoke dope or steal bikes again. But the next day, he always would. Only a *mamahuevo* backed out, only a cocksucker. Besides, he had friends now, for the first time in America, and if he went straight, he would wind up alone.

The more Carlos drifted, the more Ramón tried to anchor him, and the discipline he knew was swift and severe. He raised the belt against Carlos on many occasions. He restricted him to the apartment. He chased him one time along 105th Street, waving the sandal he would wield when he caught him. He sweated and puffed and drove his legs like pistons, and still he saw Carlos vanish across Amsterdam Avenue. Ramón was an aging man chasing a growing boy, and he was destined to lose the race.

Each year brought some greater threat. The drug dealers around the basketball court advanced from cellophane sacks of marijuana to tinfoil packets of cocaine, which one carried in his jockstrap. A hen club of heroin addicts, Miriam and Louise and Mamma, sold stolen goods door to door, slinging Lord & Taylor slacks and fake Vuitton handbags across their swollen arms. When Carlos was twelve, watching a late movie on a warm July night, he heard firecrackers through open windows. Not especially alarmed, he looked down to the street and saw two stocky men leaving, hands shoved into their pants. Two minutes later, he heard an old woman screaming, *"Ay, Dios mío! Ay, Dios mío!"* Carlos ran to the first floor and there he saw the body, tattooed with bullet holes and still spouting blood. He knew instantly it was a drug killing, and he knew instinctively not to say a thing. Perhaps the killers had spotted him in the window; perhaps they would come back with guns drawn for him. For the next five or six months, he would not enter his building alone, nor would he depart it without surveilling the street.

School offered little refuge. The first time Carlos saw crack was on a class trip to Bear Mountain, a wooded parkland rising high above the Hudson. He was hiking on a nature trail with his friend David, and when they found a solitary spot, all green boughs and pine needles, David reached into his pocket and withdrew a paper towel, unfolding it to reveal twenty loaded vials. "Try some," he said, and Carlos would have accepted, except that David had forgotten a pipe.

In a moment, temptation passed, and in its aftermath Carlos understood how his friend could afford his Zodiac shoes and Gap outfits, when everyone else settled for secondhand jeans and sneakers from the mix-n-match bin. He understood that and much more, an entire evolution in Manhattan Valley. Carlos could see BMWs on his block and ragged men who waxed them for just one little taste. He could see friends with guns, reclining in chaise lounges as they awaited clients. He could see Chi-Chi, who started him on marijuana, dealing crack around the corner from their old elementary school. No sight was so awful that it could not be bettered, if that was the word. Carlos came home one night to discover in his lobby a haggard young woman with scared sunken eyes. She tried to hide her crack pipe, and in the haste dropped her vial. "I can't believe I lost it," she moaned as she fell to the tile, rooting like a pig for truffles. "Where is it? Where'd it go?" Carlos said nothing, slowly crushing the vial under his heel.

As victory, it was pyrrhic. Carlos knew he wanted no part of crack, but he had no idea what he did want or where he might locate it. He hated his father and he scorned his mother's solace. He earned decent grades in a school he knew did not challenge. The streets that had once been his amusement now held nothing but waste. There was no going back to Boca de Mao. There was not even room in New York's low-income projects, for which his family had applied. "What am I doing?" Carlos asked himself often. "Why do I deserve to be alive?" Several were the times he could find not one reason and considered taking his life.

*   *   *

Mortality seemed to hover around him. A junior high school classmate died of a cocaine overdose. Thinking of her, so attractive, so intelligent, so unlikely, Carlos could only shudder at his own odds. Barely months later, a doctor diagnosed throat cancer in Ramón, and he checked into a hospital for emergency surgery. Ramón returned home two weeks later alive, but thin and drained, his neck sunken where the tumor had been extracted. Carlos did not stop hating his father, but for the first time he felt pity for him, seeing this strong man dependent and reduced. In his despair, Ramón reacquainted himself with a faith he had neglected, and it was on his visits to Ascension Church that he met Cipriano Lintigua, the man who would save his son.

A former teacher from Santo Domingo, Cipriano led youth programs at the church. Ramón told him that Carlos did not respect the family or the culture or the cross. He went out partying, came home when he wanted, talked back to his mother. He was hanging around with the wrong crowd. Cipriano had heard such concerns from many parents. Speaking little English, working long hours and several jobs, they saw themselves helpless to hold their children. So Cipriano had begun a club he called "Los Buenos Amigos," The Good Friends, for teenagers to explore their problems and fears.

The club members convened every Friday afternoon, drawing together folding chairs in the low-ceiling church basement. They were honors students in pleated skirts, playground ballplayers in sweatpants and tank tops, and sometimes a drug dealer or two, dappled in gold and yet guilty enough to consider change. Each meeting included discussion of a social or political issue, examination of a Bible verse, and often the reading of a research paper by one of the members who was attending college. The next time Cipriano strolled down 105th Street and spotted Carlos on a stoop, he invited him to join.

Among Carlos's crowd, "Los Buenos Amigos" were called "church boys" and "suckers," and he acceded only because he had heard the group had pretty girls. But when he went to the meeting, there was only one, and he sat there feeling haughty and superior. For his part, Cipriano judged Carlos a decent boy, obsessed with proving himself hard—a prime candidate for the plunge into robbery and drugs. He pulled Carlos aside after the meeting and told him, "You have a lot of good qualities. You should appreciate them. You should help others. And help yourself."

Carlos had to admit he enjoyed the trips to Van Cortland Park and to Orchard Beach, which the kids called "Playa de los Mojones," Beach of Shit. There was also the church basketball team. Still shorter than five feet as a ninth grader, Carlos rode the bench, but in practice at least, he found a steam valve for his anger. And when Cipriano spoke about Dominicans, Carlos felt pride in his people. He still saw the crack vials and gold chains, but he also smelled the roasting *pernil* and heard the swinging merengue and rolled every pleasure into an ineffable quality he could only call "sauce."

Then came a special meeting, just for fathers and sons. Cipriano lined them up on opposite sides of a long table, and as each one spoke, the rest listened. "Carlos is not responsible," Ramón said when it was his turn. "He doesn't take care of things. He never sticks with his family. He won't even go to the same mass. He is embarrassed by us." Ramón talked about his first son, Carlos's half brother, who was an officer in the Dominican Air Force, an intelligent, respected man. He looked to Carlos and added, "You seem like a loser, and I can't have a loser in my family." Carlos had heard it all before, but never so directly, and never in front of an audience. Tears rolled down his cheeks, and Ramón saw them. "I'm your father," he said. "I brought you into this world. I care about everything about you." Now Carlos cried harder, but with remorse and relief.

As he mended relations at home, Carlos raised his performance at school, intending to prove his worth while his father was still alive to see. He cut adrift his drug friends for a new temperate bunch. He volunteered for school plays, and finding that he could "bug out" in approved ways, stopped "dissing" his teachers. He confided often in a guidance counselor named John Scoville, sometimes spending his entire lunch period pouring out his troubles and his plans. Scoville feared sending Carlos on to Brandeis, the neighborhood high school, for it churned with tensions between Dominicans, Puerto Ricans, and blacks. He had established a pipeline from J.H.S. 54 to Seward Park, which he deemed safer and which had a College Discovery program, and he placed Carlos in it. Only dimly aware that attending Seward Park meant traveling by subway an hour each way, Carlos accepted.

He wondered whether he had misplaced his trust in Scoville when he first entered the annex in September 1985. Windows were shattered. Water dripped down classroom walls. Paint peeled and flaked. He heard girls gossiping about "punks" from other neighborhoods, and he realized their slurs included him. When he left school each afternoon, the local lowlifes stood ready to fight over a pair of new sneakers, or even the wrong sort of stare. "You got a fucking problem?" they would say, sneering, as Carlos quickened his steps to the subway.

For all the physical discomfort, the education inside the annex awoke Carlos. He learned about equations from Alex Sabatino and sentence structure from Linda Rothman, arching toward advanced-placement courses as an upperclassman. Louise Grollman, who would later direct Carlos in *The Odd Couple* and *Bye Bye Birdie,* nicknamed him "Peanut Butter" and "Dimples." Denise Simone promised to marry him once he bought a BMW. Nobody believed in Carlos more completely than his College Discovery counselor, Hal Pockriss. It was Hal to whom Carlos, all four feet ten of him, pronounced his passion to join the basketball team. Hal thought, *This humunculus?* but he said, "School comes first, and be careful."

Carlos could not remember such a spontaneous sign of concern from anyone except his parents, much less from a white stranger who had known him only as a line on a computer printout. The world of BMWs and crack and guns, the world of Manhattan Valley, now seemed so distant that Carlos could laugh about it, and his faculty admirers had no inkling of a model student's muddled past.

Then, one afternoon in May 1986, one month shy of summer vacation, the past intruded on the present. Carlos and four other Dominican classmates were walking to the subway when a dozen men in their early twenties, members of a Puerto Rican gang called the Hill Boys, surrounded them.

One of the Dominicans tried to break through the border. Punches started to fall, and the circle closed more tightly. Two of the Hill Boys had pit bulls on leashes, and the dogs barked and bared teeth, inflamed by the scent of prey.

"What the fuck you want?" asked Carlos's friend José, less in challenge than in exasperation.

"Oh, you wanna get loud?"

Then more punches rained, and hands clawed away gold chains. When the volley subsided, the Dominicans held their heads, touched their swollen cheeks and cut necks, and limped into the subway, planning revenge. They had not sought confrontation, but they could not shrink from it. That was the code, the only code most of them knew.

One friend had a friend whose family sold cocaine, and he borrowed from them a stolen car and five guns. At the hour the next morning when they normally lugged their book bags toward school, they loaded their .22s and searched for their targets. The car moved down the West Side Highway among the commuters, and then along Canal Street amid delivery trucks, and Carlos could not believe he was there. He had never held a gun except his half brother's military .45, and he withered each time he saw a policeman, certain that somehow the officer knew. *Damn,* he told himself, *I'm gonna kill somebody? This is stupid. Something's wrong.* But he said nothing as the car crossed the Bowery and then Allen Street, and swung alongside the park by the annex.

They found the Hill Boys, a dozen or more, sitting on benches. "Look," one boy's girlfriend warned, "it's those guys you jumped." By then it was too late to run. One Dominican opened the door and drew his gun, and the rest stuck their barrels out the car's windows. *Are we really gonna shoot them?* Carlos thought. *Fifteen years old. In a stolen car.* Then one Dominican noticed there was a station house for the Housing Authority police behind the Hill Boys. He motioned to the others. Now they knew they couldn't shoot. They reassembled in the car, wagged their guns in the air, and drove away shouting, "You better watch yourselves."

The Dominicans cut school for two days, hoping for tempers to cool, but on the third day, the word was that the Hill Boys were waiting. Carlos asked Richard Corbo, a business teacher of Dominican ancestry, to accompany him to the subway after school. As he waited for Corbo outside the annex, a gray Cadillac appeared, carrying three Hill Boys. First they waved their guns. Then they stopped the car five feet from Carlos and took aim.

Am I gonna get blown away? his mind flashed. *Am I stupid or what?* He blathered quickly, "We didn't shoot you, we didn't shoot."

"All right, you're too young," one of the Hill Boys said as he drew within inches of Carlos and again raised his gun. "But next time you act stupid, you know what you get."

Holstering the weapon, he ripped from Carlos's neck a twenty-four-karat gold chain with the Playboy medallion, a present from his mother for junior high school graduation.

Carlos was shorn of all innocence now, educated in every risk and danger, conversant in the nearness of death. Never had he stood farther from Boca de Mao. And seeing the terminus of one road, while excelling on another, he could choose his own destiny without ambivalence. It would be one or the other, no halfway, no dallying. Of the five friends beaten on that May afternoon, the five friends a circumstance away from firing or receiving fatal shots, only Carlos ever returned to Seward Park High School.

*   *   *

The Seward Park gymnasium barely exceeds the dimensions of the basketball court it contains. Just across one baseline, doors open into a hallway, and just across the other stands a tangle of gymnastics equipment. Three rows of bleachers flank each sideline, but even such limited space easily accommodates the handful of girlfriends who comprise the crowd. At the east basket, Carlos leads Seward Park through its warm-ups for the game against Mabel Dean Bacon. Stripped to his uniform, he looks a young seventeen, hands bony, face delicate, voice piping as he calls out the drills. He is shooting a lay-up when Jessica enters the gym, accompanied by George Vecsey of *The New York Times.*

Carlos sent George a copy of his article on the false dream of a pro sports career, told him he played for Seward Park, and invited him to a game. George arrives with curiosity and misgivings. He had warned Carlos that if he attended a game, his presence might unnerve him. He was remembering his older daughter's days on her high school team, when he hid behind the bleachers so she wouldn't freeze with fright.

In the first minute of play, Carlos records an assist, with a look-away pass on a two-on-one break. Then he misses several jump shots, loses two loose balls out of bounds. He does not score his first basket until the end of the first quarter, which ends with Seward Park trailing 24 to 13. A bad pass early in the second has the coach, Bob Macmillan, off the bench, shouting, "Carlos, relax!" This he does, scoring on several drives and keeping Seward Park in the game, although not for long. Bacon operates in gears that Seward Park has not yet discovered, making steals, snatching rebounds, sprinting the floor to a 20-point lead. With two minutes left, Carlos tries a 360-degree spin while driving the lane, and a waiting opponent strips the ball. Macmillan leaps as if shocked with high voltage. Seward Park loses 103 to 86, and Carlos's effort to impress has been futile, at least on the basketball court.

George buys Carlos and Jessica dinner at Puglia's in Little Italy, a favorite restaurant of Seward Park's teachers. A growing boy who played thirty-two minutes of basketball, Carlos must surely be famished. But overwhelmed by a real reporter's presence, he picks at his spaghetti, handling his flatware gingerly. Only conversation calms him. He tells George about Cipriano and "Los Buenos Amigos." He tells George he would like to play basketball in college, but academics must come first. George asks about the future, and Carlos talks about becoming a journalist, then applying what he learned as mayor of New York.

After the last cappuccino, George drives Carlos to the subway, then takes Jessica home. The streets are cold, the windshield steamy, the chatter now subdued. Finally, George says of Carlos, with admiration, even amazement, "Where did that kid come from?"

13

A Kind
of Grail

Second term arrives on the insinuative whispers of false spring. A Carolina breeze has reached the Lower East Side, warming the playground for handball, melting the snowbanks to cinder-topped scabs, peeling wool coats and gum boots off romantics who trust the February sun. Jessica Siegel, so romantic she sobs at long-distance telephone commercials, rides her bicycle toward Seward Park, just as she had that first morning in September. A broken bottle at Chrystie Street punctures more than her illusion, and she struggles down Delancey Street on one tire and one rim. Claiming the English department Smith-Corona by seven-fifteen, she starts typing letters of recommendation for students applying to college, a seasonal ritual and one she enjoys. She is midway through a testimonial to Angel Fuster when Loretta Sims, the business department chairwoman, enters the office, a student teacher in tow.

"See this," Loretta says, pointing to the rexo machine as one might point to a carnival freak. "Ancient." As if on cue, the machine begins to bleed purple ink. "It's leaking," Loretta tells Charlotte Hirsch, the paraprofessional. "It's leaking," Charlotte tells Jessica. Jessica examines the wound, pronounces herself puzzled, and withdraws from the spreading pool, as if behind a levee. College recommendations will have to wait, and so, for some of Jessica's seniors, will college itself. Those who floated through first term on excuses and ennui now have seen their failing report cards and plummeted to earth. Jessica knows from experience that she will meet them this morning, as they undertake the grubby business of dunning for grades. It is a false spring, indeed.

Harry Nieves, the first petitioner, presents himself with the news that he passed the Regents examination in English, and the suggestion that Jessica thus raise his failing mark in English 7. Possessed of merely a 65, he can proceed to English 8, his last required course, and graduate on schedule in June.

"The fact you passed the Regents," Jessica says, "shows how strong your abilities are. I never had any doubt about that. But I have to grade you on your work." She pauses, her silence making it clear there will be no pardon. "Who do you have for English 7 this term?"

"You."

As Harry departs, a stocky girl with coffee skin enters, with the timing of a farce's ingenue. She grins faintly, without intent, and holds at her side a schedule card. She need not speak a word for Jessica to comprehend.

"*Oy*, Rosa," she says, grinding palm against temple. "Again?" She sighs. "What is this, four times?" She inspects the schedule card. "And first period?" She shakes her head like one bereaved. "I don't want to kick you out, Rosa, but don't you want another teacher?"

Rosa merely grins. Fifteen minutes later, when the class meets, she is missing, and Jessica records the semester's first cut.

Now a thin black boy with a flat-top Afro charges the length of the hallway, halting only inches from Jessica. He is Elvin Foster, like Harry and Rosa assigned to repeat English 7. Jessica remembers how in last term's first-period class he would drape the sports pages before his face like a Moslem maiden's *chador*. When he bothered, that is, to attend at all.

"Miss Siegel," he mewls, "what did you do to me?"

"You did it to your . . ."

"You jerked me."

"You want to talk about jerking?" Jessica says. Elvin turns and stalks off on stiff legs. She follows, bouncing Big Black across the linoleum, as the mob in Times Square laughs at the spectacle. She catches Elvin at last, hurling a hand over his shoulder like a stevedore wielding a grappling hook. She turns him to face her and says, "I want to talk to you about what you handed in."

Elvin knew he would fail English 7 and in the last week of the term, he begged for an extra-credit assignment. Jessica was weary of his sloth and his arrogance, and of his groundless fantasy of joining an older buddy at college in New Paltz. But she remembered Elvin's mother from Open School Night—still in heels and a suit from her office job, so sweet, so intelligent, so clearly bamboozled by her boy. So she told Elvin to read an American novel and write a report, and when he selected the Britisher H. G. Wells's *The Time Machine,* she was willing to let him slide. He never opened the book, as far as she could tell, instead basing his report on a movie called *Time Bandits,* and even at that, delivering fewer than two pages of spaghetti squiggles masquerading as prose. There was a type of hustling that at least impressed Jessica with its devious wit; Elvin's provoked only disgust. Now she thrusts the paper toward him.

"Why don't you read what I had to say?"

He stands in petulant silence.

"Elvin, if you want to take English 7 with someone else, you can. I'm not the only one teaching it."

Elvin mumbles, "I want it with you." He removes the paper from its plastic cover, carefully turns the pages sideways, and rips them in halves and then quarters. Jessica, oblivious, returns to the office.

There she finds Ben Dachs, himself now a sort of repeater, sitting at his chairman's desk, bent over schedules and registers. Ben's interim appointment as principal at Beach Channel High School ended last week in failure, when he was not offered the position permanently. All term, his friends at Seward Park heard indirectly that the United Federation of Teachers was campaigning against him, although Ben himself was too circumspect to confirm any rumors. Despite his silence this morning, the union newspaper speaks for him, and with a certain malicious glee.

A full page is devoted to the imbroglio surrounding the selection of a principal for Beach Channel, and to the involvement of the union's highest officers in the fray. Without identifying its target by name, the account assails "a totally politicized supervisory force" in which "people in authority [are] getting jobs through politics" despite the fact they "[are] coming out of left field." As it wages a highly public campaign for "teacher empowerment"—to which the entire issue of the newspaper is devoted—the union apparently found it insufficient to argue that Beach Channel's faculty sought a principal from its own ranks. Not content with that reasonable proposition, the UFT deemed it necessary to caricature Ben as a well-connected incompetent, and to send him back to Seward Park both defeated and besmirched. In this painful period, Ben thinks best by writing, and he delivers this letter to each teacher on his staff:

Dear Friends:

Within the context of my professional life, these are both the best of times and the worst of times.

You can easily imagine the pain that comes with the loss of something for which I had worked long and hard. But the sadness is tempered with the knowledge that I can come home to a supportive family of friends. After having seen what's out there, I return in the sure knowledge that you are the best. I've missed you all and draw comfort from being back here. I look forward to working with you again and to speaking personally with each of you. The first bowl of soup is on me.

I'd like to take this opportunity to close with a public apology to Emma. If I had my way, you'd still have your job, a job I know you have earned and deserve. I'm sorry my misfortune caused you misfortune. The only words of comfort I can offer is that you have the same supportive group of friends that I believe I have. We'll both need them.

Like her colleagues, Jessica hardly knows what to say, how to approach a man who had been both guide and partner, always the strong one, salving her wounds. "I feel for you," she says, and gives him a kiss and a hug. Ben thanks her, and she retreats a pace or two. New York's public schools have no place for a man of Ben's independence and integrity, she cannot help thinking, and some suburban district whose kids need him less surely has. But if he must be back, then she is glad he is here, at least temporarily. In all her years of teaching, no one has instructed and uplifted her more. And while Ben knows nothing of her thoughts of leaving, and so cannot face the issue foursquare, his return argues for keeping an open mind.

* * *

Jessica's day begins as it did the first semester, with two sections of English 7 and a nominally free period she uses for meeting students. Next comes the Lower East Side class, which contains only nine pupils, meaning it will be filled by "equalization" transfers and over-the-counter admissions, threatening confusion and frustration again. Each afternoon, Jessica teaches two periods of journalism, and in these classes the greatest promise resides, especially when compared to the fall term's disaster. Jessica has recruited such English 7 main-stays as Wilfredo Ayala, See Wai Mui, and Addie Severino, and Addie brought along her sister, Daisy, president of the senior class. Denise Simone steered into journalism a dozen College Discovery students, known to most teachers for their willingness to work. Angel Fuster audits the beginning course in his lunch period, as does Ottavio Johnson, with his daily desktop picnic of a Blimpie and Gatorade. Carlos Pimentel, who has neither journalism period free, is taking independent study with Jessica. The feet, as Ben Dachs noted in another class years ago, have voted.

The way Jessica teaches journalism, ideals precede execution. By the second week of the term, she has not instructed her charges in the five Ws and H, in the "inverted pyramid" architecture of articles, in the elements like timeliness and proximity that define news itself. All that will come, but something else will come first, the study of actual coverage by professionals, and of the human choices hidden inside the practical craft. Through discussion and analysis, Jessica will pass along a kind of grail, a way of approaching journalism and humanity itself, first learned at Liberation News Service, then tested in the world beyond radical rooms.

Two nights ago, she assigned her students to watch the local television news, and to note how each channel ranked in importance the day's events. The top story on each station was the trial of Robert Chambers for the slaying of Jennifer Levin, a lesson in social class and news judgment more profound than any Jessica could have invented.

Levin and Chambers could have been the peers of Jessica's pupils. He was nineteen and she was eighteen on the early morning in August 1986 when, it was alleged, he strangled her to death in the course of a sexual dalliance in Central Park. Age aside, however, they inhabited another planet from the children of Chinatown and Alphabet City, a planet of private schools and posh townhouses and nocturnal revels at Dorrian's Red Hand, an Irish pub gone Ivy League. Young, sexy, and well heeled, Chambers and Levin cut a compelling couple as protagonists of what became known as "The Preppy Murder Case." There was tabloid titillation about his taste in drugs and hers in lovemaking; there was handwringing and head scratching in the more august *Times* about what the case said about child rearing and jurisprudence. Unlike other sensations, this one's wattage never really dimmed.

Yesterday, when Jessica asked the class why, it was Angel who said the word "entertainment" and Daisy who followed with "soap opera." Jessica pressed her to elaborate, and the girl grew incensed. "I hear about stuff like that happening every day," she said of the murder, "and the only reason this one gets covered is they were rich and they were white. If this was a black or Hispanic couple, you wouldn't hear about it." Soon the room was in an uproar, voices careering wall to wall, even the single white student seconding Daisy's declaration. Only rarely in her years at Seward Park has Jessica heard her students blame their woes on class and race—if anything, they tended to blame themselves—but the Chambers case drove past the calluses and down to the nerves. The corollary of its coverage, as even a roomful of teenagers could see, was that some lives were worth more than others.

Today Jessica writes on the blackboard a seemingly abstract aim: "How Can We Draw Some Conclusions About the Responsibilities of a Journalist?" She repeats Daisy's words from yesterday, a preamble of sorts, and then passes out a rexo, drawn from a book entitled *Reading The News.* The sheet consists of excerpts from several articles about the killing of a woman named Eleanor Bumpurs. If Chambers and Levin occupied another planet from Jessica's students, then Bumpurs could well have occupied an apartment down the hall. A portly black grandmother living in the projects, she achieved her unlikely notoriety in October 1984 in a fatal confrontation with police officers who were seeking to evict her. Before Jessica asks a single question, she can hear murmurs of recognition. The Bumpurs case was one of several slayings of black residents by white police officers in New York in the mid-1980s, incidents that strained the city's race relations until they snapped with the fatal mob attack in Howard Beach, Queens.

All down the rows, heads dip and eyes read. There have been few moments so calm in the past two days. The first article on the rexo is *The New York Times's* initial story on the case, which appeared on October 30, 1984, on page 3 of the metropolitan section, a setting neither obvious nor obscure.

Police Kill Woman Being Evicted;
Officers Say She Wielded a Knife

A 67-year-old Bronx woman being evicted from a city housing project for nonpayment of rent was fatally shot by a police officer yesterday after she slashed at another officer with a butcher knife, the police said.

Authorities said the woman, Eleanor Bumpurs, who was described as "violent and uncontrollable," was shot in the chest when an officer assigned to the police Emergency Services Unit fired his shotgun. Members of the unit are specially trained to deal with emotionally disturbed people.

"What do you think of the article?" Jessica asks, rising from her perch on the corner of the desk.

"Routine," says Lun Cheung, never the most prolix of Jessica's flock.

"Routine," she repeats, beginning to pace the room in cowgirl boots, long leather earrings bouncing with her gait. "What does that mean?"

"They just went in and reported the facts of what happened," says Gregg Gross, who, like all the advanced journalism students, was summoned by Jessica for this lesson.

"It's usually like that when someone gets shot or mugged," adds Alex Cruz, a bright boy Jessica and Bruce have nurtured since his graduation from the special education curriculum. "The paper just tells you it happened."

"Where did the reporter *get* the facts from?" Jessica asks.

"From the police spokesman," says Shon Walker, a friend who Gregg has dragged into class for the day.

"He didn't investigate anything," Alex says. "He just wrote down what he was told."

Jessica folds her arms, shuts her eyes, smiles, and slowly rocks her head, a conductor pleased with her orchestra.

"Not very difficult, is it?" she says, now opening her eyes and tossing her curls. "A reporter goes to a press conference and writes down what's said there. Even you beginning journalists could probably do that in a half hour."

She turns to the board and writes, "Reporters often take a routine approach—take information from official sources." Facing the class again, she asks them to read the second article on the rexo. This story, also from *The Times,* appeared two days after the first, again inside the metropolitan section.

Police and Victim's Daughter Clash on Shooting

A police official yesterday defended his department's tactics in the fatal shooting Monday of a 66 year old [*sic*] woman in her Bronx apartment and said there were no plans to revise procedures for restraining emotionally disturbed people. . . .

In an interview yesterday, Mrs. Bumpurs's daughter Mary questioned aspects of the police account, saying her mother "suffered from high blood pressure and arthritis."

"And she had trouble moving quickly," Miss Bumpurs said. "Shotguns are for elephant hunting, not for an old woman who was terrified of people breaking into her apartment."

"Now," Jessica says, "what's the difference in this article?"

"The first one just had the facts," Eric Gonzalez calls. "The second one was an opinion."

"Is that right?" Jessica pushes. "Just facts versus opinions?" She pauses. "Wasn't there opinion in the first article, too?"

An almond-eyed girl named Susan Diaz raises her hand. Like Carlos Pimentel, she was one of the few bright spots in the first-term journalism class, one of the few worth guiding into the advanced course. While her colleagues seemed sorely taxed to review a record or movie, Susan wrote an extensive and eloquent defense of abortion rights, which she is now expanding for publication.

"In the first article, the lady sounded like she was violent," Susan says, "and in the second like she was disabled."

"The two articles had different messages," adds Janice Roldán. "First it was, 'She was dangerous, we had to shoot her.' It excused her killing. The second said maybe it was the police's fault."

"What did the reporter in the second one do that the first one didn't?" Jessica asks. "Lun?"

"Went and talked to her relatives."

Jessica nods resolutely.

"Did some *work*."

She turns again to the board and writes, "What reporters need to do is investigate any incident or situation more—delve into more depth, interview more people to get more points of view."

The discussion broadens into the case itself. Lun wonders aloud if Bumpurs's daughter is a reliable source. She had not seen her mother for five months before the shooting and had not helped pay the back rent she owed. Maybe, Lun says, she was blaming the police to assuage her own guilt.

"I'll tell you," Eric adds, "if I was a police officer and someone was waving a knife at me, I'd be so scared I might shoot." He recalls the case of Officer Steven McDonald, shot and paralyzed by a fifteen-year-old on whom he had hesitated to draw his own gun. "What about that? The guy's crippled for life."

"But Bumpurs was a grandmother," Shon says. "I don't care if she had a knife."

"You know how old people are," Janice puts in. "They get scared when somebody comes into their apartment."

"The way they do evictions," Gregg mutters.

Jessica watches from the front, pleased with the dissonance.

"I'm really impressed with how you're all thinking," she finally says. "No matter what side you're . . ."

"Well, I still don't think the reporter dug in," blurts Che Sidanius, a tall boy with one earring, half American, half Swedish, and newly arrived. "He didn't find out what really happened."

"Absolutely," Jessica says, using his interruption as her transition. "It's the easiest way. What I'd hardly call journalism." She lowers herself onto the desk, spreads her arms, and feigns a yawn. "Sit back, get the press release, write it up." Now she straightens. "And as a result, who gets written about?" She halts, her silence the strongest punctuation. "Think back to yesterday. What does this have to do with Daisy's comments about the Chambers case?"

The slender arm that rises is Daisy's own.

"This woman lived in the Bronx," she says. "And if she was paying eighty-nine dollars a month in rent, then you know she was poor. And the first article, the first instinct, was to take what the police officer said."

"Why?"

"She wasn't powerful," Ottavio says.

"Didn't know the right people," Angel adds.

"And with the Robert Chambers case," Daisy says, completing her thought, "they give it more emphasis. You get every detail." She pauses, as if to censor herself, as if unsure whether to speak aloud a belief she holds within. "Because he's white."

Jessica does not disagree, but she refuses to leave Daisy and the rest feeling helpless. Thirteen years after resigning her own reporting job, she is still romantic enough to believe that words can change the world.

"As a journalist," she says, "you might not want to take the easy way out. You might not want to just print what officials say. It's a lot harder to get out and dig. To write about minorities and poor people. The kind of people other reporters forget about." She draws breath. "So if you want to be the kind of reporter who doesn't forget, then what do you have to do?"

*   *   *

Lun Cheung ambles down the hall in his bowlegged way, wearing sweatpants, a denim coat, and high-tops, and chattering with Gregg Gross about the basketball game their team just won in gym class. Sitting just inside the English office door, Jessica spots him and pounces. "Lun," she shouts, "what about the Chinatown story?" He shuffles into the room, as Gregg escapes before he, too, is collared.

"I was working on it," Lun says in his slurred, sandpaper voice. "I don't know." He kneads the brow above his aviator glasses. "I didn't feel well last week."

"Physically?"

"Yeah," he says, "but I'm not usin' it as an excuse."

"I hope not," she says. "The article's due Friday."

"I know."

"I'll help you," Jessica says, leaning forward in the chair. "I'll go to the interviews with you if you want."

"I'll handle it," he says and rises to leave.

Jessica ponders the enigma named Lun. Here is the boy who sat in the farthest corner of the English class, feet propped on his desk, playing Pluto to her sun. Yet his writing and speaking for the term deserved a 95. Here is the boy who coasted through beginning journalism, dashing off just enough work not to fail. Yet he then registered for the advanced course. Here is the boy who won't speak two words if one will suffice. Yet he confessed his gang past in his autobiography and held himself morally liable for the death of an innocent friend. Jessica remembered his words and the agony that infused them, the agony of a sinner seeking redemption and through it revenge. Lun's was an outrage, she thought, that could be forged and hammered. She asked him to report about Chinese youth gangs and he unflinchingly accepted, but now in his fashion he is being maddeningly opaque.

Her intuition was not wrong at all. Lun wanted to expose the gangs to those who believed all Chinese were docile and sweet. He wanted his byline to shine like neon so everyone would know who dared tell the truth. If there was danger, he would not run away. He was compact and tough, a Chinese whose best friends were Hispanics, who played tackle football unpadded on a field of concrete, who christened his team the Allen Street Wild Boys. And there was a part of Lun that welcomed martyrdom, the same part that years ago told his friend's parents he wished he had died in their son's place. Getting started, though, getting started was the problem. He told himself he did not like conducting interviews, but that was prevaricating. Getting started meant going back, back into a past of anger and shame and unexpiated wrongs, a past of which Jessica knew only one final piece.

Lun had come to America from Hong Kong at age four, but unlike many immigrants, his family had not fled deprivation. They had lived in Hong Kong on the largesse of a grandfather, Lun's father studying to become an engineer, his mother remaining home to rear five children. It was only for the children that the Cheungs left all that was certain and comfortable. Their first place in New York was a two-room tenement, and making the rent was a full-time ordeal. Lun's mother sewed in a garment factory, while his father cooked in a Chinese restaurant. Without a mother to manage the household, Lun's three older brothers assigned him the chores, insisting that labor elevated the soul, wrapping their bullying in Confucian cloaks. No longer was Lun's father the stable force he had been. As year after year he continued cooking, and abandoned his dreams of engineering, a withheld rage corroded him from the inside out. Sometimes he sat and looked at the portrait of his college class from Hong Kong, and complained that he had never wanted to leave. Sometimes he threw plates and broke mirrors. Eventually, he committed himself to a psychiatric hospital, to which he returned many times, often for periods of months.

Between a troubled father, overbearing brothers, and a mother straining to hold her fissioning family intact, Lun discovered his sole refuge on the streets. He had a friend in seventh grade who served alongside his father in the Ghost Shadows, one of Chinatown's two dominant gangs. First inducted a year earlier at age twelve, Lun's friend drove his own Pontiac Firebird and carried $800 in cash instead of lunch money. When the boy invited Lun to join the Ghost Shadows, Lun felt honored and pleased. There were no oaths or rituals, Lun would later remember, only the warning, "Join another gang and we'll kill you."

The threat was anything but idle. The Chinatown gangs in one ten-month period of 1977 slew thirty innocents and rivals, using guns and bats and meat cleavers alike. They ran protection and gambling, sold women and drugs. When so moved, they marched into movie houses or wedding receptions to relieve the attendees of their wallets and jewels. At the top, the gangs worked in tandem with entrenched Chinese organized crime syndicates; at the bottom, they drew on boys like Lun—teenagers born in Hong Kong, unhinged at home, bored in school, craving status and excitement and money.

Lun started his career as the junior partner in a three-man extortion firm. The ring was responsible for Mott Street, a few bustling blocks of curio stores, restaurants, and herbal medicine shops, the place any guidebook would direct a tourist to experience "the real Chinatown." Lun stood rear guard as the leader demanded money, cursing each shopkeeper's ancestors. A small business was assessed $150 a month, a large one $400. Owners who refused to pay were beaten, and for those who persisted, the leader packed a .38. Lun also served as a watchman outside basement gambling parlors, and one night while he was on duty, he saw several Ghost Shadows attack a rival gangster, bludgeoning him with a lead pipe until his head cracked like a melon. "I *lived* on that," he would say years after, still tasting the thrill. Yes, it was heady to be young and feared, to earn four times the money of men your father's age, to watch them bow in greeting whenever you approached, to unleash the fury built up at home on unfortunate strangers, safely backed up by your gang.

Lun rarely slept at home any longer, staying instead in a Ghost Shadows apartment for weeks and even months. He cut junior high school four days out of five, telling the teachers who asked, "Hey, I do what I want." In the end, to his shock, they always passed him, but it barely mattered because school seemed superfluous. Lun was making $400 a week, enough to buy Adidas sneakers and Jordache jeans, enough to gamble on sports and mah-jongg, enough to slake his thirst for Johnny Walker Red. At last, at age fifteen, he felt like his own man.

Then in the tenth grade, as he told Jessica in his autobiography, he was jumped and beaten senseless and his best friend Steve was killed. Another friend, this one a gang member, accidentally killed himself while cleaning his gun. Lun's parents sent him to Hong Kong that summer, where he boarded with cousins and vowed to straighten his ways. He returned in the fall to a hard, dull, legitimate life, doing his homework, working as a cashier, and choosing new friends who were not Chinese. He watched from the sidelines as the police splintered the Ghost Shadows with dozens of arrests, and he was relieved to see temptation sent to prisons far away. Lun showed enough promise to be placed in Seward Park's honors program, but he wanted mostly to be done with high school, done with his past. He imagined going to Syracuse University, making the football team as a walk-on, reinventing himself. His lax attitude told, and he was dropped from the honors program, and placed in classes that rarely pushed a boy who needed to be pushed very hard.

Every time Jessica pushes him on the gang article, Lun resists. As a teacher, she applauds his insistence on independence, but as a journalist, she worries about the quality of his work. Neither the threat of poor grades nor the prospect of a national award moves him. "I can handle it," he tells her time after time. One day, abruptly, he confides that she is the only teacher who knows him, and then he retreats into obliquity again. He does not want her to worry or go out of her way. He does not want her to know how he writhes with indecision, sighting his target only to return arrow to quiver.

The break comes in mid-February with the Chinese New Year. Lun has a friend who is a disc jockey for private affairs, and the friend invites Lun to the holiday party he is working. Lun walks from his housing project toward the neon signs and the narrow tenements, skirting the Lion Dancers bobbing like human centipedes, kicking aside the firecracker casings that cover the asphalt like fallen blossoms, navigating this celebration of Chinatown at its most deeply rooted and its most superficial. His friend has directed him to a restaurant, which tonight is being rented in its marble-floored, mirror-walled entirety. Once Lun arrives, his friend walks him across the ballroom to a group of young men leaning against the bar, diffidence on display in their Zodiac shoes and Ravo sunglasses and razor-creased black pants. They all smoke Marlboros. Lun recognizes the signs.

As he shakes hands with one, the gangster says, "Your friend here told me you're writing an article."

"Just a little piece," Lun says. Then he adds, "Maybe it'll give you guys some publicity."

The ruse seems to work, for several in the crowd agree to sit for interviews. In the next few weeks, Lun treats each gang member individually to dim sum, asking questions and taking notes as they eat. "Don't use my name," each tells him at the session's end. For someone with Lun's knowledge of gang terror, the addendum "or else" is unnecessary.

As Jessica sees it, the article should contain much more than horror stories, so she equips Lun with a list of political scientists, social workers, community historians, and union organizers. They frame the gang problem within the contexts of immigration, drug trafficking, poverty, and power, and at times, the complexity of their insights overwhelms Lun. But none of these experts unsettles him more than does Sergeant James McVeety, a Police Department specialist in Chinese youth gangs. Sitting across from a cop in a station house, Lun cannot shake the sense he has done something wrong, for until now, he has never met an officer as anything except a suspect. Sergeant McVeety tells him about a mother who saw her son assassinated by a gang and refused to testify against his killers for fear they would then murder her. Lun wants to leap through his skin. He, too, never identified for the police the men who beat to death his friend Steve, and the cowardice haunts him still. He wonders where Steve's parents live. He heard that they moved. He feels some obligation, wherever they are, the same obligation that propels him each year on his birthday to visit Steve's grave.

In late March, Lun delivers the article. It spans both sides of four pages, scrawled tightly in ink. Jessica edits that afternoon, suggesting a new lead, reordering paragraphs, checking information with sources, and gushing red ink from first line to last. When he returns home from his job as a messenger that night, Lun rewrites. He has never labored harder on any high school assignment. Jessica reads the finished version with more than satisfaction. Everything is there— quotations, statistics, historical scope, verisimilitude, and a penultimate paragraph that addresses her alone, as if buried in code.

> Tommy, an ex-member of the Ghost Shadows, tells about his involvement. "I used to be a gang member but my friend Richie told me to get out. I did not listen. One day we met some rivals from another gang and my friend, who was innocent, was killed. For this, I will never forgive the Chinese gangsters. I hate them with a passion."

This tale, she knows, is Lun's own.

*   *   *

During a *Seward World* meeting several weeks into March, the same meeting at which Jessica swears her staff to secrecy about Lun's authorship of the gang article, Aracelis Collado arrives with her fair brown hair dyed black. Jessica feels herself gasp, but says nothing. When the session concludes and the other students scatter, she draws Aracelis aside and manages to say, "You look very sophisticated. You look forty years old." Aracelis tightens her lips into a cryptic smile and then backpedals into the hall without speaking a word.

Jessica has been wondering for a few weeks now what could be wrong. While the other advanced journalism students use their period to research and write articles, Aracelis has been sitting in class with the beginners, listening to lessons she heard a full year ago. She owes two *Seward World* articles that were assigned a month earlier, one on illegal immigrants and another on a student storyteller, and it is unlike Aracelis to hand in any work late. Jessica knew she had had bronchitis back in January, and for awhile she attributed the girl's current pallor to that. Then, as time passed, she ascribed the torpor to a bad case of senioritis.

The black hair, though, is less easily diagnosed. This black does not shimmer and catch light; this black has about it something beaten and limp. Jessica tries to convince herself that Aracelis changed hair color to match her best friend Elizabeth's, but that hardly explains the new wardrobe of black sweaters and black pants and black boots.

Jessica spots Aracelis again that afternoon, leaning against the wall opposite the English office, almost as if she intended to be observed. "Are you having any problems?" she asks. Aracelis answers, "No." The next morning, Jessica approaches Aracelis's sister Damaris, one of her students in English 7, and asks if Aracelis is all right. Damaris says she has been sick lately, that's all.

As a journalist and a teacher, Jessica has prided herself on summoning from people the *jinni* of their internal lives and on sensing when the lamp is best left lidded. It was one thing to nag the Luns and the Greggs, to turn her pursuit into a standing joke, and the joke into a way of achieving intimacy. But Aracelis, it seemed to Jessica, had carefully created around herself an aura of being efficient, in control, well defended. And it was welcome. Aracelis was someone Jessica could count on—for delivering assignments promptly, for contributing intelligently in class, for carrying herself like a woman, not a giggly juvenile. Aracelis, in a way, gave Jessica the freedom to aid others in greater need.

But as the second term proceeds, she exerts herself only in English 8 and physical education, the two courses she needs for graduation. She drops a class in shorthand, and considers doing the same with journalism, remaining only because she fears that in leaving she may hurt Jessica. "I owed her that much," she would later recall. Her presence, however, is no more than corporeal. She sleepwalks through school and "spaces out" on her job and cloisters herself at home, listening to Hot-103 on the radio and reading romances by the score.

To speak of a problem, Aracelis believes, is only to make that problem more real; to speak of a problem is to show weakness, and her role in life is to be strong for others. As the oldest girl in her family, she started sweeping and cleaning at age eight. Four years later, when her mother went home to the Dominican Republic for her own father's funeral, Aracelis took on cooking and laundry. After her mother returned, she worked overtime in a garment factory, so Aracelis continued her domestic duties, later taking on an afterschool job, too. She grew rapidly, and in more ways than one, becoming early in her teens a beauty with the social aplomb of someone ten years her senior.

On a family visit to the Dominican Republic when she was twelve, Aracelis received her first proposal of marriage. Her suitor was a teacher, a man of twenty-three, who judged Aracelis to be fourteen or fifteen. That was an appropriate age for a girl to marry in the republic, especially in the countryside, for in her early teens she was almost sure to be a virgin, and virginity was vital in a bride. Although Aracelis's mother dissuaded the teacher, Aracelis as she grew never dated boys her own age, and those who sought her at Seward Park only embarrassed themselves. Their idea of flirtation was to holler down the hall, *"Mami, tu si estás buena,"* which translated in spirit as, "Yo, Mama, you lookin' fine." Their idea of a date was the latest sequel to *Nightmare on Elm Street.* Aracelis wanted someone who would walk with her through a park, treat her to dinner, ask what she thought about things, and care what she answered. Then she met him.

His name was Miguel, and everyone called him Mickey. In truth, Aracelis had known him for six years, because he was a friend of her two older brothers, Alex and Carlos. She never imagined Mickey as anything except *their* friend until he appeared at her Sweet Sixteen party. He escorted Damaris, as a favor to Carlos and Alex, but he really came to admire Aracelis. Not long after, Mickey went with Aracelis and Alex to visit Carlos at college in Stony Brook, Long Island. A month later, he told her he wanted to become engaged. He had already asked his mother, and she approved. Sensing Aracelis's reluctance, he changed the subject, but as months went on, he kept hinting about it, telling Aracelis that his mother was asking when he was buying the ring. Aracelis begged Mickey not to surprise her. She was not convinced that she could say yes.

The problem was that she loved Mickey. Mickey was in the Army and Mickey had plans. He was already an accomplished mechanic and he would learn to become an electrician, even an engineer. Mickey bought flowers for her, and held the door when she entered his car. He listened when she talked about her hopes of attending college and studying psychology, and he said there were lots of good colleges in the city. When she said she dreamed of going away to school, perhaps to join Carlos at Stony Brook, he said all right, he would visit her every weekend, wherever she was. Aracelis's uncle, the closest thing to a father in her household, argued Mickey's cause. "This guy is great," he told her. "He doesn't cheat on you. He wants to provide for you. What else can you want?"

She wanted time. She had little. On Valentine's Day, two weeks into Aracelis's final semester of high school, she and Mickey had a date. He arrived at her apartment bearing a skirt, a handbag, and a dozen red roses. They sat on the sofa, and he proposed. She said she was too young. Mickey said nothing. He sat for a long time and then he went into the bathroom to cry.

In the month since then, Aracelis has felt her soul severed. One half wants to marry Mickey, because she loves him and even more because she cannot bear to harm him. The other wants college and a career more fiercely than ever. She thinks of all her mother sacrificed—an immigrant alone sneaking into New York, a seamstress sending money to children left behind, a protector drawing a kitchen knife on the bullies who attacked her boys. Aracelis remembers the day she was five, the day her mother returned to the Dominican farmlands to bring her children to America. She remembers sitting on the porch of her aunt's hilltop house, remembers seeing her mother approach astride a white horse, waving a white handkerchief, a vision more magical than any in fairytales. Was all that for no more than for Aracelis to marry at eighteen?

After several weeks, Aracelis starts to write for the journalism class. The first marking period of the term is nearing its end, and Aracelis fears she is failing the course; required to submit an article each week, her output amounts to a column of blank boxes in Jessica's grade book. Always reliable, as a daughter and a student, Aracelis craves the license to make her own mistakes. But she is cautious enough to permit herself only safe foibles, and the image of an F on her report card makes her stomach sink. So she writes, and in writing she reveals. The three articles she submits to Jessica concern the fear of not being admitted to college, the risks of young marriage, and the causes of suicide.

Jessica sees the topics and shrivels. It is as if someone bleeding to death and in need of a tourniquet sent a letter to the first-aid squad, the better to save face. She reads the article entitled, "Waiting For the Result," not yet prepared to wade into the others. "At night, I fall asleep," Aracelis writes, "and what do I dream? Well—it's none other than the idea that I am not accepted to any of the colleges that I applied to. It all becomes a nightmare. I see the admissions director. I see his horrible expression of disgust and a mean twinkle in his eye. He looks at my application and rips it apart and throws it into the nearest waste basket. There I see my life thrown apart."

Atop the first page, Jessica writes: "Is this part of what's on your mind now? Why don't we call Stony Brook and see what they say." These fears, at least, are familiar to Jessica. And in Aracelis's case, she is certain they are unfounded.

She begins the second piece, "Young Marriages." At the outset, it strikes her as clinically detached, derived too closely from *Psychology Today*. By the bottom of the first page, though, the tone veers without warning into the intimate, Aracelis quoting a nineteen-year-old mother with two kids. Two paragraphs later, Damaris Collado speaks, and it is impossible for Jessica not to regard her as Aracelis's alter ego. "I think marriage, especially for a young couple, is something that should be thought over carefully," Damaris says in the article. "It's hard to think about this, because personally I would not like to get married before I'm 20. . . . You should concentrate first on school. Also, live your life more. . . . You'll need time and space to become a mature adult and the person you want to become. Rushing time and events sometimes proves to be Fatal."

Jessica scratches in the top right corner of the first page a check mark and three plus signs, her highest tribute to homework. She adds the word "Good" and to its left as an afterthought "Very." Then in small scrawl, in a gulley between the title and Aracelis's name, she writes: "I get the feeling this might come out of things you're thinking about right now—is this part of what's bothering you?" She cannot stop wondering why Aracelis, who knows better, would capitalize the "F" in "fatal."

In the story about suicide, too, Aracelis opens in a reporter's voice that is decidedly remote. "The suicide rate," her second paragraph says, "seems to show a 'negative correlation' with prevailing economic conditions." As the sentences pass, the tone wavers between term paper and diary, as if Aracelis were handling uranium through protective lead gloves. "Being caught up in a relationship at an early age," Jessica reads, "is often a sign that the boy or girl involved (or both) feel unloved and neglected by their families. If such a romance breaks up, as early romances often do, the teenager is likely to feel alone in the world, with no one to turn to. This experience may well be a crushing one, especially for girls in our society, especially when they know or fear that they are pregnant."

This time, Jessica does not answer in ink. During journalism class the next afternoon, she takes Aracelis into the hall. She leans against a wall, curtaining with her body a private spot in a public space.

"You've always been a good student," Jessica begins, "the kind I never have to worry about." She pauses. "But now I'm worried." Aracelis looks away. "I can't force you to talk about it. But if you want. . . ."

Jessica decides not to push any harder. Aracelis, she understands, needs to seem strong, even invulnerable. Denial may be the only sustenance she knows; to say to her face, "You're falling apart," may only convince her the battle is lost.

Aracelis says the articles had nothing to do with her low spirits, but knows she is lying. Aracelis admires Jessica too much; she cannot confide in an icon. Yet she realizes this one teacher has seen her despair and offered a hand of kindness, a hand that, even untaken, can soothe, if not heal. As teacher and student reenter the classroom, Jessica can only assume she has failed, but for the first time in months, Aracelis feels hope.

When she receives her report card soon after, she is amazed to find Jessica passed her with a 65. It is the lowest passing grade, true, but Aracelis interprets it as a sign of faith.

She finally interviews the student who is an award-winning storyteller. She blushes and laughs when Jessica kids her, "He wants to be a celebrity, and I think he has other interests in you." The article Aracelis submits shows humor and life. "Once upon a time. . . ." it begins. "Ooops, this story doesn't start like that. In fact, this story is about a story." At the end, she quotes the boy: "I want people to recognize me and my efforts in life. Everything in life takes a lot of sacrifice."

This tale, in its way, is Aracelis's own.

*   *   *

It was just about one year ago that Jessica wandered into the business department office to find Edgar Lassiter, a senior starter on the basketball team, and Carlos Pimentel, a younger teammate she knew only faintly. The season had just ended, graduation loomed three months away, and Carlos wanted to know what Edgar planned on doing with the rest of his life. "Go into the Air Force," he answered, and when Carlos pursued him, Edgar launched into the sort of reverie Jessica had heard too many times. "Damn, you shoulda seen their outfits," he said of the soldiers he had already met. "Everything was perfect. Wasn't a crease on it. Open the drawer, and the underwear's all in a pile. Folded up like triangles."

Carlos shook his head in disbelief, and Jessica unleashed an argument almost as practiced as Edgar's own. "That's a reason?" she said, standing over him, hands on hips. "Because their underwear looks neat?" She exhaled as if blowing steam. "You strike me as a guy who thinks for himself. You're always bitching about how teachers don't like you because you talk back. And now you want to go into a place where if you say what you think, they're gonna try to break that down?"

Then a crew-cut head poked around the door, searching for Jessica. It belonged to Vinnie Mickles, and to Jessica his timing was sublime, beyond sublime, divinely ordained. Vinnie was one of the few students she had ever encouraged to enlist, because at the time his most pressing need was to escape his family and his neighborhood. He had survived two years in the Marine Corps, and while his heart held the corps's fraternal pride, his brain recognized how it had tried to disassemble him. Jessica asked him to tell Edgar a story she knew from his autobiography.

In boot camp, Vinnie said, he had fallen ill, and during a set of several hundred push-ups he coughed up some phlegm.

"Stand up, Private," the drill instructor said with deceptive calm. Then he shoved his face inches from Vinnie's and bellowed, "Did I say you could spit, boy?"

Vinnie said no.

"I didn't think so," he continued at top volume. "Pick that up!"

Vinnie raked through the mud and leaves for the gob of mucus, finally producing it in his palm. "Now put it away!" the instructor hissed.

Vinnie stuffed the mess into the pocket of his camouflage pants.

Perhaps that tale made the difference; perhaps Jessica's appeal did. It certainly did not hurt that Loretta Sims found Edgar a night job in a bank, so he could earn money and have his days free for college. Whatever the reason or combination of reasons, he did not enlist, but the memory of that day, and the importance of that issue, stayed with both Jessica and Carlos. They have been meeting every morning during the second term, discussing Carlos's next article. His piece on sports fantasies proved to him he could comprehend and explain serious issues, and win approval in school for doing it. In a case of parallel evolution, or perhaps common vision, Jessica and Carlos agree his next subject will be military recruiting.

Since she came to Seward Park, Jessica has railed against the incessant pursuit of minority teenagers by the armed forces. In her very first year of teaching, she saw one of her most outspoken, idiosyncratic students—a boy who struck some teachers as altogether obnoxious—join the Army and return the next Christmas with a rigid mind beneath a shaved scalp. Last year, both Sammy Williams and Sammy Ryan received surprise visits at home from recruiters. This year, Angel Fuster made the mistake of accepting a complimentary pair of socks, and soon was being pressured to enlist. Military recruiters appear regularly at Seward Park's college fair and career day and in the school cafeteria, impressive in their spit-and-polish manner, laden with posters and brochures, pens at the ready to record names and addresses. The military donates a vocational aptitude test to Seward Park, among other high schools, provided recruiters can later contact those who take it and score well. Where Seward Park has drawn the line is in not permitting recruiters to address classes and assemblies, and in refusing to deliver to them a roster of juniors and seniors. Those decisions matter little, however, since the New York City Board of Education annually supplies to the armed forces a roster of all graduating seniors, complete with home addresses and telephone numbers.

Jessica understands too well the appeal of enlisting. The Vietnam veterans she met while reporting for Liberation News Service were either poor blacks and Hispanics fleeing riot-torn cities or working-class whites like Gunny Musgrave, pumped full of patriotic zeal. With the end of the war, and of the immediate risk of injury and death, the allurements and incentives grew only more attractive to teenagers like those Jessica taught. Their families battled and fell apart. Gangs and dealers dominated the streets. Legitimate jobs paid the minimum wage. College meant taking tests, seeking financial aid, completing applications, surmounting the suffocating sense of inadequacy. Weighed against all that, joining the military, signing on the dotted line, looked like the simplest decision in the world.

Carlos has seen the scenario repeated endlessly in Manhattan Valley. His former friend Chi-Chi, a high school dropout and a crack dealer, the father of a child out of wedlock, escaped into the military. A guy named Eddie, the older brother of a friend, got his girlfriend pregnant and judged his high school grades too low for college. He chose the same route. Every time a soldier comes home on leave, hard and strong in a dress uniform, the neighborhood applauds. "This guy accomplished something," Carlos can hear the parents on the stoops saying. "He's not a loser."

Like Angel, Carlos foolishly bit the bait. Back in December, when a military recruiter was plying the cafeteria, Carlos asked for a book cover because he liked the photograph of a soldier scaling a sheer rock wall. In return, he needed merely to supply his name, address, and telephone number. The calls commenced three weeks later.

"We heard you want to join," the voice began.

"I never said I wanted to join."

"Why not?"

Carlos invented a story about receiving a college basketball scholarship. The recruiter said each service branch has a team. David Robinson, the All-American center, was playing for the Navy's squad right now. When Carlos still resisted, the recruiter began arranging appointments and calling Carlos with the time and place. Every time Carlos broke one appointment, the recruiter scheduled another. When Carlos repeated the basketball scholarship line, the recruiter suggested he at least attend a college with ROTC. By now, Ramón Pimentel, too, was lobbying Carlos to enlist. In Ramón's experience in the Dominican Republic, the military, not college, was a poor person's most direct route to the middle class. Ramón had seen it work for Carlos's older half brother. The next time the recruiter telephoned, Carlos blurted in exasperation, "I'm a pacifist," having summoned the word from the murky memories of tenth-grade history. And finally, after almost four months, the dunning ceased.

Once it did, Carlos began working with Jessica on the *Seward World* article, which would be an article with a marked difference. No matter how strongly Jessica feels about most issues—abortion rights, for instance—she demands fairness from her students' coverage of them. With military recruiting, however, she suspends all pretense of balance, stressing the same points she had in refusing to accept military advertisements. "Everything around these kids," she says, "is from the other side, the military side. Every time they watch sports on

TV, there are the commercials. Every time they open a magazine, there are the ads. It's all over the place. One article with an alternative point of view is like one tree in the middle of this forest."

If it is a lone tree, she will make sure it is a redwood. She steers Carlos to David Cline, the chairman of Vietnam Veterans Against the War, and reminds him to interview Angel Fuster about free socks and other inducements. Then she lends Carlos Vinnie Mickles's autobiography, with its account of boot camp. Finally, she sends him to the War Resisters League, which supplies Carlos with newsletters, pamphlets, and, of the greatest use, a point-by-point rebuttal of an Army Reserve advertisement aimed at students.

Having completed most of his research, Carlos decides to play guinea pig. Following Louise Grollman's suggestion, he visits the military recruiting office in Times Square, posing as a potential volunteer. He wears dress shoes, designer jeans, and a sweater, because he wants to look "like an educated kid"—the sort who would invite the most interest and yet appear the least susceptible to guile. As he enters the glass-and-steel rectangle, stuck on a concrete island amid eight lanes of traffic, he tightens with fear. One window banner declares, ARMY—BE ALL YOU CAN BE, and another, THE FEW, THE PROUD—1-800-MARINES. Through the glass, Carlos can see bumper stickers on file cabinets, photographs of soldiers with faces painted for jungle warfare. Carlos has this picture in his mind of an officer closing the door behind him, turning the lock, and hauling him off to boot camp, to pick up his own phlegm like Vinnie. He is so scared he cannot imagine how he will execute this deception. He expects any second to turn and run, to lose himself among the taxis and buses and pushcarts.

Instead, the officer he meets is a friendly black man in a thickly woven green sweater. He is the kind of guy, Carlos thinks, his mother would trust. Carlos realizes he must begin before his hesitation betrays him.

"I'm thinking of joining the Army," he says.

"Well, Carlos, we can use a few good men. Why do you want to join?"

"Well," he says, trying to remember his lines, "I really want to travel and learn a skill and go to college."

"Carlos," the officer says softly, "what if I promised you a trip to Europe?" He lets the prize dangle. "Would you go?"

"Yes," Carlos says. Outside, horns squabble and brakes shriek. A crack addict leans into a pay telephone to light her pipe. A young man with a megaphone announces that a holy earthquake is coming. Even as Carlos plays the role, he feels the attraction, the attraction of getting away, of trading this madness for a fantasy called Europe.

"First you must sign up," the officer says.

"Whoa," Carlos blurts, opening his palms and thrusting them toward the desk. "How about a field?"

"What do you want?"

"Communications."

"Don't wait until June, Carlos," the officer says paternally. "Sign up now, because in June that field might not be available." He sees Carlos wavering. "But don't worry. There'll be an opening for *you*."

Carlos pauses, pretends to consider, then asks, "What's boot camp like?"

"It's OK," the officer assures him. "It gets pretty easy after awhile." He changes the subject. "Carlos, don't wait too long. Come in Friday with the necessary papers, and you'll be set."

Carlos leaves his real name, but changes a few digits in his address and telephone number. The officer gives him a poster. On the subway home, he unrolls it and thinks to himself, *Where's the fine print?* By now, he knows that more than half the vocational fields in the military are related to combat. He has calculated that the starting pay of $170 a week amounts to $1.42 an hour, about 40 percent of the minimum wage, if one considers the military a five-day-a-week, twenty-four-hour-a-day job. The money the new GI Bill sets aside for college, he learned at the War Resisters League, is lost unless a soldier wins admission to college. As for boot camp, Carlos remembers from Vinnie what "pretty easy" means. He throws out the poster and starts to write.

Unlike Lun, who labors over his prose, or Aracelis, whose work shows a streak of perfectionism, Carlos creates with relative ease and occasional laxity. The information and the voice are present from the very first draft, but the structure often strikes Jessica as a bit jumbled. So it is with the military recruiting article. She sits with Carlos in the English office several mornings in a row, isolating every element in the article, ranking each in importance, determining the order of arrangement. Each night, Carlos rewrites completely, until the article passes muster with Jessica. Much as she would loathe the analogy, as newspaper adviser she possesses her share of drill sergeant.

The final version opens with a verbatim account of Carlos's meeting with the recruiting officer, typed like a playscript. Next comes a warning, casual yet direct, student to student:

> Sometimes you have a bad day, a test you couldn't pass . . . or just one of those days! You might walk down the hallway thinking of college and getting away . . . and then of all those horrible application forms. Then a sharply dressed soldier with his shiney shoes, ironed uniform walks into the lunch room . . . Think about it before you go up to him and ask him about the armed forces, because you are only going to hear good things, the things they want you to hear.

Descriptions of basic training come next, followed by an analysis of wages and career opportunities and allegations of racial and sexual bias. Upending the "inverted pyramid" format of journalism, Carlos and Jessica place the most fundamental point at the very end of the article:

> And then, finally, there are the moral issues which are certainly ignored by the armed forces in their advertising. Most important is killing—for after all, that is what everyone is trained to do. "They use the military as a youth employment service. It's total indoctrination. It tries to change you into a machine that is built for killing," explained Mr. Cline. "Whatever field you or anyone else in the military is in, you are trained to be a rifleman, you are a machine. If they say kill, you kill."
>
> Some say that the military is the key to peace so we can protect ourselves; others say its through peace and disarmament of weapons. There are many opinions to choose from, but remember what you are there for—which may be ultimately to kill someone. Also remember that what a recruiter says is not always honest, so make your choice with your heart, not by the advertisement on Super Bowl XXII. Joining the military is no game.

This tale, told by Carlos, is also Jessica's own.

*   *   *

The third edition of *Seward World* appears the week after Easter vacation. Lun's article, sans byline, fills page 2. Carlos's piece, featuring a photograph of soldiers in gas masks and the headline, "The Military Uses Fast Talk and Hard Sell," occupies all but the bottom three inches of page 4. Across the top of the facing page spreads Aracelis's story. With the deadline past for this year's Robert F. Kennedy awards, Jessica enters Lun's article in a contest sponsored by the Asian-American Journalists Association and Carlos's in a similar competition offered by the National Association of Hispanic Journalists. And when Dr. Kriftcher criticizes Carlos's story for its obvious bias, Jessica pleads the case. At least there is no question that her tree has rattled the forest.

Jessica herself, meanwhile, comes in for salutations. The *Village Voice,* publishing columnist Jack Newfield's annual "Honor Roll" of "New York's Finest," places her in a pantheon including Paul Simon (for creating a pediatric medicine program for children in welfare hotels), Woody Allen (for an essay in *The New York Times* criticizing Israel's occupation of the West Bank), and Cedric Sandiford (for remaining calm and dignified under an abusive cross-examination during the Howard Beach trial), as well as sundry advocates, organizers, and whistle-blowers. The testament to Jessica begins:

There are things about this city's school system that arbitrary measurements like reading and math scores will never tell us. Judging by its low standing in city scoring in recent years, Seward Park High School, on Grand Street on the Lower East Side, seems an unlikely place to incubate young journalists and students who love to read and write. But for nine years, English and journalism teacher JESSICA SIEGEL has been doing just that: motivating her students with a love of the printed word and a reporter's curiosity about—and passion for—the world they live in. The same streets that formed Jacob Riis 100 years ago may now produce an Hispanic, black or Asian equivalent of the great Riis, because of Jessica.

Jessica being Jessica, she frets about her photograph, withers when the article mentions her background on Liberation News Service, and worries that the publicity will make her colleagues jealous. But Ben Dachs frames and posts the article, and all the reaction Jessica receives is supportive, except from the journalism student who chides, "How much you pay to get that?"

Payment is rather a sore subject at the moment. Jessica exhausted her $3,000 annual budget for *Seward World* with the second issue— exceeded it, in fact, by $100. Now she owes another $1,600 for the current edition. Harold Steinberg has not returned to work since he broke his hip, so carrying a debt seems unlikely. And where she can raise $1,700, plus enough for a final issue, is a question she would prefer to avoid.

14

The Opa-Opa Show

ON THE DAY before Valentine's Day, John McNamara shovels the sidewalk outside his suburban New Jersey home. The storm yesterday was a vintage East Coast changeling, starting as rain and shifting into hail, sleet, and slush before achieving its final, fluffy grace. John has sliced through the topmost layer easily enough; now he is down to the frozen foundation, slamming his shovel blade against solid ice, raising beads of sweat on his forehead, wondering if he showered too soon. Beneath his down coat, he wears a wing-collar shirt and braces; inside his galoshes, he wears black loafers; between his shirt and shoes, he wears tapered black pants, the bottom half of his tuxedo. On what the calendar says is a weekend, on what should be the second leg of a four-day school vacation, John will work his second job. He will leave his wife of fewer than four years and his son of seventeen months to serve as maître d' for the wedding reception of two strangers. He has done the same thing on hundreds of weekends and holidays in the past six years, paying the price of being an excellent teacher.

John lives in a brown-shingle, split-level house on a street of others similar in all but hue. It is a block of barking dogs and roosting birds and roaring lawnmowers, home to an insurance lawyer and a telephone repairman and a retired FBI agent. They are not an especially forthcoming bunch, the neighbors, but if one sees John shoveling the walk, he may chat about tulip bulbs or carpet remnants or John's regular job. "How can you work in a city that has so much crime and pollution?" the neighbor will say, less soliciting an answer than expressing a perplexity. Then the fellow may ask, "Is it true, everything I hear on the news?" meaning by "everything" the unending exposés about drugs, violence, and low reading scores in the New York public schools. John will explain that he loves his work, and the neighbor will smile and change the subject, as if indulging a dotty aunt. Nobody considers John any crazier than the other teacher on the street, a veteran of twenty years in a suburban high school, and an expert in doing only what is required. Sometimes when that teacher notices John lugging a laden briefcase or throwing a backyard picnic for his favorite students, he will chide, "You get paid extra for that?"

John does not bother trying to describe the surge of electricity he feels when he enters Seward Park each morning, or the excitement of seeing a lesson plan succeed. The guy has John sized up as a Pollyanna, and nothing will shake his certainty. There is no point in John telling him that at the age of forty-one, he has read 150 pieces of homework a night 180 nights a year for 19 school years. There is no point in telling him that he taught in a junior high school where students too illiterate to read *The New York Times* used copies as kindling for hallway fires. Confronted by such conditions, such reasons to resign or surrender, John stayed and grew. He earned a master's degree in American history from Fordham University, compiled thirty-three graduate credits at Kean College in New Jersey in educational administration, and has completed all but his dissertation in the doctoral program at Columbia University. Last summer, he won a Fulbright scholarship to study in Korea. John is a survivor, blessed with a survivor's equanimity and an Irishman's tolerance for hard work. Little rattles his resolve, little except for the irony of his existence.

"If I wasn't educated," goes his jaundiced jest, "I'd be a rich man." He has spent almost $20,000 on bettering himself as a teacher, precisely $15,021 of that in tuition for graduate school and about $4,800 on textbooks. Neither the New York City Board of Education nor the United Federation of Teachers provide across-the-board tuition assistance to teachers, although both espouse increasing professionalism in the ranks.* When his wife, Linda, was working as a guidance counselor in Chatham, New Jersey, its school district guar-

---

*There are specific and limited exceptions. Under the terms of its contract with the union, the board pays tuition at branches of the City University for paraprofessionals who are taking courses to become teachers. On its own, the board grants tuition aid to teachers in

anteed to pay her tuition at any state college. John's friend Eddie, who works at Bell Labs, receives rebates from the company for his tuition at Stevens Institute of Technology, a private institution. The disparity between city and suburb hardly ends with tuition grants. With deserved fanfare, New York's school board and teachers' union in September 1987 signed a contract raising the top teaching salary to $50,000. Yet a New York teacher's median salary of $37,756 still lags $3,000 to $12,000 behind the level in most surrounding communities. And the foresighted city of Rochester in upstate New York pays veteran teachers up to $70,000 annually if they work for part of the summer, serve as mentors to younger colleagues, and counsel a small group of students—things John and dozens of others at Seward Park do already for free.

During his teaching career, John has moonlighted as a mail sorter, truck driver, cabbie, waiter, clothing salesman, grocery counterman, camp counselor, and private tutor. He is hardly alone in the predicament. His chairman, Geoffrey Cabat, writes curricula to make extra money. His colleague, Bruce Baskind, buses tables on his wife's private catering jobs. One of his best friends at Seward Park, Rick Rowley, teaches at a Brooklyn yeshiva four afternoons a week. Various others chaperone bicycle trips, write record reviews, sell tennis shorts, and design jewelry, and so many teach in summer school or high-school-equivalency programs that a tally would stretch like a column of batting averages in a Sunday paper.

For awhile, John and Linda made a game of his most recent second job, as a maître d'. She would attend whatever affair he was hosting wearing the same chiffon cocktail dress in which she was married, and nobody ever proved brave or curious enough to ask as much as, "Bride's side, or groom's?" But once the novelty of the charade faded, the loneliness settled in. Sometimes Linda begged John "to give it up for a year or two," and sometimes she wondered if she had done something wrong to drive him away. All she knew was that with both of them educators and their combined salaries totaling about $60,000, she had anticipated hiking the Rockies over the summer, even taking a cruise one Christmas.

Two years into their marriage, she gave birth to a son, Bryan, and John's second job became a necessity. As a new mother, Linda left her

---

subject areas with the severest shortages, such as special education and home economics. and on an ad hoc basis, the board cooperates with area colleges in offering certain graduate courses at reduced tuition.

counseling job and its $22,500 salary. Although she now teaches developmental motor skills to infants and toddlers, the part-time position pays only $40 a week, and one-third of that flows directly to the baby-sitter. On an annual basis, John's take-home pay of $24,855* must cover a mortgage of $9,000, commuting costs of $1,600, Linda's graduate school loan of $1,560, plus his own tuition and books— leaving well under $10,000 for a year's worth of food, clothing, utilities, and other routine expenses. The $5,000 or so he can earn as a maître d' is the family's sole buffer against default. But it exacts its own price in warmth and intimacy. During the week, John gets home at five-thirty, eats dinner with Linda and Bryan, then repairs to his study to grade papers and work on his dissertation, coming to bed after midnight. His weekend job takes him away ten or twelve hours at a time. There are only so many days that Linda can spend with her relatives on Staten Island, only so many hours she can invest in needlepoint and macrame and guitar.

So they fight, not as enemies but as frustrated lovers. "Quit that job," Linda pleads. "I'll budget. I'll clip coupons. I won't spend another dime. Just quit that job." The problem is that all the coupons were clipped and all the corners were cut long ago. Their home is decorated with Linda's crafts and John's books. Linda buys the family clothes at K-Mart and Bradlee's, entering a middle-market store such as Abraham & Straus only for the twice-yearly "final clearance." She and John indulge in a take-out pizza three times a month, and except for their birthdays and wedding anniversary, their only restaurant meals are $6.95 specials at the diner. There are moments when they wonder whether their marriage will survive.

John fastens his bow tie and dons his tuxedo jacket, dressing to make another couple happy. Some days are harder than others. Bryan is just recovering from a 103-degree fever, so Linda will not leave the house. She rises from the lunch table and walks John to the door. She stands on the top step with chestnut hair and limpid blue eyes, the kind of natural beauty that could inspire Roger McGuinn or Neil Young to song. It seems like the cruelest joke in the world that she and John met when she was a bridesmaid in a wedding for which he was the maître d'.

"What time will you be back?" she asks.

"Eleven-thirty," John says, and he drives away, knowing it could well be later.

*   *   *

Perhaps education was so revered in John McNamara's boyhood home because it was the one valuable that fate denied his father. The elder McNamara, also named John, was in his third year of college when his own father died, taking with him the twelve dollar weekly paycheck as an elevator operator. The Great Depression had just struck, and the only other money for four children came from his mother's labor as a domestic. So the young academic set aside his major in industrial technology and his dreams of working in finance or utilities to become a stock boy and then an office clerk and, finally, in John's early years, a claims investigator for a freight-shipping company.

Measured by salary alone, it was not a bad job. Added to Mrs. McNamara's wages as a saleslady, it rented one floor of a brick house in Queens and paid for parochial school for John, the only child. It afforded day trips to Jones Beach and a Christmas visit to Santa Claus at Macy's. Best of all, it provided the McNamaras with free railroad travel, to Washington, D.C., Chicago, and Florida every spring. Comfortable as material life was for his family, John's father never stopped regretting aloud the different, better future he might have made with a diploma.

John could not sweeten his father's bitter past, but he did confer on his present much vicarious joy, ranking sixth in a senior class of 167, winning letters in baseball, basketball, and track, and graduating with an award as the outstanding student-athlete of Monsignor McClancy High School. When it came time to think about the future, he thought of his teachers. His inspiration came from James Murphy, who taught history and "never let a simple answer go unchallenged," and Vernon Bauer, who roamed the rows of biology class, voice rising in pitch, arms windmilling in excitement. Those men gave John the gift of life without illusions, for they explained how they supported their teaching and their families only by holding second jobs, Murphy coaching and officiating, Bauer painting houses.

Knowing all that, John wavered not a whit. As a history major at Manhattan College, a Catholic liberal arts institution, he spent one term student teaching at a public high school in the Bronx. There he apprenticed to a social studies teacher named Carl Fryburg. Short, dark haired, thickly spectacled, Fryburg prowled his room as if fevered, stroking and goading his charges at turns. He had intellect and humor and a dynamism unlike anyone John had ever seen. Here, he decided, was the man to emulate. And Fryburg, as if realizing this, shared time and insights with his tall, blond protégé. He told John: "Always have fun with what you teach. Because the kids will, too." And: "Remember you're working with young *adults*. They can learn almost anything you can teach them." And: "Every class is a performance. For you and the kids."

Three months after graduation, in September 1968, John accepted his first job, at a school that made him doubt all he thought he had learned. The times alone were terrible. The decentralization war had spread from Ocean Hill throughout the city, and three separate strikes closed New York schools for ten weeks that fall. On John's second day as a teacher, he was walking a picket line, without understanding exactly why. By the time classes opened in mid-November, one-third of the previous year's faculty had deserted John's school, J.H.S. 98 in the South Bronx. The building itself was like a museum of public education in decline. Erected by the Works Progress Administration with bas-relief panels and a dome, authorized to admit pupils by competitive examination, the J.H.S. 98 that John entered stored history books in a lavatory, used locker rooms for classes, and posted two police officers in the hall. Far from screening students, the school now was required to accept all survivors of the neighborhood's appalling elementary schools. Some arrived clad in the colors of the Turbans and the Savage Skulls, gangs well practiced in felonies. One girl brought John a note from her mother, explaining that she had been absent because the mother's boyfriend had sexually abused her. Boarding the subway home to Queens each night, to a neighborhood of edged lawns and candy stores and civil servants, John watched the Bronx burn, the latest apartment to be struck by arsonists spewing smoke and flame. "I think," he often told himself, "I'm going to quit this job."

He stayed, however, for five years, outlasting three principals and all but 15 of the 150 teachers with whom he had started. He learned how to maintain discipline with humanity, and he learned how hard young lives could be. When one girl in ninth grade asked if there could be a class trip to her wedding, three days hence, John wanted to laugh and to cry. With the gallows humor of Robert Altman's film in mind, his friends on the faculty joked about being afflicted by "The *M.A.S.H.* Syndrome."

All that was fine, but John missed a sense of accomplishment. Teaching in a junior high school, he could not share most of what he knew. At best, he realized, he was in a tiny way slowing some ghetto kids' demise. He began his doctoral studies, took 1975–76 as a sabbatical year, and passed his licensing test to teach high school social studies. But fall 1977 saw John assigned to J.H.S. 117 in the South Bronx, his third school in a decade, and as desperate as the rest. The principal, noting John's skill at securing order, dispatched him each year to the most troublesome class—math one time, reading another, social studies only if John got lucky. During those years, John received offers from several high schools, and each time his principal refused to release him. When in 1982 John heard of a colleague in mathematics being allowed to transfer to Brooklyn Technical High School, one of the most elite in the city, he ran directly to the principal to protest.

"How come you're letting that guy transfer," he demanded, "when he doesn't do one-tenth the job I do?"

"Exactly," the principal responded.

"You're penalizing me for doing well," John pressed. "If I was lousy, you'd let me go."

"Yes," the principal said, smiling.

He remembered a night back in the early 1970s, when he had bumped into an old college pal. His friend had barely graduated, limping to his degree with a 2.01 average. Now he was making $30,000 a year as an accountant, living in an $80,000 house, driving a new car, and vacationing with his wife in the Bahamas. John was making $12,000, renting an apartment in Flushing, and driving a five-year-old Volkswagen bug. All of which he was willing to endure on the assumption that he would someday teach high school, do what he had set out to do. But now, believing he would never escape the confines of junior high school, he decided to quit.

Being a cautious man, he planned. He had always followed stocks and read the *Wall Street Journal* as a would-be investor. Now he interviewed friends who were brokers and analysts. Thinking his historian's skills well suited to stock analysis, he began studying the market, especially the petroleum field. When Linda first met him, he taught her the difference between a "put" and a "call." Every time he talked about his future in finance, it seemed to her, "he'd light up, become animated, excited."

Still, the frustration of never teaching in a high school nagged John. A baseball star in his own student days, John imagined himself a prime relief pitcher, inexplicably withheld by the manager from every key game. Saying you would retire might ease your agitation, but it did nothing to satisfy the tingling, taut muscles in your arm. One lunchtime in April 1983, two months before he intended to resign, John confided his frustrations to the teacher whose classroom was next door.

"You really want to go to a high school?" the man asked.

"Yes."

"I can do it for you with one call," he promised without elaboration.

"It's impossible," John said. "I've been trying for years. I've had eight high schools want me."

The man explained. He knew someone important at the Board of Education, someone with latitude in hiring, someone more powerful than a junior high school principal. John restrained himself. Too much optimism, he knew, was dangerous.

"If I can do it," the man persisted, "what can you do for me?"

"What do you want?"

"I love scotch."

John shook his head, his hope tempered by doubt.

"If you can get me appointed," he finally said, "there'll be a bottle of Chivas on your desk in the morning."

The next day the teacher told John to visit a man at 65 Court Street in Brooklyn, and everything would then be arranged. John did, and it was. In September 1983, he reported to Seward Park, summoned at last from the bullpen.

*   *   *

What Forest Lawn is to death, the Chrystopoulos Citadel is to marriage. Two stories of smoked windows, baroque columns, marble floors, gold-leaf mirrors, brass bannisters, and stained-glass ceilings, it overlooks a six-lane highway known for its roadside "shlockitecture," as one nearby newspaper put it. To the west lies an Italian restaurant called the Leaning Tower of Pizza, with the ersatz edifice to match, and to the east waits a furniture store shaped like a pirate galleon. Cast amid such a landscape, the Citadel barely merits a second glance. Only longtime locals would remember with affection its original incarnation as an unassuming eatery, its metier a well-grilled sirloin, its mascot a toy monkey balanced like an acrobat on a clothesline above the bar. The monkey is still in residence, but surrounded now by the glitter and chintz of ambition run amok, like Rosebud in Citizen Kane's closet.

John enters the Citadel, skirting the lobby statue of a cherub holding a brook trout, their eyes locked and their mouths open, as if preparing to share secrets or a French kiss. A few men sit around the bar, watching Syracuse play Georgetown in basketball, and from the kitchen come the sounds of silverware clanking, glasses clinking, workers conversing in Greek, Arabic, and Spanish. John slips his card into the time clock, telling no one in particular, "Seems like every job I have, I have to punch in."

The catering coordinator taps John's shoulder and asks, "You have the Willis-Michaels wedding?"

John nods.

"Good luck."

John wonders what could merit such a warning. After having overseen five hundred weddings at the Citadel, he believes few surprises remain. He has seen fistfights on the dance floor and cocaine in the bridal suite. He has seen a bride vanish with the best man, and a best man douse a bride with champagne, commencing a brawl with her father. He has seen a guest die while the band took its break, returning unawares to play, "Staying Alive." There has already been one cancellation today, the groom having fled with the honeymoon tickets to Hawaii. Somehow that Help Wanted advertisement John spotted years ago did not quite suggest the dimensions of the job.

John receives a five-page information packet, providing a head count, details of the meal, names of the wedding party, and a minute-by-minute plan for preparation and service. Under a heading for special notes, John sees the order, "Do Opa-Opa Show." He groans. The Opa-Opa Show involves a Greek dance, a darkened room and Sterno; it is the Citadel's specialty, available for a surcharge of one dollar per guest. John's problem is that only the Greek waiters know the steps, and none of them will perform since the owner refused to pay them an extra four dollars apiece. That means John must prevail on the Ecuadoran porters and the Egyptian cooks and pray they can pass for Athenian.

For the moment, he busies himself in the Elizabethan Court, in which the reception will be held. It is a two-level room divided by a balustrade, with a view of the parking lot and a highway cloverleaf. Already the tables are set, and in the center of each sits a metal candelabra and a bouquet of cloth flowers. John counts the chairs, then checks the table configuration against a diagram.

"How many people?" a waiter asks John, breaking briefly out of Spanish.

"A hundred twenty-five."

"What kind of fountain we got?" asks the bartender.

"Whiskey sour."

The smell of roasting beef wafts into the room. The wedding cake arrives, its frosting tinted a hot pink that reminds John of Pepto-Bismol. The waiters arrange napkins like open fans inside goblets. Brandishing two of them, one waiter calls to a companion, "Para la photo! Para la photo!" They laugh, and John cringes. As usual, few of the waiters speak fluent English, and one has never before worked a wedding. John recalls the results from previous affairs: Customer asks for a coffee refill and receives a salt shaker; Customer asks for ice water and receives a coffee pot; Customer complains to John about lousy service for $10,000.

He steps into the hallway to place name cards on a reception table. As he aligns the cards in rows, evening the borders with a fingertip touch, a fellow maître d' approaches. He is a tall, stocky man, his balding head fringed by dark, curly hair. Like the catering coordinator earlier, he warns John about the wedding.

"So better me than you?" John asks.

"It's like when I was in Korea," the maître d' says. "Last night before the armistice. In my foxhole. Shells all around. Wife pregnant in Japan." He purses his lips and nods. "First time I ever prayed. Whenever someone got killed, we'd say, 'There but for the grace of God.' Same thing here."

"So it's gonna be one of *those*," John moans.

The maître d' says nothing, but simply mimes mortars whizzing toward their targets. It is The *M.A.S.H.* Syndrome once again.

Two banquet managers presently appear, attired in standard-issue black suits, white blouses, and gold hoop earrings. One of them, John knows, teaches in a preschool full time.

"I think she's very on edge," the first manager tells John of the bride, "because she got jilted once before."

"Wait until you see her," adds the second. "You'll understand."

"So you'll have to use some extra understanding," the first resumes.

"In others words," John says, "grovel."

The three lean against the balustrade and discuss each bridal request.

"She was very concerned about when the main course will be served," the first manager explains. "She said, 'Does that mean we have twenty minutes to eat?' I said, 'Don't worry, we'll wait for everybody to finish up.'" She sighs, then indicates several tables toward the corner. "And see those? She wants them taken out. She's afraid people will sit down and 'have a party of their own.'" She rolls her eyes. "And I don't know if they want the Viennese table. They may say to you at some point, 'We've had enough.'"

John chuckles dryly, then speaks with a bitter edge one never hears from him in school.

"Or I may say, *I've* had enough."

* * *

John McNamara opens each school day teaching two periods of advanced placement American history. As soon as he closes the door and collects the homework, he leaps into his lesson. Right hand in pocket, left free for visual punctuation, he paces before the blackboard, as if treading a path worn deep into the planks. His shoulders are hunched, his head is thrust forward, his short graying hair falls into stray strands. For this day's lesson on the outbreak of the Spanish-American War, as for most others, he distributes both a typed outline and original source materials—tabloid accounts of the sinking of the battleship *Maine* and excerpted speeches about Manifest Destiny by an admiral, a senator, and a minister. His own lecture includes references to George Washington's farewell oration and Theodore Roosevelt's inaugural address. John rarely writes notes on the blackboard. He expects his students to attend and append, and his method is largely Socratic.

"Why did the U.S. have an isolationist foreign policy during the nineteenth century?"

"What role did geography play in it?"

"Why did American policy become expansionist in the 1890s?"

"The Monroe Doctrine said, 'America for Americans.' What does that mean? Do you agree?"

As he frames a question, his hands knead the air before him, as if he were shaping thought itself. When arms rise in response, he surges down the aisles with long, athletic strides, the muscles clearly visible in his shoulders and thighs. He is not precisely graceful, nor is his speech classically eloquent, for it erupts from inside him in tight, thorny bursts. Yet he holds eyes and ears by his energy alone, and in an evangelical way. His is not the practiced smoothness of the television preacher, but the unrehearsed fervor of the tent revivalist, who believes souls must be fought for before they can be won.

John has to admit his lengthy wait for a high school position provided him at least one backhanded advantage: Never would he take the job for granted. He remembers the day in April 1983 when he went to the Board of Education's hiring hall and asked for an assignment to any high school. "Even Boys High?" taunted one of the office apparatchiks. "I mean *any* high school," John repeated. As far as he knew, it was only coincidence that Seward Park had an opening at the time. In fact, Dr. Kriftcher had heard of John's reputation during John's years of freedom seeking, and although he considered it bad form to meddle with another principal's faculty, he made certain he knew the moment of John's manumission.

Once ensconced at Seward Park, John promised himself he would teach every class as if it were his last, and for him, those words were not a hollow cliché. Finally, he could devote his courses to content instead of conduct, beginning terms with the query, "Is Government Necessary?" and ending with the prosecution of the Vietnam War. He developed Seward Park's first advanced placement history course, and regularly filled two sections a year. Working almost entirely with children who were new to America and the English language, John saw better than 90 percent pass the Regents examination and about 30 percent score highly enough on the Educational Testing Service's advanced placement test to earn college credit. Some years, he wrote college recommendations for as many as sixty pupils.

The demands, and the satisfactions, extended beyond school. Having faced in the South Bronx so many children accommodated to defeat, John was struck by the verve and the will of the Lower East Side's young immigrants. They bombarded him with questions in class and appealed to him for instruction after school. They depended upon him to decipher the mysteries of labor laws, voter registration forms, income tax returns, health insurance plans, even subway maps. "In a limited way," he says, "I felt like I was their bridge of assimilation."

As part of the process, in the spring of 1987 John encouraged several students to enter a citywide essay contest to mark the Constitution's Bicentennial. He held scant hope that any would actually win, not pitted against the elite of Stuyvesant and Bronx Science, but he thought the effort important. That September, two weeks into the current school year, John learned that one of his pupils, Anna Yuen, had placed first for her analysis of the Constitution's evolution through amendment. Anna was a short girl, and shy by nature, with an improbable fancy for punk fashion. Whenever she raised her hand in class, John sensed it was an involuntary reflex, as if some primal need for knowledge was overwhelming a conscious preference for privacy. She had emigrated from the People's Republic of China only three years earlier, after all, and her parents ran a cubbyhole of a restaurant.

John accompanied the Yuens to a reception at City Hall, where they drank champagne, ate pâté, and mingled with politicos and reporters. After Anna mounted the podium to receive her award and a $1,500 prize, she walked the half-mile home to her Orchard Street walk-up. All along the route, her father hailed friends on sidewalks and in stores, boasting of Anna's triumph and hoisting aloft her plaque. Watching him glow, understanding what he said without knowing his language, John told himself it was true, one person *can* make a difference. He had never felt better about being a teacher. He tried to sustain the sensation the next time he punched in at the Chrystopoulos Citadel.

*   *   *

The bride and groom, trailed by an aunt deeply concerned about locating a hanger and cellophane for the wedding dress, arrive at five-forty. Playing bellhop, waiter, and social director, John drags their bags upstairs to a waiting suite, serves champagne and caviar, and welcomes the ushers and maids. He can hear the sounds of full-tilt matrimony from a half-dozen banquet rooms—dishes colliding, great clouds of chatter, dress shoes shuffling to salsa, polka, and "Twist and Shout." When John dashes to the kitchen for more champagne, he passes another maître d', who grimaces and says, "Somebody wants ketchup with capon."

Barely has John corked the second bottle when the captain summons him to confront an unexpected guest, the bride's ex-boyfriend. John asks the fellow if he has an invitation and is shown a mimeographed Christmas letter sent by the bride. John suggests this is not quite adequate, but the former beau refuses to budge. A forced exit may ruin the entire evening, and, much as John loathes needing this job, he possesses a genuine pride about performing it well. He proposes as a compromise that the interloper remain for the cocktail hour and then discretely disappear. Now satisfied, the man makes for the whiskey-sour fountain.

John meets the band, greets both sets of parents, coaches the wedding party on its entry, fetches a chair for a table one short, and serves a soda to Mr. Chrystopoulos himself, who visits every reception under his roof. By then, it is time for John to trek from table to table dusting Parmesan cheese atop onion soup and ziti. Next he races into the kitchen to tell the waiters to hold back the prime ribs for ten or fifteen minutes. Finally, he slips to a telephone booth to call Linda, who tells him Bryan's fever is rising again.

Then it is back to the Elizabethan Court to ensure marital bliss. The couple shares its first dance to "Moon River." The bride and her father waltz to "Daddy's Little Girl," the groom and his mother to "Sunrise, Sunset." The groom's father, jacket off and shirttails flagging, totters from table to table, eventually clamping his arms around the newlyweds like vise-grip pliers. John pries him loose so the two can slice into the wedding cake. Then he turns to the bandleader, a full-time teacher himself, and sighs, "I guess it's time."

The bandleader introduces John, passes him the microphone. The lights dim, except in the entry portal where John stands.

"I hope that all of you are having a very enjoyable time tonight," he intones, following a script he memorized many weddings ago. "In Greek, we have the words 'Opa-Opa,' which means to have a good time, and we hope all of you are having a good time." There is a smattering of applause. "In Greece, when people are celebrating a good time, they wave white handkerchiefs in the air and say, 'Opa-Opa.' The management of the Chrystopoulos Citadel wants to celebrate the wedding of Ken Willis and Carol Michaels, so would you please wave your napkins, say 'Opa-Opa,' and welcome the . . ." Perhaps twenty napkins flap, and as few voices rustle. "Could we try it again? 'Opa-Opa.'" A bit better. "One more time. 'OPA-OPA!'" Still sparse, but as good as it's likely to get. "And welcome the 'Opa-Opa' dancers!"

John jumps aside as two porters and one cook bounce into the room. Each carries in one hand a napkin and balances on the other palm a pizza tray, into which is bolted a chafing dish, inside which burn several chunks of Sterno. Without lights, few of the celebrants can see the conscripts' awkward steps and bumping knees and terrified eyes.

They see only the ripples of white linen and blue flame. Now their own napkins rise. The dancers retreat to the kitchen, followed by lusty applause. But the Opa-Opa Show is not yet concluded. John wheels in a cart loaded with 125 dishes of frozen ice cream and cherries and two pitchers partly filled with a mixture of grenadine syrup, cherry brandy, and seventy-one-proof brandy flambé. He sets these afire, and pours the burning libation from one pitcher to the other, gradually moving them a yard apart, until a thin waterfall of flame topples through the air. There are isolated oohs and aahs. Finally, he ladles the concoction onto each portion of ice cream, melting the hard mass so the guests will believe it was fresh.

After the Viennese table and the coffee and cordials, the lights rise, and the guests leave. John packs leftover wedding cake and commemorative champagne flutes for the new Mister and Missus, then unlocks the bridal suite so they can change into street clothes. He helps clean off the tables and stack the chairs so the floor can be mopped. At 12:30 A.M., eleven hours after he started, John punches out. He will receive one hundred dollars for his night's work. He did not get a tip, as usual, because on their itemized bill the bride's parents were assessed two hundred dollars for his services. The one hundred dollars difference belongs to Mr. Chrystopoulos. Even bandleaders and photographers have to kick back their share, if they expect continued employ at the Citadel, and the cooks and waiters, green to America, rent beds in houses Mr. Chrystopoulos owns. John has to admit the guy has one hell of a system. It reminds him of a lesson about the exploitation of the Third World.

Sliding onto the icy vinyl seat of his car, John feels his back ache and his feet throb. Those marble floors are unforgiving. He enters his house quietly, hangs his tuxedo outside a closet, showers off the cigarette smoke and kitchen grease. He looks in on his son, touching his forehead for fever, then covering him with the blankets he has kicked off. He stops briefly in his study, where atop a book on slavery lies an unpaid Visa bill. He finds Linda awake in bed, reading a magazine, and they talk for a half hour.

On the morning of Valentine's Day, John will give Linda a dozen red roses. Then, at eleven, he will drive again to the Chrystopoulos Citadel to work another wedding while his own wife waits alone. As a husband, he wishes he could have turned down the day's work. As a teacher, he could not afford to say no.

15

Soupin' 'Em Up

A DIM DISK of sun hovers in the pale overcast sky, the sky outside Jessica Siegel's classroom on the early afternoon of March 18. Jessica sits in the last row as a guest speaker from *Newsday* entertains her beginning journalism students, her mind on the forecast for rain changing into snow and continuing through the night. She has 180 miles to drive by then. The *Newsday* reporter is talking about writing a feature story about the 100th anniversary of the Blizzard of '88. The storm struck with such surprise, he says, that people left their homes in the morning unprepared and wound up stranded or frozen stiff. Hearing this, Jessica stares up from her Delaney book and rolls her eyes. Talk about omens.

When this period ends, at one-twenty-seven, Jessica will meet Wilfredo Ayala, See Wai Mui, and Angel Fuster and embark in her parents' car for the State University of New York at New Paltz. She has pled and wheedled and whined with the associate director of the campus's program for economically disadvantaged students to grant interviews for her three pupils. Admission is supposed to rely solely on transcripts and recommendations, but Jessica has a special credibility at New Paltz, based on having steered a dozen students to the college in the past four years. They have variously landed on the Dean's List, the student government, the Latin-American club, and the radio station. So a friend will do a favor.

Jessica knows she will need personal entree and reflected glory and more. More than 1,500 applicants are competing for 150 places in New Paltz's Educational Opportunity Program (EOP),* with its tuition waivers, study groups, and personal counseling, and officially none are to be admitted with averages below 75. Jessica's brood has a collective average of 74. Neither their autobiographies nor her letters of recommendation can alter that fact. Wilfredo, See Wai, and Angel must, in effect, talk their way into college. Since the campus offices close at four-thirty, they will have at the very most one hour.

It has been agonizing enough for Jessica to select her three candidates. She worried less about omitting the Carlos Pimentels and Aracelis Collados, who have superior records and designs on other colleges, than the Ottavio Johnsons and Gregg Grosses, who might settle for a junior college or no college at all. She actually consented to bring Nancy Caban, a solid student in English 7 and beginning journalism; since Nancy and Wilfredo flirted so often in class, she figured she could sit on his lap. Then Nancy cancelled for her grandfather's funeral, and the rumor of an open seat in Jessica's car whirled through school. The most persistent pursuer has been Francisco Ramirez, a mainstay in the first-term humanities class. Francisco showed up today shaved and moussed, clad in pleated checked slacks and a tennis sweater, advertising his desire to join the expedition. Having skipped an ice-skating outing led by his favorite teacher, Leah Gitter, he paced the hall outside Room 336 as Jessica taught journalism sixth period and even peeked into the room once or twice. Finally, in the break before the seventh-period class, Jessica had to turn him down. There was simply no more room. And at least, in Leah, Francisco had another teacher to fight for him. Who would drive Angel or See Wai or Wilfredo to a college interview but Jessica?

Francisco trudged down the hall and around the corner. "She said something about the car's too small," he told a friend. "I'll go up there on my own." He paused. "You can't trust teachers anymore." Back in the portal of Room 336, Jessica thought of triage. *How many,* she asked herself, *can you save?*

Angel and See Wai follow Jessica into the English office after the seventh period ends, but there is no sign of Wilfredo. Nor, inexplica-

*The basic program, established by the New York State Legislature in 1968, operates under various titles at 90 percent of the state's public and private colleges. A student's eligibility is determined on the basis of family income. A family of four, for instance, cannot earn more than $18,180 annually.

bly, did he attend journalism sixth period. All term he has been so earnest, so trustworthy. *What a time,* Jessica thinks, *for him to fuck up.* Maybe Francisco will get to visit New Paltz after all. Suddenly a breathless Wilfredo bursts into the room, his denim cattleman's coat open, his shirt wet with sweat. He went to the bank to cash his paycheck, he blurts, and boarded an express train by mistake. Next thing he knew he was at Thirty-fourth Street. Then he had to ride the slow local five stops downtown to Grand Street and run the last six blocks to school. Then he couldn't take the elevator to the third floor because he's a student.

"All right," Jessica says briskly. She cares less about explanations than making good time. It is about one-forty and the drive to New Paltz takes two hours. Ten minutes of interview time is already squandered. "Does everybody have their financial-aid form? Their autobiography? Recommendations? The application? All filled out? In pen?"

"I don't have anything," Wilfredo says. "I haven't been home since this morning."

"Great," Jessica says pointedly. Wilfredo drops his backpack and races down the hall, bound for home. "Ten minutes," he calls.

She reaches into the office refrigerator for half a cantaloupe filled with cottage cheese. Phlegmy and feverish, she has little appetite, and sends Angel to a grocery for black coffee and vitamin C, which will pass for lunch. With Angel and Wilfredo gone, See Wai sits alone beside Jessica, wearing a light blue windbreaker, new jeans, and the striped sweater that was his Christmas present. He reads from a battered paperback anthology of Ibsen, its cover cobwebbed with creases, its binding secured by scotch tape. His English 8 class is studying *An Enemy of the People.* Jessica senses he is already clenching with nerves and tries a little levity.

"You gonna criticize my driving, See Wai?"

"Maybe," he says, returning to his book.

"You know woman drivers," announces Angel, coming through the door.

As Jessica washes down a fistful of vitamins, Angel pages through his folder until he finds Jessica's recommendation. He wears new Florsheims, checked slacks, and a double-breasted John Weitz jacket, half of his single suit, which he bought after feeling so inadequate in his DECA blazer at Friends Academy. "What do you mean, 'He thinks at a *fairly* sophisticated level?'" he cries. Jessica tilts her head slightly and says, "Angel, we've got to deal with the reality of what your grades are."

The same is true of See Wai and Wilfredo and many of the students for whom Jessica wrote letters of recommendation. Nothing attracts Jessica to a pupil more strongly than what she calls "independent thinking," the ineffable "spark of intelligence that throws me in some way." Such traits do not necessarily translate into high marks, however, and when combined with impatience or caustic wit have quite the opposite effect on certain teachers. So each year at college-application time, Jessica becomes Seward Park's Saint Jude, its patron of lost causes. She assigns and edits autobiographies, oversees the completion of standardized forms, solicits letters of recommendation from other teachers and counselors, and produces her own endorsements by the score. Facing each blank page in the typewriter, she searches for new words to explain away averages of 69 or 74, words that will seduce and beguile a college into embracing precisely the petitioners it would normally shun. "Soupin' 'em up," is the Seward Park slang, and Jessica soups up so well because she believes so totally in her students and in the necessity of their higher education. She does not lie; she merely tells selective truth. She does not invent; she merely inflates. She acknowledges deficiencies the better to diminish their import. Almost every letter begins with some variation on the sentence, "There are times when grades and grade point averages, SAT scores and credits, don't communicate who a student is."

With his 75 average and his rank of 299 in a senior class of 593, then, Angel comes recommended as "one of the most creative and intelligent minds I have run into as a high school teacher." See Wai, ranked 230 with a 77 average, "shows a sensitivity towards, and an inquisitiveness about, American literature that is rare in someone born here, no less someone who learned English as a second language." Wilfredo, the hardest sell of all with his 71 average and 410 rank, has "maturity, intelligence, perceptiveness and insight." Jessica concludes his letter with a particularly direct pitch: "If you accept Wilfredo, in a sense take a chance on him despite his record, you will not be disappointed. . . . Such chances should be taken. You will not be making a mistake."

Jessica's partner in salvage and reclamation is Hal Pockriss, a wry and literate man who once had a play produced Off Broadway. Only See Wai is in College Discovery and so officially one of Hal's 200 students, but when Jessica asked him months ago to begin plotting on behalf of Angel and Wilfredo, he hesitated not at all. As he had for her pupils many times before, as far back as George Vega in 1978, he wrote letters and made calls and suggested strategies and boosted hopes. "If Jessica thinks a kid has a brain," Hal says, "the kid has a brain."

From his own days as a student with a 66 average, Hal had learned to distrust grades as a barometer of intellect. And from his first experiences as a guidance counselor at Haaren High School in Hell's Kitchen, which closed several years ago, he had delighted in championing the purported losers. "You relive your life through these kids," he says. "Getting kids with sixty-nines and seventies into college is like a displacement of anger for me. It's like fucking the establishment, all the know-it-alls. It's the feeling of power, of ego, to see kids everyone else gave up on doing so well."

Neither Hal's advocacy nor Jessica's will matter if Wilfredo does not return soon. The eighth-period bell has just rung, and the clock hands near two-fifteen. With dry road and no traffic, perhaps she can reach New Paltz by four. That leaves thirty minutes to be split three ways. It is better than staying home, but not much.

With a fresh shirt and a sheaf of papers, Wilfredo hurtles into the office at two-twenty. Jessica hurries down the stairs, leaping steps two or three at a time, and shoves her students into the seats of the family Cutlass Classic. With only 49,000 miles, the car's suspension is punishingly stiff and its speedometer reads seven miles per hour at rest. "OK," Jessica says, unfolding directions written by Bruce Baskind, "we've got to get to the FDR Drive."

"North or south?" asks Angel.

"New Paltz, Angel," she says with mock irritation. "What do you think?"

Jessica slurps her coffee at the first light, swallows yet another vitamin. "Wilfredo," she says, turning to the back seat, "you asked in class if I ever did drugs." She pauses. "Now you see."

"I asked if you were a hippie," he corrects. "Because hippies used drugs."

Involved in cheering her charges, Jessica mistakenly turns east on Delancey Street instead of continuing until Houston. Delancey has no entrance onto the northbound FDR. She must circle back around Seward Park like a hot-rodder cruising for chicks. At the corner of Grand and Ludlow, she gets stuck behind a school bus that is loading.

The traffic light changes twice without her budging. Her watch shows two-twenty-five.

"I think you're a defensive driver," Angel says in both humor and anxiety.

"I want you to go to college," she replies. "Dying might be a drawback."

"Oh yeah," See Wai says, pursing his lips and nodding. "That's one good point."

Soon the car turns northward on the FDR, an asphalt ribbon along the East River. The Lower East Side and its housing projects shrink in the rearview mirror, soon disappearing as if they had slipped off the earth, and the windshield beholds a grandiose Gotham, framing Sutton Place and Tudor City, the United Nations and Gracie Mansion. Wilfredo gazes across the water to Roosevelt Island, a colony of stores and apartments tethered to Manhattan by a tramway as fanciful as an Alpine funicular. "Is it expensive to live there?" he wonders aloud.

Roosevelt Island gives way to the surging waters of Hell Gate and Wards Island across the strait. From its banks rise several sand-colored buildings of ten or twelve stories, all of them surrounded by a barbed-wire fence. This is one landmark Wilfredo knows too well.

"It's for the criminally insane," he says softly.

"How you know?" Angel asks.

"My uncle's there."

"Why?"

"He tried to kill my mother," Wilfredo says, looking out the window. "He's been there a long time."

"My friend's brother is in a place like that," Angel says. "He went crazy on drugs."

"If that me," See Wai says, "I'd suicide. Too painful live there. So one bullet."

Jessica says nothing. *The stuff they have to deal with,* she thinks. *These lives people in school have no idea about. Much as I know, I don't know the half of it.* She crosses the Willis Avenue Bridge into the Bronx and turns onto the New York State Thruway. She indicates a sign marked "Upstate," and says, "Well, this is it. We're upstate."

"Whaddaya mean?" Angel asks, assuming she was serious. "We're not there."

Jessica tells them the genesis of the joke. It was last year at this time, and she was driving Sammy Ryan and his friends Sammy Williams and Winford Cropper to New Paltz. Jessica had arranged a private tryout for Sammy Ryan with the basketball coach. If he was nearly as good as he claimed, she figured, it might help his chances of being admitted. Twenty minutes from Seward Park, Sammy Williams saw the road sign and declared, "Hey, we're upstate." When Jessica finished laughing—she just couldn't help it—she informed him, "We're still in the Bronx."

Now the mood buoys. Angel asks Jessica to switch on LITE-FM, but See Wai and Wilfredo outvote him for HOT-103. The first song is by Michael Jackson, and Angel cannot resist teasing. "You know what I don't like about that guy? He doesn't want to be black." See Wai slaps him five and says, "You should be proud of what you are."

Angel's attention is claimed next by a Porsche 914 roaring past. "That's how I wanna drive to New Paltz," he says. See Wai leans onto the front seat near Jessica and adds, "Miss Siegel, maybe you drive in middle lane, you go better." She obligingly accelerates until the speedometer shows 72.

"Am I going fast enough now?" she calls.

"No!" Angel and See Wai shout in unison.

With the hour close to three, their jive has justification.

*   *   *

They are truly upstate now. They have left behind Yankee Stadium and Yonkers Raceway. They have crossed the wide Hudson on the Tappan Zee Bridge and begun to roll west across the Rockland County suburbs. The six-lane road is flanked by bare trees and dried cattails and brown grass, blown flat by the slipsteam of passing cars and flecked with crumpled napkins, flattened coffee cups, and empty jugs of antifreeze. Off the shoulder and behind the second growth stand motels and discount stores, aluminum-sided homes and red-brick schools with football fields still faintly lined. The traffic is the traffic of bedroom communities, station wagons carrying children, panel trucks delivering pastries and dry cleaning. The landscape reminds Jessica of her own hometown, stolid and predictable, but to the boys it appears as quaint and foreign as "Little House on the Prairie."

The road swings north at Suffern in a great sweeping arc. Ridges rise both east and west, and the highway runs as a river would. Sometimes the asphalt lifts from the flood plain to cut a notch through the rock, where falling water is frozen into a dozen bridal veils. The Cutlass passes stone churches and mill races and colonial graveyards.

The sky now has swallowed the sun, and the roadside is encrusted with old rock salt. The commuters have all exited, and the remaining cars speed toward the slopes, one with a license plate exclaiming, SKINUT. The temperature must be in the twenties. With an hour of driving left until New Paltz, Jessica prays that the snow will start late. It is three-thirty.

She listens to her students chatter about movie stars like Charles Bronson and Arnold Schwarzenegger, blissfully unaware of how little time there is to spare. "Michael J. Fox is a great actor," Wilfredo says. See Wai replies, "Commercials, yes. Movies, no." As Jessica slows for the toll booth at Harriman, See Wai complains that she brakes too abruptly, much to the delight of his companions.

"What is this shit?" Jessica says, affecting great pain. "Is this the payback for all the red ink on your papers? I've been driving for a long time."

"Since before we were born," Angel says. He waits a beat, then adds, "Since before there were cars."

"You wanna get to New Paltz or not?"

The car pushes north through valleys and glades, through fallow fields broken by the yearning arms of black oaks. The conversation wanders from Shakespeare to Northern Ireland to the film *The Last Emperor*, ideas condensing on windows side and rear. With her passengers momentarily relaxed, it is now Jessica's turn to worry. For all the energy she devotes to pushing her students toward college, all the unqualified optimism she exudes, the process fills her with conflict. She would never speak aloud these doubts, for fear of confirming whatever insecurities her pupils already harbor, yet she cannot banish them. A mother may smile stoically as her son boards the troop train, the expectation of courage etched in her eyes, and still cry privately awaiting word from the front.

Just this week, Jessica has been teaching *Bread Givers*, Anzia Yezierska's 1925 novel, to the Lower East Side class. It is a fiction deeply rooted in autobiography, an autobiography that Jessica's students invariably find familiar. Born in a Polish shtetl in 1885, Yezierska emigrated with her family to the Lower East Side. There her existence evolved into two struggles, one against the religious and romantic strictures of her Old World father, the other against the American deprivations of tenement and sweatshop. She eventually achieved the college education she had sought, and won national renown in the 1920s for her genuine renderings of Jewish immigrant life. Her protagonist and alter ego in *Bread Givers*, Sara Smolinsky, undertakes a similar odyssey, and her introduction to an upstate college is particularly trying. Setting out "like the pilgrim fathers . . . in search of the New World," Sara is chastened to encounter her affluent classmates, "children of joy" in "spotless, creaseless clothes, as if the dirty battle of life had never yet been on them." Alone on the sidelines of a dance, she laments: "The whirling of joy went on and on, and still I sat there watching, cold, lifeless, like a lost ghost. I was nothing and nobody. It was worse than being ignored. Worse than being an outcast. I simply didn't belong."

When Jessica teaches *Bread Givers*, it humbles a class like nothing except *The Great Gatsby*, and for some of the same reasons. She can tell her students about programs like EOP and assure them they will not be as isolated as Sara Smolinsky, but she wants them to be aware of the realities, too. The past few years have seen racist outbreaks at the sort of colleges that normally define Eastern liberalism—a Jewish *succah* and an anti-apartheid shantytown desecrated in separate incidents at Dartmouth, eight Asian-American students spat upon at the University of Connecticut, black students beaten by whites at the University of Massachusetts for celebrating the Mets' World Series victory. Troubling as such events are, Jessica worries less about the obvious and malicious affronts than the subtle, unintended ones. She has heard from Angel about the visit to Friends Academy and the well-meaning questions that cut so deep. She remembers getting lost in farm country on last year's trip to New Paltz and Sammy Williams joking nervously about being in "redneck country." And the campus at New Paltz is more welcoming than most, with a student body that is one-quarter minority. Carlos Pimentel has set his eyes on Colgate, a private and rather tweedy college where George Vecsey's brother is a professor. Angel has applied to the University of Vermont, kidding about opening Burlington's first bodega. Wilfredo is trying the State University of New York at Binghamton, the most competitive campus in the state system. Jessica wonders which might be worse: being rejected or being admitted.

"Going away to college," she once told me, "means going up against people who have never doubted themselves, have never seen anyone different from themselves, have never, ever questioned their privilege. They have a certain ease about life kids from Seward can't even imagine. I tell them it may be hard to make friends at first. I tell them they may be the only poor person in a class or in a dorm. I tell them they have to be strong. I tell them that eventually they'll find people they can relate to. Because, ultimately, that's what they'll face in the larger society. What's the option? Stay on the Lower East Side? Never venture from where you're born? If you want to stretch yourself intellectually, you're not going to get much excitement working in a store on Orchard Street. If you want your life to be better, how long can you turn down $500 a week to sell crack?"

But all this, she reminds herself as she drives, is premature. None of her seniors have yet been accepted by any college. And with her watch showing four and the New Paltz campus fifteen miles away, her three current companions are losing their opportunity minute by minute.

At the first chance, she veers into a service area. A one-story brown building houses a snack bar and gift shop and beside it are gasoline pumps. Set as it is along a frozen marsh, buffeted by a north wind, it looks as forlorn as an Edward Hopper diner. The boys, not yet alarmed, head for food and bathrooms. Jessica runs to a telephone booth and dials Ed Olmo, the associate director of EOP at New Paltz. Having traded on Olmo's friendship once already in arranging this afternoon's interviews, she is hardly in the position to ask him to stay late. So she tells him that traffic was terrible in the city, that she is running a bit behind schedule, and then waits for him to volunteer to linger. He does not; at four-thirty his day ends.

She hops into the car and shouts for the boys, who are ambling out of the snack bar, sodas in hand. Seeing her panic, they toss their drinks in the trash and run, as if racing for a root cellar with a funnel cloud on their heels. Before the side doors close, Jessica pushes the speed past twenty, and she enters the highway at sixty-seven. The scenery passes in a blur—the yellow willows, the brown brambles, the signs for resorts and vacation homes. Jessica flogs the Cutlass to eighty-six, until the tires shimmy and the chassis shakes. Nobody speaks. It is the silence of a family after the parents have fought without reconciling. It is a silence that could suffocate. See Wai tries to lighten the mood with comments about the clouds or some trees or a fast-food franchise. Unanswered, his words hover and vanish.

"If you hadn't had to go home to change your clothes," Jessica finally says to Wilfredo, eyeing him in the rearview mirror.

"It wasn't for my clothes," he answers in a whisper.

"You said it was only gonna take ten minutes," she pursues.

"Ten minutes for me to get home." Wilfredo breathes. "I'm sorry, everybody." His voice, small at best, is now Lilliputian. "If I made us late."

There is another long pall. Something in the air is taut, stretched to the threshold of snapping. The time is four-ten.

"This guy at New Paltz," Angel says. "He wouldn't go home without seeing us." He drags his fingers through his hair, then looks to Jessica. "Would he?"

*   *   *

Alone as only a first-day freshman could be, Jessica Siegel dragged her suitcases toward Woodward Court, her dormitory at the University of Chicago. It was early September 1966, and never before had she been farther from home than Camp Najewah, which was on the near side of the Delaware River. She watched with emptiness and anxiety as other students emerged from station wagons with parents and siblings, carrying footlockers and record players, and parting with kisses. Jessica had flown by herself to a college she had never seen. An admissions officer had interviewed her in New York the previous spring, and his initial question should have been her initial clue. "We're next to a slum, and there's a lot of crime," the officer had said. "How do you feel about that?"

She had been full of bravery then, talking about her forays into New York for sheet music and Broadway shows. It was harder to summon the same courage 800 miles from home, in a place that exuded suspicion and isolation. Woodward Court was a perfect precis of the university itself, a low gray building accessible only through a guard station, its three wings drawn in a tight, insular U. Try as it did to impersonate Oxford with its Gothic stonework and copper roofs, ivied walls and leaded glass, iron gates and period lampposts, the University of Chicago could never entirely succeed. To the east lay Lake Michigan, conferring not the soft green climate of England but the barbed lash of the American Midwest. In all other directions— north, south, and west—sprawled an immensity of slums. Buffered on the outside by a demilitarized zone of abandoned tenements, defined on the inside by a rebus of cul-de-sacs, the campus was a hard place either to enter or to escape.

Having managed the first, Jessica craved the second, for nothing had ever so overwhelmed her, academically or socially. The dean greeted incoming students with a lecture on C. S. Lewis's *The Screwtape*

Letters. The president's wife welcomed undergraduate women with the warning, "Don't go south of the Midway." The college newspaper printed a crime map. Jessica's classmates had on them the burnish of Deerfield Academy and Elizabeth Irwin and the United Nations School. Surrounded by such company, the assurance she had known as an intellectual—perhaps *the* intellectual—in a middling suburban high school evaporated.

She was deposited as if by parachute into a curriculum of Thucydides and Herodotus and Plato, Hobbes and Hume and Burke. She rounded out her schedule with the dual torments of physics and French. For perhaps the only time in her scholastic career, she earned her highest marks in gym. An evening's study lasted from 5 P.M. until 3 A.M., and a night's sleep from 4 A.M. until 8. She worried away thirty-seven pounds. So depleted was her paltry store of self-confidence that when "fiduciary" was misspelled "ficudiary" in a text, she ran for a dictionary and panicked to find it contained no such word. The fault, she had to assume, was her own.

While others might have transferred or withdrawn, Jessica dared not: The University of Chicago was her mother's school; the University of Chicago had a reputation. "It was a question of could I do the work," she would remember. "All I saw was the intellectual part of going to college. Not the atmosphere, not the personality. Why was I there? To study. And if I wasn't doing well, then the answer was to study more. And if I still couldn't measure up, then it said something about my abilities." She committed herself to a reading clinic, where she was tested for comprehension and armed with study stratagems. Feeling no more relieved, she unburdened herself to a dean. He seemed compassionate enough, but then he wrote to Jessica's parents:

As far as I can see, Jessica has no real troubles. However, that is not so important as what she herself thinks. To her, her troubles are very real, no matter what I, or you, may think about them. According to her, she is having great difficulty in understanding the materials of her various courses. Consequently, she gets depressed and questions her ability to understand anything whatsoever. I did point out to her that all students have varying degrees of incapacity in grasping the materials of their courses. However, this point seemed to make no impression on her, since she feels that she should not have a problem concerning her school work, no matter what the difficulties of other students may be.

So you see, this is a very real problem to her, although a more mature person would see such a problem in its due proportions and from a proper perspective. I pointed out to her that she is a pretty girl and that she has a great deal of charm. This point, also, I thought made very little impression on her, since she cried throughout most of our conversation. I assure you that I offered what sympathy I could to her and asked her to come and see me again so that we could talk over all her problems again. As you may understand, there is little anyone can do for Jessica. She herself will have to deal with her own problems and surmount them.

After two years of travail, something gave way. All the Bs and Cs on Jessica's transcript, the grades that had weighed like a millstone of mediocrity, now liberated her. She would never be a star student, no matter how much midnight oil she burned. She began to enjoy her classes, most especially Shakespeare, as taught by David Bevington, a slight, gentle, solicitous professor who demonstrated "you could be an intellectual *and* a human being." She sought pleasure and fulfillment outside the lecture hall and library. In spring 1968, she volunteered for Eugene McCarthy's presidential campaign, working through the tumultuous Chicago convention. She joined antiwar teach-ins at a political coffeehouse called the Blue Gargoyle and even addressed one rally outside the Administration Building. "Some rhetoric about unity," she would later recall.

The truer unity she found among friends. One of them, Ilene Kantrov, had known Jessica since her freshman year as the girl with bright tights and fifty pairs of shoes, all from garage sales or junk shops. The others—Ellen Bogolub, Judy Ferber, and Carolyn Brown—had transferred to Chicago as sophomores. After their junior year, all except Judy traveled together to London and France. From there, Ellen and Ilene took the "fascist route" through Spain and Italy and Jessica and Carolyn the "Communist route" through Hungary and Czechoslovakia. Theirs was an adventure of third-class trains, bread and cheese, trading jeans for verse with a poet, and being tear gassed in Prague during protests against the Soviet occupation. Appropriately enough, the four travelers reconnoitered in nonaligned Yugoslavia.

The next year, their last in Chicago, Jessica and her friends shared an off-campus apartment. They sewed paisley curtains and hung Bosch prints and listened to Laura Nyro. They laughed and drank with the boys downstairs, who belonged to a satiric society called Students For Violent Non-Action. In one closet, Jessica discovered the immense Army overcoat that would become her trademark. Ilene's lasting image of Jessica in college was watching that coat and the body it mummified trundle to a political meeting or a play rehearsal. The former introvert acted in *The Elephant Calf, The Shoemaker's Holiday,* and *The Duchess of Malfi,* essaying a madwoman. "I had to drool and scratch myself, and I wasn't very good," she later said of the role. "Not uninhibited enough."

Most often, Jessica could be found at *The Maroon,* the college newspaper and her surrogate home. Its offices had the dark wood beams and heavy oak tables and sorrel tile of a Tudor alehouse, bringing a rare warmth to a chill academy, and its staff created an ambience just as uncommon. *The Maroon* was a place of Marx Brothers jokes, late-night hamburgers, breathless voices bearing the latest news. Never, perhaps, was there a more exhilarating time and place for the undergraduate journalist than Chicago in the late 1960s. *The Maroon* reported on the 1968 convention, the Chicago Eight trial, and the Days of Rage; its printshop maintained a standing logo, "The Student Revolution." All the while, in the somewhat hermetic tradition of its university, *The Maroon* editorialized for increased funding for the yearbook and recorded the triumphs of the chess team.

Jessica found two bailiwicks. One was as the author of the "Culture Vulture" column, in which upcoming events provided the pretext for irreverent commentary. Jessica on Judith Malina and Julian Beck of the Living Theater: "The Mr. and Mrs. Mao Tse-tung of their own Cultural Revolution." Jessica on the film *Rashomon:* "A woman is raped and her husband murdered, or are they? The story is told, true to any UC (University of Chicago) discussion, from three viewpoints. Which one is true—well, what is truth anyway?" When not being a wag, Jessica was serving as managing editor of the *Grey City Journal, The Maroon's* weekly magazine. The title itself, drawn from T. S. Eliot's *Murder in the Cathedral,* was her benediction on the university:

> Here is no continuing city, here is no abiding stay.
> Ill the wind, ill the time, uncertain the profit, certain the danger.
> Oh late late late, late is the time, late too, late and rotten the year;
> Evil the wind, and bitter the sea, and grey the sky, grey grey grey.

Her selection, meant with a certain humor, proved rather too prophetic. Ilene Kantrov was robbed at knifepoint. Ellen Bogolub discovered a radical professor, Richard Flacks, lying in a pool of blood in a secluded library tower; an assailant, never identified, had slashed his wrists and fractured his skull. During a campus strike after the

Kent State killings in May 1970, a mob vandalized the think tank named for Jessica's hero, Adlai Stevenson, on the unsubstantiated claim that it conducted war research. Her own academic career ended when the English majors refused en masse to sit for their final examination. "Half of it was the outrage about Nixon's invasion of Cambodia," Ilene Kantrov recalled, "and half was not wanting to take the test."

Such was the temperament of the times, a mix of informed dissidence and rampant juvenilia. Jessica would leave Chicago with a profound ambivalence about both her university and college itself. After the fact, she could appreciate the education and wonder how much of the pain was her own fault. But in her moment of departure, what she longed for was nothing less than a painful world to be remade into utopia, much as she would try to remake her students' worlds years later, if not into utopia then at least into something more decent and more colorful. As she wrote in one of her final "Culture Vulture" columns:

> After hanging around this place for the length of time I have, I finally discovered a major cause of the place's greyness, besides pollution, the weather and just the emotional atmosphere. [This alluded to the Administration Building.] There are many solutions to this problem. Sink it down under the ground so you have to descend six floors, or paint it bright yellow or turquoise or chartreuse. Anybody got a lot of paint?

*   *   *

Four tollbooths stand at the New Paltz interchange, and only one is open to exiting traffic. Trying to save seconds, Jessica digs change from her wallet and listens to Wilfredo read Bruce's directions while steering into line. When she turns to hear better, the Cutlass rams a red pickup. "Shit," she says. A chunky blond man wearing a fire department sweatshirt bounds from the truck, glaring. He inspects the bumper and hitch, finds no damage, and returns to the wheel. On the far side of the booth, he waits for Jessica, and as she passes he rolls down his window and gives her the finger. Where she turns left, following a "S.U.N.Y." sign with a silhouetted student in gown and mortarboard, he turns right. Thank God.

Jessica scours the sides of Route 299 for a drive-in bank opposite a shopping center. There, the directions say, she should turn left and drive a half-mile to the campus. By the time Jessica sees the bank and mall, she has overshot the intersection. It is four-fifteen. Maneuvering through four lanes of slow traffic, she veers into a beauty salon's parking lot for a U-turn, and tailgates back to the corner, squealing as she makes a right. The street narrows from two lanes to one, wanders through a housing development with no college in sight, and deposits her back at Route 299, beside the beauty salon. It is four-twenty. Jessica can't imagine what she did wrong. Could Bruce have made a mistake? He went to college at New Paltz, but that was eight or nine years ago.

Without alternatives, she turns left on Route 299, and shortly comes to another drive-in bank opposite another shopping center. This time there is also a "S.U.N.Y." sign with an arrow pointing left. Jessica follows it, and soon she spots a brick-and-glass tower, obviously part of the college. She steers into a cluster of older, smaller buildings, none of them identified, and asks a girl in a punk overcoat, "Where's the EOP office?" "Two lefts," she replies. It is four-twenty-five.

Two lefts later, Jessica idles beside a generating station. Nowhere within view is the EOP office or an administrative building of any kind. She drives alongside another girl and asks for directions. "EOP? Oh, sure," the girl says, inexplicably giggling. "It's, um, around there."

"Where?" Jessica demands.

"There," the girl says, pointing into the middle distance. "And then you go left."

"Left?"

"Why don't I get in and show you."

Angel tumbles onto See Wai's lap to make room for the girl. She guides Jessica around the circumference of the campus. Near a cluster of dormitories, she offers, "You could park now, if you want to walk."

"We can't walk," Jessica snaps.

"OK, then," the girl says, confused and offended. "Just let me out." She indicates a modern nine-story building about a quarter-mile ahead. "There it is."

Jessica speeds away, spattering the girl with road sand and dead leaves. She parks illegally in front of the building and leads the boys at a gallop up a flight of concrete stairs, across a brick plaza, and into the lobby. Workers heading home pour out the glass doors. One elevator is stalled on the seventh floor, the other is rising from the third. Jessica watches each's position register on a round dial like a gambler playing the slots.

Finally one arrives, and the four shove their way aboard. They leap out on the fourth floor, dash down the hallway, and burst into the EOP office to find people cleaning off desks and zippering coats, filling purses and closing briefcases. "Ed Olmo," Jessica heaves, and a secretary walks to the rear of the office. Meanwhile, a woman approaches, smiling. "Hi, I'm from admissions," she says, extending her hand. "You're the adviser from Seward?" Jessica nods. "Well, ah, as you know, we've got to leave. I have my kids to pick up, and Ed does, too." She tugs on a wool hat and tucks a thermos under her arm. "Is there anything I can do before I go?"

"Interview them," Jessica says, sweeping her arm before Angel, Wilfredo, and See Wai.

"How about a campus tour?" the woman responds. "You can take one every Monday or Wednesday."

"But we drove up here," Jessica says. "We got caught in traffic."

"You could come back another time," the woman says cheerfully.

"I work," Jessica says in a voice both aggressive and pleading. "We left after my last class. And all three of them work. They already missed one day from their jobs to be here now."

Ed Olmo strides through the office, buttoning his overcoat. He is an olive-skinned man with a thick mustache and aviator glasses. When he sees Jessica, he scowls.

"I *told* you," he says reproachfully. "I *told* you. You had to be here by four-thirty. I have my children to pick up. My baby-sitter has to be to another job by five. So if I'm late, she's late. And then I'm in hot water."

Jessica stands in the portal, clutching Big Black. Angel and See Wai flank her, and Wilfredo looms behind, peering over shoulders. They have Ed barricaded. They will not let him leave without seeing them. Feeling their challenge, Ed bristles. He tried to do a favor; he held up his end; he wasn't the one who showed up an hour late. The standoff lasts for a long half-minute.

Ed's face softens and he retreats a few paces. He hands the boys some course catalogues, tells them about an EOP open house in April, with free bus service from New York. Then he accepts from Jessica a folder containing their applications, autobiographies, and recommendations. "I'll read these this weekend," he promises, "and give you a ring on Monday."

They part to let him pass. Waiting for the elevator, he turns again to face them. "But you should know our cutoff is high this year. Nobody below seventy-five."

Silently, Jessica and her students watch him leave. They ride the next elevator down and walk across the brick plaza and descend the concrete steps to the parking lot. A damp wind saws through the open air.

"I have a seventy-five," Angel mutters.

"That's why we were coming up for an interview," Jessica says.

"Seventy-seven," See Wai says. "I didn't do so well in tenth grade."

"Seventy-one," Wilfredo adds.

"That's why we were coming," Jessica repeats.

They walk toward the Cutlass. The lot, packed ten minutes ago, is nearly empty now. Ed trots past, coat flapping, black gym bag under one arm, briefcase in the other. "On the road again," he calls, nodding to the four. "Nice meeting you."

"Thanks, but," Angel says so only the others can hear. "He didn't even have the idea of interviewing us."

"It's like he thought we came for fucking nothing," Wilfredo adds.

Jessica stops. The wind reddens her face, whips her hair into tangles. Exhaustion films her eyes. The boys regard her.

"No," she says firmly. "He was gonna do it as a favor. We blew it."

She unlocks the Cutlass. She feels guilty about blaming Wilfredo and furious at herself. She never should have let him go home. She never should have ceded control. After all these years of teaching, all these years of seeing teenagers act like teenagers, she should have known better. She was the one who blew it.

"I'll see if I can get a friend of mine to drive us up," Angel says to Wilfredo and See Wai. "If you wanna come." Neither answers.

Angel tosses an imitation leather folder onto the seat and then loosens his tie. He no longer needs the camouflage.

"Seventy-five," he says to himself. "But I had all these tough classes. Chemistry. I didn't have to take that." He slams the door. "I was gonna tell him that."

*   *   *

Jessica is disheartened enough to drive straight back to Manhattan. But she promised Sammy Ryan a visit and promised his foster mother she would deliver some spending money, so she sets out for his dormitory with her enervated entourage. The building is locked, and Jessica cannot remember his telephone number or room. She slips into the lobby as a student exits, and slumps with the boys onto a vinyl sofa. Just one more fiasco, she thinks. Then Sammy suddenly appears, loping down the hall in pressed jeans, a bomber jacket, and Reebok basketball shoes. "Hey," he says, enfolding Jessica, "my favorite teacher."

He loosens his hold, steps back, and says, "Where were you? I gave up waitin'."

"Don't ask," Jessica answers.

Between the soul shakes of introduction, Jessica reminds Angel that Sammy was in his Lower East Side class, "the guy who sort of lounged across three chairs." Sammy and Wilfredo establish that they share several friends, including Jayson Williams, a neighborhood teenager now playing college basketball at St. John's. Sammy explains he was on his way to the gym, but agrees to delay his game in favor of leading a campus tour.

It is certainly not what the admissions woman had in mind. Sammy's tour comes with a nonstop, free-associative, forty-five-minute monologue. Some of it is social ("When they're single, they love to mingle"), and some of it is strategic ("You don't have to take girls to the basement, like at Seward; you can bring 'em to your room"), and the boys bellow. Interspersed, though, is common sense from a survivor. "Lots of people, they tried to bring the city with 'em here," Sammy says of the EOP program. "They're gone now." And later: "Nobody gonna make you go to class, like in high school. You don't go, you just fail." And later still: "Profs get paid to teach you, not to baby-sit. You gotta take care of business yourself." Now Jessica beams. How many times did she say the same things to Sammy? How many times did she wonder if he listened? Here is the boy who last June was convinced he would flunk out of college by July, rising to the role of sage. Sammy is the first thing that has gone right all day.

But the uplift does not last long. Jessica buys everyone dinner at a McDonald's on Route 299, returns Sammy to campus and basketball, and then heads toward New York under starless skies. The Thruway is like a long tunnel, a black tube through black stone, illuminated only fleetingly by trucks that bore past and disappear. There is no talk and there is no radio. The day has ended a failure, and everyone knows it.

"Miss Siegel," See Wai eventually says, "I don't think you should drive so far to left."

She sucks her teeth. She has had just about enough driver's education for one day. She pulls into the right lane, just to silence See Wai.

"Slow down," Angel now cries, pointing to a truck with "Flammable Material" stamped above its taillights. "You wanna blow us up?"

"Gimme a break," Jessica says, laughing almost against her will.

Following her cue, the boys begin to chatter again. They talk about childhood pranks—Wilfredo burying a live rat, Angel burning the antennae off roaches—and they talk about adult issues. The topic migrates from Oliver North to political propaganda to the Soviet Union, and that starts Wilfredo describing his dream of studying there during his junior year of college. For the moment, he needs to believe he will be going to college.

The Cutlass rolls through the night, past the Harriman toll plaza, past the Suffern exit, into the suburban smear of Rockland County. When Jessica stops for gasoline, the boys take up a collection, thrusting a nine-dollar bundle of green at her. Back on the highway, they handicap Seward Park's teachers, moving from the worst to the best and ultimately to their driver.

"I can say this," Angel tells the others as Jessica eavesdrops. "And I'm able to say this because I don't have her this term and I already passed her class." He pauses. "Not by a lot, but I passed." There is laughter. "Miss Siegel is a good teacher." See Wai and Wilfredo murmur assent. "I mean, you start out, the subject is boring. And Miss Siegel makes it interesting."

"She gets your attendance," adds See Wai, meaning "attention."

"She cares about you," Wilfredo puts in.

She listens and stares at the road, unfolding 100 yards at a time in her high beams. It discomfits her to hear herself being souped up, yet she knows these boys are not the ass-kissing kind. In the dim dashboard light, she blushes.

"Some teachers claim they care," Angel continues, "but when she teaches you, you *know* she cares. She tells you to do your homework to learn. Not just to pass."

"Miss Siegel's way of teaching," See Wai announces. "The first time the students are quiet. But she grab their attendance. She get them to express their opinion."

They speak among themselves. They speak of Jessica in the third person, as if she were not inches away, as if she were not present at all.

"A lot of teachers teach because that's their job," Wilfredo says. "They think, 'I'll get paid whether you learn or not.'"

"Some teachers want revenge," See Wai says.

"You didn't have to take us up there," Angel says, finally directing the conversation to its subject. Then he halts, as if this outpouring has been too direct, too intense, too naked. "So you get an A," he says, and everybody laughs.

Their testimony only deepens Jessica's disappointment. All she has to show for today's misadventure is a sore throat and two throbbing temples. Tomorrow she has this car to return, and Sunday she has articles to edit and papers to grade. And for what? Where is the reward? Knowledge for its own sake is a wonderful thing, as Jessica surely agrees, but in the workaday world of getting a job and buying a house and raising a family, it is no replacement for a college diploma. Nearly seven months of work, starting in September, pointed toward this one day. All the writing assignments, all the private confidences, all the nagging and nudging, what was it for if not to push three students like these off the margin and into the mainstream? She told herself hours ago that today's trip felt like triage, but maybe she was wrong. Triage is supposed to save the fortunate few, not pronounce them dead on arrival.

As emotional a person as Jessica is, her fears are grounded in more than impression. Not long ago, she read a book by William Julius Wilson called *The Truly Disadvantaged*, which confirmed what she had already suspected: The solid jobs in hard industry, the jobs that had supported the dropouts and undistinguished graduates of Seward Park in earlier decades, were dying off by the hundreds of thousands. Jessica herself could see that the metropolitan landscape was littered with the carcasses of the manufacturing economy—the Brooklyn Navy Yard, the Steinway piano factory in Queens, the Ford Plant in Mahwah, New Jersey—even as it was giving rise to skyscrapers built on high finance and high technology, waiting to employ the highly educated. The only choices that awaited her students, if she could not hurl them into college, were the menial rungs of the service economy, the abusive "immigrant industries" typified by Chinatown's garment sweatshops, or the lucrative trade of selling drugs. It was all well and good for her to teach Martin Luther King's "I Have a Dream" speech, but that dream went only so far. *The Truly Disadvantaged* contained another quote from King, less famous, but perhaps more pertinent to the consequences of today's disaster: "What good is it to be allowed to eat in a restaurant if you can't afford the hamburger?"

"The street is always there," Jessica often says in explaining her obsession about getting students into college. "You can be as supportive, as encouraging, as attentive as you want. But the realities of life intercede and sometimes take over. You walk on the wrong street, you get in the wrong fight, someone pulls a knife instead of using a fist. People die. People get killed. I know that. The chance to get out, the chance to change class, the chance to have a chance, depends on a college education. And if you don't catch that ring on the merry-go-round, you're lost. You're lost."

When her mind returns to the road, she finds the Cutlass pushing south on the FDR Drive, the streets of the Lower East Side stretching beside her. Friday night lights twinkle in restaurants and dance clubs and bars with a foreign joy. After all the dire predictions, not a single snowflake fell. "Feels like it must be midnight," Angel says wearily. It is actually eight-thirty, but nobody disagrees.

Jessica drops off Angel at his building in the Vladeck projects. The next stop is the LaGuardia projects, where Wilfredo lives. "Sorry again, Miss Siegel," he says as he walks away. "Wilfredo," she shouts. He turns. "Don't worry about it." Last, she drives up Essex Street, past Seward Park to the Delancey Street subway station, where See Wai will begin the ninety-minute trip home to Flushing.

"Miss Siegel," he says, "please you should drive more careful."

He opens the car door, shoulders his backpack.

"And you need some rest this weekend."

"No kidding, See Wai. No kidding."

16

The Verities

On a March morning hinting at spring, one of those mornings when streetcorner society first emerges from hibernation, an instructive event occurs at the corner of Ludlow and Delancey, a block from Seward Park. Wedged into a small opening between a lamppost and a mailbox, two groups of teenagers are squaring off like rugby players readying for a scrum. One side is Hispanic, the other Chinese, and the leaders of each stand only inches apart. Their shouts carry down the street, the words indistinct, the anger palpable. Then the Hispanic leader delivers several stiff, two-handed shoves into his Chinese antagonist's chest, knocking him toward moving traffic.

In a momentary lull, the Chinese boys begin retreating down Delancey, not daring to turn their backs. The Hispanics match them stride for stride. The Chinese move off the sidewalk and into the street. The Hispanics mirror their steps. The Chinese start to run, weaving through cars. Now there are a dozen Hispanics giving chase, appearing from parking lots and side streets, one hobbling stiffly and carrying a crutch. From taxis and sidewalks and store windows, people watch, paralyzed by this sudden fury.

All the Chinese escape on the far side of Allen Street, except for the leader. Two Hispanics tackle him outside a hamburger stand, pinning him until the rest arrive. They take turns kicking him, boots striking his stomach as relentlessly as a machine stamping molds. The limping boy lifts his crutch above his head with both hands, like a giant scythe, and whips it against the unmoving body on the asphalt. Again and again the crutch slashes through the air, a brown blur, until it splinters into pieces. Then a metal blade glints in sunlight, and seconds later the Chinese boy holds his face, blood squirting out between his fingers.

Two men in suits suddenly leap out of their car and into the mob, peeling away attackers like so many artichoke leaves. They are undercover police officers, who have been patrolling for drug dealers. The Hispanics now flee, with one of the officers in pursuit, while the other drags the Chinese victim to his feet. The boy's legs buckle, and he clutches his ribs. His cheeks and temples are cut deep and clean. Between the streams of blood something shiny catches light. It is half of a contact lens, which was sliced, evidently, as it sat atop the boy's eye.

*　　*　　*

Within moments, Dr. Noel N. Kriftcher has learned of the beating. Police officers are on their way to Seward Park to brief him. The boys' dean, Len Greif, is walking the streets outside school, paying particular attention to several gathering spots for gang members. Dr. Kriftcher's first concern is whether any students were involved, and the initial indication is that they were not. That is a relief, but not altogether a surprise.

By New York's admittedly warped standards, Seward Park is a safe school. During the entire 1987–88 academic year, Seward Park files twenty-eight "incident reports" with the Board of Education, or one for each 128 pupils, and the vast majority chronicle trespassing, small thefts, or false alarms. The greatest fear at Seward Park, that of racial fighting, is realized only once, in a brawl between Dominicans and Chinese in the cafeteria, and it never widens or recurs. An attendance clerk is punched by an irate parent. A substitute teacher is shoved by a student, although the victim by his own admission incited his attacker by comparing him to a crack addict. The most serious offenses are four slashings of student by student with a knife or box-cutter, and in each instance the cause is a feud that began outside school.

The most violent high schools in the city, in contrast, record "incident reports" at rates of one per thirty to fifty pupils, and must contend with crimes as severe as rapes and shootings. Many, then, are the envious colleagues who tell Dr. Kriftcher, "Your school is always going to be good, as long as you get those Chinese kids." Such an assumption would be news to Norman Wong, an alumnus who saw

Chinese gangs regularly shake down his uncle's restaurant, or to Lun Cheung, who lost his best friend to a gang hit that he barely survived. As for Dr. Kriftcher, he used to try to explain that Seward Park's Chinese population was a diverse and complex group, until he realized few outsiders wanted to listen, preferring their panaceas untainted by truth.

What diminishes violence in Seward Park is something more subtle, more slippery—an urban version of natural selection in which the most dangerous teenagers on the Lower East Side do not bother going to high school. The appeal of disrupting a lesson or robbing a classmate or assaulting a teacher cannot compete with the big money to be made in drugs and extortion. And the parents of the neighborhood's young felons generally are not the sort to insist that their children attend school for the sake of appearances. Almost every student at Seward Park, even those with one foot in crime, harbors some desire to succeed. Consider Richie Morales, one of Jessica's students in English 7 and the Lower East Side class. Richie is a proud member of Here To Chill, with an array of criminal summonses for disorderly conduct and resisting arrest. He was almost killed last summer when a rival stabbed him four times during a gang brawl. Yet he is so obsessed with taking neat notes in class that he deploys a ruler to straighten the bottom of his letters, and when he received a 92 on a composition about his near-death, entitled "My Turning Point," he brandished the paper like a loving cup. Perhaps, he told friends, he would submit it to the school literary magazine.

Seward Park, at best, could tilt the pH of Richie's values toward the decent. But every afternoon he went home to Avenue D and every morning he arrived with the aura of Avenue D on him. He personified the true dilemma for Seward Park, which is not the infrequent violence within the building but the incessant violence beyond its walls, floating like a toxic cloud. Somebody calls somebody a bitch. Somebody flirts with someone else's girlfriend. Somebody insults somebody's brother-in-law. Somebody gets burned in a drug deal. None of these incidents have the least to do with Seward Park, yet any one has the potential to convulse it, for Seward Park is the crossroads of neighborhoods, ethnic groups, and extended families. And while school may teach the virtues of mediation, negotiation, and jurisprudence, the street teaches retribution and vengeance.

For most of the 1980s, contrary to conventional wisdom, the incidence of violence in New York schools actually fell by 40 percent.

When the frequency and severity abruptly rose in 1987, the variable was not a mystifying breakdown in school security but the onslaught of crack, the same drug that sent violent crime soaring citywide. More than 1,650 weapons are confiscated in public schools in the 1987–88 year, ranging from an Uzi submachine gun to a .357 magnum to a crossbow. On consecutive days in May, a special education teacher in the Bronx is slashed twelve times by a robber and a seventy-one-year-old remedial reading teacher nearly loses her hand when two boys who are cutting class toss an M-80 firecracker into her room. Park West High School in Manhattan becomes the very symbol of lawless students and ineffectual leaders. After searches of book bags turn up guns, brass knuckles, and even a meat cleaver; after a fourteen-year-old pupil is sought by the police for threatening to murder a classmate; after one seventeen-year-old boy attacks another a block from school with a machete, the principal has this blasé response: "School is a microcosm of society. Kids have been bringing weapons to school for years. It's almost a habit."*

Mortifying as such events are, they account for only part of the heightened concern with violence in the schools. The other reason, it seems clear, is the emergence of a principal named Joe Clark. A month before the fight on Delancey Street, Clark graced the cover of *Time* magazine, carrying his two trademarks, a bullhorn and a baseball bat.

Clark became principal of Eastside High School in Paterson, New Jersey, in 1982, not long after the Passaic County prosecutor had described the institution as "a cauldron of terror and violence." He expelled more than three hundred students during his first year and regularly inveighed against "hoodlums and thugs and pathological deviants." He also posted photographs of Eastside graduates in college, hung charts showing the student body's improvement on standardized tests, and greeted his charges by name with a high-five and the salutation "Peace." His contribution, of which harsh discipline was only one part, was in being surrogate father to teenagers from unstable or nonexistent homes. "It's that simple," he once acknowledged to a reporter.

Then fame turned his head. In early 1988, the Paterson school board charged Clark with insubordination and threatened to dismiss

*The principal, Edward Morris, drew so much criticism for his comments, which were conveyed in *The New York Times* in December 1987, that he asked for and was granted a transfer several weeks later.

him for expelling sixty "leeches, miscreants, and hoodlums" without due process. He refused to back down, warned he might resign, and opined that he hoped the school would suffer in his absence: "If it didn't plummet to the depths of despair, if it didn't become violence-ridden, if drugs and stabbings, all the things that I inherited did not reappear, I would be chagrined." Clark's resistance landed him in *The New York Times* and on "60 Minutes." Already the unacknowledged inspiration for a pulp movie called *The Principal,* he sold his own story to Hollywood, where it would be filmed under the title *Lean On Me* by John Avildsen, the director of *Rocky.* William J. Bennett, then the U.S. secretary of education, telephoned Clark with advice to "hang in there," and a White House adviser, Gary Bauer, promised him a job in the Reagan Administration if he decided to leave Eastside. "Sometimes you need Mr. Chips," Bennett had said of school administrators several weeks earlier. "Sometimes you need Dirty Harry."

There was the rub. Clark had become a folk hero less for his legitimate educational achievements than for his baseball bat. The same man who argued so passionately for the potential of ghetto children had happily accompliced himself to those who believed ghetto children were best reached by a thirty-six-inch Willie Mays Big Stick. It was a comforting, simplistic, and demeaning idea, and one that unfortunately would outlast Clark's fleeting celebrity. George McKenna, the acclaimed principal of an inner-city high school in Los Angeles, put it succinctly: "If the students were not poor black children, Joe Clark would not be tolerated." Much less revered, one might add.

Nobody who saw that Chinese boy hunted and savaged by a virtual lynch mob on Delancey Street could harbor any illusions about the violence in and around an urban school. What intrigued me was how little of that violence ever infiltrated Seward Park. The school did not have armed guards. It did not have metal detectors. It did not search book bags and lockers. It could not summarily dismiss students. Seward Park's approach began with its principal, a man whose favorite instruments of discipline were not bat and bullhorn but sarcasm and guilt.

*   *   *

Noel Kriftcher strides into the first-floor hall for his 11 A.M. constitutional. His blue sport jacket remains behind in his office, and his shirt sleeves are rolled to his elbows, as if he were a suburban homeowner abruptly enlisted for yardwork. He walks past a display case with photographs of students with perfect attendance and beneath the portraits of outstanding recent graduates. It was his idea to salute the current students in this fashion, and to increase the visibility of the alumni "Wall of Fame" he inherited. The principal of an inner-city school, he often says, cannot afford to be timid and reactive. He must be an advocate.

He also must be a guard, an interrogator, and a physical presence, as this daily stroll illustrates. When the Park West principal blamed his school's violence on "society," Dr. Kriftcher did not disagree. Where he differed was in seeing "society" as a challenge rather than as an excuse. One part of him says a neighborhood school must be a welcoming refuge, what he calls "mother with a light on in the kitchen," another that it must be a fortress defended against barbarism.

Watching him move through the halls, it becomes clear how personally he takes the charge. In most matters, Dr. Kriftcher delegates responsibility and shares credit, enjoying reflected glory as much as the direct variety. His appearances at events like China Night and Latin-American Night are brief and gracious. When students are interviewed during two weeks each May for scholarships and graduation prizes, he vacates his office for ninety minutes a day so it can be used for the screening process. The one area in which he assumes more direct control, the area that he considers the foundation of a credible school, is in ensuring safety.

Some of his means are, by design, invisible. Should one of the staff parking spaces in front of school happen to be vacant, for instance, Dr. Kriftcher will recruit a staff member to fill it before some drug dealer or gang member does. When the police installed a stop sign at Ludlow and Broome a few years ago, he whisked off a letter of thanks to the precinct, with copies up the chain of command. When he shops in the neighborhood, it is not only bargains he seeks. Storeowners know to call him with complaints and suspicions and, in one case, praise for two students who foiled a mugging. Dr. Kriftcher's hall walking, however, is meant to be as overt as possible.

"Where are you supposed to be?" he asks a boy without a hall pass.

"Excuse me, young man," he says to another drifter, "Where are you going?"

"We don't wear hats here," he informs a third, and he remains rooted to the spot until the boy sullenly complies.

Every single encounter, no matter how mundane, carries the seeds of confrontation. Every single interchange requires Dr. Kriftcher simultaneously to project resolve, respect, and a trace of threat. The Lower East Side is a neighborhood of ready violence and macho mores. Seward Park is a school with many children deserted or beaten by their fathers and inordinately adoring of their mothers. A female teacher or administrator, particularly one popular with her students, can often maintain order by assuming a maternal pose. When colleagues could not dislodge loafers from the third-floor hangout known as Times Square, Louise Grollman, hardly imposing at five feet tall, could scatter them merely by singing a high A. A male, however, must exude strength and will, must suggest that he is capable of meeting a physical challenge without ever inviting one. That, to Dr. Kriftcher, is the problem with a baseball bat.

He addresses wayward students with polite words and sardonic tones, like a radio talk-show host condescending to an unwelcome caller. He stands only inches from such students, his arms folded and his back arched, near enough to see anger flicker across their faces. And yet a punch has never flown, not in Dr. Kriftcher's twenty-eight-year career.

Much of what he knows about posture and persona he learned from the three strong men of his youth. His father, Irving, grew up on the Lower East Side, working from childhood as a newsboy when being a newsboy meant being an orphan, economically at the least. His friends used to joke that Irving went through more pairs of glasses than pants because of his penchant for fistfights, and as a father he demonstrated similar self-reliance, if a bit more discretion. He worked six days a week running a candy store, did not indulge in a vacation until age thirty-eight, and jumped the counter to confront a man stealing cigarettes when he was nearing fifty. Slashed in the process, Irving still subdued the robber until the police arrived. Noel would later distill the lesson of his father's life as, "Get up in the morning and check the obits; if you don't see your name, get to work."

The one thing Irving could not provide was an academic model. This Noel found in two rabbis. The first, who taught him in Hebrew school from ages eight through thirteen, was Jacob Hecht, a Hasid of the Lubavitcher sect. With his burning red beard and arrowhead eyes, with his unstinting orthodoxy delivered in fervent Yiddish, Rabbi Hecht loomed like a figure from the Old Testament. Yet he was canny enough to know that his students would arrive early if he placed a basketball hoop outside his synagogue. Rabbi Hecht's place was taken in Noel's teenage life by Rabbi Abraham Bloch, someone less from the Old Testament than from the Age of Reason. A clean-shaven man who spoke clipped, unaccented English with oratorical flourish, Rabbi Bloch held a doctorate from a secular university and led the first Conservative synagogue in the neighborhood. From a distance, Noel admired how Rabbi Bloch commanded the silent attention of his congregation, an acknowledgment that he was the most educated man for blocks around, and how he demanded that the worshippers carry a moral compass from the temple into their daily lives.

Outside synagogue and on the street, resolve of a different sort was required. The Kriftcher family lived in Brownsville, a section of Brooklyn that was being abandoned by its more affluent families after World War II and left to the Jewish and Irish working class and to survivors of Hitler's concentration camps. When blacks began moving into Brownsville in the mid-1950s, and Long Island became the magnet for white flight, the Kriftcher family's business, Izzy's Olde Sweet Shoppe, allowed them to move no farther than East Flatbush, ten or twenty blocks away. In that middle ground stood Lincoln Terrace Park, where Noel played basketball. The proof of central Brooklyn's grit was in its basketball players, young men like Red Holtzman and Sid Tannenbaum and Billy Cunningham, scrappy kids with elbows as sharp as their minds. The single rule governing the court was, "Winners stay, losers walk." Being defeated could mean waiting forty-five minutes or an hour for a second chance. And Noel Kriftcher won often enough to start on a Lincoln Terrace team that finished second in a boroughwide tournament.

Still, his world was a confined one, demarked by the family store, the basketball court, the synagogue, and the public library. Noel knew only one family who visited museums. It took New York University to introduce him to Shakespeare, and a summer job in Manhattan to introduce him to Broadway. When he wrote "G-d" in his term papers, for a pious Jew considers it sacrilege to spell out the name, professors chastised him. For better and worse, he was moving now among the secular and in some respects, the profane.

As he turned twenty in 1959, he took his first teaching job in Williamsburg, a Puerto Rican slum in Brooklyn, and it was a chastening, if illuminating, experience. The children entered the school so poorly prepared that he had to lower the junior-high lessons to the fourth-grade level, sometimes teaching a child to write his or her name. On Open School Night, he waited in vain for parents to whom he had sent personal invitations. Not once in five years did his principal observe or aid him or even dine in the faculty cafeteria. Order was all, and Noel Kriftcher could keep order. "I was a terrible teacher," he would recall years later. "I didn't know shit from Shinola." He did know, at least, that order had its limits. Discipline did not replace learning; it only made learning possible. To invoke discipline without offering education in return made a school "nothing but a penal colony."

Now Dr. Kriftcher steps toward a stairwell in Seward Park, where a blond, blue-eyed boy cowers, holding a class schedule flat in his two hands. Clearly he is a newcomer and clearly he cannot speak English. "German?" Dr. Kriftcher asks. No response. "Rumanian?" Again, no answer. Finally, the boy gets the idea. "Hun-gar-y," he says haltingly. *Hungary.* Dr. Kriftcher can only shake his head and make a note.

He ascends the stairs, plucking a matchbook off the floor without breaking his gait, spotting the graffiti signature of "Redjack HTC" and jotting himself a reminder to have it eradicated. Now on the second floor, he nears a teacher. "Mr. Molters," he says. The teacher starts to say hello, assuming this is a social call, but before he can push out a pleasantry, Dr. Kriftcher instructs him, "If you turn around, you'll see someone wandering. Could you find out why?" And the principal paces on, charming and chilly by turn, here berating a teacher for his opened classroom door, there praising one for her elaborately decorated bulletin board.

Word reaches the English office on the third floor that Dr. Kriftcher is making his rounds. A teacher who has been tutoring a slow student instead of monitoring the halls, as he is assigned, bounds through the door and to his post. Dr. Kriftcher passes with a greeting. The teacher slides back into the office and tells a friend, "Cover thy ass." Neither laughs.

Up in the cafeteria, one of the security guards hails Dr. Kriftcher. A table of Chinese boys is playing poker and refuses to stop and surrender the deck. Dr. Kriftcher approaches the table and holds out his hand. A boy relinquishes some cards. "A dozen?" Dr. Kriftcher says sourly. "You can't have much of a game with these. Where's the rest?" The entire table answers with flat, uncomprehending eyes. Their strategy is to feign ignorance of English—we're all just *sun ding,* brand-new—and it proves not only effective but frustrating because it is partially true. Dr. Kriftcher goes to another all-Chinese table and asks for an interpreter. Everybody plays dumb. He gets the same blank stares at a third table. Finally, a short boy with a crew cut offers his aid. A package containing the remaining forty cards is passed forward. "Next time," Dr. Kriftcher says, through his young assistant, "I tear them up."

On other days, Dr. Kriftcher may lunch in the staff cafeteria, but today there is no time. Descending the stairs, he talks about the psychologist Will Maslow's theory of the "hierarchy of needs," a hierarchy in which physical safety and well-being must be assured before education can commence. "I prefer fighting the small battles now to the big battles later," he says, nearing his office. "You can't bar the 'mean streets' at the schoolhouse door. But you want to get across the idea that this is not 'Out There.' This is 'In Here.'"

*　　*　　*

Noel Kriftcher's office must have been conceived with an Oxford don in mind. Dark, grainy wood girdles the room, except on its east wall, where two sets of built-in bookcases flank a fireplace. Above the mantle is a bas-relief bust of William Henry Seward, governor of New York, secretary of state under Abraham Lincoln, namesake of this high school. If the furnishings necessarily tend toward the relatively modern—a coffee machine, a lithograph of city rooftops, a poster of the principal's beloved Brooklyn Dodgers—then the overall effect nonetheless remains formal, weighty, and grave.

Perhaps the architects imagined the chamber would lend itself to great ponderings and rigorous debate, all part of the public school's mission of moral uplift. This morning, however, finds its occupants discussing a slashing that occurred four days ago. In the aftermath of every violent incident at Seward Park, Dr. Kriftcher holds a series of hearings, one for each student involved. The severest cases, those involving weapons, may proceed to the borough superintendent, while the police consider criminal charges independently of the school system's deliberations.

In Dr. Kriftcher's years at Seward Park, he can recall only a handful of incidents as serious as this one, less for the event itself than for the gang tensions it exposes. From what he has learned from deans and several student witnesses, a girl named Jane Oquendo got into a fight with a girl named Lisa Carerra. As they grappled, Jane drew a boxcutter and sliced Lisa above her left eye, across her lip, and down her chin. Then she hurled the weapon out the window. As severe as the attack was, the rumors made it sound far worse. Jessica Siegel, who had had Lisa in English 7 in the first term, was told that the girl would be permanently disfigured. Friends of the foes began taking sides, intent on earning their pyrrhic brand of honor. And there the problems only started. The fight began with Jane and Lisa trading accusations of flirting with each other's boyfriend, and since the two boyfriends belong to the separate and rival gangs of Here To Chill and The Smiths, there is plentiful tinder for a larger blaze.

Jane Oquendo's case is already in the hands of the borough superintendent, who will ultimately assign her to another high school.* Now Lisa Carerra sits beside Dr. Kriftcher at a long wooden table, proper enough for a law firm, in what the principal calls "the hot seat." It is the one closest to the drawer with the tissues. No scars are visible on Lisa's face except a two-inch red mark across her chin. Otherwise she retains a moody beauty of ink-dark eyes, high cheekbones, and lustrous black hair. From a physical standpoint, at least, she has little cause for retaliation, which is a relief to Dr. Kriftcher. To Lisa's left is her mother, wearing worn jeans and a chamois shirt, her face ruddy and creased and drawn. Across the table are Bernice Portervint, the dean of girls, and Muriel Salzman, Lisa's guidance counselor.

The dean briefly recounts the incident, then Dr. Kriftcher asks Lisa for her version.

"I was walking behind Jane," she says. "She kept looking at me. Calling me curses. Saying, 'C'mon and fight me. Pussy. Pussy.'"

"Is this a longtime feud?"

"Yes," Lisa says. She fidgets in her chair, as if wondering if the answer will help or hurt her cause. "Goes back to gym class. She don't like me."

"You live in the same neighborhood?"

"No."

"You see her outside school?"

"No."

Dr. Kriftcher nods, a bit distracted. Students almost always see this room as a court, these hearings as trials, and they plead and contort in pursuit of the verdict of innocence. The principal strives for such an atmosphere, privately calling suspension hearings "The Supreme Court," but his designs are not legalistic. He already knows the

---

*At the time, reassignment was the severest long-term penalty. In June 1988, after a series of attacks on teachers, Chancellor Green announced new regulations that allow for the expulsion of students who assault school personnel.

essential details of the slashing. He cares less about reconstructing what happened than preventing it from happening again on a grander scale. Two girls arguing about boyfriends is nothing new in any high school; the rapid escalation to violence and weaponry is the unfortunate province of an inner-city school like Seward Park. The kids with decent grades and decent attitudes can usually graduate and attend college and get out. For the ones who stay behind, and who define the neighborhood by their tenancy, life's verities are knives and taunts and gangs and drugs. A principal ignores them at his peril.

Bernice Portervint now hands Dr. Kriftcher a manila folder. He inspects the papers within. When he lifts his head, he is grimacing, and he turns that grimace toward Lisa.

"How is it you're a student here," he asks, "if you live in Brooklyn?"

Lisa explains she used to live on the Lower East Side with her aunt, but recently moved to Brooklyn to be with her mother. The point of the exchange is the unspoken threat. Lisa can be ousted from Seward Park simply because she lives outside its district. She attends at the sufferance of, among others, Dr. Kriftcher. Nothing more need be said for everyone to understand.

"Is there any way you could've avoided this?"

"If she hadn't found me in the morning," Lisa says, "she would've later. In gym class. Or after school."

"Couldn't you have avoided it?"

Lisa says nothing.

Dr. Kriftcher withdraws from the folder a copy of Seward Park's discipline code, signed by Lisa. Each student must promise to abide by its sixteen rules, ranging from returning textbooks to not wearing a Walkman, and to ensure that all 3,500 comprehend it, the code is available in Chinese and Spanish translations. Dr. Kriftcher directs Lisa's attention to a section that poses the question, "WHAT DO I DO IF I have a PROBLEM with another student that may lead to a FIGHT?"

"Do you remember what it says?" he asks. She nods no. "It says you go to a teacher, you go to a counselor, you go to a dean, you go to me." With each phrase, he unrolls a finger from his fisted left hand and strikes it with the index finger of his right. The motions are brisk and brusque. And with the last, he leans on his elbow to peer into Lisa's eyes. "It doesn't make sense to me," he says with a mix of exasperation and pity. "There are cars outside on Ludlow Street and Grand Street." He indicates the corner through a window. "And as long as one car stops at the intersection, there's no collision. If neither stops, there's a collision."

Now he requests Lisa's disciplinary records from Portervint. There are a dozen pink slips, most related to lateness or talking in class. It is not an awful record, all told, but Dr. Kriftcher wants Lisa to feel like a grand jury has just indicted her. His fingers snap the pages smartly, and his head wags slowly, as if burdened with unspeakable anger or sorrow. Silence becomes his ally.

Finally he thrusts a particular pink slip toward Lisa. The slip reports that she told a teacher, "I'll wring your fucking neck."

"You remember this?" he says. "Your use of language was unfortunate." He breathes, wipes a hand across his forehead. "What was happening?" She does not answer; her eyes fall to the table. "You just didn't like the teacher?" She nods.

"Sleeping in first-period algebra," the principal declaims, reading from another pink slip.

"I think she was late because she had to come over from Brooklyn," Lisa's mother says with contrition.

Dr. Kriftcher leans back in his chair, the pink slips arrayed across his thighs. He selects and reads as if at random. He is a leisurely inquisitor.

"Eating in class and leaving wrappers," he recites with a distaste suitable for assault and battery. "Is that true?"

"That was true," Lisa confesses. She places an elbow on the arm of her chair and presses one finger across her lips. If nothing else, Dr. Kriftcher has won her attention.

"You instigated a fight with Maria Perez," he continues.

"I don't talk to that girl," Lisa insists. "I don't even look at that girl."

"This is the day before the fight with Jane. And Maria is saying that Lisa is spoiling for a fight. What does this mean? *What does this mean?*"

"OK," Lisa's mother says, straightening in her chair. "Lisa tells me the day before that girl was in class and said if you're gonna have a fight, I've got you backed."

"So why did this happen?" Dr. Kriftcher asks, his gaze on Lisa alone.

"I don't know."

"Is there a boy involved?"

"No," Lisa says.

The principal's silence tells her he knows she is lying.

"OK," she resumes. "Jane always thought I was after her boyfriend. But I was just friends with him."

"Did you talk to him?"

"Not when she was around. She got jealous."

"Who is he?"

"Eddie. The guy in the cafeteria."

"He must be terrific," Dr. Kriftcher says in mock tribute, spreading his arms wide. "If he's worth fighting over."

Muriel Salzman, the counselor, hands Dr. Kriftcher Lisa's academic records. He peruses them as the girl waits. Removing her most recent report card, he closes the folder.

"You know, Lisa," he says in a softer voice, "even your elementary teachers say great things about you. You're bright. You're eager. Did you know they said those things about you?" She shyly nods no. "Did you get into fights then?" She cannot meet his eyes. Now he lifts the report card by two fingers, dangling it before her. "This is very unusual. Usually, if a student wants to cut class they go to official." Official, or homeroom, is where daily attendance is taken. "*You* go to class, but not to official. Absent twelve times. I know you weren't absent twelve times. How come you don't go to official? Where do you go?"

"The cafeteria," she almost whispers.

"What do you do there?"

"Nothing."

He guesses she visits Eddie, but does not say so.

"Where else do you go?"

"Nowhere special. Outside."

Dr. Kriftcher faces Lisa's mother. He speaks to her as much as a parent as a principal. It is a favorite gambit.

"Do you want your daughter hanging out on the street?"

"Not when she's supposed to be in class."

"Who do you hang out with?" he asks, swiveling back to Lisa.

"Friends."

"I take it on faith," he says. "No one hangs out with enemies. What are their names? You don't know?"

He pauses, satisfied the mother has heard. The interrogation is really for her benefit. It is for her, Dr. Kriftcher knows, that Lisa will study and behave. And if playing the heavy helps, that is fine. He seems actually to enjoy the role.

"When do you expect to graduate?" he asks.

"June."

"Not with this." He taps the report card, as if touching it longer would soil his hand. "Not with this." He waits a beat. "You're a smart girl, but you don't always act smart."

He lays both arms atop the table. He is now a father presiding over holiday dinner.

"What do you want to do after you graduate?"

"Go to college."

"Where?" he asks with genuine curiosity. "What do you want to study?"

"I don't know."

Lisa wipes a tear from her eye. Her fingernails are painted bright red. Dr. Kriftcher removes the tissues from the drawer, reaching deep into the box to fetch one for Lisa. The supply has been depleted by her predecessors in the hot seat. Tears are always a good sign, especially from a girl as tough as Lisa. Tears are the sign of an active conscience.

"You see," Dr. Kriftcher says as Lisa dabs at her eyes, "the fight is nothing. Yes, you got bruised. Yes, you got cut. Yes, you had to go to the hospital. Five years from now, that fight won't matter. But you have a clean record up till now. And should I write 'Suspended' on it today? So people can see it for the rest of your life?" He pauses. "I don't think that will be necessary. I'm going to return you to class because I think you're smart enough to learn from this."

He tells Lisa she will receive a "probation card." She must have her teacher in each class, including official, sign it every single day. Lisa's head lies limply on her right shoulder, as if her bones have turned to straw. Dr. Kriftcher has examined the minutiae of her years at Seward Park; he has threatened by inference; he has served as confessor, and like a confessor, he has pointed the route to absolution.

"However," he adds, "if you get into another fight by the end of this year, I'm going to enter the suspension on your record. You and Jane Oquendo are married to each other now. If something happens to you, I come looking for her. If something happens to her, I come looking for you." He rises. "You can go to Room 128 to reregister."

Lisa and her mother disappear down the hall. Dr. Kriftcher returns the tissues to the drawer, which he closes with a click. He has another hearing in five minutes, involving two boys who had a fistfight in the Delancey Street subway station. After that, there is a third hearing, for a class cutter. His mother, Dr. Kriftcher knows, is a heroin addict now trying methadone maintenance. The world without, as always, affects the world within. But long ago, he stopped expecting those who judge schools from a distance to realize.

*   *   *

The attack on Delancey Street never intrudes into Seward Park, but it continues to rub around its edges for days. The Hispanic assailants, at least those caught by the police, are not students, but they live in the projects beside Avenue D and probably know many. The Chinese victim, it develops, is a Seward Park alumnus. It also develops that he is widely thought to be a gang member and a drug dealer. And it appears that he stirred up the fight by fondling a Hispanic gangster's girlfriend.

The victim never presses charges. Nor does he noticeably avoid the neighborhood. Only hours out of the emergency room, in fact, he rejoins his gangster friends at a restaurant near Seward Park. Preening like a model, he shows off his wounds.

17

Leaving Trains

SPRING ARRIVES ON the Lower East Side not as a time of renewal but of dissipation. Neighborhood landmark and commercial lifeline, the Williamsburg Bridge is shut down by the city, its steel frame infirm. Just when shoppers should be flocking over the span to the alfresco markets of Delancey and Essex and Orchard streets, the blocks stretch in near desertion. The aromas of joss sticks and new leather coats drift undisturbed through the air, as touts pace the sidewalk, impatient to importune. Only the Off Track Betting parlor, its doorstep littered with yesterday's tip sheets and empty malt liquor cans, claims a brisk business. Only the OTB parlor, that is, and its next-door neighbor, the methadone clinic.

Seward Park, too, seems heavy with weariness and disrepair, as if the old building itself were trying merely to survive until summer, a terminal patient clinging for one final visit from a spouse. The faculty elevator breaks. One year to the date since a contractor stalked off the job in a snit with the Board of Education, the roof still leaks. In Jessica Siegel's English 7 classroom, three overhead lights expire, two windows shatter, and one blind sags. Faster than custodians can tighten them, the screws that secure desks and chairs to the floor worm loose, and students who sit down too heavily find the entire assembly groaning and shimmying and rearing in rebellion.

Jessica feels every bit as worn. The cold she carried to New Paltz has worsened in the days since, turning her voice into a sickly croak and finally a faint rasp, which she depletes further each period. Her head wobbles; her bones throb. And if ever Jessica required her powers and her charms, it is now. Her favorite students remain unchosen by colleges. More than half her English 7 pupils are failing the course, and unless they can levitate their grades they will not graduate in June. The second term has unfolded far enough to reveal the freshest crop of tragedies, any one of which could occupy a social worker for weeks. There is a chronically truant girl possibly being abused by her stepfather, a boy who has missed class twenty-one times because he works nights supporting his baby daughter, a girl whose parents are threatening to ship her back to the Dominican Republic if she does not break up with her boyfriend, a boy who survived the Khmer Rouge's genocide in his native Cambodia only to have his mother denied an emigration visa by Vietnamese "liberators."

And there is Ruby Mayes, who has disappeared altogether, just when Jessica had her convinced to apply to college. Ruby took advanced journalism in the first term, and through her assignments and journal entries told Jessica that she and her mother had been living for two years in a welfare hotel, an experience that so warped her standards of civilized existence that she could call it "not so bad." Her mother died toward the end of the first semester, and Ruby went to live in Brooklyn with her older sister and the sister's boyfriend. As they idled on welfare, she took graveyard shifts as a supermarket cashier and somehow clung to a passing average at Seward Park. Jessica envisioned college—any college—as the answer to Ruby's needs for education and escape. Only a few weeks ago, though, the older sister resolved to move herself and Ruby back to relatives in Mississippi, and she refused to delay their flight long enough to let Ruby complete high school. It is probably a futile gesture, but Jessica tries writing one last letter.

Dear Ruby—

I'm very worried about you. After you were gone a few days, I called your number to find it disconnected. I really want to know what is going on with you.

Please call me at the English office 674–7000 x 35 or come by. Don't give up now!

Ms. Siegel

That plea, underlined and exclaimed, might well address its author, as well. For nearly a year, and particularly in the four months since Thanksgiving, the prospect of resigning has never been far from Jessica's mind. It has shimmered before her like the mirage of a jade pond on a desert highway. It has flowed beneath her feet as a river runs under limestone. It has been both real and illusory, reassuring in its promise of a life of fewer demands, depressing in its risk of a life with fewer rewards. Jessica has spoken these thoughts aloud to her old college roommates over dinners and even to casual acquaintances at holiday parties, and it appeared she did so less to declare a certainty than to ponder an option, for she has let slip not a clue to the friends in teaching who might argue with her to remain, who might say in so many words, "Don't give up now!"

*   *   *

On Saturday afternoon March 26, Jessica trudges to a B. Dalton bookstore a half-dozen blocks from her apartment. She needs to buy a new copy of Bobbie Ann Mason's novel *In Country* because she gave her own to Wilfredo Ayala and its replacement to Carlos Pimentel. With Wilfredo's curiosity about the Vietnam War era and Carlos's pacifist sentiments, she felt they would be most moved by Mason's story of a teenage girl discovering the war that killed her father and damaged her uncle. Now she is considering teaching the book to her English 7 classes—provided, of course, that she can find seventy free copies, since, as usual, Seward Park cannot afford them.

Wandering the fiction aisle, Jessica bumps into Frances Mayer, an English Department colleague on leave this semester to attend graduate courses at Hunter College. Jessica asks her about life as a student, and Frances confesses she doesn't like it as much as teaching. As a teacher, she says, she can dictate her world, and so confine it, but as a student, she must react to someone else's agenda.

Nodding agreeably for appearances, Jessica bridles within. What could be better than going back to school? Nothing to do but read and think and talk. If you want to stay up till three in the morning, you can. If you want to slide for a week, you can. You are responsible to nobody but yourself. Those summer seminars Jessica took on Shakespeare and Melville were like fine brandies whose aftertaste turns all else to tap water. Teaching is the thing she can't control. You come to work late or woozy, you coast for awhile, and you let down 170 people who depend on you every day. Winning the Robert F. Kennedy awards would have been easier had Jessica actually done what some cynics believed—written the articles herself. No, it's far harder, far more draining, to take an intellectually insecure child and educate and inform and push, push, push. And with forty-five *Seward World* submissions and thirty Lower East Side tests to read this weekend, and preliminary term grades due on Tuesday, Jessica needs no reminder that her job is her taskmaster.

Maybe, she thinks, the difference is that Frances is only in her second year, still riding the adrenalin of novelty. Maybe the difference is that Frances has often taught reading, the most rote and contained of English classes. Teaching writing—real expository writing—is something else again. "The importance of writing isn't debatable," Jessica tells me several days later. "I can't say, 'I'll keep teaching as long as I don't have to teach humanities; I'll keep teaching as long as I don't have to teach journalism.' I taught in a reading program as a para [paraprofessional] and I connected with kids individually. But as far as empowering kids with content and ideas, I wasn't doing that. You can't in a reading class. But if you also want an easier life, then what is your choice?"

Her despair only deepens on Sunday. It is a bracing, blustery day outside. Families stroll together from Palm Sunday services. Crowds line the Upper East Side for the Greek-American Day parade. Fans flock to bars for the college basketball tournament games. A black-tie audience cheers the new August Wilson drama, *Joe Turner's Come And Gone,* on opening night. Jessica does none of those things. She does not have time to jog, or to read the Sunday papers. She does not step outside her apartment the entire day. She does her work, or most of it, grading half the Lower East Side exams, and editing every single *Seward World* article—articles on subjects as complex and volatile as abortion rights, homelessness, illegal immigration, teenage pregnancy, drug use in sports, and the history of the civil rights movement. One of the pieces, by Daisy Severino, concerns academic preparation for college. Daisy quotes Norman Wong as saying of Seward Park: "There is a gross insufficiency in concentration on grammar and sentence form. I have read many Seward graduates' papers, which are pathetic failures of the system. More concentration on writing should be stressed."

Jessica nods and tells herself, *That's my job.* She covers the pages with red ink, a kind of blood. She spills serum drop by drop, transfusing enthusiasm and knowledge and ability. But the donor of time, unlike the donor of blood, cannot regenerate what is given. Jessica must finally save something for herself before there is nothing left worth saving. And if she cannot ration her commitment or equivocate in her devotion, if she cannot revive herself with whatever elixir Ben Dachs and Hannah Hess and her other idols have discovered, then, as she wondered after seeing Frances yesterday, what is her choice? There is only one choice: to walk away. And in this sunless apartment on a sunny afternoon, the vision of deliverance stimulates in her something uncommon.

Bitterness is no more than a trace element in Jessica's periodic table, but she feels laden with it now. She thinks of an encounter with Dr. Kriftcher last week. She was wheeling her bicycle past his office late one afternoon, and he asked how she was doing. "Well, you know, it's really hard to put out the paper and teach five classes," she said. He chuckled and told her, "What do you say we just abbreviate it from now on? Just say, 'WYKIRHTPOTP and teach five classes.' So when I ask how you're feeling, all you have to do is repeat it." Now she promises herself that if she gives notice, she'll strew on Kriftcher's desk all the papers she read today, each drenched in red ink. Not as a way of saying, "Fuck you," but, rather, "This is what it takes"—to publish a professional-quality newspaper while responsibly teaching five classes. And she's not even a perfectionist, because she hears, and sometimes from Kriftcher, about whatever gaffes escape her.

But when her anger cools, Jessica knows that even if the principal relieved her of a class in exchange for advising the paper it would not make much difference. A decision to stop teaching would be the product not of anything as temporal as being denied a point-two. It would be the product of working conditions that are largely beyond a principal's control—five classes a day times thirty-four pupils a class times nine years, all without money for enough guidance counselors or social workers or new textbooks or xerox machines, all for a pittance in salary and respect. Jessica has occasionally likened herself to a marathon runner, and like a marathoner, she possesses a tolerance for pain, isolation, and deferred gratification that a spectator may confuse for masochism. If she drops out of the race, then, it is not because a boulder fell on her head, but because she has been plodding for twenty miles with the same pebble in her shoe.

The next morning, back at Seward Park, Jessica teaches two difficult classes on Melville's short story, "Bartleby the Scrivener," as if to underline that after all these years, the performance part of teaching still taxes her, still makes her long for the anonymity of the wings. Then she meets Bruce Baskind in the English office to review the scores on the Lower East Side test, to see yet another class failing by half, and to remind herself of friendship in eclipse. Almost against her will, Jessica is lifted by Bruce's humor, especially when he says of one boy, "He's so far out to lunch that lunch isn't a nearly long enough meal." But then Bruce excuses himself to the bathroom, and in his brief absence Jessica tumbles. The jokes that used to be so constant between them have for months been all too rare, and in a way it hurts more to hear one than none at all, for laughter invites memory. Bruce returns to their wooden work table to find exhaustion etched beneath her eyes, tears about to fall.

"Is something the matter?" he asks softly.

"No," she whispers hoarsely, struggling for control.

"Is there anything I can do?" he asks.

"No."

*   *   *

Watching Jessica's troublesome early years at Seward Park, Hannah Hess struck upon a truth. Jessica would not quit her job, no matter how painful its conditions, if she believed she was failing. Jessica, Hannah understood, could resign only from a position of success. And so as abject and enraged as Jessica now feels, she still cannot utter the oath of departure. There are still tasks to be completed. There are still futures to be arranged.

The first step is to call Ed Olmo at the State University of New York in New Paltz. Nearly two weeks have passed since Jessica's misbegotten trip with Wilfredo Ayala, Angel Fuster, and See Wai Mui. She needs to know whether any of them has miraculously won admission, with their low averages and without personal interviews. If they did, she can celebrate; if they did not, she must plot anew.

The telephone in the English office is rigged to abort long-distance calls, so Jessica goes to the College Discovery office, where Hal Pockriss and Denise Simone never refuse her an outside line. Angel is already at work, starting a job as a motorcycle messenger, but Wilfredo and See Wai accompany her. As she dials Olmo, Wilfredo leans against the doorjamb, unfolding a paper clip, shaping it into a circle, then turning it between his fingers like a gyroscope. Behind him, See Wai stands erect, right hand locked over left. The first eight times Jessica tries the call, she gets a busy signal. The ninth time she hears a young voice and begins to explain herself before realizing she is talking to a student who picked up the extension on Denise's desk. On the tenth attempt, she gets through.

Olmo begins by saying he felt so guilty about going home just as Jessica arrived that March afternoon that he went into work the next day, a Saturday, to review all three applications. *A good sign,* Jessica thinks. And the fact that all three boys presented complete transcripts and financial-aid forms puts them ahead of dozens of disorganized competitors. *So maybe it wasn't a mistake letting Wilfredo go home for his material.* Judging by grades alone, it's not clear that these boys can survive at New Paltz, and survival is important to the EOP program. *That was always the rub.* But very few students ever submit autobiographies or essays, and all three boys did, and the autobiographies were pretty impressive. Especially Angel Fuster writing about the future. Most kids only talk about the past and present. *Yes? And?* And the other students you've sent us, like Sammy Ryan and Vinnie Mickles, have succeeded even when their high school grades predicted they shouldn't have. *Yes? And?* So the State University of New York at New Paltz accepts See Wai Mui and Angel Fuster and places Wilfredo Ayala on the waiting list.

"See Wai!" Jessica shouts from inches away. "You're in."

She loops her arms around his slender shoulders, drawing him toward her, but he resists.

"I don't know this," he says in a flat tone, his head faintly nodding no.

"I just found out. Just now. You and Angel are in!"

See Wai examines the information, as if handling some strange orb. The pupils of his eyes track back and forth across Jessica's face. For seconds that feel as long as minutes, he says nothing.

"Miss Siegel, are you sure they accept me?"

"See Wai, believe me."

"But when we went there, right, I didn't think I do so well."

"Well, it doesn't matter."

"Then I feel happy," he says, although his face remains creased and fretful. "What about him?" he abruptly adds, indicating Wilfredo.

"He's on the waiting list," Jessica says. "But he can still get in. Or he could get in at Binghamton." She faces Wilfredo. In his anxiety, he shifts his weight from side to side, as if pacing in place. "We'll try them, too."

See Wai disappears down the hall. Once he is beyond earshot, Hal sighs and says to Jessica, "Just one sour note. We gotta get this kid to pass his RCT in writing."

"I promise," Jessica says.

She now calls Sharon Williams of the EOP program at Binghamton. Wilfredo had made the four-hour trip to the campus last week and stumbled into an interview with Williams's boss, the EOP director. Wilfredo has been wary of expressing any hope, as if it could hex his slender chances, but Jessica knows from her own reactions as Wilfredo's teacher how his maturity and sincerity can impress. As she waits for a secretary to connect her to Williams, she flips through a pamphlet about Passover, distributed every year by a Spanish teacher who is Hasidic.

"Sharon? Jessica Siegel."

Then, as Sharon speaks, there is a long silence in Hal's office. Wilfredo retreats from the portal and braces himself against a table in the waiting room. His jaw is locked, and his hands are balled so tightly the veins rise.

"Can I tell him?" Jessica says.

There is another pause as Sharon resumes.

"Can I tell him that, too?"

There is an even longer pause.

"And Carlos?"

She listens, nods, hangs up. Then she bolts to Wilfredo and kisses both cheeks.

"You're in!" she squeals.

"I can't believe it," he says, cracking his knuckles and squinting with doubt. "They had people applying there with eighty-fives."

"I'm telling you the truth," Jessica says. "You really made an impression."

"Well, I'm not saying anything till I get a letter."

"But they loved you, Wilfredo."

"They did?" he says with the fragile trust of a child pushing open the door of a darkened room. "What did they say? Word for word."

" 'He made such a good impression. We're gonna let him in. Just have him send the financial-aid form.' "

"They said that?"

"*Yes!*"

"Binghamton," Wilfredo says, rubbing his chin. "Binghamton."

His eyes widen and flicker. "Never had a doubt in my mind." And he departs to Jessica's laughter, moving toward home with strides so long he can hardly keep from breaking into a sprint.

Jessica calls Angel Fuster's mother with word of his admission to New Paltz, then embarks on a quest for Carlos. He told her he would be staying late, rehearsing with the chorus for *Bye, Bye Birdie,* the school's spring musical. Scooting down empty halls, swiveling her head quickly as a Wimbledon watcher, she checks every classroom on the third floor, finding only Bruce Baskind closing windows. On the fourth, nothing. On the fifth, she sees a music teacher, writing in her Delaney book. The chorus just left, she tells Jessica, for the auditorium. Too impatient for the elevator, Jessica swirls down five flights, hurls open the auditorium door, and spots Carlos onstage in the middle of his solo number. She waits and waits and waits, and when he descends to the aisle she rushes him.

"Talked to Binghamton," she blurts.

Carlos, collecting his breath, asks, "What happened?"

"You're in!"

She showers Carlos with kisses. He stands limply, arms at his sides, not quite prepared to believe. For weeks now, he has been lingering on the waiting list at Colgate and waiting for any word from Binghamton, calling his mother every day at lunchtime to see if mail from either college arrived. It takes some time for him to trust this news, even coming from Jessica, but gradually he hugs her back, laughing throatily and smiling until his trademark dimples show like tiny whirlpools.

"Every time I mention your name to the EOP people," she says, "they go crazy."

"Good to be in somewhere," Carlos sighs, raising his eyebrows and rolling his eyes upward in relief. "Good to be in." Before he can say more, his scene is called again.

Early the next morning, Angel finds Jessica at work in the English office. Standing in the doorway, he lowers his head and fixes his gaze upon her, hoping she will see him and speak first. But he cannot bear to wait, and once she lifts her eyes, as if feeling his presence, the words rush from him.

"My mother told me. I didn't believe her."

"Your mother's gonna lie to you?" she answers.

"But I don't understand it." He plants his hands in his pockets.

After waiting so long for an acceptance letter, he just assumed he had been rejected. "Why'd they let me in?"

"Because of your recommendations and your writing. Your writing shows your abilities, your intellect."

"I still can't believe it."

"Believe it. You got in."

"I'm not good at mushy things," he says, averting his eyes. "But thank you."

She hugs Angel and he hugs her and when they part, he unzips The Entity. "Won't need these anymore," he says, and together, he and Jessica place his dozens of college catalogues in the garbage. They work with an odd daintiness, as if laying offerings on an altar.

That night, Jessica thinks of trains. She sees Angel and Wilfredo and See Wai and Carlos all running toward a leaving train, grasping at its closing door and charging down the tracks in pursuit, missing it barely at a second station and a third. She sees herself running with them, watching the caboose light grow more and more distant, and then watching it come closer with the train stopped at the next station. She sees her students scramble aboard safely now, sees them totter down the aisle looking for seats. She sees herself stand between the rails, lungs beating like bellows, as the train churns away.

What incredible kids, she thinks, *what incredible kids!* Them and Aracelis and Addie and Daisy and the rest. Had she ever had a more amazing bunch of seniors? And she did not recruit them. Why, she hardly knew any of them a year ago. The encounter had been purest kismet. Sure, there are loose ends, and many failures, too, failures who in other moments depress and infuriate her. But in this reverie, there is no room for footnotes. If leaving Seward Park might ever feel a little easier, it will after seeing this group off. Now she can begin thinking about herself. Now she can board her own leaving train.

*   *   *

For the next month, the decision remains her private possession, a bomb in a briefcase. She surreptitiously applies for a counseling job with the I Have A Dream Foundation, which provides financial aid and support services to college-bound ghetto children, and she checks with a friend about vacancies in the admissions office at Fordham University. She starts compiling a list of organizations that might give her a grant to create a book from her students' oral histories. But by daylight, inside Seward Park, she carries on as if she will return in September.

She treks to the annex, as she has every spring, to woo next year's juniors for journalism and humanities, and she laughs when one boy asks, "Which class don't have tests?" She nominates two of her current juniors, Yuet Lo and Alvin Aponte, for a summer journalism workshop at New York University. Concerned that she does not adequately prepare pupils for college term papers, she revises her English 7 curriculum to include a three-page research paper, drawn from a new two-week unit on literature of the Industrial Revolution. Having massaged a donation of seventy books from its publisher, Jessica adds *In Country* to the course. She arranges for Ottavio Johnson, her black nationalist in residence, to review both *School Daze,* Spike Lee's movie about an all-black college, and *Sarafina!* a South African musical on Broadway, for *Seward World.* She steers See Wai into a part-time job at the New York Chinatown History Project, a far more ideal employer than Arby's for someone of his cultural consciousness, and she begins his intensive tutoring for the Regents Competency Test in writing.

The test is composed of three sections, each providing a student with the raw data from which to construct a business letter, a report, and a composition. Each section is graded by a panel of Seward Park English teachers on a 100-point scale, and the total is divided by three for the final mark. See Wai passed the test with a 70 in the first term, but his mark was later reduced to a failing 55 by state evaluators in Albany. So many Seward Park students were "reversed," as the lingo has it, that Ben Dachs recently devoted an entire departmental meeting to discussing a strategy for June's exams. Jessica has been tailoring See Wai's assignments for journalism class—Pathfinders, Chinese class, and the Yankees—in the hopes that acumen will follow interest. But the results leave her less than sanguine about the RCT. The test has no place for insight and invention, See Wai's greatest gifts, but places a premium on verb conjugation and sentence structure, the areas that most bedevil students who were reared in Chinese. Jessica decides her best hope is to rehearse See Wai on past RCT writing tests, to drill him in the approvable, passing form.

She yanks him out of eighth-period gym class one April afternoon for his first session. He wears light gray sweatpants and a white cotton windbreaker, and he drums his felt-tip pen on a desktop as she reaches into a green file cabinet and says, "RCT's Greatest Hits." See Wai does not get the joke.

"Read it over carefully," she says, handing him the test booklet. "Make sure you're clear about what they're asking you to do." She pauses. "Let's try the business letter. You can really clean up here."

"I know last time my letter was low," he says. "Like a seventy."

"You probably didn't go over. . . ."

"This time," he interrupts, "a hundred."

He reads, then writes, as Jessica talks cheesecake recipes with Pat Ng, another teacher. He waits for her to finish chatting before he hands her the letter. She slaps her palms across her eyes like a minister who stumbled into *Deep Throat* by mistake.

"Not until you read it over," she declares. "I won't look at it."

He obliges, excising an unnecessary comma and correcting his spelling of "truely." Then Jessica reads the letter, which asks a manufacturer to replace a defective radio he has bought. She advises him not to repeat the company's name in the text since he already used it on the letterhead. "Make it 'your company,'" she says. "Don't repeat the same information. People will be looking for that. And don't begin 'Dear Gentlemen:' Use 'Gentlemen:' or better yet, 'To whom it may concern:.' And mention that you're returning the defective radio with this letter."

She cannot quite believe that for a student who comprehended *Walden, Fences,* and *The Great Gatsby,* high school graduation may hinge on the difference between "Dear Gentlemen:" and "Gentlemen:." This is not teaching; this is teaching to the test. But there is no point sharing her distaste with See Wai. These tests are the law. She tells him to try writing the report. His eyes follow his capped pen across each line and slowly down the page. Jessica knits together her fingers and rests her chin upon them.

"This is a hard one," See Wai says.

"Are there any words you don't understand?"

"No. But the beginnings, right, they give me trouble."

Jessica reprises with See Wai the four-paragraph form that his reading teacher, Bob Dehler, has been recommending. He returns briefly to the paper, then looks again to Jessica. "The last RCT," he says, "the report it was on driver's license."

"Ah," Jessica says, smiling, "you're an expert on that." She pauses. "But they can give you a report on something you know nothing about."

"Nothing," See Wai echoes.

Before he finishes the draft, the bell rings for the ninth period. See

Wai must leave for his job at the Chinatown History Project. He returns the test booklet to Jessica, crosses out his half-done report, and throws away the wadded page.

"Time goes so fast," he says with concern.

"When you're having fun."

*   *   *

One morning Jessica sees a notice from Ben Dachs that all English teachers must submit their course preferences for next fall within five days. Any other year, she would simply write down journalism, humanities, and English 7 and think no more of it. This year, it means she must announce her resignation. Keeping a secret she can justify; deceiving her friend and mentor she cannot.

For an impetuous person, she plans with surpassing care. First she will tell Bruce, because whatever the condition of their friendship now, he is her oldest friend at Seward Park. Ben will come next, then Dr. Kriftcher. Between these farewells, she will recruit Mark Fischweicher to become the journalism teacher and *Seward World*'s adviser. She has sensed Mark's humanity since he apologized for not supporting her in the Teachers Choice debate; she has appreciated how much he stresses writing in his bilingual English classes, using Jessica's favorite tool of the journal; and she has considered him a political peer since she spotted a calendar from the group "Nebraska Cat Lovers Against Nuclear War" in his apartment. It is not in Jessica's power, of course, to hire and assign her replacement, and even in positioning Mark for the job before it is declared vacant, she risks running afoul of Dr. Kriftcher, Judy Goldman, or both. But this is not a matter of logic as much as of conscience. She is settling her estate.

The next Friday morning, Jessica finds Bruce in the social studies office, working on his campaign against Judy in the election for UFT chapter chairperson. With his back to her and the rexo machine whirling out a position paper aimed at secretaries and paraprofessionals, he does not see or hear Jessica's approach. She looks and thinks for a moment, and suddenly, her departure becomes a reality. Here is Bruce, backing up all his big talk, not only staying at Seward Park but trying in a direct way to improve things. Here is she, quitting. She winces with the irony. She sees scissors cutting cord.

"Bruce," she says finally, "can I talk to you?"

He turns to her, speaking excitedly about one particular secretary he had always disdained and Jessica had always liked. "I must tell you," he says, "your take on her was right."

Jessica cuts him short. They need to meet. "In private," she mouths, so the other teacher in the office, Maureen Lonergan, cannot hear.

They move to the humanities classroom. Bruce leans against the blackboard, his arms crossed just above the waist, one eyebrow lifted in inquiry. Jessica sits in a student's desk. Then she rises to open a window. Chilly as the morning is, the room feels furnace-hot.

"I just have to tell you," she sputters, "I'm leaving teaching."

She heaves a moist sigh. Bruce lowers his head to hers.

"Does it have anything to do with us not getting along?"

"No."

"I know we haven't been getting along these last few months."

She starts to sob. No, they haven't. And this is the first time she can recall Bruce saying a thing about it. And now it isn't even the point.

"I'm really tired. I work all the time. I have no life." She sucks in air, wipes a few tears. "And I just can't take it anymore."

Bruce moves from the board, one hand extended toward Jessica, the other twirling the tip of his beard.

"Aren't you confusing two things?" he asks.

"No."

She starts to cry again. She wishes she could stop, wishes she could prove to him how relieved she is with her choice.

"Have you thought of what you're going to do?"

"I think I really want to sell the book." They both know she means the oral history collection that in better times was to have been their joint project, their baby. "It means a lot to me."

Bruce wipes his forearm across his brow. Crescents of sweat dampen his shirt.

"Farther down the road," he says, "I hope that we can be friends. Keep up with each other. Despite what's happened between us."

"Yes."

Then they talk about the union election, about the enthusiasm for Bruce at the annex, about the teacher who told him, "I don't care who you are, if you're running against Judy, I'm voting for you." Then it is almost eight, and time to part for their separate classes.

"Come here," Bruce says, drawing Jessica into a hug. "I really love you, baby."

She cannot hug him back. She just cannot.

*   *   *

A weekend passes before Jessica regains nerve enough to tell Ben. He has seen her despondence of late and has often invited her to lunch at the Grand Street Dairy, their old haunt for cabbage soup and sympathy. When Jessica accepts the offer this particular Monday, Ben simply assumes that for once she has not filled her free period with student conferences.

"How're things going?" he asks as they descend the stairs.

"Well, I have something to tell you."

"Uh-oh," Ben says with mock gravity. "Sounds ominous. So lunch was just a subterfuge."

He laughs his full, lusty laugh as they cross the street. Inside the restaurant, Jessica searches for a secluded table in the back. All full. Ben chooses one beside the front window, usually favored by Chinese gangsters. *Why*, Jessica thinks, *couldn't they be here today?* If she cries, the whole world will see, and her eyes are tearing already.

"Well," Ben says amiably, "what do you have to tell me?"

"I'm leaving teaching."

There is a long, dead pall. Ben draws both hands through his hair and locks them behind his neck. He leans far back into his chair, until the two front legs lift off the floor. And then he stares, grasping for words.

"What? Why? I am totally stunned."

"I'm tired of working this way," Jessica says, appropriating a paper napkin as a tissue. "All I do is work. I have no life."

Her words leave Ben no room for appeal. If she had said the problem was her workload, he could have renewed the fight for a point-two or a separate class for advanced journalism. But this kind of unhappiness, something soul deep, even Ben cannot remedy.

"I can't believe it," he keeps repeating. "I can't believe it." He leans forward, dropping his elbows to the table and shaking his head. "There are so many people I could think of. But never you. Never you. I know you work too hard. But I never thought you would do this. So many people before you."

Jessica tells Ben now how close she came to leaving Seward Park two years ago for the Columbia journalism school.

"I didn't know," is all he can manage.

"Two years ago, I couldn't go," Jessica continues. "I still had too many feelings about Seward. But I have to do this. To survive."

Ben asks about her plans, and she tells him about the oral history book.

"What else?"

"I thought I'd try going back into journalism." She inhales heavily. "At the very least," she says, trying to sound casual, "I could fall back on my secretarial skills."

Ben's eyes glint in anger, and Jessica needs no explanation why. She always says there's nothing wrong with being a secretary, but how would she feel if one of her best students wanted to forgo college to become one? And that must be how she looks to Ben, all insecurity, just like the day she first met him. And hadn't she come farther than that? Hadn't she?

Carlos Pimentel and Sammy Martinez wander by the window and wave. As Jessica catches sight of them, Ben watches her overcast face burst into sunshine. She leaps from the table and runs outside to tell Carlos that she called the National Association of Hispanic Journalists earlier today and learned it has not yet chosen its award winners. So don't give up hope. *Don't give up now!*

When Jessica returns, Ben asks simply, "And what about the kids?"

She loses control all over again.

"It's gonna be hard," she finally says. "But I gotta do it."

*   *   *

The next morning, Jessica sits outside Dr. Kriftcher's office, awaiting her appointment. She is still feeling twinges from a chat twenty minutes earlier with Tommy Gjonaj, a student in English 7 and beginning journalism. When she had him the first term in the Lower East Side class, he disappointed her, cutting regularly to practice with his rock band. But lately, he has been dominating the discussion about *In Country* and today he told her he wanted to write an article "Inside *Seward World,*" so people would want to join the newspaper and take journalism. He already registered for next fall's advanced class, he added, just to have Jessica as his teacher again. She feels like a mother who set the table for dinner and then snuck out the back door with a packed suitcase.

Dr. Kriftcher sees the wet streaks across her cheeks when she enters his office. He reaches for tissues, the same box usually reserved for students having suspension hearings. Before he can speak, Jessica says, "I just want to tell you I'm leaving."

Slowly, Dr. Kriftcher settles into a chair at the head of his work table. Jessica takes a seat around the corner. The only sound is the faint squeak of a custodian cleaning the windows outdoors. No less emotional for having covered the same ground twice before, Jessica explains her reasons for leaving and enumerates her prospects for the future. When Dr. Kriftcher says he has a point-two for Jessica "on my long list of things to do," she tells him she did not come to bargain but only to say so long.

"Is this leaving as in quitting?" Dr. Kriftcher asks. "Or is it a leave of absence?" Before she can answer, he proceeds. "Why don't you take some time to think about what you really want to do? You feel so exhausted now."

"I want to be straight. As far as everyone here is concerned, I'm leaving for good. But if it's for the Board of Ed, then I'm asking for a leave. It's my understanding, though, there are only three reasons for a leave—medical, study, or teaching abroad."

"No," says the principal, with the cryptic smile he reserves for bending rules. "There's also 'adjustment of personal affairs' and that's up to me. And I'll sign it."

Dr. Kriftcher's self-interest in arranging a leave of absence is that he can reclaim Jessica for Seward Park if she reconsiders anytime until September 1989. Jessica's self-interest in accepting a leave is that she will be able to maintain her medical insurance as she begins a new, untethered existence.

"Obviously, you're going to be missed," he says. "There'll be a big hole. Especially for the kids."

That remark reminds Jessica that fourth period is near. She has to give a test in humanities. As she rises to leave, Dr. Kriftcher kisses her cheek. Then he pulls open his special drawer.

"And if you ever need a Kleenex. . . ."

*   *   *

The tribal drum beats.

Steve Anderson tells Rick Rowley, who says, "A real loss." Rick tells Denise Simone, who cries and writes Jessica a letter. Denise tells Hal Pockriss, who tracks down Jessica to make certain it's true. "God, I'm depressed," he says when she confirms the rumor. "I know it's a cliché, but it's like doing a play and everyone pulling together and then the play ends and everyone goes their way."

Mark Fischweicher asks Jessica if she can teach him about teaching journalism. Harriet Stein tells her, "Hearing this depresses me. Looking at you, I wonder what'll happen to me." Helen Cohen stops Jessica in the hall and begs her to drop *Seward World* or to teach less-demanding courses or do anything to stay. "Writing is the survival skill," Jessica answers. "I could stay if I was willing to give multiple-choice tests or not use the newspaper to teach writing. But I couldn't." As they speak, Dave Patterson arrives with a face knotted in concern. Like few others at Seward Park, he has known Jessica from her very first day as a paraprofessional. "What's this I hear about our girl?" he asks, tilting his head slightly. And when Jessica says he heard correctly, he can only moan, "Oh, now, Jessica. What're we gonna do?"

Word of her resignation spreads soon from those who know Jessica best to those who know her least, and see in her departure a reflection of their own bitterness. "Congratulations," one says. "Oh, you're so lucky," another adds. "You're smart to get out while you can," contributes a third. She cringes to think of her juniors, and all the other kids behind them, passing into hands so coarse and gnarled.

Within a few days, everyone in school knows Jessica is leaving. Everyone, that is, except her students.

18

Greatest Miss

Aɴɢᴇʟ Fᴜsᴛᴇʀ sᴛʀᴏʟʟs into the English office during the fifth period to talk money, and Jessica Siegel is only too eager to listen. Although she has assigned, read, edited, reread, and finally typed enough articles to fill a twenty-page issue of *Seward World,* which would be the largest ever, she holds not a cent toward its $2,500 cost. The November and January editions consumed $3,100, $100 more than her annual allocation from the school's Student Organization. The April newspaper, with a printing bill of $1,600, swallowed every dollar raised since September in advertising. Without a windfall, she will be lucky to produce the last *Seward World* of her career on a rexo.

Anticipating the current crisis, Jessica weeks ago started pressing her advanced journalism students to contact prospective advertisers, equipping them with lists of neighborhood businesses supplied by both Dr. Kriftcher and Loretta Sims. But Carlos Pimentel has rehearsals for *Bye, Bye Birdie* and Aracelis Collado works after school, and Gregg Gross and Lun Cheung are cutting so many classes they may not graduate, and Rosie Sanchez—introverted, reliable little Rosie, the editor-in-chief—is refused entry to school several times for wearing dresses that cover her as spottily as a fast paint job. Even when Jessica corrals the bunch of them during homeroom period, she cannot generate enough excitement to win one sale. She scripts a pitch, provides a telephone number, and eavesdrops as each utters the appeal with the energy of a narcoleptic. Their collective sloth makes her wonder if these seniors were so special, after all. Only Angel, the one who was supposed to be such a "get-over," only Angel shows a shred of responsibility.

They hunch now over the work table, two coroners examining a common corpse. Angel points out that the Senior Prom will be held June 10. Florists, formal-wear stores, and car services may all want to advertise. The only question, he concludes, is whether *Seward World* will appear before prom night.

"I don't know," Jessica says, "but I'm not above taking their money anyway."

"Some of me's been rubbing off on you," Angel says proudly.

"What about selling things in school?" Jessica asks. "Somebody's always selling something here. Candy bars. Pretzels. Flowers. What were those things Wilfredo was selling? Those salt-and-pepper things. What'd he call them? Condiment containers."

"Condom containers?"

"*Condiment,*" Jessica corrects. Then she waits and considers. "As long as your mind's on condoms, see if Planned Parenthood wants an ad."

Back on the subject of promotions, Jessica and Angel cannot settle on a product. And Jessica doubts the value of the Fuller Brush method even if they could. When *Seward World* tried T-shirts last year, the cheapest wholesaler was an hour away in Brooklyn; the arguments about color and design wore on for weeks; and even with Sammy Ryan selling sixty by himself, the effort brought in only $450. What's needed here is a quick killing, and it is when Angel jokes about running numbers that Jessica gets the brainstorm: *Seward World* will sponsor a raffle. Convince stores to donate prizes in exchange for free advertisements. Charge students and teachers a dollar a chance. There has to be $1,000 or $1,500 worth of curiosity afoot in Seward Park. Jessica and Angel make a date after school to dun the local merchants.

It looks like a bad day for charity on Essex Street. With the Williamsburg Bridge still closed, the shops are losing thousands of dollars a week, and beneath drizzly skies, what few buyers live within walking distance are staying dry inside their tenements and housing projects. Skirting purveyors of falafel and brisket and prayer shawls, Jessica and Angel step into an electronics store. It is run, like many on Essex Street, by a Hasidic Jew, a tall, balding man with just enough hair left for the sidelocks called *peyes.*

"Hi, I'm Jessica Siegel," she says, approaching the counter. "I'm the faculty adviser to *Seward World,* the school paper at Seward." She unfolds a copy atop the display case. "We were wondering if you could donate something for a raffle. We'll give you a free ad in return." He does not respond. "Two free ads."

"How many copies of that you print?" he asks, appraising *Seward World* as if it were written in Urdu or Tagalog.

"Four thousand."

The Hasid raises his eyebrows and his yarmulke slides a bit on his bare head.

"A raffle I can give you."

He lumbers into the storeroom and reemerges a moment later with dust on his shoulders and a set of socket wrenches in his hand.

"We thought maybe something like a Walkman," Jessica says, flipping a palm as if the idea had just occurred to her.

"This costs the same as a Walkman."

They thank him mildly and walk outside.

"Would you pay a dollar for a chance at that?" Angel asks.

"You need to have a car first. And nobody's gonna donate one of those."

The next stop is another electronics store run by another Hasid, a portly man with bushy gray hair, Frack to his predecessor's Frick. Jessica repeats her plea until the man slashes his hands through the air to halt her. "My question is," he announces, "do they read it?"

"It's the school paper," Jessica says huffily.

"But do kids read newspapers anymore?"

"This one." She folds her forearms. "Cover to cover."

"All right, all right," he says as if suddenly annoyed. "I give you a scientific calculator."

Jessica and Angel depart satisfied. A calculator has some appeal. And next door they have a third electronics store run by a third Hasid. They wait out two transactions in Yiddish before making their appeal and being offered their choice of stereo headphones or a white plastic Walkman, each worth thirty-five dollars. They select the Walkman as the sexier prize.

"We can say, 'State of the art,'" Angel says once outside. "And underneath in little letters, 'If the state's Ethiopia.'"

Their next destination is a video store operated by an Indian and two Chinese assistants. Its fare ranges from *Casablanca* to *Zombie Lake, Dragon Fist,* and *Pasión Prohibida.* The only customers are two boys in Seward Park gym T-shirts, evidently on a sabbatical.

The Indian resists Jessica's rap, claiming he has donated raffle prizes to *Seward World* before. Jessica informs him that *Seward World* has never *held* a raffle before. The Indian scowls. Angel points to the two class cutters. Obviously, the store does business with Seward Park students. The Indian nods faintly, not quite acceding but inviting further persuasion.

"How about a month's membership?" Jessica says, beginning the bargaining.

"A day."

"That's not worth very much," she says.

"How much is the ad worth?"

"Seventy-five dollars."

"Show me the size."

She does. He yawns.

"How about a gift certificate?" Angel puts in. "Fifty dollars."

"Five."

They compromise at twenty-five dollars and proceed down the street. Before they finish at the corner of East Broadway, they add an iron and a watch as prizes and give away enough advertisements to fill two or three full pages. Jessica remarks how easily the donations came. Seward Park still touches some sentiment in the neighborhood. "I'll bring my mother here at Christmas," Angel says, "and try this with her."

The next day, when Jessica asks Jules Levine for permission to hold the raffle, she learns that public schools cannot by law promote games of chance. So the whole afternoon with Angel was wasted, and she is no closer to the $2,500 price tag for *Seward World*—and actually farther away for the time squandered. Meanwhile articles keep arriving, many of them in the nature of personal farewells.

*   *   *

Lun Cheung
Journalism
Ms. Siegel

Graduation is always a time of happiness and a sense of fulfillment. It is that special time of the year when the graduates are relieved that everything is over with and are ready to step to the next plateau. Whether it be grammar school to junior high to high school or from there to college, the feeling is the same.

The road to the ultimate sense of achievement is too often a long and hard one. For many this never happens and dropping out is the solution. No one or at least not many drop out because they want to. Sometimes they just can't help it. For example many students have serious family problems. The next day is hard to face. This is not an excuse because I realize the students are mature enough to handle it.

Or you're a student who has a nine period day working after school. Straight after school you go to work until 11:00 P.M. You come home and realize there is a lot of homework to do. You just don't have enough strength left and you fall asleep. Before you realize it you're falling behind. The teachers get on your case. You want to explain to them but you are just too afraid because you think they feel you are just making excuses. And so the inevitable words come out, "Who cares, forget about it." How annoying it is when people tell you "Why don't you just quit your job." If you quit where will the money come from, who will pay the phone bill, sometimes who will pay the rent.

Do not take this as an excuse, instead as a better way to understand a student. A student feels lousy when a teacher embarasses a student by saying "Hey look who showed up" or "No, I don't believe you." Instead of facing up to the problem students take the easy way out.

There are some teachers who really care though, those teachers who believe in you and have complete faith. They are the ones who want to see you go to college and will help you to achieve those means. But there is that little feeling inside of you that you can't help but feel and your problems pile up and up. This is when the dilemma pops up because you just don't want to disappoint those teachers who have been pushing for you.

Still I strongly believe that the students really do realize the importance of education. Students are mature enough not to make excuses for their mistakes. They really do want to graduate and start on a new future!!!!

*   *   *

Jessica swore it would never come to this. But now it has. She is so desperate she has decided to hold a bake sale.

She will solicit contributions and assign work shifts in her journalism classes and set up shop during the four performances of *Bye, Bye Birdie,* which bows two days from now. She writes "Wed," "Thurs," "Fri," and "Sat" on the blackboard and calls for offers.

"Ketchup," says Lun Cheung.

"What about beer?" hollers Silvio Estrada, who has annoyed Jessica all term long.

"I'd suggest a kissing booth," says Tommy Gjonaj, "but you can't do that these days."

Lun raises his hand again. Jessica thinks he is finally getting serious.

"Alka-Seltzer."

"Pepto-Bismol," seconds Che Sidanius.

"Wilfredo," Jessica says. He just got into college. He owes her.

"I don't know."

"It doesn't have to be dessert," she coaxes.

"Toast."

"Folks," Jessica declares, and she surveys the room. Bodies lay sideways across desks. Sunglasses shield eyes. Sneakers jut into aisles. Room 336 resembles Orchard Beach, and it infuriates Jessica. Senioritis is senioritis, but she has just finished telling these kids that *Seward World,* which is *their* newspaper with *their* articles, cannot be published unless they *raise* the money. And they don't give a damn. She drops like lead into her seat. Maybe she shouldn't feel so guilty about leaving. Maybe all these years she's been fooling herself. *Seward World* has been nothing but the pilot light of her journalistic ambitions; she has been teaching others how to do the job she herself wants.

Nancy Caban raises her hand.

"Yes," Jessica says warily.

"I can bring cream puffs."

"Flan," Addie Severino says.

"I can get a cake for Wednesday or Thursday," Tommy adds.

Touching chalk to blackboard, Jessica commits him to both days.

"I'll get my mother to bake one day," he shrugs, "and my sister the other."

Still, all is chaos the morning the bake sale is to begin. Jessica has been awake since 3 A.M. producing cheesecakes, while her students bring barely enough sweets to cover a card table. She throws a twenty-dollar bill at one student with orders to empty Gertel's bakery and dispatches three others to the lobby to start selling before the *Bye Bye Birdie* matinee. Only moments later, they return to the classroom with word from Jules Levine that the bake sale cannot be held because Jessica did not submit the required form.

Then she remembers what she forgot. She had received a blank permission slip two days ago from Dr. Kriftcher's secretary, Ellen Silva, and in her cheesecake frenzy neglected to return it to the principal for his signature. She runs now to Jules Levine and pleads for a break, since this is only a matter of some donuts and cupcakes on a folding table, but he insists she must see Dr. Kriftcher, who is eating lunch. So she charges up five flights of stairs to the staff cafeteria, where he informs her today's bake sale cannot proceed because she contravened "procedures."

So she is out twenty dollars in cash, four cheesecakes, and five hours of sleep; the various desserts donated by her students are going stale; and *Seward World* is still broke. She has the permit signed in time to resurrect the final three days of the bake sale, but the take barely exceeds one hundred dollars. It would have been even lower had Norman Wong not appeared to play carnival barker. As Jessica counts the money, feeling crestfallen and mean, she hears from the auditorium one of *Bye, Bye Birdie*'s first songs.

> An English teacher!
> An English teacher!
> If only you'd been
> An English teacher!
>
> We'd have a little apartment in Queens,
> You'd get a summer vacation,
> And we would know what life
> means. . . .
>
> . . . An English teacher
> Is really someone.
> How proud I'd be
> If you had become one.

Whoever wrote that song, she thinks, didn't know shit.

*   *   *

Wilfredo Ayala
Journalism
Ms. Siegel

Seward Park High School has been graduating seniors for over 50 years. Now, once again Seward Park is ready to graduate the class of 1988.

Many seniors had misunderstandings about this school before they came here. Many seniors didn't want to come here. Now, although happy to leave, many seniors are finding it hard to say goodbye.

"When I was in junior high school I didn't want to come to this school," said Susan Diaz, an 18 year old senior. "I was really upset when I didn't make it into Stuyvesant. I was even more upset about the fact that I was heading toward Seward Park. I had heard rumors of a lot of drugs, a lot of fights, and a lot of muggings. When I got here, I was a little bit nervous because of that, until I found out that there was a good environment here, and the people welcomed you. It's funny because I didn't want to come here under any circumstances. Now, although I am happy to be graduating, I am going to miss this place a great deal."

While in junior high school, many students were led to believe that Seward Park was a bad school, one of the worst in the city. It wasn't until later on that they found out that it wasn't such a bad school, and that it is one of the best in the city.

"This school is not as bad as everyone says it is," says Gladys Franco, an 18 year old senior. "I have grown a lot in this school, it has become a second home to me. This is a place where you come to discover who you are. This is a place where you discover your goals and your abilities. Although I am relieved, and happy that I am graduating, I am going to miss this place a lot. The people, the teachers, and the activities. The people that say this school is bad are the people that don't go to the school, and know nothing about the school. I will always have a lot of memories of Seward Park H.S. and I thank the school for helping me to grow."

Although graduation is a time to rejoice, and celebrate, it is also a sad time. Many friends will be missed, and the environment and atmosphere that the seniors have been in for three years will no longer be.

"Seward Park High School has prepared me very well for the real world that I am now about to face," says Nancy Caban. "When I was in the COOP program in eleventh grade, it made me experience what life is like out there in the outside world. Now, I am taking a journalism course, which has taught me to be more open minded. Those are only two of the many courses that prepared me well to be a successful person. I am graduating now, and because of Seward Park I can walk down that long road ahead of me with confidence, and not be afraid. I know that whatever achievements I make, whatever road I go down on, and whatever path I take, it would lead me right back to the place that got me started on my journey, Seward Park High School. Thanks a lot."

Both the faculty and the seniors knew the day would come where they would have to say goodbye to each other, where the faculty would point down that long road of success and watch as the seniors walk away. . . .

. . . Clearly, some seniors will miss this place more than others. But, I think that on behalf of all the seniors, I for one would like to say thanks Seward Park High School. You have been good to us. The environment, atmosphere, students and faculty will be missed. 90% of all Seward Park High School graduates go to college. So Seward Park can rest assured that the 90% of the graduates that go on to college and even the 10% that don't will make Seward Park High School proud of its graduates. From all of the seniors, BYE!

*   *   *

Ben Dachs had advised Jessica not to let her students know she was resigning until June. She saw the logic in waiting, for with Gregg and Lun at risk of not graduating and dozens of others teetering between passing and failing her courses, she did not want her own departure to provide one more reason for their surrender. But events have overtaken her. Last Thursday, as she was helping Jessica clean up the day's bake sale, Daisy Severino asked if it was true that Jessica was leaving. The next day in the seventh-period journalism class, one of the advanced students, Mike Lagoa, blurted, "I heard you're not doing the paper next year." Jessica mumbled and fudged her way through both incidents, but she knew there would be more questions, harder to dodge. After all, she taught these kids how to interview.

So, on Monday morning May 23, Jessica summons her advanced journalism pupils. Just before the meeting, she conferred with Hal Pockriss, fretting about how much support students would need from her in the coming weeks, what with finals and Regents and RCTs. "Who're you kidding?" Hal chided. "You'll need *them.*"

Now, sitting at the work table in the English office, surrounded by her progeny, she realizes how right he was. The sun throws squares of light on the dull varnish, and a sultry wind shoots through the half-open window. From the classroom across the hall sounds the horse-track fanfare of a computer game. As Jessica gazes at the faces around the table, all the anger she has lately held drains away.

"I want to tell you that I'm leaving," Jessica says.

"Leaving Seward Park?" asks Angel Fuster, his voice rising.

"Yes."

"For another school?"

"No."

"Leaving forever?" Mike Lagoa asks delicately, expecting the worst.

"Maybe," Jessica says, her voice growing round with emotion. "Maybe."

She reaches for one tissue from the five open in her lap. Angel folds and unfolds a letter from the University of Vermont; he was all set to tell Jessica he was going there instead of New Paltz. Carlos rolls a *Seward World* advertising contract into a tube and presses an open end to his lips. Jeanette Rosado offers an unfocused smile. Mike Lagoa drums his fingers on his jeans. Her eyes moistening, Aracelis Collado lets her head fall against her shoulder. She thinks about how she first heard about Jessica from her brother Carlos, about how her sister Damaris was planning on taking journalism next fall, about how Jessica has always known when something was the matter with her.

"I wanted to tell you all," Jessica resumes, "because I didn't just want to disappear into the sunset. I didn't want to let you know too soon because there are some people—the people who aren't here—who are on the verge of not graduating. And I don't want to do one more thing to pull them down."

She explains that Mark Fischweicher will assume the journalism classes and the newspaper, since her students would want to know *Seward World* is being left in good hands. Then she mentions the oral history book and the possibility of reentering journalism. "Obviously, I'm really excited and happy about doing this," she stammers.

Tears race down her face and roll off her chin like a deluge down a storm sewer. She gropes for a second tissue, then a third. Her face glows crimson. She sits as if paralyzed. Confused and embarrassed to see their teacher crying, the students trade quizzical glances at each other and mouth the obvious question. *If you're so happy, how come you're crying so much?*

"Where you gonna stay?" Angel asks at last. "New York?"

"Yeah, in New York," she says. "I have to find an apartment. I have to ask you about your neighborhood." She laughs. "I don't think I'd drag it down too much."

Now everyone laughs, but only briefly.

"I'm just glad you're leaving after I had you," Angel says.

"Me, too," Aracelis adds.

There is a long silence.

"A lot of kids are gonna miss having you," Carlos says.

"I wish you could teach my little sister," Angel says.

"My little brother *and* sister," Carlos says, as if raising the bet.

The submarine siren announces the end of homeroom period.

Nobody moves or says much. Four minutes later, another siren marks the beginning of fourth period. Gradually, the students rise.

"So we gotta make it a really great issue," Angel announces to the rest.

"Wanna help me rob a bank?" Jessica says.

Over the next two days, Jessica breaks the word to all her classes, falling apart each time. In more restrained moments, she tells Sammy Ryan and Alex Iturralde, who are home from college and visiting Seward Park. Although she does not rob a bank, she does start selling classified advertisements, the brainchild of Tommy Gjonaj. And this time, dozens of students join the effort, bringing in such notices as "Jose Duran has a tremendous crush on Lisa Bello," "To the bitchest Gym class period 1," and "Will you marry me, Shelly?"

After Memorial Day, Jessica sends all the copy to Official Press to be set in type. The next weekend, she convenes her staff to lay out the twenty-page issue. Between the bake sale, the classifieds, and three pages worth of advertisements sold by herself and Angel, she counts less than five hundred dollars. She asks Mark Fischweicher if he would be willing to start the next school year with a newspaper two thousand dollars in debt, and remarkably he says yes. Now Jessica must hide the huge deficit from everybody else. She had managed such deception in the past, but that was for five hundred dollars, and that was before Harold Steinberg left Official Press with a broken hip, and that was when she was returning to Seward Park the next September.

*   *   *

Tommy Gjonaj
Journalism
Ms. Siegel

Journalism—newspapers, magazines, television, radio—it helps each and every one of us to understand the world and how different events and happenings affect and change our lives. If you don't believe that now, you will after you have taken journalism.

But what goes on in journalism class? A day usually starts off when one of the class puts a journal topic on the board. For example, "What do you think of the fact that many of President Reagan's decisions might have been influenced by an astrologer?" Sometimes a soothing hush comes over the classroom as the journalism class's heads are bowed down over their note books in deep concentration.

After the journals, Ms. Jessica Siegel, the journalism teacher, brings up possible articles, fundraising methods for the newspaper and reminds the students to get their pending articles in before the DEADLINE. . . .

. . . A number of students were asked why they liked journalism. "Class participation and the great ability to express yourself in writing, ideas and in speech," explained Ottavio Johnson. "I enjoy the class because there is a good amount of class participation and feedback." Rosa Jerez said she liked journalism because, "I like to interview people and get to know them." That's one of the great advantages of being in journalism—you get to meet very interesting people when you do your assignments.

Everything might sound clean as a whistle and real dandy but it isn't. The Student Organization gives *Seward World* approximately $3,000 for the production of the newspaper, but the money was used up a long time ago on the fat issues of the paper. Ms. Siegel and her students have kept *Seward World* alive. We've had to sell ads to different stores, had a bake sale and we've created and sold our own classified ads, all in order to bring this very interesting, exciting, overwhelmingly intelligent diary of events to you, oh great Seward Park High School student. . . .

. . . "Working for *Seward World* was the first time at Seward that I felt really important," said Lun Cheung. "I felt like I was a great part of this school. It made me realize as well as other people what my capabilities were as a writer."

Aracelis Collado agreed. "Once a teacher called me a 'star of the *Seward World*' right in front of a class of 30 as I was entering. It was embarrassing and I was speechless. I've always enjoyed expressing my feelings in writing and I thought taking the class would be exciting. I enjoy having no tests, and if you go on to advanced journalism, working on only one story a week." It's true, believe it or not, there aren't any tests in this class, but there are articles which you have to write, which are the most enjoyable part of the class.

Rosie Sanchez has been in journalism for a year and a half and is now editor in chief. "Being in journalism has encouraged me in a positive way and has made me strive to do better academically and socially. Ms. Siegel has expressed a genuine interest in me and has made me become aware of my own potential." Daisy Severino explained, "I get to express my feelings a lot and talk about things that I want to change and things I'm upset about."

There is a special quality of teaching and learning in journalism that is second to none at Seward. When a teacher is dedicated to a course, as Ms. Siegel is, then a student can't help but learn. The kids are as dedicated and they, each and every one of them, has their own special gift. Check out the other articles in this latest issue of *Seward World* and see if you agree.

*   *   *

On Monday morning June 7, Jessica carries the completed layouts for *Seward World* into the English office. From Gregg Gross on the civil rights movement to Daisy Severino on the Robert Chambers case, from Che Sidanius on pollution to Wilfredo Ayala on drug abuse, from Susan Diaz on abortion to Aracelis Collado on feminism to Carlos Pimentel on hope and despair in Manhattan Valley, all rounded out with nearly two pages of farewells to Seward Park, the final issue under Jessica's tutelage amounts to a kind of greatest hits album. The $2,000 debt, for a moment, falls from her thoughts.

Then she overhears Shawn Gerety confessing to Ben Dachs that *Folio,* the student literary magazine he advises, is $400 in the red. Ben lectures Shawn on fiscal responsibility and then requests a detailed explanation of how he could have exceeded a budget whose limits he had known for months. Jessica loses track of Shawn's answer, for she is thinking, *And he's only down a couple hundred dollars.* There will be no keeping her $2,000 secret, she realizes now.

"I gotta tell you something," she says to Ben after Shawn departs. "I hate to say this, but if you think Shawn's debt is bad, do you know how much we're in debt to Official Press for the paper?"

"Sit down," Ben says affably, "and tell me all about it."

"Two thousand dollars."

Ben, much to Jessica's shock, laughs. He laughs the way a drenched man laughs at a redundant downpour.

"How do you get me into pickles like this?"

His question is metaphysical, but her answer is earthbound. She describes all her misbegotten attempts at fund-raising—the raffle, the bake sale, the classifieds, the months of nagging students to sell display advertisements. Her sentences wind and snarl. Then she switches from logic to emotion, painting herself as the victim of a sudden calamity, rather than the engineer of her own petard.

"We're gonna have a twenty-page paper," she pleads. "Incredible articles. What're we supposed to do?" She grabs the sheath of dummies. She sees the greatest hits becoming her greatest miss. "You want me to throw this in the garbage?"

"I feel like there's a shotgun to my head," Ben says. "I just can't believe you did this to me. I've been back since February. Why wait until now to tell me?"

He censors himself from saying all else he feels—how negligent

Jessica has been, how irresponsible, how unfair to lay this catastrophe at his feet. Just because she knows he'll cover her ass. Just because he always has.

As Ben seethes, Jessica reddens. What could make her feel so weak with shame, with guilt? She is living her recurrent nightmare, the nightmare of awakening for the last day of school having forgotten to write her term paper, the nightmare of failing. *How can I be so stupid? How could I have let this happen?* And hiding the deficit from Ben was worse than forgetting, it was dissembling. Her failure was a failure of trust.

"So?" she finally asks Ben.

"It's too much for me to think about now."

Rick Rowley, who has been grading papers, crosses the room to Ben and Jessica.

"I couldn't help hearing," he says. They both regard him. "I just want to tell you." He rubs his mustache. "I'd, um, be willing to go class to class for you. Collecting money."

"Let's hope it doesn't come to that," Ben says, knitting together his fingers.

That afternoon, Ben calls on Dr. Kriftcher. He explains the situation, reminds the principal of their common admiration for *Seward World,* and asks if he can draw money from a special administrative fund. Jessica has already incurred a $1,000 bill for typesetting, Ben argues, so canceling the newspaper would still leave a deficit. And cutting the size of the paper to sixteen or twelve pages would save no more than $600. So isn't the least of all evils to pay and publish?

"The answer is no," Dr. Kriftcher tells Ben. "And you should know better than this. The money's for emergencies. Emergencies by definition couldn't have been foreseen. This could've. Why did you even bring me this thing? Deal with it yourself."

Ben does, by visiting Jack Lessner, the adviser to the student organization. The organization receives $9,600 annually from the Board of Education, and this year it raised another $13,000 through various sales, shows, and dances. Ben wants to know if there is anything left for *Seward World.* Jack says he is sorry, but the money is already spent, and besides, *Seward World* already got $3,000 this year from the student organization, more than any single team or club or activity.

"Jack," Ben says. "We've worked together for years. I've done you a thousand favors."

"I'll present it to the kids. We'll see."

The next day he informs Ben that *Seward World* can have $1,810. Although the student organization has indeed exhausted its budget for the current school year, it has a reserve account, accrued over fifty years and defended against Board of Education auditors. The $1,810 represents accumulated interest, interest reserved for emergencies. "It's a good thing the stage lights or sound board didn't blow out this year," Jack adds. "There'd be nothing left to give."

Armed with Jack's commitment, Ben returns to Dr. Kriftcher. For all the public abrasiveness of the principal, Ben knows, there is a private magnanimity and an appreciation of persistence. Dr. Kriftcher is like a basketball player who throws an elbow and only respects the opponent who answers in kind.

"I've got a different deal for you," Ben says.

This one Dr. Kriftcher accepts. He will provide $400 from an endowment created during Seward Park's fiftieth anniversary celebration and $100 from the administrative emergency fund, enough to complete Seward Park's version of the Chrysler bailout. The principal's largesse, however, comes with one contingency. From now on, *Seward World's* pursestrings will be held by Ben alone.

Jessica knows nothing of Ben's orchestrations, and she independently appears in Dr. Kriftcher's office, suffused with dread. The principal is famous among his faculty for his excoriations, and he has little reason to soften the lash for Jessica, who is leaving anyway. Instead she receives a desultory scolding and a rundown of the financial rescue package.

"It's all going to work out," he says. "You can thank Jack Lessner."

"God. Thanks. I can't believe it. I can't wait to tell the kids."

*   *   *

For the last time in Jessica's career, she waits in the Seward Park lobby for the white delivery van from Official Press. When it arrives, she helps the driver unload the bundles onto a dolly and then rolls the dolly into Room 128 to begin stuffing papers by the score into the mailbox of each homeroom teacher.

As always, Jessica pauses long enough to inspect a single copy, its crease crackling, its ink still drying. Everything looks perfect. Except for the box on the bottom of page 1. There wasn't supposed to be any box. She pulls the paper closer and reads the boldface print inside the border:

This issue is dedicated to Ms. Jessica Siegel, who is leaving Seward to pursue a career in journalism. For instilling in students a desire for excellence, a caring for others and for making "The Seward World" a better place, we all thank you.

So begins the end.

19

Part of Something

I N THE SIDE room of Puglia's in Little Italy, where she had watched Carlos Pimentel impress George Vecsey over spaghetti and cappuccino one January night, where she had joined in saluting Ben Dachs on his principalship at Beach Channel way back in September, it is now Jessica Siegel's time. On this torrid June afternoon, with the sky bleached white and the street tar softened to putty, Denise Simone has convened a farewell toast and roast. Around a long table, weighted with platters of pasta and bottles of homemade red wine, sit Ben, Denise, Emma Jon, Pat Ng, Shawn Gerety, Steve Anderson, Louise Grollman, Laura Ryan, Liz Rothberg, Jennifer Emmanuel, and Norman Wong. Dr. Kriftcher has already put in an appearance, Mark Fischweicher and Rick Rowley are in transit, Hal Pockriss has family obligations on Long Island, and Harriet Stein has sent regrets and a gift, for she has a graduate school class at Columbia. There has been no word from Bruce Baskind.

The narrow room, meant to evoke a taverna with its whitewashed walls and imitation trellis, is oddly dominated by a mural of mountains and parrots and orchids, altogether more Guatemalan than Sicilian, and rather akin to the print dress Jessica wears. For the moment, though, she remains only the nominal object of this gathering. The conversations wander from credit-card interest rates to the upcoming Mike Tyson–Michael Spinks fight to the correct way of indicating the possessive state in words ending in two s's, a topic Ben and Shawn address with great relish. "Don't you just love going out with English teachers?" Denise says to no one in particular.

A waitress appears asking, "Is there a Miss Siegel? We have a telephone call."

"Must be the printer with another bill," Ben says.

It is actually Rick Rowley reporting that he is stuck in traffic returning to Manhattan from his second job at a yeshiva in Brooklyn. Returning to the table, Jessica is followed by Mark Fischweicher.

"Am I late?" he asks.

"Not for dessert," Ben answers.

As the cheesecake, cannoli, and tortoni arrive, Denise commences her duties as emcee, standing beside Jessica at the center of the long table. Having begun to make the open-mike circuit as a stand-up comic, she savors this role. At least this crowd gets all her teacher jokes.

"Things are kinda quiet," she says, arching her back and tossing her curls in feigned petulance. "Whatsa matter, Ben? No more *grammar* to talk about?"

When the laughter subsides, she turns to her primary target. Privately, Denise composed a letter to Jessica when she first learned of her resignation. "The saying goes, 'Everyone is replacable,'" she wrote at one point. "Obviously, the person who coined this phrase never knew you." But for this occasion, Denise has only affectionate taunting.

"I've got to get back at Jessica Siegel for having to have my mailbox under hers for five and a half years," she says to raucous laughter. "She's got her bedroom furniture in there somewhere. But I know our insurance rates will go down now, because we won't have Jessica's bicycle to trip over. And we can get our work done in the morning, because all of her advanced journalism students won't be sitting in our laps."

"Some," Jessica interrupts. "I don't exactly get a full house."

"But we will miss the leftover banana bread," Denise resumes.

"Cranberry, too," Louise Grollman calls.

"And another thing about Jessica," Denise continues in her best Borscht Belt manner, "is some poor substitute won't have a job the day before marks are due." Jessica blushes fiercely, having thought that over all these years nobody had noticed the curious pattern of her sick days. "And when Jessica took over *Seward World,* she wanted to make it like the *New York Post.* Every cute guy on the faculty was in there. The whole paper was beefcake."

"It wasn't *my* idea," Jessica protests. "A couple of the girls came up with it."

"But seriously, Jessica," Denise concludes, "we will miss you brightening up our office. Speaking on behalf of everyone else, I can say that I shed a tear for Seward students, all of them. To see you go is so hard. And I just cry." She gathers herself. "But we should laugh, so the night doesn't end with crying."

The next satirist is Steve Anderson. He peers through horn-rimmed glasses at a lone index card, on which he has painstakingly printed his text in letters small enough for a newspaper column of stock prices. As if this script were not sufficiently precise, he has also underlined key words and phrases in red ink. Where Denise favors the wrecking ball, Steve prefers an X-acto knife.

"Leonardo with canvas, Michelangelo with marble, Paganini with violin, Callas with voice, Siegel with rexograph stencil," he intones with unwavering aridity. "She transformed what was originally the mere duplication of data into a transcendent art form of breathtaking originality."

Jessica nearly spits out her cannoli, she is laughing so helplessly. Steve must wait for applause to ebb before he can continue.

"Many mornings, as dawn broke over the projects on Avenue D and sunlight trickled through the lone window of Room 329, there you'd find Jessica toiling at her craft, turning out copy after purple-stained copy. Her fingertips were worn with the pressure exerted to create the perfect imprint; her hands were stained that color I think of as pedagogical lavender.

"In some dark, damp basement room in Seward Park High lies an old, sad, unused rexograph machine I think of as the Siegel Memorial. The earth turns, seasons turn, the Wheel of Fortune turns. But none of these turned like that old machine's roller as operated by Ms. Siegel. It was on that machine that Madame disclosed to me the secrets of her art: How to position the stencil; how to hold the can so the fluid passed correctly through the hose; and, when the stencil supply was decimated, how to steal extra ones from Loretta Sims's closet.

"Like any artist, La Siegel had detractors. Some said she rexoed too zealously. Some suggested that near the end, her style waned in the way Callas's last performances, though full of emotion, were lacking in technique. And certainly, when Teachers Choice came around, no one screamed louder for a Xerox machine."

Everybody bellows. Jessica's face falls to the table, landing between her coffee cup and a decanter of vinegar. Even her ears blush.

"Let's not consider the coda of her career, but rather the whole. At its least, a Siegel rexo was functional. But at its best, it had an ineffable beauty. I only hope that we who follow you in the art of rexography can become worthy of comparison with your *Pietà*, your *Gioconda*, your Sistine Chapel."

From around the table, others offer their homages. Laura Ryan, nearing the end of her second year, talks about Jessica as a role model. Shawn Gerety recalls Jessica's telling him when he first applied for a job that Seward Park was a good place to work. Liz Rothberg hails her as "one of the great mothers of Seward Park High School." Louise Grollman and Pat Ng both gag on tears early into their testimonials. Mark Fischweicher reads a poem about teaching that his wife, June, gave him years ago. Eventually, it is Emma Jon's turn to speak, Emma with whom Jessica had squabbled so often in the first term.

She starts by invoking the names of other colleagues who have left Seward Park, including Jessica's early patron Lanni Tama, and describing how each of them succeeded in their new lives because "they brought along the people they had become as teachers." Then Emma draws breath and addresses Jessica alone. "While we had different ideas about how to relate to kids," she says, "I always respected you. And I wish you good luck and much happiness."

Jessica's mouth goes dry, and her throat muscles thicken. She wishes she could reach to Emma and pull her close. Separated by a length of tabletop, she leans forward far enough to align her eyes with Emma's own and says, "That means a lot."

Ben stands now and his presence fills the room. He is someone of whom eloquence, wicked wit, and great heart are expected.

"I had a whole bunch of humorous things to say," he begins almost laconically, "but everybody said them."

"Try 'em again," Jessica calls. "I can take it."

"So instead I'll say some things that border on the maudlin and the syrupy." Ben pauses. "Seven years ago, I came to Seward. I met a lot of interesting people, and one of them ran up to me that first day, hair frazzled, yelling something about, 'Are you a good chairman? Will you teach me to teach?' She introduced herself as someone greatly in need, hopeful that I could show her some of the mechanics. And I have to admit I practiced a lot on her."

"Hmmm," Denise says.

"I watched her grow over the years, as a teacher and as a person. I came to count on her. And when someone says they learned everything she knows about teaching from you, it's hard to criticize her on the observation report.

"But I have to admit I learned a lot from watching her. I learned from Jessica what gifted teachers are like. I always had a sense of what a master teacher was like. Jessica showed me. You don't have to be a person who plans lessons perfectly. As I discovered." He is interrupted by laughter, loudest from Jessica. "You don't have to give homework every night. As I discovered." Again. "You don't have to be organized. As I discovered." A third time. "What you do have to have—and it's indispensable—is the ability to show your caring to the kids in your charge. And Jessica gave herself to her kids. To the point where some of the vermin of the school became some of the brightest lights.

"All of us have a teacher like that in our past. Jessica's legacy to us is that she has hundreds of kids who will look to her as the great teacher in their life." Looming above Jessica, he now casts his eyes down toward her. "What you came by naturally is something the rest of us had to work at. Please come by to visit us. And to save us."

Ben kisses Jessica and hands her a bouquet. Someone passes forward Harriet's present, a bracelet from Nepal. Mark hands Jessica a laminated copy of the poem he had read; it is, she realizes, the very copy June had given him and he had carried in his wallet. She reads it to herself.

> When I grow tired of my students, as I always do—
> staring at their faces till my eye sockets burn,
> I remember one girl told me
> how she followed a boyfriend home—
> found him in tears—
> He rocked on the bed,
> screamed at her to *Get away*.
> So she turned off his light
> and closed the door,
> and sat on his floor till morning.
>
> When I think of this girl speaking
> in her gentle voice with its rough edges

I think how teaching is like crouching sleepless
in a darkened room refusing to get up
knowing nothing will come of this,
—or only a story, maybe.

Then Denise rises and by way of introducing the major present of
the evening indeed tells a story. She and Jessica were watching a
basketball game, maybe it was Seward Park against Queens Vocational, and talking about what kind of kid they most liked to teach.
And they spotted this one boy on the Queens team, his face a mixture
of false bluster and devilish merriment, his gait a sequence of long
strides and hip hesitations, ending in shots that were stylish if not
always successful. *Oh, yeah,* they agreed, *he's the kind who slouches
down the hall with a baseball cap worn backwards and a letter jacket
hanging off his elbows. He's the kind who's a wise-ass; he's the kind
who's fun.* Her preamble completed, Denise hands Jessica a small box.
Jessica opens it to find a teddy bear, the bear being Seward Park's
mascot, attired in a tiny letter jacket sewn by Pat Ng. Pinned to the
bear is a card signed by dozens of faculty members, entitling Jessica to
an official Seward Park letter jacket, which will have her name and
"Seward World" stitched on the front. The one catch is she must come
back to Seward Park next fall, at least for a day, to collect it.

"I guess I have to say something," Jessica offers as she struggles to
her feet, her hair askew and cheeks red from so many bouts of
laughter. "The last time I did this, I fell apart." Breath ripples in her
chest. The playful syncopations of a tarantella can be heard from the
next room. "It's strange when people come up to you and say, 'Congratulations, you're leaving, you're escaping.' There are a whole lot of
ways I feel that this job is overwhelming. But I certainly don't feel like
I'm escaping. I learned a tremendous amount from my students and
from the people I worked with. It had an enormous effect on my life.
And what I'm doing now is a continuation. I don't want to cut off. I
don't want to even read this stuff until I get home, because I'd be too
embarrassed."

She laughs and fingers the farewell card.

"I feel like laughing and crying. I feel excited and sad. I'm gonna see
you all and come and visit and pick up my letter jacket so I can walk
down the hall and. . . ." Her composure dissolves. She cradles the
bear in her palms. She stares at it for a long moment before she can
face her friends again. "So thank you."

Everybody applauds, and when they cease, they leave their eyes expectantly on Jessica.

"Do I have to say any more?" she asks.

"Just bake a cake for tomorrow," Ben says.

"You never know."

*   *   *

On a Sunday afternoon shortly before graduation, Bernandita Pimentel receives a telephone call. A woman from the National Association of Hispanic Journalists is looking for Carlos. Bernandita explains that he is in Central Park with his girlfriend, and the woman leaves a number in Arizona and a message to call it tomorrow.

Carlos finds Jessica at nine-thirty on Monday morning. It is only seven-thirty in Arizona, too early for an office to be open, but Jessica cannot bear waiting another hour or two to learn if Carlos has received one of the association's scholarships. After all, she has been calling for two months and getting a full spectrum of evasive utterances, only driving her to a higher plane of harassment.

Now she ushers Carlos into Loretta Sims's office and dials the association's office in Washington, D.C. She asks for the same woman she has bothered every other week since Easter, and this time what she hears is anything but evasive. Carlos has been awarded a $500 scholarship. The only other winner is a sophomore at the University of Texas. Normally, the woman tells Jessica, high school students are not even considered for the scholarship, but Carlos's portfolio, including his *Seward World* articles on military recruiting and the elusive dream of a professional sports career, was too outstanding to go unrewarded. "We couldn't *not* give it to him," she says, "because of his writing and his passion."

Jessica passes Carlos the receiver so he can hear for himself. When he hangs up, she hugs him. "That's why I kept nagging them," she says. "I never lost faith."

*   *   *

On the final day of classes, Jessica leaves the Grand Street Dairy, heading back into school for the sixth-period journalism class. As she enters the first floor hallway, she encounters Susan Diaz and Rosie Sanchez, who spin on their heels and race upstairs. Jessica slowly climbs after them, until she is halted by Carlos Pimentel, who insists she sign his yearbook.

"Right now?" she asks.

"Right now," he says.

Five minutes of encomia later, Jessica ascends to the third floor, enters Room 336, and is all but knocked horizontal by a tsunami of "Surprise!!!" She sees dozens of students clapping. She sees atop her desk cake, cookies, donuts, and soda for the multitudes. She sees on the blackboard a chalk drawing of a quill and scroll, the emblems of the journalist's trade, and beside it a voluptuous valentine inscribed with the words, "Seward World Loves Ms. Siegel."

Before she can speak, Carlos steps forward and says, "We wanna give you this because we love you and we'll miss you." He presents her with a plaque with a carved wood figure of a winged woman holding aloft a wreath. Unknown to Jessica, Carlos had been collecting money from classmates for weeks, and traveling from the Lower East Side to Harlem in search of an appropriate gift. Now Jessica realizes where he was when he was supposed to have been out selling advertisements.

As the other students draw around him, Carlos reads aloud the dedication:

Presented to
Ms. Jessica Siegel
For Contributing A Part of Her Life
To Us And for Caring
And Her Love
From
Seward Park Students
1988

First comes applause, then barks of "Speech! speech! speech!"

"Well, I'm surprised," Jessica says, raking her fingers through her curls. "I'm moved and impressed." She halts. "You all saw me cry a couple of times already." She speaks to herself now. "Um, try to be articulate here." She inhales, starts anew. "Obviously, I'm going to miss you all. I'm just glad so many of you are graduating. And I want to keep up with you. I'm not dying. I'm not leaving town. I'm not going to California. So it's not the end of anything."

She tilts her head back and thin streams roll down her cheeks.

"To say I've learned a lot from all of you puts it mildly. Even though you're supposed to be in school to grow, I feel I've grown a lot being your teacher." The stream becomes a river. "So instead of crying anymore, I'll cut the cake. How about that?"

Even after she finishes slicing, she cannot move from the desk, as students surge toward her, yearbooks in hand. She signs for See Wai, Daisy, Rosie, Aracelis, Angel, Wilfredo, and many more. She writes each message deliberately, filling the odd spaces between the triangles and trapezoids of others' comments. Her students wait with great patience, fanning themselves with notebooks and open palms.

Janice Roldán, a junior who helped plan the party, clears the food off one corner of the desk, and there she places two farewell cards that have been passed from student to student for days. One card shows the cartoon cat Garfield reclining on the sand, a line of turquoise surf behind him. He says, "I am seriously considering pursuing a career on the beach." The other card, drawn by Janice, resembles a diploma.

SUPER * STAR
TEACHER
AWARDED TO: Ms. Siegel
Seward World Loves you
and we will miss you.

The party flows into the seventh period, bringing Ottavio and Lun and other favorites, and subsides only halfway through the eighth period, as students head for jobs or ballgames or study sessions for the Regents and RCTs. Left alone, a hot breeze swirling through the room, Jessica begins to read the two cards. There are scribblings on the front and back, crammed in corners and pressed along sides, abutting each other like chunks in a stone fence.

"Thanks for everything you have done for me," writes Wilfredo. "Without your help, support & love I don't think I would have made it through my senior year in the position I am in. You believed in me when I didn't and I am going to miss you alot."

From Tommy Gjonaj: "You've taught me so much in such little time, I truly regret parting. You're the only teacher who has given me hope. If I ever shed a tear, it'll contain millions of atoms of profound feelings for you."

From See Wai: "One of my Greatest teacher I ever had! I miss you very much. Wish you happy forever."

From Carlos: "I love you, I love you, I love you. When you need me, just look for me. When you're lost just keep looking up at the sky and you will find me. I will try to win. If I don't win in the future, I will be brave in the attempt. This I learned from you."

Jessica also opens two gifts. One, from Rosie Sanchez, is a ceramic sculpture of Buddha surrounded by disciples. Rosie's card is a photo-graph of herself holding *The New York Times*, a larger version of which will be hung on the Wall of Fame in acknowledgment of her term as editor-in-chief. "To the best teacher in the world," it says on the back. The second present, from Aracelis, consists of an embroi-dered T-shirt and two matching belts. Her card has a painting of three orange chrysanthemums flanked by irises. Aracelis wrote carefully, not letting ink cross the flowers.

> Saying goodbye is a hard thing to do, especially when it's someone like you. May all your future plans be granted. Ms. Siegel, not only do I say good-bye, but more important I say THANKS! I thank you for being such a great teacher and friend. You were the only teacher who cared, listened & understood. For example, that time when I was going through a struggle and gave up, you cared to ask me what was wrong. Not only did you ask, but you gave me a chance. For this and much more, I thank you. I know that I haven't been the perfect student, but I want you to know that you were my perfect teacher.

That evening, Jessica sits in her apartment and writes homemade cards to her advanced journalism students. The air conditioner wheezes fecklessly against the heat. Marmalade pants. Dusk topples from the sky into the concrete courtyard. Just days short of one year ago, Jessica had looked at a pile of those cards and said, "I used to be an artistic person. In a past life. That's what I yearn for. That and a few other things." Soon she will have the time. Soon she will have a new life, or at least a different one. Yet all she can think about is the past, and not the yearnings denied but the yearnings fulfilled. So she writes for the last time.

To Carlos: "Having read your articles in the newspaper, your autobiographical essays and speaking to you, it's clear you have an understanding of all the people and experiences that helped to con-tribute to whom you are today. I'm glad to have added a little piece to that or perhaps to have pushed what was there further along. Yet when I look at you, it's clear to me that no one can ever really understand how the pieces fall together in a particular person, what gives certain people a spark. I'm glad I got to be your teacher . . . and I will look for you in the sky."

To Angel: "Thinking of you will always bring a smile to my face. Not just for your sense of humor and wit, which will break me up, even if I'm bummed out, but especially for the way you surprise me with the depth of your intellect & sensitivity of your mind and your feelings. As much as I think I know you, you always surprise me and I can only laugh at my own surprise. . . . Angel, because of the depth of your understanding of the world, you know what you may encounter up at Vermont—a taste of which you got at Friends Academy. You can deal with it, Angel—in the mature, intelligent way you've learned to do. You know some of the reality out there—never doubt yourself. You've come far enough & know yourself well enough not to."

To Aracelis: "I've been really moved by some of the things you've written to me. I guess teachers are never sure if they really have had an impact on students. I guess with more needy students you are more sure; with ones with tremendous resources on their own less so. Thanks for communicating your feelings to me. It means a lot to me. It makes leaving both harder & easier. Harder, of course, because of what & who you are saying goodbye to, but easier in a sense that for the time I've been here I have had some impact."

*   *   *

See Wai arrives in the English office at 9:03 A.M. on June 17, fifty-seven minutes before the RCT in writing begins. A weeklong hot spell broke overnight, and he wears a sweatshirt with the words, "The Winning Edge." He must triumph on the RCT or he will not be permitted to graduate next week or start college in September.

"I have a feeling, See Wai," Jessica says. "At least an eighty!"

"I'm still worry about beginning the report."

"Make a list before you start," she says. "And read everything over. Revise. Use all the time."

He is worried, however, about more than he revealed. Last night, See Wai and a friend were coming home from fishing at Rockaway. They stopped at a Chinese take-out place in Flushing, and See Wai went inside to order. As he stood at the counter, he heard what sounded like firecrackers, followed by plate glass shattering and people screaming. Then came another burst of firecrackers. A wall telephone, a foot from See Wai's head, exploded into pieces. The firecrackers, he knew now, had been bullets. When he turned, he saw a man supine on the sidewalk, blood pulsing from holes in his back. A gang hit, someone said.

Still rattled after a sleepless night, See Wai must now focus his thoughts on the three components of the RCT—a letter seeking the replacement of a pair of defective gloves, a composition about improving physical education courses, and a report written as an article for the school newspaper. He reads the test booklet closely. He revises his answers often. He works so slowly all the students but one finish before him.

The minute he leaves, he searches for Jessica and, finding her, pours out his worries. Did he get the address correct on the letter? Is self-defense good for physical education? Was it a good idea to write the newspaper article about himself? Jessica can hardly tell without seeing the completed test, but she says, "I know it'll be an eighty. I have faith."

That afternoon, when the English teachers convene to grade the RCTs, she locates See Wai's paper. His score on all three sections totals 195. His average, then, is 65. He cannot afford to lose a single point when the tests are checked by state officials—and he lost 15 when he took the RCT in January.

As far as Seward Park is concerned, if See Wai is "reversed," he can still walk through the graduation ceremony with the gown he has already rented; there would be no point in compounding the boy's shame. But See Wai would know that the whole exercise had been a fraud; it would feel like that day in China when he came home crying because he had failed first grade and thought he would end up a beggar.

The RCT tests do not return from Albany for six days, until the afternoon before graduation. And it is not until the next morning, on the sidewalk outside the Hunter College auditorium, that Jessica locates See Wai to tell him that he passed. He shoves a clenched fist into the air and shouts, "Now I graduate one hundred percent!"

*   *   *

The commencement exercises for the Seward Park High School Class of 1988 are held on Thursday, June 24.

Angel Fuster arrives late with a graduation gown that has been masticated by his pet hamster. Carlos Pimentel and Daisy Severino both address the audience as representatives of the graduating seniors. Among the students from Jessica's flock who receive awards are Angel, Carlos, Daisy, Wilfredo Ayala, Nancy Caban, Aracelis Collado, Helen Moy, See Wai Mui, Susan Diaz, Rosie Sanchez, Jose Santiago, and Addie Severino. The faculty marshals, two men and two women chosen by student ballot, are Steve Barry, Peggy Breen, Louise Grollman, and John McNamara. Her bobby pins dispensed and her tissues just opened, Jessica watches the ceremony from the next-to-the-last row. After the recessional, she walks into the brilliant June morning to take some pictures and pose for many others. She introduces herself to Gregg Gross's mother, a frequent ally by telephone, and they immediately hug. In the end, he managed to graduate, as did his partner in brinksmanship, Lun Cheung.

But nearly 40 percent of those who entered Seward Park as freshmen back in September 1984 did not. Some fell behind, some transferred, some dropped out, and some vanished. One of the absent is Elvin Foster. One of them is Ruby Mayes. One of them, most tragic of all to Jessica, is Mary Tam.

Three days remain in the school year, and nothing stops on Jessica's behalf. Bruce Baskind commences his term as chapter chairperson of the United Federation of Teachers, having vanquished Judy Goldman by 160 to 68 in the election. Laura Ryan asks Jessica if she can borrow her lesson plans for *In Country*. Dr. Kriftcher interviews candidates for teaching positions, including one immigrant from Yugoslavia and another from Malaysia. Ben Dachs posts the fall English Department schedule. The alphabetized roster skips from "Schwartz" to "Simone." Beside Mark Fischweicher's name is the code "EJR01"— beginning journalism.

Jessica feels a twinge, but not a big one. She never wanted to be the solitary heroine; she never wanted to be the last of the just. She only wanted to be part of something.

October 8, 1987
Dear Gloryia,

If you look at the signature, I'm sure you will be more than a little surprised. We haven't been in touch for so long, this must feel like a blast from the past.

I can't remember the last time we were in contact but for the last 9 years, I have been working at a high school on the Lower East Side of Manhattan—yes, a high school teacher, hard to believe. Seward Park High School, where I work, has a long tradition of serving what has traditionally been one of the poorest communities in New York City, as well (at least for me) one of the most interesting.

It was a long road to me becoming a teacher. I worked for a small independent news service for four years, had various administrative assistant-cum-secretary jobs, ending up at an organization which ran group homes for adolescents where I decided I really liked teenagers. From there I went to Seward Park where I have been all this time.

What do I teach? Yes, English of course. I currently teach (have done so for a while) American Literature, Journalism (I'm the faculty advisor of the newspaper, which I'm proud to say has won some national journalism awards) and an interdisciplinary course I designed and teach with a history teacher on the history and literature of the Lower East Side. The last two courses, as you can well imagine, I've put a tremendous amount of work into and mean a lot to me. Most of the time it's worth it because of the kids. I'm constantly amazed by the young people who, despite so many things going against them, manage to surprise me with their intelligence, perceptions, sensitivity and strength.

Though I've often thought about you in the past, especially since I've ended up in your profession, I've thought of you even more recently since I've been thinking about some of the significant influences on my life. God, I know that sounds ominous, but in fact it is quite the opposite.

Sometimes I think the memories of my high school years are rather dim, probably because of all the family illnesses that were going on at the same time. But standing out in the blur is the year I spent in your class and the friendship which followed, which broadened my horizons and encouraged me to think and reach for the sky. Sometimes I step back from the kids I have developed relationships with and think about how you performed that role for me over 20 years ago in New Milford, New Jersey.

I'd love to get back in touch and possibly come down to Washington for a day so we can renew our friendship and talk over old times. How are John and Libertie? She must be out of college and in the work world. Are you still teaching? Drop me a note, along with your phone number.

Sincerely,
Jessica Siegel

Oct. 12, 1987
Sweetest and Dearest Jessica,

How can I ever thank you for your Lovely letter!!! I can't tell you how very deeply I appreciated it. For the most part, a teacher certainly senses but seldom knows the long term effects she has on her students. Then comes that shining, glorious glimpse of a former student and she knows that her work has taken root and continues on—perhaps into eternity. . . . You were Special at 15. You are far more Special now!!! . . .

I was teaching part time at Montgomery College for several years but am now teaching full time at a small private school only 2 blocks from my home. I am as enthusiastic as ever! (one of my 1st objectives was to undo the prejudice many of these kids have against public school kids). . . . Liberty is getting her Masters at U. Penn. She too is considering teaching. (Lord knows, the world needs us!!!). . . .

How is Norm? Ma? Pa?

I would be so very delighted to see you. Do come for a visit! — We've plenty of room. Jonathan & I are looking forward to it!

Hugs & Kisses,
Gloryia Okulski

P.S. I still talk about you whenever a kid is a Sherlock Holmes fanatic.
P.S.S. I hope someday you get a letter from a student like the one you sent me. It will bring tears to your eyes & gladden your heart. . . .

Afterword

As of this writing, nearly sixteen months have passed since the Class of 1988 graduated from Seward Park High School.

Among Jessica Siegel's students, Angel Fuster is a sophomore at the University of Vermont, Aracelis Collado and See Wai Mui are sophomores at the State University of New York at New Paltz, and Carlos Pimentel, Wilfredo Ayala, and Susan Diaz are sophomores at the State University of New York at Binghamton. Sammy Ryan and Vinnie Mickles are both juniors at New Paltz.

Gregg Gross, who has been working as a mail sorter, will begin attending Borough of Manhattan Community College in the spring term. Rosie Sanchez and Lun Cheung, both of whom deferred college admission for a term, are second-semester freshmen at Fashion Institute of Technology and Brooklyn College, respectively. Ottavio Johnson, who studied last year at New York City Technical College, is attempting to transfer to either Howard University or Morgan State. Daisy Severino goes to Hunter College, and her sister Addie Severino goes to Kingsborough Community College. Raquel Tamares and Lisa Carerra both attend LaGuardia Community College. José Santiago manages a pharmacy.

Mary Tam graduated from Seward Park after the 1989 summer session. She is working in a bookstore.

Shortly after the 1987–88 school year ended, Noel N. Kriftcher was appointed superintendent of high schools for Staten Island and part of

Brooklyn. During the search for a permanent successor, Helen Cohen served as interim acting principal. She has returned now to the position of assistant principal for guidance services, making room for Jules Levine to become principal of Seward Park. Ben Dachs, treated so unfairly in his tryout as principal of Beach Channel High School in Queens, got another chance at leading a high school, and is now in his second year as principal of Wingate High School in Brooklyn. In September 1988, Emma Jon was named English Department chair at Seward Park. John McNamara, appointed social studies chairman at Brooklyn's Edward R. Murrow High School in September 1988, was finally able to resign from the Chrystopoulos Citadel.

Dave Patterson, now in his third decade at Seward Park, received a telephone call from Darnell Reese in late 1988, more than a year since he had last seen him. The boy told Dave he was on probation from a burglary conviction and anxious to enter a vocational school. Dave promised to help, but he never heard from Darnell again.

Bruce Baskind, Denise Simone, Harriet Stein, Hal Pockriss, Mark Fischweicher, Steve Anderson, Louise Grollman, Shawn Gerety, Pat Ng, and many other teachers, counselors, and administrators remain at Seward Park, continuing to defy all expectations by sending 90 percent of each graduating class on to further education, carrying with them more than $100,000 worth of scholarships and grants.

As for Jessica Siegel, she has written free-lance articles for the *Village Voice* and *Columbia Journalism Review* and serves as coordinator for ArtsConnection's Young Talent Journalism Program, which aims to enrich the quality of high school journalism in New York City's public schools by bringing professional journalists into partnership with teachers and students. From time to time, Jessica still teaches a lesson.

S. G. F.
October 17, 1989

Bibliography

Abdur-Rahman, Amina. "Lost in the Labyrinth: New York City High School Admissions." New York: Educational Priorities Panel, May 1985.

Anson, Robert Sam. *Best Intentions: The Education and Killing of Edmund Perry.* New York: Random House, 1987.

Asbury, Herbert. *The Gangs of New York.* New York: Alfred A. Knopf, 1927.

Barron, James. "Bronx Kindergartner Shows Up With Loaded Gun." *New York Times,* January 12, 1989, B3.

Baskind, Bruce, and Siegel, Jessica, eds. "Our Lives, Our Stories, Our Neighborhood." Typescript.

"Beach Channel HS Chapter Seeks Voice in Selection of School's New Principal." *New York Teacher,* February 1, 1988, 11A.

Bell, Teresa. Unpublished study of Chinese garment workers (untitled). New York: New York Chinatown History Project, 1987.

Berger, Joseph. "Educators Call Bennett Too Negative." *New York Times,* April 26, 1988, A23.

Bernstein, Nina. "DAs, Inspector General Widen Probe Into School Districts." *New York Newsday,* November 29, 1988, 3.

Berube, Maurice B., and Gittell, Marilyn, eds. *Confrontation at Ocean Hill–Brownsville.* New York: Praeger, 1969.

Bettmann, Otto L. *The Good Old Days—They Were Terrible!* New York: Random House, 1974.

Birmingham, Stephen. *The Rest of Us: The Rise of America's Eastern European Jews.* Boston: Little, Brown, & Co., 1984.

Black, Jan Knippers. *The Dominican Republic: Politics and Development in an Unsovereign State.* Boston: Allen & Unwin, 1986.

Blair, Jill F., and Amlung, Susan. "First Steps Toward Fairness: High School Funding, 1985–86." New York: Educational Priorities Panel, March 1986.

Bluestone, Barry, and Harrison, Bennett. *The Deindustrialization of America: Plant Closings, Community Abandonment, and the Dismantling of Basic Industry.* New York: Basic Books, 1982.

Bogen, Elizabeth. *Immigration in New York.* New York: Praeger, 1987.

Boyer, Ernest L. *High School: A Report on Secondary Education in America.* New York: Harper & Row, 1983.

Brand, David. "The New Whiz Kids." *Time,* August 31, 1987, 42–51.

Breslin, Susan, and Stier, Eleanor. "Promoting Poverty: The Shift of Resources Away from Low-Income New York City School Districts." New York: Community Service Society of New York, July 1987.

Brown, Ezra. "Getting Tough: New Jersey Principal Joe Clark Kicks up a Storm about Discipline in City Schools." *Time,* February 1, 1988, 52–58.

Brumberg, Stephan F. *Going to America, Going to School.* New York: Praeger, 1986.

Butterfield, Fox. "Year of Snake Marks Decade of Change in Chinatown." *New York Times,* February 8, 1989, B1.

Carter, Barbara. *Parents, Pickets and Power.* New York: Citation, 1971.

Chan, Anita, Madsen, Richard, and Unger, Jonathan. *Chen Village: The Recent History of a Peasant Community in Mao's China.* Berkeley: University of California Press, 1984.

Chavez, Lydia. "New York City Schools Lose Fast Way to Hire Teachers." *New York Times,* March 3, 1988, B4.

Chin, Ko-lin. "Chinese Triad Societies, Tongs, Organized Crime and Street Gangs in Asia and the United States." Unpublished Ph.D. dissertation. The University of Pennsylvania, 1986.

"Comparative Analysis of the Organization of High Schools." New York: New York City Board of Education, Office of High School Allocation, Management & Planning, 1988.

Cremin, Lawrence A. *American Education: The Metropolitan Experience 1876–1980.* New York: Harper & Row, 1988.

Daley, Suzanne. " 'Couch People': Hidden Homeless Grow." *New York Times,* June 17, 1987, B1.

———. "Leaving a Welfare Hotel, Reluctantly." *New York Times,* September 14, 1988, B1.

———. "New York Schools Faulted on Teacher Recruitment." *New York Times,* July 10, 1988, 26.

———. "On the Road Back: Alvarado Vitalizing a School District." *New York Times,* July 18, 1988, B1.

———. "The Ruin of a New York–Owned Building." *New York Times,* February 8, 1988, B1.

Dickens, Charles. *American Notes.* New York: St. Martin's Press, 1985.

Eberhard, Wolfram, ed. *Folktales of China.* Chicago: University of Chicago Press, 1965.

Edsall, Thomas Byrne. "The Return of Inequality." *Atlantic Monthly,* June 1988, 86–90.

Falletta, John. "Ranking of Schools by Reading Achievement, 1987." New York: New York City Board of Education, Office of Educational Assessment, January 1988.

Feingold, Harry L. *Zion in America: The Jewish Experience from Colonial Times to the Present.* New York: Hippocrene, 1974.

Ferretti, Fred. *The Year the Big Apple Went Bust.* New York: G. P. Putnam's Sons, 1976.

Fessler, Loren W., ed. *Chinese in America: Stereotyped Past, Changing Present.* New York: Vantage Press, 1983.

Finder, Alan. "Apartments Left Vacant As Shelters Fill." *New York Times,* March 16, 1988, B1.

———. "Dreyfus Seen Likely to Quit New York City." *New York Times,* September 30, 1987, B1.

Fishman, Katharine. "American High." *New York,* March 2, 1987, 78–94.

Fiske, Edward B. "Report Warns School Reforms May Fall Short." *New York Times,* August 24, 1987, A1.

Fitzgerald, F. Scott. *The Great Gatsby.* New York: Charles Scribner's Sons, 1925.

Foner, Nancy, ed. *New Immigrants in New York.* New York: Columbia University Press, 1987.

Freedman, Samuel G. "Bridgeport Fights Order to Educate 2 Expellees." *New York Times,* June 17, 1982, B1.

———. "Dist. 200 Given a C by Some." *Suburban Trib,* May 12, 1980, 1.

———. "Immigrants and Industry: Old Formula Reviving a Mill Town." *New York Times,* June 2, 1986, B1.

———. "The New New Yorkers." *New York Times Magazine,* November 3, 1985, Part 2, 24–28, 95–97.

Gargan, Edward A. "Asian Investors Battle for Footholds in Chinatown." *New York Times,* December 29, 1981, A1.

———. "New Money, People and Ideas Alter Chinatown of Tradition." *New York Times,* December 28, 1981, A1.

Glazer, Nathan, ed. *Clamor at the Gates.* San Francisco: ICS Press, 1985.

Goldstein, Tom. "Inquiry Pursued in David Kennedy Incident in Harlem." *New York Times,* September 7, 1979, B3.

Goodman, Roy M. "Teacher Recruitment and Retention: A Failing Grade." Albany: New York State Senate Committee on Investigations, Taxation and Government Operations, July 7, 1988.

Gottlieb, Martin. "A Decade After the Cutbacks, New York Is a Different City." *New York Times,* June 30, 1985, A1.

————. "New York's Rescue: The Offstage Drama." *New York Times,* July 2, 1985, A1.

Greer, Colin. *The Great School Legend.* New York: Basic Books, 1972.

Hamill, Denis. "Trying to Live, Learn in Shadow of Heroin." *New York Newsday,* June 1, 1988, 2.

Hancock, LynNell. "A Dream Dies in Brooklyn." *Village Voice,* September 15, 1987, 15–18, 22–24.

————. "Education Plantation." *Village Voice,* January 18, 1988, 10–14.

————. "Teacher Power: The Woman Who Runs the Schools." *Village Voice,* September 20, 1988, 21–27.

————. "The Teachers Union Connection." *Village Voice,* December 27, 1988, 10–12.

Hechinger, Fred M. "Coming to Terms with Bilingualism in New York City Schools." *New York Times,* April 10, 1988, sec. 4, p. 6.

————. "New Challenge to Board of Examiners." *New York Times,* March 6, 1988, sec. 4, p. 7.

————. "Schools Remain Bedeviled by Old Ills and Old Solutions." *New York Times,* December 6, 1987, sec. 4, p. 6.

————. "Toward Educating the Homeless." *New York Times,* February 2, 1988, C11.

Hendricks, Glenn. *The Dominican Diaspora.* New York: Teachers College Press, 1974.

Hess, Hannah S. *The Third Side of the Desk: How Parents Can Change the Schools.* New York: Charles Scribner's Sons, 1973.

Hollenbeck, Donald T., and Johnson, Julie West, ed. *Literature, Yellow Level.* Evanston, Ill.: McDougal, Littell & Co., 1984.

Howe, Irving. *World of Our Fathers: The Journey of the East European Jews to America and the World They Found and Made.* New York: Harcourt Brace Jovanovich, 1976.

Jackson, Kenneth T., and Schultz, Stanley K, eds. *Cities in American History.* New York: Alfred A. Knopf, 1972.

Johnson, Edgar. *Charles Dickens: His Tragedy and Triumph,* 2 vols. Boston: Little, Brown & Co., 1952.

Kelley, Tina. "A Teacher for the Apple: Why New York City Can't Staff Its Schools." New York: Educational Priorities Panel, November 1987.

Klein, Joe. "The Power Next Time." *New York,* October 10, 1983, 38–45.

Kozol, Jonathan. "The Homeless and Their Children." *New Yorker,* January 25, 1988, 65–84.

Kriftcher, Noel. "The Principal as Instructional Leader: The School as Learning Community." *CSA Education Review* (Fall 1987), 30–35.

———. "Politicizing the New York City School System: A Review of Decentralization." Unpublished Ed. D. dissertation. Hofstra University, 1976.

Kurlansky, Mark. "The Dominican Republic: In the Land of the Blind Caudillo." *New York Times Magazine,* August 6, 1989, 24–30, 43.

Kwong, Peter. *The New Chinatown.* New York: Hill & Wang, 1987.

Lamming, George. *In the Castle of My Skin.* New York: Schocken, 1983.

Laquian, Aprodicio. "Two Booms in China Are One Too Many." *New York Times,* May 27, 1988, A31.

Lauro, Shirley. *Open Admissions.* New York: Samuel French, 1984.

Lueck, Thomas J. "New York's Job Market: Why So Many Are Sitting Out." *New York Times,* August 14, 1988, sec. 4, p. 24.

Lewis, Neil A. "For New York City, the Lessons Are Hard and Gold Stars Few." *New York Times,* September 4, 1988, sec. 4, p. 7.

———. "School Board Counts Workers for Trims." *New York Times,* August 18, 1988, B2.

Lyall, Sarah. "Man Charged in the Death Of 3-Year-Old." *New York Times,* April 9, 1988, 33.

Mann, Arthur. *Immigrants in American Life.* Boston: Houghton Mifflin Co., 1974.

Manoff, Karl, and Schudson, Michael, eds. *Reading the News: A Pantheon Guide to Popular Culture.* New York: Pantheon, 1987.

Mason, Bobbie Ann. *In Country.* New York: Harper & Row, 1985.

Metzger, Isaac, ed. *A Bintel Brief: Sixty Years of Letters from the Lower East Side to the Jewish Daily Forward.* Garden City, N.Y.: Doubleday & Co., 1971.

Miller, James. *Democracy Is in the Streets: From Port Huron to the Siege of Chicago.* New York: Simon & Schuster, 1987.

Mo, Timothy. *Sour Sweet.* London: Sphere Books, 1982.

Moore, Donald R., and Davenport, Suzanne. "The New Improved Sorting Machine." Wisconsin Center for Education Research, University of Wisconsin, Madison, April 1988.

Morris, Jan. *Destinations.* New York: Oxford University Press/Rolling Stone, 1980.

Nasaw, David. *Children of the City, At Work and At Play.* Garden City, N.Y.: Doubleday Anchor Books, 1985.

National Commission on Excellence in Education. *A Nation At Risk.* Washington, DC: U.S. Government Printing Office, April 1983.

"New York Ascendant." Commission on the Year 2000, June 1987.

"New York: The State Of Learning." Albany: University of the State of New York and the State Education Department, January 1989.

Oreskes, Michael. "Fiscal Crisis Still Haunts the Police." *New York Times,* July 6, 1985, 23.

Newfield, Jack. "New York's Finest: Jack Newfield's Annual Roll." *Village Voice,* February 16, 1988, 1, 22–24, 27–30, 32.

Oser, Alan S. "About Real Estate: Renovation of the Prince George Hotel of E. 28th. St." *New York Times,* July 29, 1981, A21.

Perlez, Jane. "A New School for Stuyvesant to Be Speeded." *New York Times,* October 2, 1987, B1.

———. "Knives and Guns in the Book Bags Strike Fear in a West Side School," December 10, 1987, B1.

———. "New York City Begins School Year Amid Persistent Problems," September 14, 1987, B1.

———. "Quinones, Under Attack, to Leave As Schools Head 6 Months Early." *New York Times,* August 14, 1987, A1.

———. "School Bans a New Peril: Flashy Gold." *New York Times,* April 12, 1988, B1.

———. "Schools Chancellor Job: Does Anyone Even Want It?" *New York Times,* September 7, 1987, 21.

———. "Schools in New York Urged to Care for Teachers Better." *New York Times,* April 20, 1988, B2.

———. "Teacher Tells Commission of Ordeal in the System." *New York Times,* May 13, 1988, B1.

———. "Thousands of Pupils Living in Hotels Skip School in New York." *New York Times,* November 12, 1987, A1.

Postal, Bernard, and Koppman, Lionel. *Jewish Landmarks in New York.* New York: Hill & Wang, 1964.

Postman, Neil. *Amusing Ourselves to Death: Public Discourse in the Age of Show Business.* New York: Viking Penguin, 1985.

Purnick, Joyce. "The Deepening Troubles of Chancellor Alvarado." *New York Times,* March 11, 1984, sec. 4, p. 6.

Raab, Selwyn. "Brutal Drug Gangs Wage War of Terror in Upper Manhattan." *New York Times,* March 15, 1988, B1.

Rabb, Harriet. "Promoting Integration in the New York City High Schools." New York: Columbia University Law School, July 1987.

Ravitch, Diane. *The Great School Wars: New York, 1805–1973.* New York: Basic Books, 1974.

———. *The Schools We Deserve: Reflections of the Education Crisis of Our Times.* New York: Basic Books, 1985.

Regan, Edward V. "The Board of Regents and The State Education Department Oversight of New York City Schools." Albany, N.Y.: Office of the State Comptroller, July 1988.

——. "New York City Board of Education Community School District Budget Deficits." Albany, N.Y.: Office of the State Comptroller, August 28, 1987.

Reimers, David M. *Still the Golden Door: The Third World Comes to America.* New York: Columbia University Press, 1985.

Rimer, Sara. "Paterson Principal: A Man of Extremes." *New York Times,* January 14, 1988, B1.

Roberts, Sam. "Manufacturing Reclaims Pasture in East New York." *New York Times,* July 30, 1987, B1.

Rogers, David. *110 Livingston Street: Politics and Bureaucracy in the New York City Schools.* New York: Random House, 1968.

Rogers, David, and Chung, Norman H. *110 Livingston Street Revisited: Decentralization in Action.* New York: New York University Press, 1983.

Rosenberg, Terry J. "Poverty in New York City: 1980–1985." New York: Community Service Society of New York, 1987.

Rosten, Leo. *The Joys of Yiddish.* New York: McGraw-Hill Book Co., 1968.

Rothman, Jane. "Those Who Didn't Care About Good Teachers." *New York Times,* December 8, 1987, A38.

Sachar, Emily. "After 85 Years, She Finds Old Way Is the Best." *New York Newsday,* September 10, 1987, 9.

——. "8 High Schools Face Closing." *New York Newsday,* December 17, 1987, 22.

——. "One Panelist Went to City Schools." *New York Newsday,* September 11, 1987, 7.

——. "Schools' Disturbing Arithmetic." *New York Newsday,* June 7, 1988, 3.

——. "Schools Seize More Weapons; Officials Blame Drug Trade." *New York Newsday,* May 4, 1988, 3.

Schanberg, Sydney H. "The School Charade." *New York Times,* April 26, 1983, A23.

Sheehan, Susan. *A Welfare Mother.* Boston: Houghton Mifflin Co., 1976.

Shefter, Martin. *Political Crisis/Fiscal Crisis: The Collapse and Revival of New York City.* New York: Basic Books, 1985.

Shenon, Philip. "East Side Drug Sweep Hailed by Morgenthau." *New York Times,* March 14, 1984, B4.

Shulman, Harry. *Slums of New York.* New York: Boni, 1938.

Siegel, Jessica. "It's Real and the People in VVAW/WSO Are Real: An Interview with John Musgrave, a Regional Coordinator of VVAW/WSO." *Liberation News Service,* 551 (September 8, 1973), 1.

————. "Massacre at Attica." *Liberation News Service,* 375 (September 15, 1971), 9.

————. " 'No One Contributed More to Law Enforcement': J. Edgar Hoover Is Dead." *Liberation News Service,* 433 (May 10, 1972), 9.

————. "The Best Fucking Cop in America." *Liberation News Service,* 391 (November 13, 1971), 9.

————. "The Gainesville 8 Acquitted." *Liberation News Service,* 550 (September 5, 1973), 1.

————. "The Gainesville 8 Go to Trial." *Liberation News Service,* 543 (August 4, 1973), 1.

————. "The Occupation of Wounded Knee." *Liberation News Service,* 511 (March 24, 1973), 1.

————. "The Siege of Wounded Knee Continues." *Liberation News Service,* 509 (March 17, 1973), 1.

————. "Vets and Supporters End Week of Protests." *Liberation News Service,* 545 (August 11, 1973), 4.

————. "Voices from Inside Attica." *Liberation News Service,* 402 (December 24, 1971), 1.

Shear, Jeff. "For the Chinese, School Days Are a Time of Model Pressure." *Insight,* June 6, 1988, 18–20.

Simon, Kate. *A Wilder World: Portraits in an Adolescence.* New York: Harper & Row, 1986.

————. *Bronx Primitive: Portraits in a Childhood.* New York: Harper & Row, 1982.

Smith, Hedrick. *The Power Game: How Washington Works.* New York: Random House, 1988.

Smith, Matthew Hale. *Sunshine and Shadow in New York.* Hartford, Conn.: J. B. Burr, 1869.

Smits, Edward J. *Nassau: Suburbia, U.S.A.* Garden City, N.Y.: Doubleday & Co., 1974.

Spann, Edward K. *The New Metropolis: New York City, 1840–1857.* New York: Columbia University Press, 1981.

Stegman, Michael A. "Housing and Vacancy Report: New York City, 1987." New York: New York City Department of Housing Preservation & Development, April 1988.

"Study of New Jobs Since '79 Says Half Pay Poverty Wage." *New York Times,* September 27, 1988, A22.

"Streets: The Magazine of the Lower East Side." New York: Columbia University Graduate School of Journalism, Spring 1988.

Sung, Betty Lee. *Mountain of Gold: The Story of the Chinese in America.* New York: Macmillan Co., 1967.

————. *The Adjustment Experience of Chinese Immigrant Children in New York City.* New York: Center for Migration Studies, 1987.

"The Forgotten Half: Non-College-Bound Youth in America." New York: William T. Grant Foundation Commission on Work, Family and Citizenship.

Turetsky, Doug. "The Dealer Next Door." *City Limits,* November 1988, 12–15.

Tyack, David B. *The One Best System: A History of American Urban Education.* Cambridge, Mass.: Harvard University Press, 1974.

Uchitelle, Louis. "Reliance on Temporary Jobs Hints at Economic Fragility." *New York Times,* March 16, 1988, A1.

Uhlig, Mark A. "At Least 6 Freeze to Death in Cold Snap, Officials Say." *New York Times,* January 16, 1988, 29.

Viteritti, Joseph P. *Across the River: Politics and Education in the City.* New York: Holmes & Meier, 1983.

Vogel, Ezra F. "On China's Southern Coast, Dramatic Progress." *New York Times,* March 15, 1988, A26.

Wade, Tanya. "When Home Is a Hotel." *New Youth Connections,* June 1988, 3.

Weinstein, William. "Why My Wife Quit." *New York Times,* August 6, 1988, 25.

Weiss, Samuel. "New York Panel to Urge Broader Role for Teachers." *New York Times,* March 11, 1988, B1.

Weitzman, Phillip. "State of the Stock." *City Limits,* October 1988, 12–15.

Weyr, Thomas. *Hispanic U.S.A.: Breaking the Melting Pot.* New York: Harper & Row, 1988.

Wiarda, Howard J., and Kryzanek, Michael J. *The Dominican Republic: A Caribbean Crucible.* Boulder, Colo.: Westview Press, 1982.

Willner, Robin. "Ten Years of Neglect: The Failure to Serve Language-Minority Students in the New York City Public Schools." New York: Educational Priorities Panel, October 1985.

Wilson, William Julius. *The Truly Disadvantaged: The Inner City, the Underclass, and Public Policy.* Chicago: University of Chicago Press, 1987.

Wines, Michael. "Against Drug Tide, Only a Holding Action." *New York Times,* June 24, 1988, A1.

Wolff, Craig. "Drug Arrests Mounting on the Lower East Side." *New York Times,* March 5, 1984, B1.

WPA Guide to New York City. New York: Random House, 1939.

Yezierska, Anzia. *Bread Givers.* New York: Persea, 1975.

ABOUT THE AUTHOR

Samuel G. Freedman is a former reporter for *The New York Times*. Educated in the public schools of Highland Park, New Jersey, he graduated from the University of Wisconsin. He lives in New York City with his wife, Cynthia.